Chichester Excavations I

Chichester Excavations I

Alec Down and Margaret Rule

Introductory chapter by
Professor B.W.Cunliffe

Phillimore

Acknowledgements

The Committee wish to record their thanks to the undermentioned bodies and individuals whose generous advance donations and subscriptions made publication of the first edition possible.

H.M. Ministry of Public Building and Works
West Sussex County Council
City of Chichester
Chichester Rural District Council
Chichester Museum Society
Chichester Civic Society
Adorian Archaeological and Educational Trust
Butlin's Ltd.
Messrs. Thomas Eggar & Son
Kenwood Manufacturing Co.
Mason's Garage Ltd.
G. A. Neal & Sons
C. Shippam, Ltd.
Tansley & Cook Ltd.
Wingard Ltd.

ISBN 0 85033 696 1

Published by
PHILLIMORE & CO. LTD.
Shopwyke Hall, Chichester, Sussex

Printed and bound in Great Britain by
UNWIN BROTHERS LTD.
Old Woking, Surrey

Dr. A. E. Wilson f.s.a. *Frontispiece*

Foreword

Dr. A.E. Wilson, D.Litt. F.S.A.

This volume is published as a tribute to Dr. A. E. Wilson from the City of Chichester, his friends and admirers and in gratitude to him for his outstanding contribution to our knowledge of the history of Sussex and particularly of Chichester.

Dr. Wilson joined the Sussex Archaeological Society in 1937 and when elected a member of its Council in 1945 he was already well known for his activity in archaeological field work in the county. He had been admitted as a Fellow of the Society of Antiquaries the previous year. Two years later he became a founder member and vice-Chairman of the Sussex Society's Archaeological Research Committee, which has continued to do valuable work in co-ordinating and recording all field-work in the county, and in the same year he was appointed Honorary Director of Excavations in Chichester, a post which he held until 1961. From 1957-66 he was Honorary Secretary of the Sussex Archaeological Society and on his resignation owing to failing eyesight he held office for a year (1967/1968) as its President, an office to which he was elected in recognition of his long service to the Society.

Apart from a season with Sir Mortimer Wheeler at Maiden Castle, all Dr. Wilson's work has been in Sussex. From 1936 until 1962 hardly a volume of the *Collections* of the Sussex Archaeological Society is without a contribution from him. In 1935 he was associated with G. A. Holleyman in excavating an early British agricultural village site near Telscombe and with G. P. Burstow in the excavation of a Celtic village at the Dyke, Brighton, and in 1937 with Dr. E. Cecil Curwen and G. P. Burstow in the first of two seasons' work on the Caburn. Later he worked on the Angmering Roman Villa, Highdown Hill and Sidlesham, the report on which is still in preparation. At the same time as publishing the results of his field work, his reports in the *Collections* are interspersed with historical papers drawing together these results and relating them to the Sussex and national scene. These are: 'The end of Roman Sussex and the early Saxon settlements' (*S.A.C.* 82): 'Sussex, Kent and the Continent in early Saxon times' (*S.A.C.* 83): 'Sussex on the Eve of the Roman Conquest' (*S.A.C.* 93). The work of his Local History Seminar at Brighton Technical College, members of which remember the easy friendly feeling and his impressive knowledge, led to two volumes of translations of Sussex Manorial Custumals published as volumes 57 and 60 of the Sussex Record Society (1958 and 1961) and his paper on 'Farming in Sussex in the Middle Ages. The working of a manor in the second half of the thirteenth century' (*S.A.C.* 97). But from 1947 it was Chichester which claimed his main attention and the later reports all refer to discoveries in the city.

The Excavations Committee established in 1947 under the chairmanship of Dr. Bishop, then Headmaster of the Chichester High School for Boys, had the object of taking advantage of the opportunity given by the clearance of sites of buildings damaged by enemy action to explore the early history of the City. At the same time it was foreseen that a good deal of rebuilding was likely to go on during the next twenty years and in fact the number of 'rescue digs' resulting from this has been even greater than was first anticipated. Dr. Wilson's width of interest and knowledge of the Sussex background made him admirably qualified for work in this City with its history of continuous occupation from the Roman period. As he warned supporters in 1947, the work of an archaeologist in Chichester is often frustrating and although a great deal lies hidden under modern buildings and streets, it is seldom that a site available for excavation is large enough to tell a whole story. Frequently the work has had to be done in cramped conditions and an important feature like a wall cannot be pursued as it disappears under an adjoining property. Often the ground is pitted by more recent rubbish pits, the undisturbed areas may only be narrow strips between old cess pits, and the eighteenth-century cellars removed the Roman levels entirely. Nearly always the work has had to be carried out under pressure for time just ahead of the builders. Dr. Wilson however proved that by being on the spot whenever a building is taken down or a hole dug, gradually a coherent account of the City's history can be pieced together. In particular his excavations, as opportunity occurred, at various points on the City walls – East Walls, Cawley Priory, Market Street and North Walls – the results of which were collected in No. 6 of *Chichester Papers*, 1957, gave for the first time a clear history of the City's fortifications.

From the first he established excellent relationships with the ecclesiastical and civic authorities, and their representatives and officers were invited to become members of the Committee. The list of helpers who took part in the earliest of the Chichester excavations (1947/50) is impressive: masters and boys from the Chichester High School and Brighton College: Lecturers and students from Bishop Otter and Bognor Training Colleges, undergraduates from University College, London. Loyalty, originally inspired by Dr. Wilson, has been a characteristic of workers for the Excavations Committee. It is fitting to use this opportunity to record for example that a master at the High School, Mr. A. H. Collins, F.S.A., who was associated with Dr. Wilson in his first excavations in Chichester and was his agent to watch for any new opportunities for excavations, has been Secretary for the twenty-three years of the Committee's existence.

One of Dr. Wilson's last tasks as Director of Excavations in Chichester was to organise the appeal for funds to excavate the site of the Roman Palace at Fishbourne and to make arrangements for Mr. (now Professor) Barry Cunliffe to carry out the work. The fact that the Chichester Excavations Committee was in a position to organise a major excavation of this kind is again a measure of the recognition he had secured for its work. When he handed over the Directorship to John Holmes, F.S.A., in 1961, the future of the Committee was in no doubt and its reputation high. John Holmes was Field Director until 1965 and on his resignation it was decided not to appoint a successor but to work with Mrs. Margaret Rule, F.S.A., and Alec Down as site controllers for each excavation, and with Professor B. W. Cunliffe, Ph.D, F.S.A., and K. J. Barton, F.S.A., as co-ordinators and consultants for Roman and Medieval finds respectively. This volume is evidence of the continuing vitality of the Committee. We have therefore to thank Dr. Wilson not only for his own achievements as excavator, but also for his foresight, example and organisation in ensuring that opportunities for throwing further light on the history of Chichester and its environment will continue to be used, and that the objects found will be cared for and the reports published. The foundations he laid have a quality of Roman solidity.

K. M. E. MURRAY
Chairman of the Excavations Committee

Authors' Note

The excavations reported in this volume represent slightly over half of the total archaeological activity which has taken place under our direction during the period 1963-69. All the work has been carried out by properly trained volunteers working throughout the whole period at weekends and holiday times, in bad weather and good. Nearly all the diggers are from Chichester and the surrounding district, but some travel regularly each week from farther afield. The majority have taken courses at the College of Further Education or sponsored by the W.E.A., in order to achieve the necessary standard in archaeology, but many of the team bring to the task individual skills associated with their everyday work which are often of great value when special problems have to be dealt with. The wealth of goodwill and "knowhow" that we can now draw upon devolves directly from the work and example of Dr Wilson himself, and we take pride in carrying on in the pattern which he laid down; that of local people with a great love and interest in their own local history, excavating it with their own hands. It is most heartening in an age where almost everybody expects to get paid, to find people who are eager to contribute so freely in time and money towards enriching the cultural heritage of our city and county.

Much of the work is of a rescue nature, mounted at short notice to extract what archaeological evidence there is before the site is re-developed, but in some cases it is possible to undertake long term research within the city, well in advance of development. For these oppportunities we are always grateful as the yield in knowledge is correspondingly higher.

It has been the settled policy of the Committee that all sites within the City and its environs should be investigated whenever possible, and whilst this sometimes imposes strains upon the organisation the ultimate result cannot fail to be a great advance in the understanding of our city and the various phases of its history. Hitherto the Roman period has received the major share of attention, largely because the remains are more prolific, but also because the late Saxon period has been difficult to define and because the medieval remains are almost always destroyed by later Georgian buildings. Nevertheless, a start has been made, and the formation of a documentary research study group under the leadership of Dr Clough may eventually assist us to a better understanding of the lay-out of 13th and 14th century Chichester.

In this volume we have attempted no more than to clear some of the backlog of reports which have accumulated over the last six years and to produce for the convenience of students a comprehensive Gazetteer of the Roman material from the city, known and reported on in a number of publications over the years. The next task is to produce a further volume in 2 to 3 years time which will include some excavations not hitherto published and work currently in progress. It is also intended that this volume will include a comprehensive survey of all the medieval and post-medieval pottery from the city, which the Committee's Consultant on these wares, Mr K.J. Barton F.S.A. F.M.A. is preparing, and for this reason we have not attempted to deal in detail with these pottery types on sites where the emphasis has been on the Roman period and where the medieval pottery has been so featureless as not to warrant special attention. Volume 2 will also contain a detailed study of the samian wares found within the city.

In a series of operations extending over six years it would be impossible to individually acknowledge the help given us by everyone. Certain specialist assistance has been acknowledged in the text, and in addition we should like to record our thanks to the many individuals both in public and private capacities who have smoothed our path over the years.

We are grateful to the West Sussex County Council, the Chichester City Council, the Dean and Chapter, Messrs Tamplins and the Trustees of St. Mary's Hospital for permission to excavate on their land. We are indebted for help and advice from Professor J.M.C. Toynbee, M.A., D.Phil, F.B.A., F.S.A., Mr Norman Cook V/P.S.A., the Director of the Guildhall Museum in London, Dr Graham Webster M.A., F.S.A. of the University of Birmingham, and Professor B.W. Cunliffe M.A., Ph.D., F.S.A. of the University of Southampton. Mr K.J. Barton F.S.A., F.M.A. and Dr G.C. Dunning B.Sc., L.Litt., F.S.A. have advised on various aspects of medieval and post-medieval ceramics, and Mr G. Dannell B.Sc., F.S.A. has kindly reported on the samian ware. Other specialist reports have been provided by Dr. Helena Ginns M.B.B.S., L.R.C.P., M.R.C.S. (osteology), Mr Alan Outen, Assistant Curator of the Bognor Regis Museum (food bones), Mr. R.P. Wright M.A., F.S.A., (gaming counters and inscriptions), Mr Ralph Merryfield F.S.A. and Mr Richard Reece F.S.A. (coins). Of the teams of diggers, special mention must be made of the Supervisors, Bronwen Jenkins, Sheila Morgan, Josephine Draper, Gina Adams, Brian Boddy, Keith and Roger Lintott, Roy Morgan and Jack Eschbaecher. The tremendous task of dealing with the pottery and finds has been at various times the responsibility of Jane Lawton, Marianne Charles, Brigetta Reynolds, Ann Street, Mrs Glue, Pauline Carder, Thalia Polak, Pat Gunn and Elizabeth Westall. Drawing of the small finds and pottery was carried out by Joy White, Margaret May, Roger Reed and David S. Neal; Geoffrey Claridge, Roger Worsley, Thelma Westmore and Jerome O'Hea undertook the photography, and Joy Kidd much of the typing. Specialist assistance with architectural drawing was provided by Richard Meynell and Baron Victor van Lawick. Our thanks are also due in no small measure to Mrs Margaret Culver and Miss Janet Wallace M.A. who carried out a considerable amount of documentary research on the Cathedral Cloisters, St. Pancras and St. Mary's Hospital sites, from which we have abstracted certain sections for inclusion in the reports. Their full reports will be attached to the remainder of the excavation records and it is intended that these will be housed in the West Sussex Record Office. It is hoped that all the finds from the excavations will eventually be deposited in the Chichester City Museum.

Chichester, 1970.

Alec Down.
Margaret Rule F.S.A.

Contents

1

The Origin and development of Chichester

The purpose of this short essay is to provide a skeleton back-cloth against which the details of the most recent series of excavations in Chichester can be seen. This is neither the time nor the place to attempt a definitive statement of the city's growth: much more excavation, historical research and sifting of the vast quantities of material recovered over the years will be required before anything approximating to a full and balanced account can be produced. Nevertheless, great strides forward have been made in our understanding in recent years, largely as a result of the work of the Chichester Civic Society's Excavation Committee, which owed its initial impetus to the direction of Dr. A. E. Wilson.[1] Because of the Committee's work, it is at last possible to see the main threads of the story even if the detailed texture is still elusive.

The Pre-Roman Situation

Everywhere, when the original ground-surface has been exposed beneath the city, it has been found to be barren of pre-Roman material – with the exception of a few scraps of pottery recovered from the site of the West Gate. The implications are clear enough: while small-scale peasant occupation, common on this part of the coastal plain, may have occurred, the urban community did not exist on its present site before the beginning of the Roman occupation. Indeed, as the first part of its Roman name implies, Chichester, *Noviomagus Regnentium,* was a new establishment—new, presumably, by comparison with the pre-Roman capital which is thought to have lain in the vicinity of Selsey Bill. Sadly, little is known of the predecessor of the Roman town. The evidence, such as it is, points to a native *oppidum* close to Selsey, but apart from a scatter of coins washed up on the seashore little else has survived the devastating erosion to which this part of the coast has been subjected. The great earthworks, known as the Chichester Entrenchments, which divide up and protect the plain from Bosham to Aldingbourne Rife are, however, in the tradition of the pre-Roman dykes like those defending the Belgic town of Camulodunum in Essex. Recent work[2] has shown that here at Chichester they form part of a complex sequence which evolved over the years preceding the Roman invasion, to offer protection not only to the Selsey *oppidum* itself but also to its territory and outlying settlements and homesteads. The situation at the time of the Roman invasion of A.D.43 is therefore tolerably clear: the nucleated settlement with a mint lay at Selsey, surrounded by arable land (the old field patterns of which are still recognizable from the air) with a denser wooded area to the north where the flocks and herds could obtain fodder and pannage. Scattered within this territory were a number of isolated homesteads.

The First Settlement

Politically it would appear that the Chichester region, the southern part of the Atrebatic tribal territory, maintained a pro-Roman attitude which in the year of the invasion would have been of enormous value to the incoming armies[3]. While the first stages of the conquest were being fought out in Kent and Essex, the Southern Atrebates provided a stable buffer preventing the tribes of the hostile South-west from supporting the rapidly assembling resistance in Eastern Britain. When, late in A.D.43 or early in 44, the conquest of the South-west was undertaken, the Chichester region came into its own. The South-west campaign undertaken by the second legion under the command of the young Vespasian, later to become Emperor, destroyed two tribes and more than twenty fortified native capitals, as well as conquering the Isle of Wight. The campaign was presumably strongly supported by sea-borne supplies ferried along the coast and landed at strategic points. In such a situation a stable supply base was needed, linked to a harbour and sited in friendly territory. This was the context for the first settlement at Chichester. While it must be admitted that military structures beneath the town have not been definitely recognized, the ditch beneath the St. Pancras cemetery may be of military origin. Moreover, there is now an impressive series of military bronze fittings from very early occupation levels in the eastern part of the walled area, particularly from Little London, and other military objects are currently turning up in the Chapel Street excavations. There can therefore be little reasonable doubt that a military base lies beneath the town, while a mile away at Fishbourne contemporary military harbour installations and store buildings have been recognized. Until much more positive evidence of the early structures beneath the town is available, it would be unwise to argue the significance of these remains too closely, but it is tempting to see Chichester as the site of a temporary camp, possibly the winter quarters for the Second Legion in the initial stages of the westward thrust, with Fishbourne serving as its supply port.

Within a year or two, the West was firmly under Roman control and by A.D. 47 a frontier zone had been established along the Fosse way. While garrisons were probably left in the hostile areas to keep an eye on recalcitrant natives, it is most unlikely that troops would have been wasted in the friendly territories. In all probability the military presence would have been removed from the Chichester region by A.D. 47, at the latest[4].

Early Development

It is well known that Chichester formed the centre of government of a client kingdom ruled by Tiberius Claudius Cogidubnus, who was in all probability a member of the Atrebatic aristocracy, acceptable both to his people and to Rome. His function as a client king would have been to rule the territory as a provincial canton on behalf of Rome, to keep order, pay taxes and encourage the growth of Roman life. The region now became known as the territory of the *Regnenses* ('the people of the kingdom') and its tribal centre, *Noviomagus* (the new market), was established on the site of the military base at Chichester.

The nature of the early development is not well known. Occupation levels associated with timber buildings are widely distributed over the area of the later town and the main streets, at least, must have been laid out, but as to the detailed planning we are at present ignorant. The town, however, seems to have developed rapidly and by the late 50's it must have possessed many public works and benefactions, among which is included a statue to Nero, the inscribed base of which was found in the eighteenth century[5].

The main impetus for urban development came to Chichester, as it did to many other Roman centres, in the 70's and 80's of the first century A.D., by which time Rome was firmly committed to maintaining the province. It is to this period that the more important public buildings probably belong: the forum and basilica, the public baths, the temple to Neptune and Minerva and the ampitheatre[6]. By now the street grid would have been firmly established and the cremation cemetery at St. Pancras was in active use. Of the shops and houses, however, little survives apart from fragmentary traces, but there can be very little doubt that Chichester of the first and second centuries was a town built largely of timber and clay. Remains of this kind, though easily recognizable, are often difficult to interpret except in large area excavations which are seldom possible in a densely built-up modern town.

The Late Roman Town

Towards the end of the second century Chichester, like many other towns in Britain, was enclosed within an earthen rampart fronted by two V-shaped ditches[7]. On analogy with more extensively excavated town sites, it is probable that the four main gates were built in masonry at this time, but apart from a small part of the North Gate, seen in a recent excavation, nothing is known of the form or exact siting of the Roman gates, unless Grimm's sketch of the West Gate is thought to depict a modified Roman structure still in use in the eighteenth century. Not long after the construction of the earthen defences the rampart face was cut back and a flint and mortar wall was built, exactly following the original line. This sequence can again be paralleled elsewhere. Precisely when and why these defensive measures were taken is still in some doubt, but a late second-century date is suggested by the stratified pottery from the earthen bank while the insertion of the wall is thought to follow on quickly in the early years of the third century. Since there is no sign of the work being rapidly carried out, external threats are unlikely to be the cause. Possibly the encirclement was connected with the formal definition of the town boundaries and it may be that the walls are a mark of civic pride, constructed in A.D. 212 or 214 when Caracella gave the right of citizenship to all free-born people in the empire.

Throughout the third and fourth centuries the face of the town changed. Gradually timber buildings were replaced by masonry as more money accumulated in the hands of the urban rich, enabling them to adopt the luxury of stone buildings together with private bath suites, central heating and polychrome mosaic floors. In all probability the public buildings received their share of aggrandizement. It may have been in the third century that the statue or column to Jupiter was erected in the forum[8]. One of the elaborately inscribed and carved blocks of its base, 3½ ft. square, was found in an excavation in Chapel Street in 1935, providing a hint of the architectural and decorative glories of the late town.

In 367 A.D. the nerve of the province was shattered by the great 'barbarian conspiracy' which led to the over-running of Hadrian's Wall by Picts and Scots, causing chaos in the countryside as far south as the Thames. Two years of upset and uncertainty followed until order was again restored by Count Theodosius and his army. Among the reforms which he carried out was probably the reorganization of the towns, turning them into strongly fortified enclosures by the addition of forward-projecting bastions and probably by billeting troops on the urban community to form a militia. At Chichester a number of the bastions have been recognized, all clearly added to the existing town wall. Their construction necessitated the refilling of the inner ditch and the recutting of the outer ditch in a wide, flat-bottomed form designed to keep would-be attackers within the optimum killing range of *ballistae* mounted on top of the walls and towers. A hint of the presence of a militia is provided by the discovery, within the town, of a belt-fitting characteristic of those worn by Germanic mercenaries, a category of object found in many of the Romano-British towns at this time[9]. Thus by the late fourth century the character of the town had changed. In contrast with the expansive days 70 years or so earlier, the community was becoming inturned, masonry buildings were being robbed to provide stone for the bastions and a general unease must have been in the air. From the 380's until A.D. 409 armies were amassed in Britain and carried off to the continent to fight for the cause of their leaders, always to be soundly beaten. This, together with the general decline in the birth-rate from which the Roman world as a whole was suffering, must have created acute problems of manpower. Following the departure of the last force, in 409, there was rebellion in the province which some writers believe was a peasant revolt against the large landowners and the urban aristocracy. At any event, the plight of the towns was serious, for they wrote to the emperor Honorius asking for help only to be told, in his famous reply of 410, to look to their own defence.

But 410 does not mark the temporary cessation of urban life. In all probability the communities continued to live much as before; indeed there is evidence from other towns, such as Verulamium and Bath, of rebuilding work going on well into the fifth century. The main difference would have been the breakdown of the complex economic structure of the Roman era. Money ceased to be commonly used after 430 A.D. and mass-produced commodities such as pottery must have faded at about this time. There was also a political fragmentation – tyrants appeared, to hold the reins of government in much the same way as they had done during the last 30 years of Roman rule. For some time at least the policy of bringing in Germanic mercenaries for protection continued, but the revolt of those already settled in the east of the country in the middle of the fifth century changed all this. The incomings were no longer by invitation but were now forced on the remnants of the sub-Roman population. How the towns fared throughout the fifth and sixth centuries is one of the most fascinating problems facing British archaeologists today. Whilst Chichester is at present silent on this period it can only be a matter of time before positive evidence begins to come to light.

The Saxon Period

The town probably continued in some kind of use throughout the Saxon period, but what form this occupation took and the size of the population is at present unknown. A charter of the late seventh century refers to a grant of a parcel a land in the southern part of the town made by king Ethelbert to Wilfred, Bishop of Selsey[10]. But the structure of the town at this time is uncertain. The defences were probably still in a reasonable state of repair and the two main streets running between the sites of the Roman gates may have remained in use. Along them there may have been a scatter of simple timber buildings with much of the internal area left wild or cultivated as garden plots.

If there is still much to learn of the four centuries following the collapse of Roman government, the picture of the town in the last two centuries of the Saxon period is somewhat clearer. By the end of the ninth century Chichester had become once more a strongly fortified settlement – fortified, that is, against threat of Danish attack. As a burgh it formed one of a chain of similar sites which ringed the Saxon kingdom of Wessex. In 894-5 men from the town drove off a Danish raiding party which had been harrying Saxons near Chichester, killing several hundred of them. In the early tenth century document, the Burghal Hidage, it is assessed as 1,500 hides which would have provided an insufficient force to man the circuit of the old Roman wall. A likely explanation is that the marshy Lavant valley formed a suitably impenetrable barrier along the south side to render manning unnecessary.

By the early tenth century the major land divisions within the walls were already laid out. The positions of the Roman gates would have determined the north-south and east-west axes of the town street grid but the other lines, particularly those running at right-angles to the east-west street, were probably in origin newly constructed land divisions, bearing no relation to the Roman pattern. Quantities of tenth-century pottery attest a fairly dense occupation at this time, but structures are yet to be defined. On documentary evidence we know that somewhere within the town lay a mint originating during the reign of Aethalstan (925-39) and a charter, supposedly of 956, refers to 'Bretheren residing in Chichester'[11] which suggests the existence of a pre-conquest minster, probably situated on the site later to be chosen for the Cathedral. Thus the urban layout had begun to take on an aspect which is still dimly recognizable in the present-day town plan.

The Medieval Town

With the Norman conquest[12] the town grew considerably in importance. Sixty new houses are recorded to have been built during the twenty years preceding 1086, and within a decade of the conquest the see had been translated to Chichester from Selsey, the new church being consecrated by Bishop Stigand probably on the site of the Saxon minister. The whole of the south-west corner of the town now belonged to the ecclesiastical authorities. The Cathedral was finally dedicated in 1108, but six years later a fire caused damage to the building and to the timber houses of the town. Later in the century, in 1187, an even more serious fire resulted in substantial rebuilding.

The other change to the Saxon townscape which the Norman invasion caused was the construction of a castle of motte and bailey type in the north-east corner of the walled area. The truncation of the Saxon streets to form an adequate outer bailey is still evident in the street-plan today. Little is known of the castle, which was never of much importance, but at various times during the twelfth century sums of money were spent on rebuildings and modifications. It was finally destroyed in 1217 after it had been recovered from the French king Louis, and in 1269 the site was given to the Grey Friars[13], part of whose priory still stands close to the remains of the castle mound.

The period from the twelfth to fourteenth centuries also saw the establishment of a group of Black Friars in the south-east corner of the town, the rebuilding or extension of many of the churches in masonry and the construction of specialized buildings such as the Vicars hall[14] and St. Mary's Hospital, also in masonry. We must not, however, forget that the town was still predominantly of timber, the houses and shops, at least along the main streets, being packed close together with yards extending far back from the frontages. All this time the walls were kept in a tolerable state of repair, financed largely by murage grants, the last of which was made as late as 1443. But the medieval town was not wholly retained within the walls. Suburbs grew up outside the gates, particularly at St. Pancras along Stane Street beyond the East Gate, and the recent discovery of a pottery kiln just outside the north-west angle of the wall is an interesting insight into medieval town planning. It is not unlike the present-day idea of concentrating heavy industry clear of settlement, in what would now be called an industrial estate.

Georgian Revival

Throughout the fifteenth and sixteenth centuries the town saw no major alterations and by the end of the early seventeenth century Speed's map shows a remarkable amount of open space within the walls, suggesting a decline in prosperity which is borne out by the documentary evidence. Nevertheless the massive walls still remained sufficiently intact to protect the community during the Civil War, until the besiegers' artillery proved too much for the nerves of the defenders.

It was during the eighteenth century that the town we know today began to reach its mature form. Fortunately the whole of the metamorphosis from the decaying sub-medieval timber slum to the spacious elegance of the Georgian brick-built facades was witnessed by James Spershott, a Baptist pastor who was born in 1710 and died in 1789[15]. In his boyhood he remembered the old low timber houses and open shops, the lack of paving and the large number of public houses. It was a mean and rather squalid place. Rebuilding seems to have begun about 1724 and by the time of his death almost the entire city had been rebuilt or refaced, the gates had been removed, the streets properly paved and the old defences laid out as pleasant walks. It is a story of revival that can be paralleled in many of our towns at this period.

The town changed little until the end of the last war. There had been some rebuilding within the walls but it was mostly on a small scale, the principal development lying in the surrounding suburbs. But in the last 25 years the pace of change has quickened – large areas, particularly in the north-west and south-east quarters, have been developed, disturbing and usually destroying the structures and occupation levels of the ancient city. Archaeological recording and excavation has therefore had to be almost continuous. Not always have the investigators met with the support they would have liked (p. 19) but nevertheless much has been salvaged from the rapidly disappearing evidence of the past and a record of some of the most recent discoveries is offered in the following pages. Much of it is necessarily fragmentary but there are many points of more than local interest, like the early Roman buildings on the St. Mary's Hospital site, the city defences sectioned near the West Gate, the important Roman cremation cemetery at St. Pancras with its underlying early ditch, the medieval kiln from Orchard Street and the new excavation work at the Cathedral. These are major contributions to the study of the city, but the smaller reports are of no less significance – they are all pieces of the jigsaw. Some of them must stand in isolation for a while, but gradually as excavation proceeds more will be found and the picture of the city and its development will begin to take on a new clarity.

Notes and References

[1] A.E. Wilson, 'Chichester Excavations 1947-50', *S.A.C.* 90, 164-200; 'The Beginnings of Roman Chichester', *S.A.C.* 94 100-143; 'Roman Chichester', *S.A.C.* 95 106-143; The Archaeology of Chichester City Walls (*Chichester Paper* No. 6, 1957).

[2] Richard Bradley, 'The Chichester Entrenchments' in B. Cunliffe, *Excavations at Fishbourne 1961-1969*, Vol. I, 17-36 (London 1970).

[3] These problems and a discussion of the significance of Cogidubnus are considered in more detail in B. Cunliffe, *Excavations at Fishbourne 1961-1969*, Vol. I (London 1970).

[4] The excavations hint (p. 26) at the possibility that military occupation may have continued longer. This would be surprising but not impossible. Firmer evidence is required.

[5] *RIB* 92.

[6] Brief summary of the forum and baths in J. Holmes, 'Chichester: The Roman Town' (*Chichester Paper* No. 50). See also *RIB* 91 (Cogidubnus stone referring to the temple of Neptune and Minerva) and G.M. White 'The Chichester Ampitheatre: Preliminary Excavations' *A.J.* 16., 149-159.

[7] A.E. Wilson, 'The Archaeology of the Chichester City Walls', (*Chichester Paper* No. 6).

[8] *RIB* 89 and G.M. White, 'A new Roman Inscription from Chichester', *A.J.* 16, 461-4.

[9] S.C. Hawkes and G.C. Dunning, 'Soldiers and Settlers in late Roman Britain' *Med. Arch.* 5, 1-70.

[10] The charter (BCS 212, KCD 1011) is now thought to be spurious (Darling, *Handbook of British Chronology*, 1961, 20.)

[11] This charter, too is thought to be a later copy – D. Whitlock, *Guide to Anglo-Saxon Charters* 214.

[12] For a full account of the medieval history of the Cathedral and the town see *VCH.* 3.

[13] F.W. Steer, 'The Grey Friars in Chichester' (*Chichester Paper* No. 2).

[14] F.W. Steer, 'The Vicars Hall, Chichester, and its Undercroft', (*Chichester Paper* No. 12).

[15] F.W. Steer, (ed.) 'The Memoirs of James Spershott' (*Chichester Paper* No. 30).

2

Gazetteer

Roman Sites and Finds within the City Boundary

List of Abbreviations

S.A.C.	*Sussex Archaeological Collections.*
S.N.Q.	*Sussex Notes and Queries.*
Proc. Soc. Ant.	*Proceedings of the Society of Antiquaries.*
A.J.	*The Antiquaries Journal.*
J.R.S.	*Journal of Roman Studies.*
V.C.H. Sx.	*Victoria County History of Sussex.*
Hay.	Hay, *History of Chichester.*
Camden.	Camden, *Brittania.*
Dallaway.	Dallaway, *History of West Sussex.*
B.A.A.J.	*British Archaeological Association Journal.*
Holmes 1965	*Chichester Paper* No. 50. 'Chichester, the Roman Town'.
Wilson 1957.	*Chichester Paper* No. 6 'The Archaeology of Chichester City Walls'.
S.C.M.	*Sussex County Magazine.*
C.I.L.	*Corpus Inscriptionum Latinorum.*
Arch.	*Archaeologia.*
A.N.L.	*Archaeological News Letter.*
Horsefield.	Horsefield, *History, Antiquities and Topography of the County of Sussex.*
J.B.A.A.	*Journal of the British Archaeological Association.*

The finds are dealt with in geographical sequence through the four quadrants within the City walls, and the area of the quadrants extended out to the City boundaries. This Gazetteer is restricted to Roman finds only, although it is intended to collate all the finds of other periods in the subsequent volumes as well as bringing the Roman Gazetteer up to date. Published sites and finds are abstracted without alteration; the author's conjectures are stated in italics. Where the location is known the Gazetteer number is entered on the map (Fig. 2.1.).

North East Quadrant

1. *North Gate. S.A.C.* 100, 75; *S.A.C.* 106 122.

Excavations for a petrol storage tank on the east side of Northgate under garage forecourt (now Blue Star Garage) exposed remains of stone walling which Dr. A.E. Wilson concluded was the south-east corner of the Roman gate tower, adjoining the remains of the Roman wall on the East side of the Roman North gate.

2. *City Walls. East of North Gate. S.A.C.* 100 75.

Four courses of the inner face of the Roman wall examined. Constructed on a trench-built foundation of unmortared flints. Wall constructed of large flints in cream mortar with one course of roughly dressed sandstone, (*? Mixen rock*).

3. *City Walls, Priory Park. S.A.C.* 75, 116.

Trench cut through the bank against the City wall. Belgic girth beaker on original ground surface. Quantities of pottery included in bank; nothing later than 2nd century.

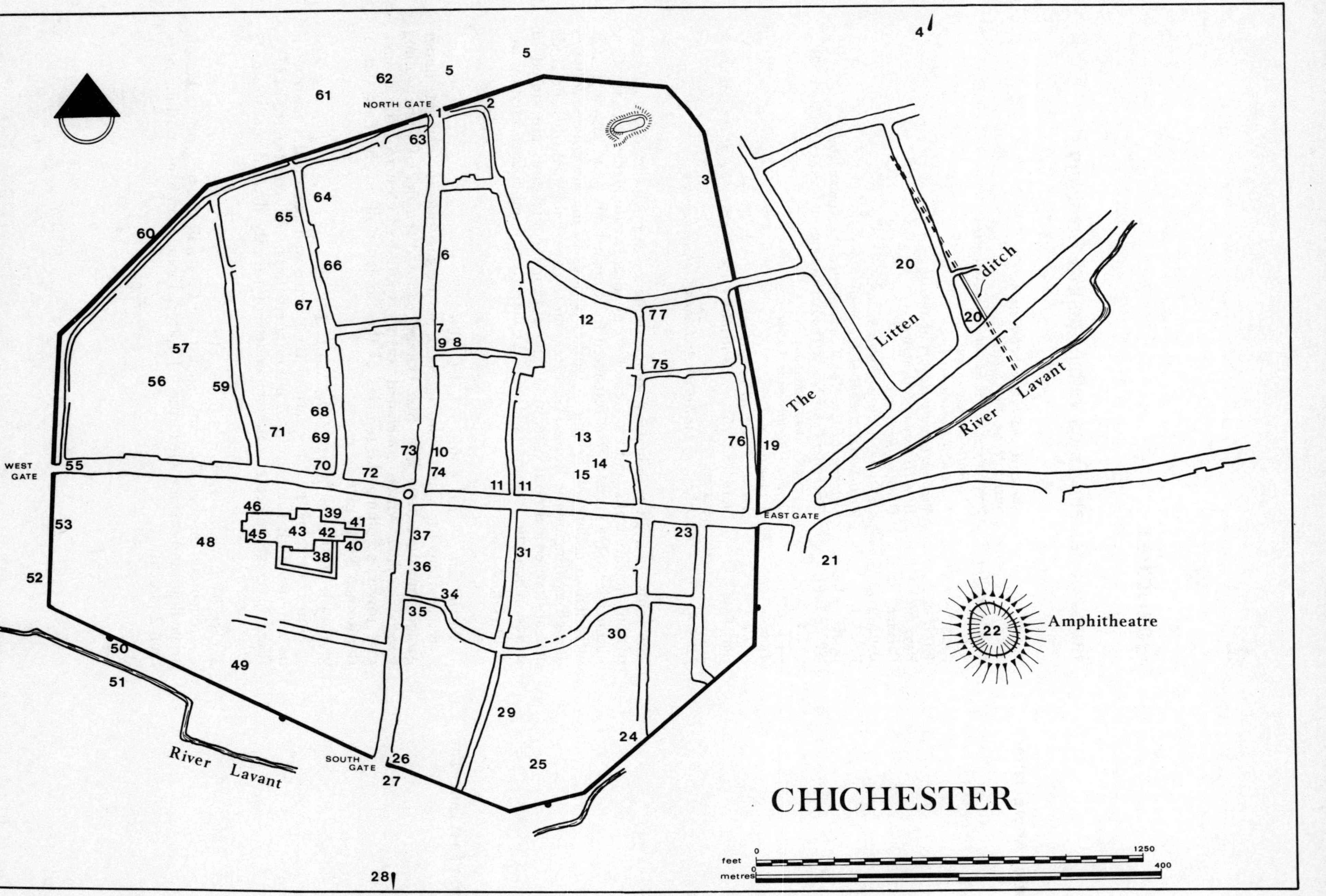

Fig. 2.1 *Plan of Roman Sites and Finds*

Photo: A. W. Rule

PLATE 1. Aerial view of Chichester 1969.

PLATE 2. Section through North Wall, Orchard Street.

Photo: M. H. Rule

4. *St. Richards Hospital.* Unpublished site..

Large pit 22 feet in diameter contained fragments of engaged columns now in the City museum collections. Discovered in 1968 when pier bases for new operating theatre were excavated. Further contractors excavations failed to produce evidence of Roman structures and it seems probable that a large Roman or medieval pit originally dug for clay or gravel was later filled with rubble brought from inside the town. The masonry clearly derives from an important classical building, possibly it formed part of the facade of a temple.

5. *Franklin Place. Wells.* Unpublished sites.

Two wells discovered in 1967 when a public service trench was cut along the south side of Franklin Place. One was constructed of water-worn blocks of Alveolina Limestone (Mixen Rock), the other of roughly dressed greensand from the weald. Lower levels of rubble included only Roman material, *tegulae, imbrices* and greyware.

6. *St. Peter the Less. S.A.C.* 100, 93-99; *J.R.S.* 50., 234.

Sequence of occupation from mid 1st-4th century; early timber structures. Late 1st century iron working site; 2nd century oven, 3rd century house/shop. Eastern edge of Roman North Street with side ditch. 2nd century re-metalling and widening of earlier street.

7. *North Street, Atkins Shop* (see page 51)

Foundations of flints set in creamy yellow mortar with a tile bonding course, seen in public service trench in 1967.

8. *Lion Street, Liberal Party Headquarters.* (see page 51)

Excavation 1967 in advance of development. 2nd/3rd century occupation debris; no structures.

9. *North Street, Temple Inscription.* (Pl. 8.) *V.C.H. Sx.* 3, 13; *S.A.C.* 94, 100-103.

1st century inscription dedicating a Temple to Neptune and Minerva. Discovered in 1723 at the North corner of Lion Street and North Street, now housed beneath the portico of the Assembly Rooms. Found at a depth of 4 ft close to wall foundations 3 ft thick running north-south and south-west. Probably the site of a first-century classical temple, but there remains a possibility that the inscription was in a secondary position when discovered.

10. *83 North Street, Storrey's shop.* Unpublished site.

Mechanical excavation of trench across the road from east to west sectioned a wall foundation at a depth of 4 ft. The foundations were 2 ft 6 ins deep and 2 ft wide and lay obliquely beneath the modern kerb at the east side of the street.

11. *East Street, corner of East Street and St. Martin's Lane. S.A.C.* 94, 104-5, *V.C.H. Sx.* 3, 14.

Dedicatory inscription from an official building or an imperial statue. Discovered 1740 and lost soon afterwards, this inscription is clear evidence for the early Romanization of Chichester. Dated 58-60 A.D. NERONI CLAUDIO DIVI (CLAUDI F G) ERMANI (CI) CAES N) EPOTI TI (CAES P) RONEPOTI DIV (I) (AUG ABNEPOTI) CAESARI AUG (T) R P IV IMP IV COS S C V. 'To Nero Claudius, son of the divine Claudius, grandson of Germanicus Caesar great-grandson of Tiberius Caesar, great- greatgrandson of the divinė Augustus Caesar, Augustus with Trionician power for the fourth time, Imperator for the fourth time, Consul for the fourth time'.

12. *St. Mary's Hospital* (see page 19)

Pre-Flavian ditches and timber structure. East-west street in excess of 15ft 6ins wide with timber buildings on the south side. Bronze harness hook (military) and Gallo-Belgic pottery.

13. *Central Car Par, Little London,* formerly Sadler's Garden.

Excavation by the late Mr. Fred Sadler pre-1939 (unpublished) and by J. Holmes and A. Down (1959-64) (forthcoming), are summarized as follows:–

a) Pre Flavian and probably military.

Sadler excavations. Sealed below second-century mortar floor were found sherds of pre-Flavian wares, i.e. Gallo-Belgic butt beakers and Terra Nigra, together with a number of brooches, some probably Claudian *SNQ*, **XIV**, 109 (sold privately) and some items of bronze military equipment (see Fig. 3.18 p. 48). It is not known whether these were from a ditch or pits.

1959-64 excavations. Early ditch running approximately east-west across the site. Bottom silt contained pre-Flavian samian and imported Gallo-Belgic wares similar to those found by Sadler. A bronze brooch (La Tene III type) was found in the ditch, and a military harness buckle below a gravel area to the north of the ditch, probably from associated military occupation layer. Bronze cuirass hook also found in robber trench.

b) 3rd-4th century

1959-64 excavations Remains of Roman house with tessellated floor, probably corridor, and with timber and clay walls and a hypocaust. This house is contemporary with the bath house behind No 30 East Street, see No. 14.

14. *30 East Street (David Greig's shop)* (J. Holmes, unpublished)

Excavation for a new sewer in 1959 cut through a mosaic pavement belonging to a bath house. The floor probably belonged to the *frigidarium*. Traces of a hypocaust were also found. Date of mosaic uncertain. This has now been raised and is in the City Museum in the Guildhall. This bath house is part of a complex of buildings stretching westwards under the car park, (see No 13) and the tessellated floor under St. Andrews church probably also belongs to this building. (see No. 15)

15. *East Street, South of St. Andrews Church. S.A.C.* 8, 291.

Tessellated pavement at a depth of 4 ft 5 ins extending from Mr. Mason's garden under the adjacent churchyard and St. Andrew's church.

16 *East Street. Proc. Soc. Ant.* 7, 292. *V.C.H. Sx.* 3, 13.

Two kilns (? ovens) discovered in 1877 during construction of a house 150 yards east of the Cross on the north side of East Street.

17. *East Street. S.C.M.* 10, 269.

Bronze figure of a horse two inches long, now in British Museum.

18. *East Street. S.A.C.* 32, 230.

Tessellated pavement 5 ft 3ins below surface showing marks of burning, discovered in 1888 'on the premises of Mr. Faulkner' and extending under adjacent buildings.

19. *East Walls.* Wilson 1957.

Foundations of City Wall overlaying 1st century occupation.

20. *Roman Cemetery at St. Pancras.* (see page 53)

Roman cremation cemetery alongside Stane Street, dating from c.70 A.D. to 4th century. Approximate extent 4.3 acres. The cemetery overlays earlier periods of gravel digging (c.60-70 A.D.) and an early 'military style' ditch running north-south and probably belonging to a military base camp.This ditch has a palisade trench on the east side and may have enclosed a defended area east of the City. After a short life, the ditch was filled in and probably dates from c. 43 A.D. Later 4th century gravel pits have destroyed part of the cemetery.

South East Quadrant

21. *Cattle Market. S.A.C.* **24**, 295.

Bronze ligula found during construction of new cattle market.

Cattle Market, S.A.C. **72**, 275.

Extensive excavations in 1930 yielded abundant pottery and tile, possibly the result of a Roman rubbish dump outside the Eastgate. No structures found.

22. *Amphitheatre.* S.C.M. **10**, 139-142; *A.J.* **16**, 149-159; *S.A.C.* **95**, 129-30.

Excavated 1935. Gravel arena floor 4 ft below Roman ground level. Inner wall faced with timber, plastered and painted, 185 ft by 150 ft. Erected *c.* 70-90 A.D. and abandoned by the end of the second century.

23. *Blackfriars Burial Ground, St. John's Street, A.N.L.* Aug. 1949, 63.

Occupation debris 1st-4th century. Traces of timber buildings 1st century.

24. *Friary Close. S.A.C.* **95**, 132. *J.B.A.A.* 1886, 134; *C.I.L.* 7, 14. V.C.H. Sx. 3 14.

Fragment of tombstone found in 1809 built into south east city wall, later built into a wall on the garden of the Bishop's Palace. (D) M........NUS AT ......ARIUS (AN) LXXXV. Broken when found and reused as building rubble.

25. *Cawley Priory. S.A.C.* **90**, 200-206; **100**, 80-92.

3rd and 4th century occupation associated with drainage ditch and (?) street. Section through town bank dug in 1959 showed the bank had been cut back when the wall was built at the end of the 2nd century. Bank made of contemporary topsoil and rubbish including quantities of 1st century pottery.

26. *Southgate, former site of Roman Catholic Church.* Unpublished excavation (J. Holmes)

Foundation of the Roman wall and bank overlay earlier occupation and a deep silt-filled ditch-like feature. No trace found of the South gate which must lie to the west, under the existing street.

27. *Southgate, Roman Tombstones. S.A.C.* **95**, 130, *C.I.L.* 7, 13. *V.C.H. Sx.* 3, 15, *Arch.* **26**, 466, *J.B.A.A.* 2, 85.

Two tombstones found in 1833 at a depth of 7 ft near Southgate. Both broken and probably re-used as building material. Late 1st century.

a) (3ft 1in. by 2ft 9in) (BODI)CCA AELIA CAVVA FIL(LA) AN (NORUM) XXXVI. Bodicca Aelia Cauva, daughter of...... aged 36 years.'

b) (Original size, 4ft 5in by 1ft 10in by 1ft) CATIA CENSORIN(A) AN XXIII. 'Catia Censorina aged 23 years.'

28. *The Canal Basin. V.C.H. Sx.* 3, 16.

Cremation and inhumation burials discovered in 1819.

29. *South Pallant. V.C.H. Sx.* 3, 13.

Drainage trench opposite No 5 South Pallant revealed the remains of a hypocaust, samian vessel form 37, a flanged bowl form 38 and other occupation debris. At this point the modern street is not on the line of a Roman street.

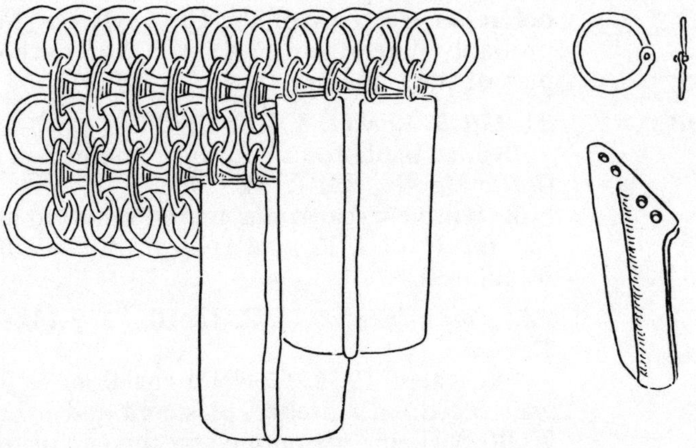

Fig. 2.3
Bronze Chain and Plate Mail

30. *East Pallant House. S.A.C.* **90**, 167.

Tessellated corridor of a house occupied in 2nd and 3rd century and demolished early 4th century. A 4ft-square cement-lined pit 3ft deep contained a deposit of fullers earth. A nearby pit of similar date contained traces of a burnt timber framework. A well lined with chalk blocks contained 15 4th-century coins.

31. *2 North Pallant.* Unpublished.

Re-building and service supply trenches in 1969 yielded native Roman coarseware and samian 1st-2nd century date. Rubbish pits, and (?) robber trenches.

32. *The Pallants. A.N.L.* April 1949.

Coin of Carausius, pottery and lamp found in 1949.

33. *The Pallants. S.C.M.* 6, 41. *V.C.H. Sx.* 3, 12.

Coin of Trajan 96-98 A.D. found in 1931 with a samian cup Drag. 27, stamped DONNAVCVS.

34. *West Pallant*. All Saints Church, *S.A.C.* 72, 275.

Public works trench dug in 1930 yielded several fragments of Roman architectural material including a massive piece of stone richly tooled with acanthus decoration (*possibly from the proscenium of the theatre*)

35. *West Pallant*, Portsmouth United Brewery site. *A.N.L.* Aug. 1949, 63.

The northern edge of a well-laid foundation exposed at a depth of 10 ft overlaying a layer of clay containing early Roman native ware. A mass of rubble masonry 'several tons', lay alongside the foundations.

36. *62 South Street.* Boots Chemists Shop, unpublished.

South Corner of Cooper Street and South Street, foundations, (?)Roman, 6ft below modern ground level. Associated with samian pottery. and coarseware.

37. *69 South Street.* Portsmouth and Sunderland Newspaper Offices, unpublished.

Redevelopment of site yielded unstratified Roman building debris coarseware and occupation debris including a fragment of plate mail (Fig. 2.3). Constructed of rectangular bronze plates with medial ridge and holes for attachment to bronze rings. Rings rectangular in section.

South West Quadrant

38, 39, 40, 41. *Chichester Cathedral.* (see page 127)

Polychrome mosaic floor at a depth of 4ft, hypocaust and three other rooms of a second-century building overlaying earlier occupation including Claudio/Neronian samian pottery.

42. *Chichester Cathedral S.A.C.* **19.**

Red tessellated floor discovered at a depth of 4ft whilst digging foundation for the reredos of the high altar in 1866.

43. *Chichester Cathedral S.A.C.* **19**, 197-98.

Red tessellated floor discovered when central pier of tower rebuilt following the collapse of the spire in 1861.

44. *Chichester Cathedral B.A.A.J.* 35, 94-95.

Red tessellated floor and flue tiles discovered in 1878.

45. *Chichester Cathedral B.A.A.J.*, 94-5.

Tesserae in a grave at west end of south aisle.

46. *Chichester Cathedral V.C.H. Sx.* **3**, 13.

Tiles and samian at west end of north aisle.

47. *Chichester Cathedral. S.A.C.* **8**, 291.

Samian pottery discovered whilst digging a vault.

48. *Bishop's Palace.. S.A.C.* **30**; Hay, Camden, Dallaway.

Several rooms of a town house, including a mosaic floor 30ft square associated with coins of Trajan and Domitian, 20ft from south east angle of bishop's palace. Discovered in 1725-7.

49. *Deanery Gardens. S.N.Q.* **3**, 55.

Foundations visible as crop marks following severe drought in 1929. Apse 15 ft across and open to the east. 10ft south of south west corner of the Deanery.

50. *Palace Bastion. S.A.C.* **100**; J. Holmes, *The defences of Roman Chichester*.

Excavator concluded that there were 2 phases in the Roman defences; Phase 1, two V-shaped ditches and a bank, the front of the bank being revetted by a wall 7ft thick, dated c. 200 A.D. Phase 2, inner ditch filled in and bastions erected at intervals along the wall; a wider flat-bottomed ditch being dug partly into the outer phase 1 ditch. Dated to c. 4th century. (Wilson 1957). A 3rd phase of defensive work occurred in 1378 when the walls and gates were repaired. A new ditch was dug, 50 ft wide around the city, which destroyed most of the earlier Roman ditches.

51. *Westgate fields. S.N.Q.* **9**, 183., *S.N.Q.* **10**, 68.

Provincial (? Gaulish) votive figurine. Now in Chichester City Museum collections.

52. *Link Road Site. J.R.S.* **50**, 234. Ibid. **53** 151. *S.A.C.* **100**, 81-2.

Stone and timber lined well 2 ft diameter and fragmentary foundations of house aligned on north side of a *supposed* east-west street pre-dating the city wall. Associated with Hadrianic samian pottery. Earlier underlying structures provisionally dated by the excavator (J. Holmes) to c. 60 A.D.

53. *Bishops Garden*, unpublished. (see p 147)

Collapse of wall on south side of Castle Inn car park revealed a section across the defensive bank, and the cut-back to facilitate the construction of the wall. The bottom inset at the rear face of the wall was seen. The

18th-century brick wall at present revetting the bank is built on the back edge of the Roman footings, which do not show above ground level.

North West Quadrant

54. *Fishbourne Roman supply base and 1st century Palace.*

One mile west of the City Cross, within the city boundary, discovered in 1960 when a water pipe was laid. Nine seasons of excavation have revealed the partial plan of a mid-1st century supply base situated at the head of an arm of Chichester harbour. Abandonment of military function and development of civil buildings on the site between 50-60 A.D. Masonry palace covering site of 6½ acres constructed c. 74 A.D. Four wings around central courtyard garden. Harbour to south of palace partially filled and landscaped to provide seaside garden, with colonnades and ornamental water-course. Gradual conversion to private use from early second century onwards. Finally destroyed by fire c. 270 A.D.

55. *Westgate 1964* (see page 143)

Excavations in advance of street works after demolition of nos 1 and 2 North Walls. Roman town wall found below cottage foundations suggests that Roman West gate occupied the same site as the later medieval gate. Sealed below bottom layers of bank were remains of timber structures and burnt layers associated with iron slag from a forge. Pottery in bank material confirms date of c. late 2nd century for establishment of defences.

56. *County Hall, West Street. S.A.C.* **76**, 135-156.

Gallo-Belgic and early native pottery discovered when the County Hall buildings were constructed, 1934-5.

57. *County Hall extension. J.R.S.* **51**, 189, Holmes 1965.

Excavations in advance of building to extend County Hall northwards in 1960, discovered a cambered gravel surface, possibly part of an east-west street parallel to West Street. A ditch approximately 4ft 6ins deep and 9ft wide ran along the south side of the street. Remains of a burnt medieval building with red clay floor partly overlaid the filled in drainage ditch in one place, the building being immediately over the street. A Roman bronze belt buckle of c. late 4th-early 5th century date found in top fill of ditch.

58. *West Street.*, Horsefield. **I**, 42.

Tessellated pavement found in 1811 during construction of a cellar.

59. *Public Library, Tower Street, S.A.C.* **104**, 46-55.

Burnt timber buildings associated with pre-Flavian samian pottery and sealed by a layer of clay make-up. Possibly the result of deliberate site clearance when the Roman town was laid out c. 70-80 A.D. Large ditch-like feature found at north west corner of the site.

60. *North walls, Orchard Street.* (see page 149)

Collapse of modern wall facing in 1968 revealed medieval wall rebuilt on Roman foundations.

61. *Northgate, corner of St. Pauls Road. S.A.C.* **87**, 39. *S.N.Q.* XI 8, 175.

4th century coin. Obverse Urbs Roma. Reverse, wolf suckling Romulus and Remus. Cohen VII, 330. Now in the museum of the Sussex Archaeological Society at Lewes.

62. *Fire Station, St. Pauls Road*, unpublished.

Levelling of the site prior to construction of the new Fire Station removed 2 ft of top soil. A number of truncated pits were observed and several excavated. A quantity of late Roman pottery of 3rd and 4th century date indicates either a late Roman settlement outside the north gate or the use of the area as a rubbish tip (See No. 21).

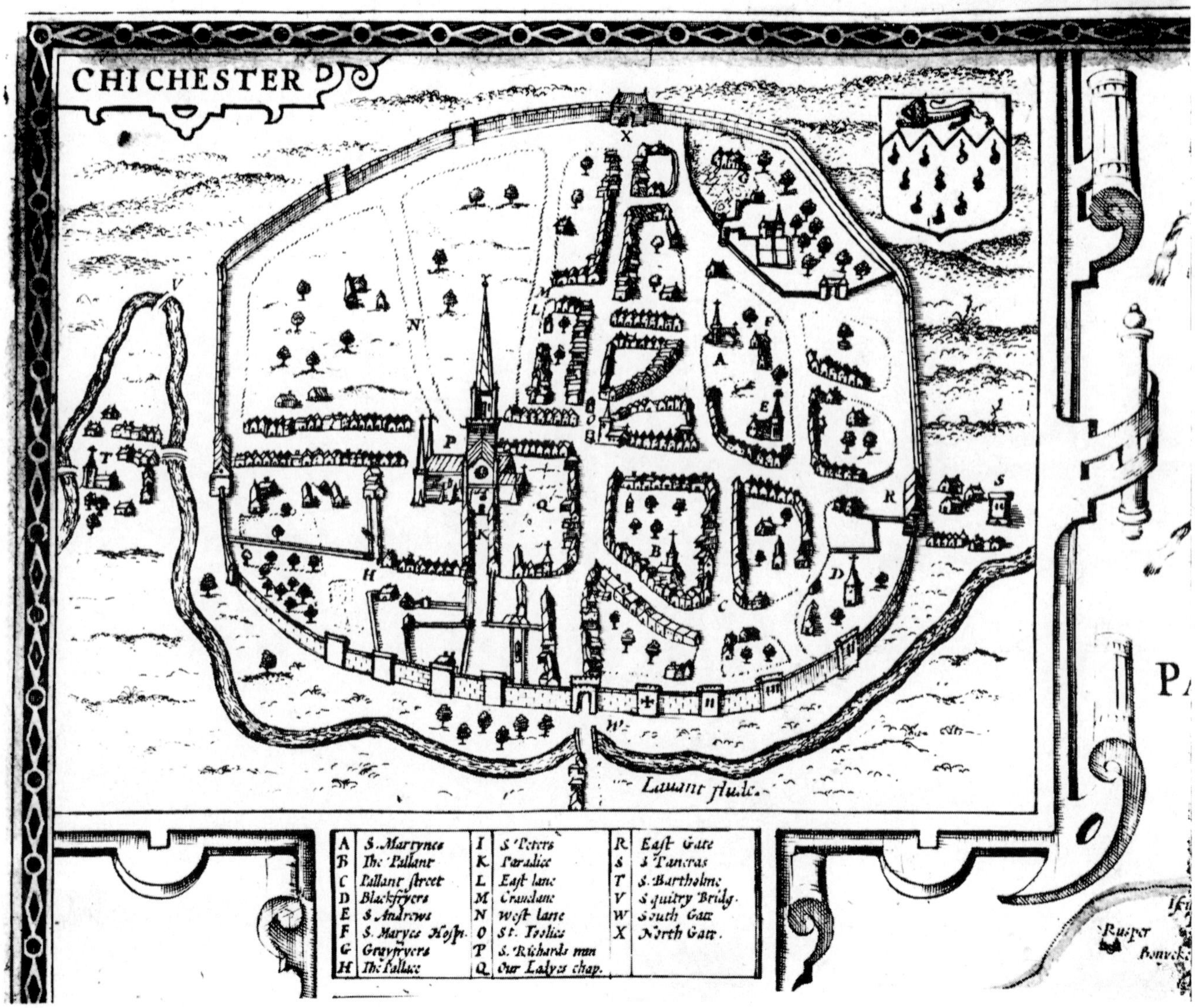

Fig. 2.2. Speed's map of Chichester 1610.

Fig. 2.5. Gardner map of Chichester 1769.

63: *Northgate, City Wall 1968*, unpublished.

Excavation of a trench by the County Council 2ft east of west kerb opposite the Blue Star Garage in North Street, cut through a hard foundation of flints and mortar approximately 9ft wide, on the line of the City Wall.

64. *43 North Street. S.A.C.* **90**, 207.

Two phases of Roman cobbling laid down at some time after the middle of the 2nd century. Metalling was 5 – 6 ins thick with a thin layer of clay between, and sealed occupation layer containing sherd of South Gaulish samian, c. 120 A.D. Evidence of earlier excavations below, probably for gravel. Coin of Cunobelinus found in earlier occupation layer. Norman oven cut through Roman cobbling, possibly bread oven.

65. *Chapel Street. S.N.Q.* **5**, *112.*

Tessellated pavement discovered in 1934, with walls running obliquely to modern Chapel Street.

66. *34-38 Chapel Street. S.A.C.* **106**, 113-132.

Excavations in advance of development in garden west of 34 to 38 North Street. Timber buildings alongside Roman street, c. 80 to late 2nd century. Pre-Flavian occupation sealed beneath the street and late Saxon pits cut through street metalling. Excavation of adjacent site to the south currently continuing (September 1969). Extensive timber buildings and a hearth.

67. *Chapel Street, Central Girls School.* Current excavations (Sept 1969).

West side of street discovered on site 66 above. Large 4th century house aligned on west side of street with 4 tessellated pavements and 4 *opus signinum* floors. This may be part of the building discovered in 1934 (see 65 above). Masonry structures overlay several phases of earlier timber buildings, one building very substantial. Part of the area used for metal working or enamelling. Pre-Flavian occupation associated with a bronze military harness strap in levels below timber buildings.

68. *Chapel Street, Telephone Exchange. J.R.S.* **53**, 156.

Three-feet thick layer of gravel (Forum) extending northwards beyond the limits of the site and sealing early occupation material. Amphora stamp 'C Semp. Poly' found below the gravel.

69. *Chapel Street. G.P.O. S.A.C.* **95**, 131-3; **A.J. 15**, 461-4; *S.N.Q.* 13, 15-16.

Square stone pedestal for column base or statue of Jupiter of late 2nd or early 3rd century date discovered whilst digging foundations for the Chapel Street frontage of the G.P.O. in 1935. Now in the Chichester City Museum collections.

70. *West Street. G.P.O. S.A.C.* **76**, 159-171; Ibid **80**, 175; Ibid **93**, 75.

Excavations in advance of building in 1935. Gravel layer 2 – 3ft thick, laid at two periods and sealing early occupation material. (Probably site of Forum, laid out c. 70-80 A.D.)

71. *West Street, Morants shop. J.R.S.* **53**, 151; Holmes 1965.

Excavations in 1960 and 1962 to extend Morants shop to the north east revealed a partial plan of a large 4th century bath building, probably the town baths. An apsidal cold plunge bath with walls 5 ft thick overlay the foundations of an earlier bath building. A fragment of black and white geometric mosaic floor still preserved in situ beneath the modern showroom floor was interpreted as part of a range of rooms associated with the baths. (*Stylistically the floor would seem to be earlier than the 4th century and it is*

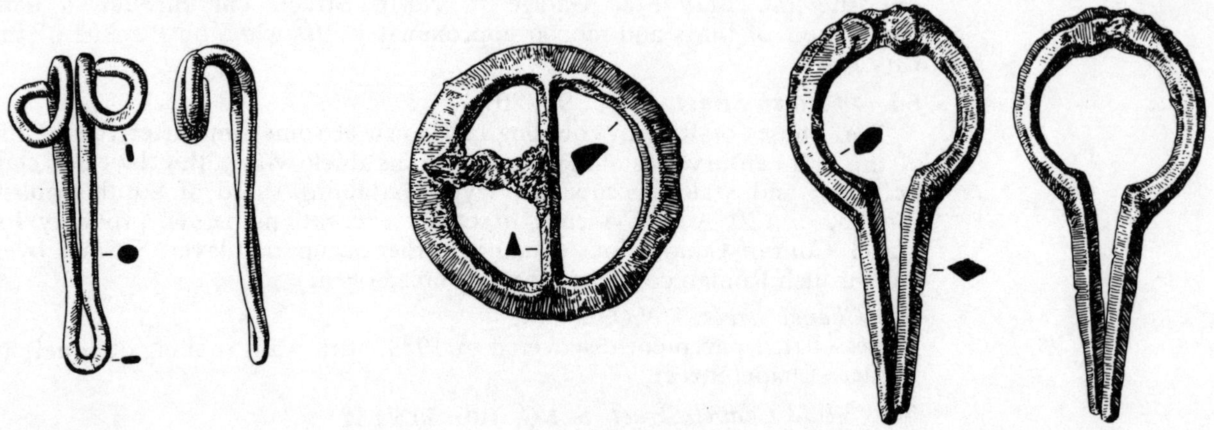

Fig. 2.4

possible that reception rooms or dressing rooms of the earlier baths were incorporated into the later baths.)

72. *West Street, Dolphin and Anchor Hotel.* Holmes 1965; *S.N.Q.* 13, 332.
Construction of an air-raid shelter in the cellars of the hotel in 1940 revealed massive flint walling at least 6 ft thick running along the West Street frontage of the hotel. (This foundation, which is still partially visible in the hotel cellars could be part of the foundations for a collonade on the south side of the Forum.) A fragment of undated stone walling was recorded in a gas pipe trench along the West Street frontage of the G.P.O. in 1934. (This could be part of the same structure.) *S.N.Q.* 4, 112.

73. *North Street 3,4 and 5.* (see page 15)
Re-development of 3, 4 and 5 North Street in 1967 revealed a spread of gravel 2ft 9ins below modern ground level, about 3 ft thick, badly cut away by medieval pits and later cellar foundations. The corner of a massive foundation constructed of water-worn blocks of Alveolina limestone (Mixen Rock) was seen in the excavation for a modern pier base foundation. This foundation, situated in an open gravel area is more likely to be the base of an altar or massive statue than a wall.

Addenda

74. *North East Quadrant.*
North Street, Little Anchor Inn. S.A.C. 95, 131; *C.I.L.* 8s,; *V.C.H. Sx.* 3, 14; Horsefield 1, 43; *Arch.* 26, 466.
Altar, 3ft 6ins x 1ft 6ins found in 1823 at a depth of 4ft. Now in City Museum collections. 1st century A.D., GENIO S(ACRUM) LUCULLUS AMMINI FIL(IUS) D(E)S(UO) P(OSUIT). 'Sacred to the Genius, Lucullus son of Amminius at his own charge places this stone.'

75. *East Row, No. 1.* (unpublished site)
Unstratified Roman coarseware and bronze objects found during building operations in 1969. (see Fig. 2.4).

Hunston 1969. Gas pipe trench being dug at the time of writing, (September 1969), has sectioned two ditches 78ft apart on the presumed alignment. NGR SU856007

The Roman Road System

East gate. Stane Street Road to Londinium, Road number 15 Margary 1967. No firm archaeological evidence exists for the route immediately east of the City Gates, although the presence of the Roman Cemetery on the North side of the present road suggests that the present line of St. Pancras coincides with the Roman Road. See discussion on page 67 of this volume.

In spite of continued excavation within the City by public works authorities and private developers, disappointingly little evidence of the Roman Street grid has so far been found.

North Street. Gazeteer No. 6
Eastern camber of street metalling sectioned.

St. Mary's Hospital. Gazeteer No. 12
East west street in excess of 15ft 5ins wide.

Chapel Street. Gazeteer No. 66 and 67
Roman north-south street circa 35ft wide. Side ditch on west side.

County Hall. Gazeteer No. 56
Possible Roman street running east west with drainage ditch on south side.

Link Road site. Gazeteer No. 52
Vestiges of flint metalling. 'Presumed' surface of east-west street.

The Roman Street System

The present street system of Chichester is not Roman, but may have had its origins in the burghal hideage town established by King Alfred in the 10th century. However, there is no doubt that its lay-out was decided by the position of the four Roman City gates. The four main streets which divide the City are therefore roughly aligned along the original Roman grid which was laid out in the years between A.D. 70 and A.D. 80 as part of a deliberate re-planning of the native town of Cogidubnus. (Holmes, 1965, p. 17; this volume pp. 69, 70.

For the approach roads to the City, the archaeological evidence is summarised below.

Northgate. Road to Silchester. (*Calleva*) Road number 155 Margary 1967

Somerstown, see page 165. Excavations on West side of Broyle Road show a ditch running North-South, possibly the side ditch alongside the Roman road, with a thin capping of graded flints on rammed clay alongside. This may have been a pedestrian way alongside the *agger*.

Westgate. Road to Clausentum. Road number 421 Margary 1967. No archaeological evidence exists for the route of this street immediately after it leaves the Westgate.

Southgate. Road to Roman settlement at Selsey. Road number 156 Margary 1967
No archaeological evidence for route immediately south of the presumed position of Southgate, but presence of Roman burials in the vicinity of the Canal Basin (No 28) and the finding of two tombstones near Southgate (No 27) suggests the existence of a road in the vicinity.

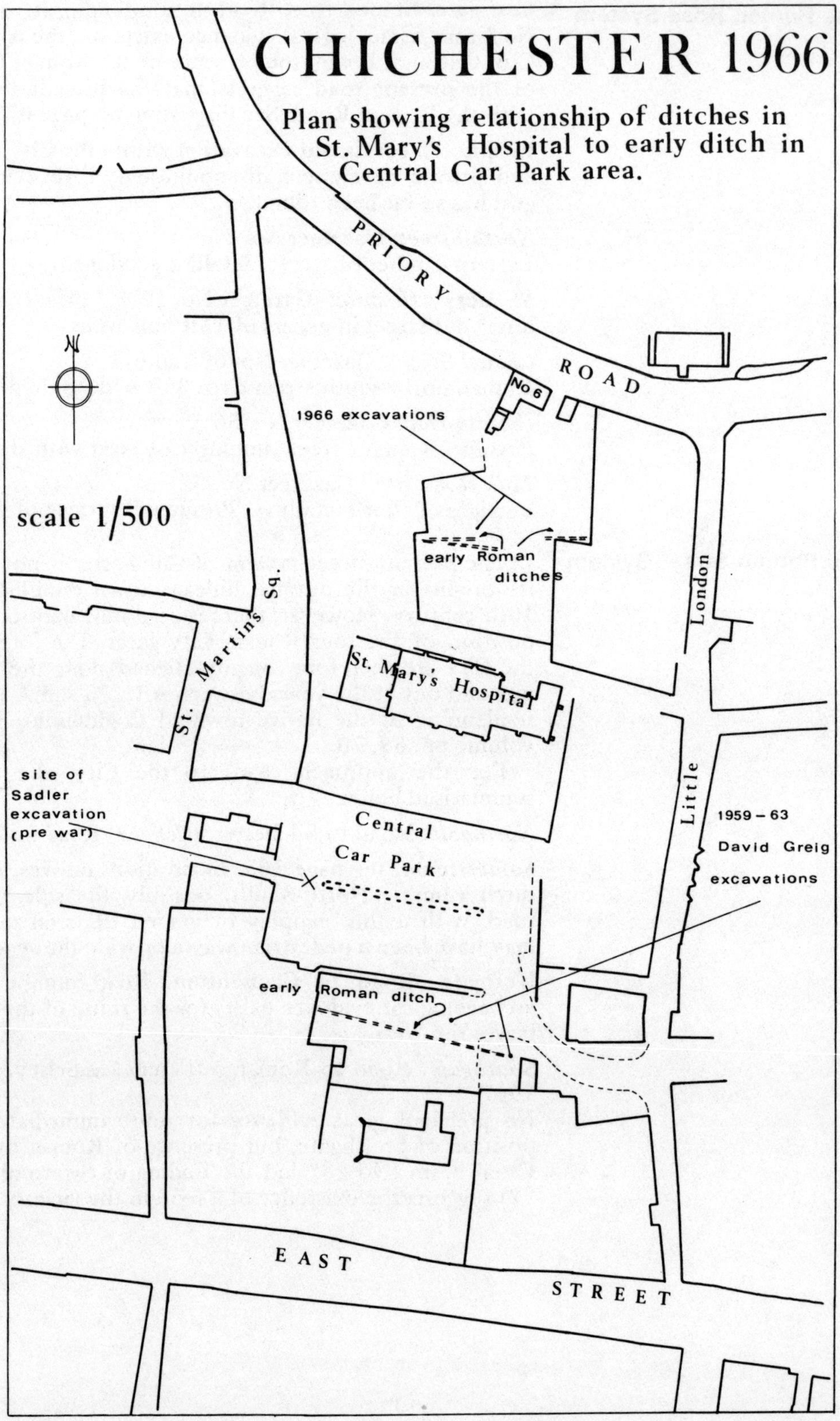

Fig. 3.1 Based on the Ordnance Survey, by Permission of the Director General

3

Excavations in the grounds of St. Mary's Hospital

In the Spring of 1966 the Excavations Committee were invited by the Trustees of St. Mary's Hospital to carry out excavations on land to the north of the hospital (formerly Pennicott's Coal Yard and the garden south of it), which was to be sold to developers.

A period of 1 to 2 years for excavation was indicated, and in view of the size of the land a joint project was planned by the site directors. Mr. Down excavated Area 1 at weekends during spring and summer, while Mrs. Rule excavated Area 2 as a full-time project during August. It was planned to complete this work with a third phase of excavation to be carried out jointly during the autumn and winter, as it was becoming increasingly obvious from the results coming in from both Areas 1 and 2 that the whole site was of great archaeological importance, and would add considerably to our knowledge of the military phase of Roman Chichester.

Before Phase 3 could commence, permission to excavate was withdrawn by the Trustees on the grounds that the land was about to be sold and developed. Although representations were made to them, no further work was allowed, and much information about the beginnings of Roman Chichester has consequently been lost. The authors regard the decision of the Trustees as particularly lamentable when it is recalled that the land subsequently stood derelict for almost three years before building operations began in the summer of 1969.

Period 1, Phase 1, c.43–60 A.D. Figs 3.2 & 3.4

At some time after 43 A.D., and probably not more than a year or so later, a ditch was dug across the site from east to west. Although it was not possible to complete the excavation of trenches G and H in Area 2, the natural brick earth beneath and to the south of Slot G38 was carefully examined and no trace of ditch was found. The eastern arm, noted in L 17, 18 and 19, must have ended east of trench G, and the western arm either ended in Trench H, which was never completely excavated, or in the unexcavated area on the west side of this trench. The ditch was approximately 2.4m (8ft) wide and 1m (3ft 3ins) deep, and was dug into the natural brick earth, coming down into clay-with-flints at the bottom, which was approximately .8m (2ft 8ins) wide.

The rapid silt contained samian ware of pre-Flavian date, associated with Gallo-Belgic wares and native imitations of these fabrics, together with 'Belgic' style bead-rimmed coarse wares and native fine-burnished wares, normally found in association on Chichester sites in a pre-Flavian context. The fill above the rapid silt was a dirty brown/yellow clay, and the pottery from this layer contained similar wares to those in the rapid silt. Two sherds of pre-Flavian samian were found, one a Dr. 17 in Montans fabric dated Claudius-Nero, and a Dr. 29 'very early', c. 40-55 A.D., together with a Dr. 27 of Flavian date.

To the west of the eastern area of Ditch 1 was a slot for a timber structure together with its associated postholes (G38 and G39). The slot was 40cms (15.75ins) wide and was cut 8cms (3.26ins) into the natural brick earth; it contained a posthole 19cms (7.5ins) diameter, cut to a depth of 11cms (4.35ins), that is to say 3cms below the bottom of the slot. A similar

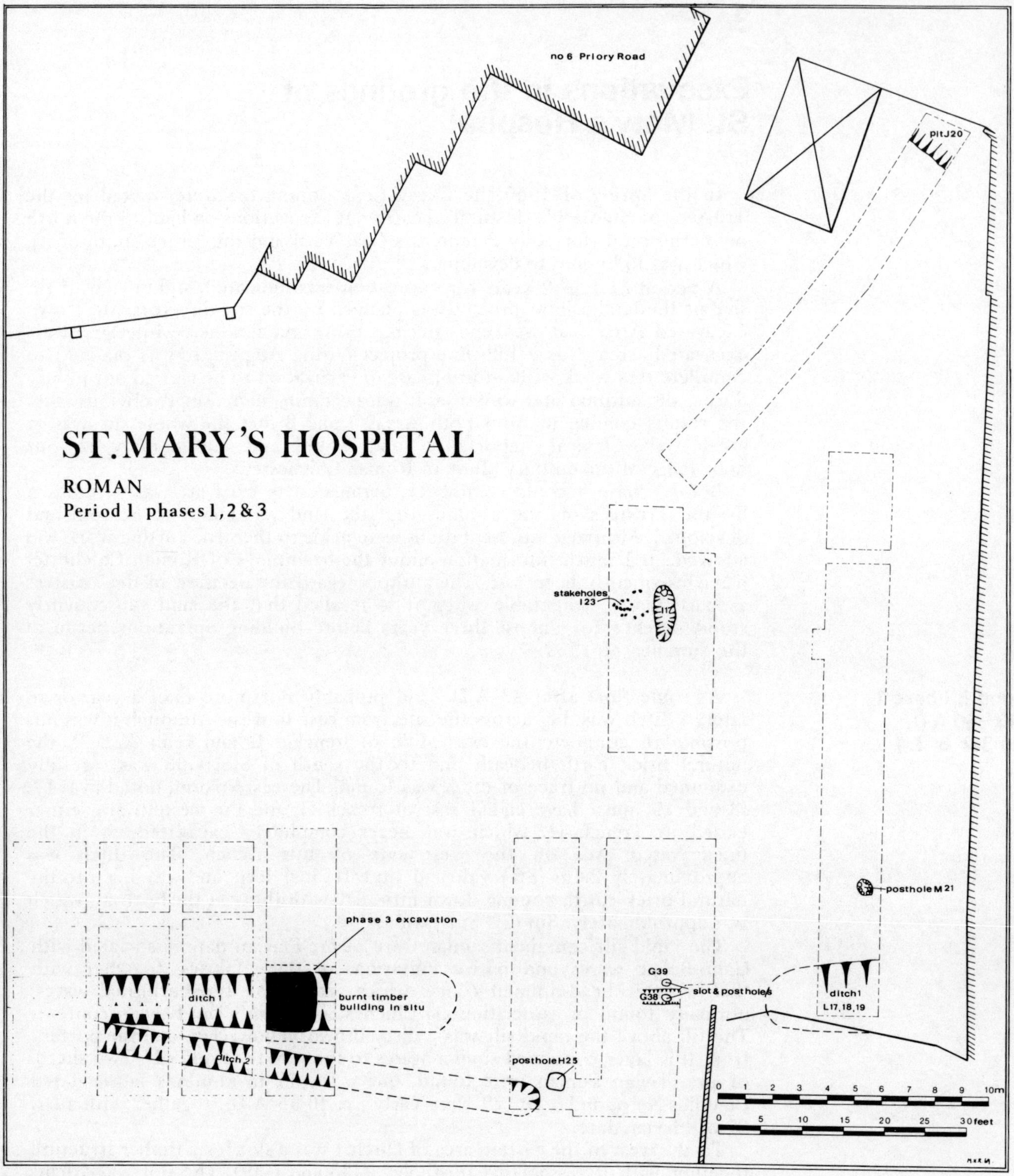
no 6 Priory Road
pitJ20
ST.MARY'S HOSPITAL
ROMAN
Period 1 phases 1,2 & 3
stakeholes
I23
posthole M21
phase 3 excavation
ditch 1
burnt timber
building in situ
ditch 2
G39
G38
slot & postholes
ditch1
L17,18,19
postholeH25
0 1 2 3 4 5 6 7 8 9 10m
0 5 10 15 20 25 30feet

Fig. 3.2

posthole, 26cms (10.25ins) diameter was found to the north of the timber slot, cut to the same depth as the posthole within the slot, (Fig 3.2). In the soft silty fill of the slot was found a bronze harness hook (Fig. 3.15 no. 2), a mid-1st century piece of equipment common on legionary sites, and found at Colchester associated with other military equipment in a pre-Flavian context (*Camulodunum*, 339, Pl. 103, 7).

This timber structure is tentatively regarded as contemporary with Ditch 1. Its function is uncertain, but it occupies a position between the two arms of the ditch and may have some connection with an entrance way, later altered (see discussion below). All these features were sealed by a turfline (L.15) and the later street metalling (G16, 20; L10, 14).

Period 1, Phase 2, Ditch 2. Figs 3.2 & 3.4

Shortly after Ditch 1 was dug, Ditch 2 was dug at a slightly different angle. The point where it cut into Ditch 1 on the west side could not be determined exactly, as later Roman pits had completely destroyed the evidence. On the east side it ran out of Area 1 and the end of it was just visible in Area 2. This ditch was narrower than Ditch 1, being approximately 1.9m wide (6ft 3in) and 1.2m deep (4ft). The primary silt again contained pre-Flavian samian, while the fill above the primary silt (A13 and 14) which was similar in colour and texture to that in Ditch 1, contained sherds from 5 pre-Flavian samian vessels, and similar Gallo-Belgic and native imitation wares to that found in Ditch 1. Layer A14 in A3 contained a *dupondius* of Vespasian in mint condition (A.D. 71). The condition of the coin and the absence of Flavian samian in the lower levels suggests that the ditch was out of use by late Neronian times and had been almost filled in by A.D. 70. A considerable amount of food waste was thrown into this ditch and it was noted that the top fill contained a number of small lumps of burnt clay. Extensive burning was also noted along the north side of the ditch in Trench A7, where the side was partly cut away by a later Roman pit.

North of the end of Ditch 2 in Area 2 an associated posthole (H25) was found, cut 1.35m (53.13 in) into the brick earth. The posthole originally contained a post, about 63 cms (24.5 in) in diameter, and the rectangular impression of the post was still retained in the bottom 5 cms (2 in) of the postpit. The lowest fill around the base of the post contained a fragment of human cranium, and the upper clay packing of the postpit showed signs of lateral compression as if the post had been withdrawn from its socket by a 'rocking' action. The cavity left by the removal of the post was filled with a re-deposited silty clay. The clay sealing the top of the postpit contained one sherd of 1st century samian.

At the extreme northern limits of the site a feature, (J.20) was sectioned which might possibly have been a ditch, or alternatively a latrine pit. It was cut 30 cms (35.4 in) deep into the natural clay, but adjacent buildings made it impossible to investigate fully. The primary fill consisted of a thin band of brownish organic loam, 4 cms (1.5 in) thick. The secondary silt contained yellow silty clay, 8 – 10 cms (3.1 – 3.9 ins) thick, and 2 sherds of a pre-Flavian Dr27, while the upper fill contained occupation rubbish; tile, coarseware, and 8 samian sherds. These included a Dr.27 (Claudian), a Dr.18 (early Flavian) and one sherd of 1st century date. A small bronze mount was also found in this layer, (Fig. 3.16 no. 6)

This upper fill was markedly different from the lower levels and represents a deliberate filling up and levelling of the site after the end of Period 1, phase 2. The feature was truncated by two pits, both containing nothing later than Saxo-Norman pottery.

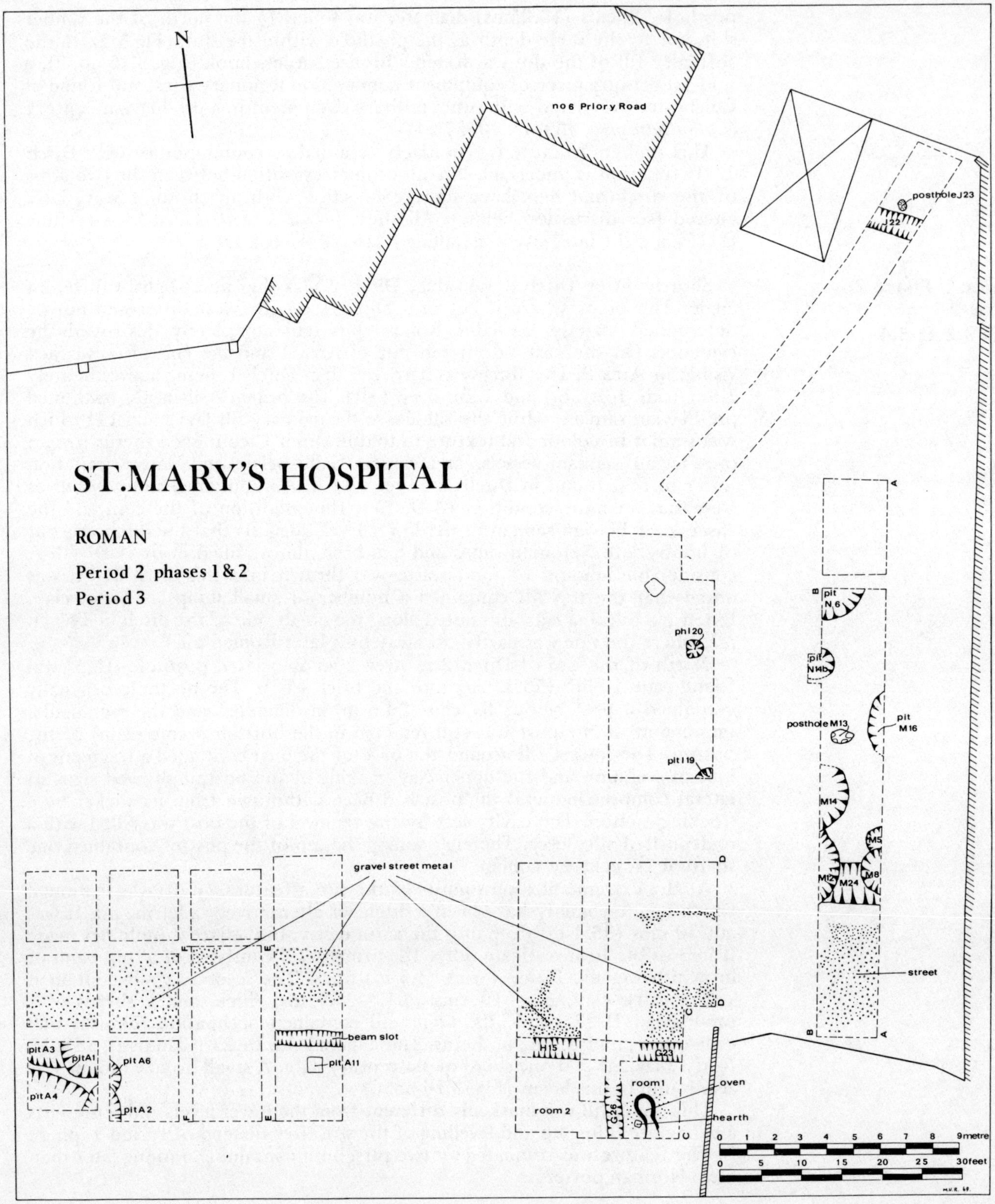
N
no 6 Priory Road
posthole J23
J22
ST.MARY'S HOSPITAL
ROMAN
Period 2 phases 1 & 2
Period 3
A
B
pit N 6
ph l 20
pit N14b
posthole M13
pit M16
pit l 19
M14
M5
M12
M24
M8
gravel street metal
street
beam slot
pit A3
pit A1
pit A6
pit A4
pit A2
pit A11
H15
G21
room 1
room 2
G26
oven
hearth
0 1 2 3 4 5 6 7 8 9 metre
0 5 10 15 20 25 30 feet

Fig. 3.3

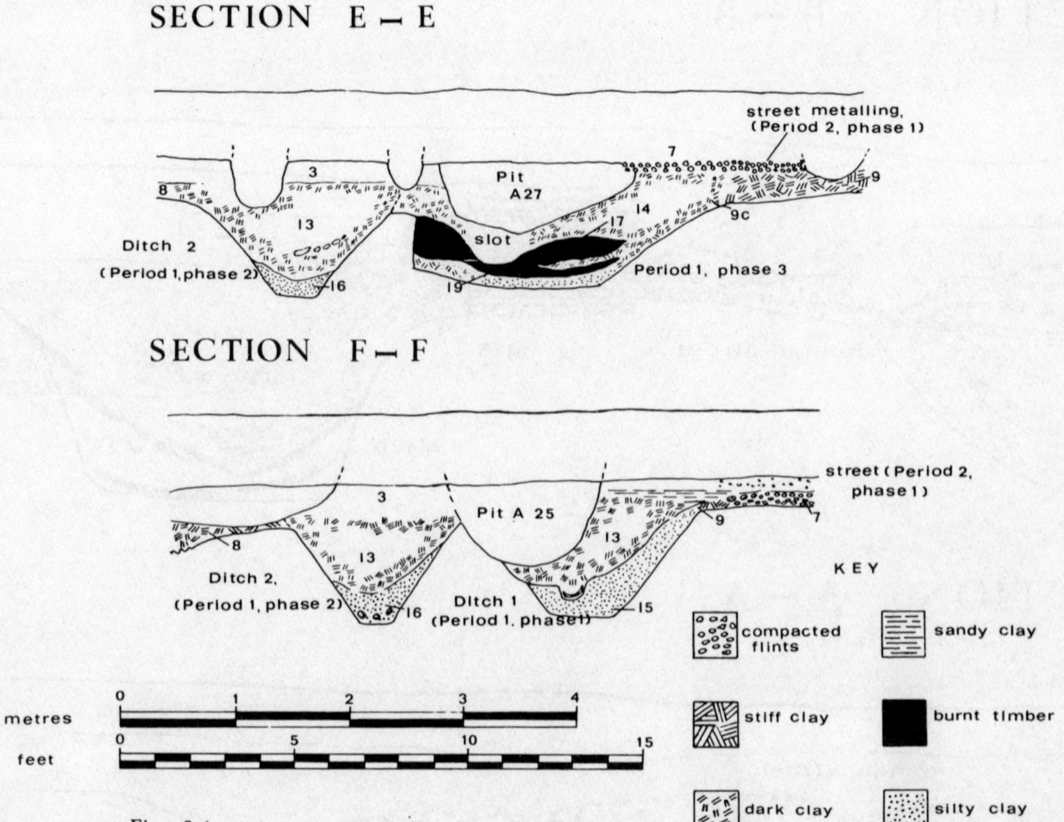

Fig. 3.4

Period 1, Phase 3, Flavian to 2nd Century. Figs 3.2 & 3.4

Whilst Ditch 2 was still open, but after it had begun to be used as a rubbish tip, an excavation was made into Ditch 1, cutting back the lip of the bank on the north side and also cutting into the undug area between the two ditches. This excavation was a local one, and was slightly larger than trench B 7. Its purpose is obscure, but it appears that some sort of timber structure was erected in it, and that this subsequently burnt down and fell into the excavation. Where it had burnt *in situ* it had baked the clay hard for a considerable area around, and it is considered that the digging of later pits through the baked clay was the origin of the re-deposited lumps of burnt clay in the top fill of Ditch 2. The separation of the burnt timber layers by a layer of clay suggests that when the partially burnt structure collapsed there were air gaps between the beams which were later filled by silting clay. There was the impression of a beam in the soft carbonised wood; this was aligned east–west, (see below under Period 2, phase 2). The fill above the excavation was very similar to that in the top fill of the two ditches, but it contained later pottery, including a number of samian sherds of Antonine date, indicating that the final backfilling did not take place until well on into the 2nd century. There were a number of other features in Area 2 which appear on the evidence of the pottery or the stratification to fall within the same phase. A stone-packed posthole (M 21), 54 cms (21.25 ins) diameter was cut 31 cms (12.2 ins) into the natural brick earth and carefully packed with 11 small fist-sized flints. This feature was cut away on the north side by Ditch M 24.

SECTION B – B

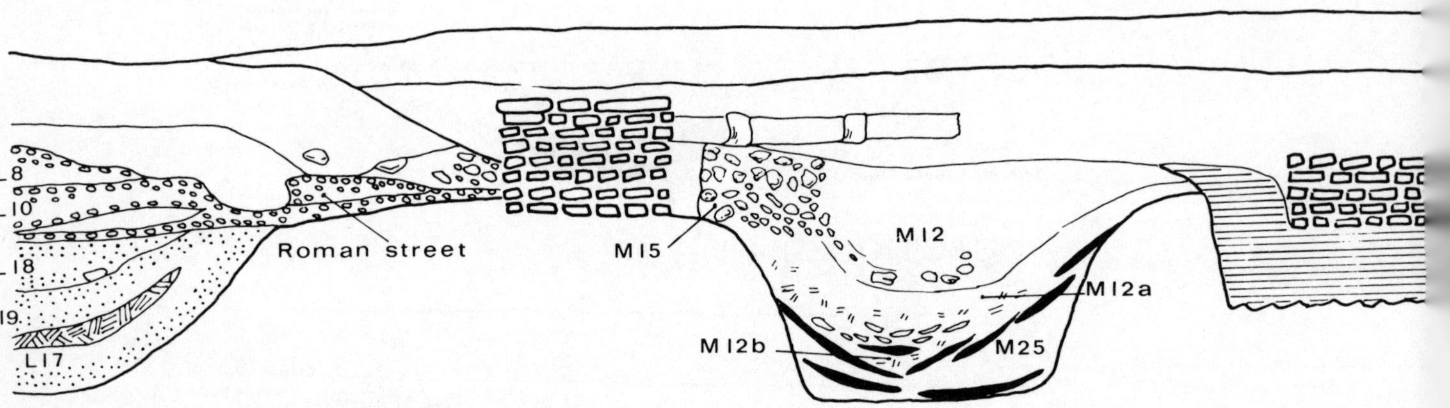

SECTION A – A

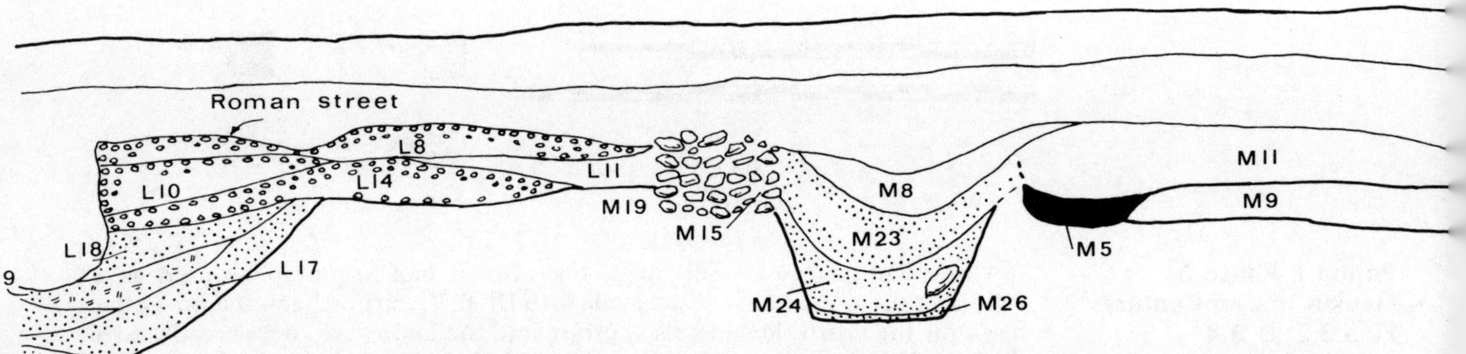

SECTION C – C & D – D

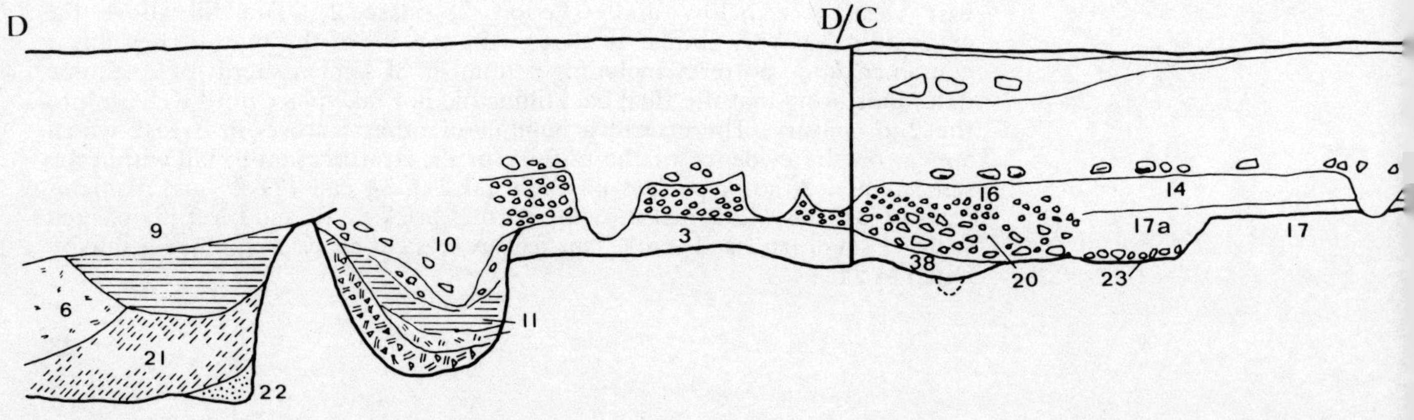

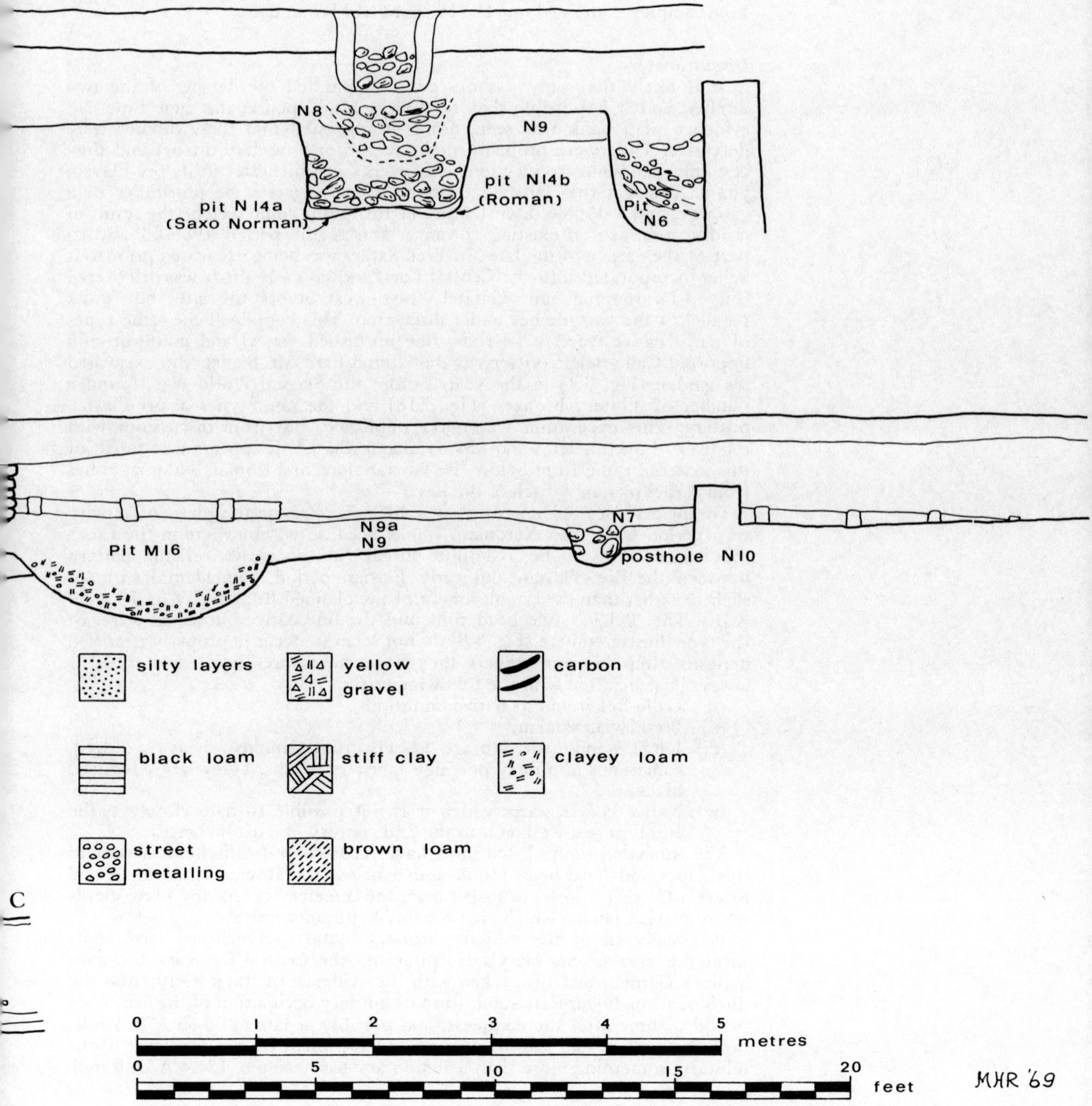
N8
N9
pit N14b
(Roman)
pit N14a
(Saxo Norman)
Pit
N6
N7
N9a
N9
Pit M16
posthole N10
silty layers
yellow gravel
carbon
black loam
stiff clay
clayey loam
street metalling
brown loam
0
1
2
3
4
5
metres
0
5
10
15
20
feet
MHR '69

Fig. 3.5

A shallow pit (I.17) which may have been a truncated posthole, was cut 4 cms (1.5 ins) into the natural clay and was associated with a complex of 16 small stakeholes (I.23), cut to the same depth. The pit contained two sherds of pre-Flavian samian and a sherd of an imitation Terra Nigra dish; the stake-hole complex contained one Dr. 18 sherd of Flavian date.

Discussion

It is likely that only a short period separated the digging of the two ditches, and it is possible that they were both open at the same time. No evidence of a bank was seen, nor is it suggested that these ditches were defensive. They were probably drainage and/or boundary ditches and they certainly had some connection with events in Chichester in its pre-Flavian phase. The fact that Ditch 2 ends in Area 2 suggests the possibility of a gateway, and a double ditch feature at this point could well be the result of modifications to an existing entrance. During the period 1959-63[1], when part of the garden of the late Mr. Fred Sadler was being excavated prior to it being incorporated into the Central Car Park, an early ditch was discovered (Fig. 3.1), running approximately east—west across the site, not quite parallel to the two ditches under discussion. This contained the same types of early native ware (bead rims, fine burnished wares) and imitation and imported Gallo-Belgic pottery as that found here. Mr. Sadler who excavated his garden (Fig. 3.1) in the years before the Second World War, found a number of military bronzes (Fig. 3.18) and the same types of pre-Flavian pottery. This excavation was never published, but from discussions with relatives of Mr. Sadler[2], and Mrs. Grahame Clark[3], it appears that much of this material came from below the mortar floor of a Roman building, either from earlier pits, or a ditch or ditches.

On the evidence of the pottery it is difficult to assign this phase of activity to a period later than Neronian. It has been noted elsewhere in the City[4] that there seems to be a definite 'break' in the native ceramic pattern between the pre—Flavian and early Flavian period, coincidental with, or slightly earlier than the establishment of the planned Roman city (c. 70 – 80 A.D.). The 'Belgic' style bead rims and the fine native burnished wares of the type illustrated here (Fig. 3.8) do not seem to occur in properly stratified deposits after this time. Where they do occur in pre-Flavian contexts it is always in association with the following wares:

(i) Gallo-Belgic and its native imitations,
(ii) Pre-Flavian samian,
(iii) Large hand-made storage vessels, rope rimmed, heavily gritted, sometimes in a dirty porridgy fabric or in a hard grey fabric reduced black.
(iv) Native coarse wares which it is not possible to date closely as the forms persist well on into the 2nd century in most instances.

The associated groups listed above have occurred in the ditches discussed in this paper and have been found sealed below the Roman street in Chapel Street[5]. Groups 1 to 3 are absent from the cemetery except for a few sherds of pre-Flavian samian which are probably heirloom survivals.

Practically all of the military bronzes found in Chichester have come from the area of St. Mary's Hospital and the Central Car Park formerly Sadler's Garden, and this, taken with the evidence of the pottery from the ditches, strongly suggests some form of military occupation of the area for a period of time after the conquest, and possibly as late as 60-65 A.D. Whilst no firm terminal date can be put forward at present for the departure of the military, something more than a temporary base camp *c*. 43-44 A.D. is indi-

Photo: M. H. Rule

PLATE 3. St. Mary's Hospital: Section through street in trench L.

cated. It would be politically viable and strategically sound for a depot of some kind to remain in operation, in friendly territory, and within easy reach of a convenient harbour with properly constructed port facilities. This depot may have co-existed with the growing native town of King Cogidubnus, possibly well on into the late fifties, and the fine native wares discussed above may have been specifically provided for a military market which demanded them. When the soldiers moved away the demand fell off, and they were no longer imported from other areas or made locally.

Period 2, Phase 1, The Roman Street Antonine Pl: 3 Fig. 3.3 & 3.5

Traces of compact gravel metalling were found in Areas 1 and 2 running across the site from east to west. In the western half of the site the upper levels had been badly disturbed by medieval and later pits but a comparatively undisturbed section through the metalling was cut in trench L. (Plate 3 Fig. 3.3 & 3.5).

Above a single layer of large flints rammed into the turfline overlaying undisturbed clay and the Period 1 ditch, a layer of compact orange-yellow gravel 20 cms (7.9 ins) thick (Layer L 14) had been laid with a definite camber on the northern edge. Above this layer of coarse gravel aggregate, a layer of finer sandy gravel 32 cms (12.5 ins) was laid (Layer L 10). Fragments of a large globular amphora in coarse greyish buff fabric with many small grits and a badly eroded and weathered surface were found in layers L 14 and L 10, showing that both layers of street metal had been laid at the same time. The silt layer accumulated at the northern edge of the street (Layer L 11), contained a fragment of samian pottery of late first century date, and a sherd of globular amphora derived from the upper levels of the street metalling.

At the south side the edge of the street had been cut away by the foundations of a timber framed house or workshop of second century date. In Area 1 a thin layer of gravel (Fig. 3.4 Section E-E, Layer 7) overlay pit A 27, cut into the top of Layer 14 which contained pottery of Antonine date. An occupation spread on the north side of the street in Area 2 (Layers N 9 and N 9a) contained fragments of Antonine samian and second century coarseware. The maximum width of street recovered was 470 cms (15ft 5ins); no side ditches were found.

It is possible that the street remained open until the early medieval period. In trench H, occupation trampled into the upper street metal contained two sherds of coarse ware which have been examined by Mr. K.J. Barton[6] who has expressed the opinion that they are late Saxon, and posthole G 15, cut through the street, contained two sherds of coarse ware of pre-10th century date.

Period 2, Phase 2, Timber Building South of Street Fig 3.3

South of the street a simple timber framed building was constructed with its northern foundations cut through the edge of the street metalling. The northern wall was constructed on a foundation of unmortared flint rubble set in a shallow foundation trench 60 cms (23.6 ins) wide. The partition wall between rooms 1 and 2 was narrower, being 29 cms (11.4 ins) wide, and constructed on a sill beam foundation with a posthole at the northern end. A timber sill beam was seen as an impression in the layer of burnt timber (Layers A17 and A19) in trench A/B7, and it appears that after the destruction of the timber structure in the top of ditch 1 a timber beam 26 cms (10.25 ins) wide and 12 cms (4.75 ins) deep was laid over the charred remains of the earlier building. This beam slot aligns with the north wall of the timber building excavated in area 2, but it lacked flint foundations, and

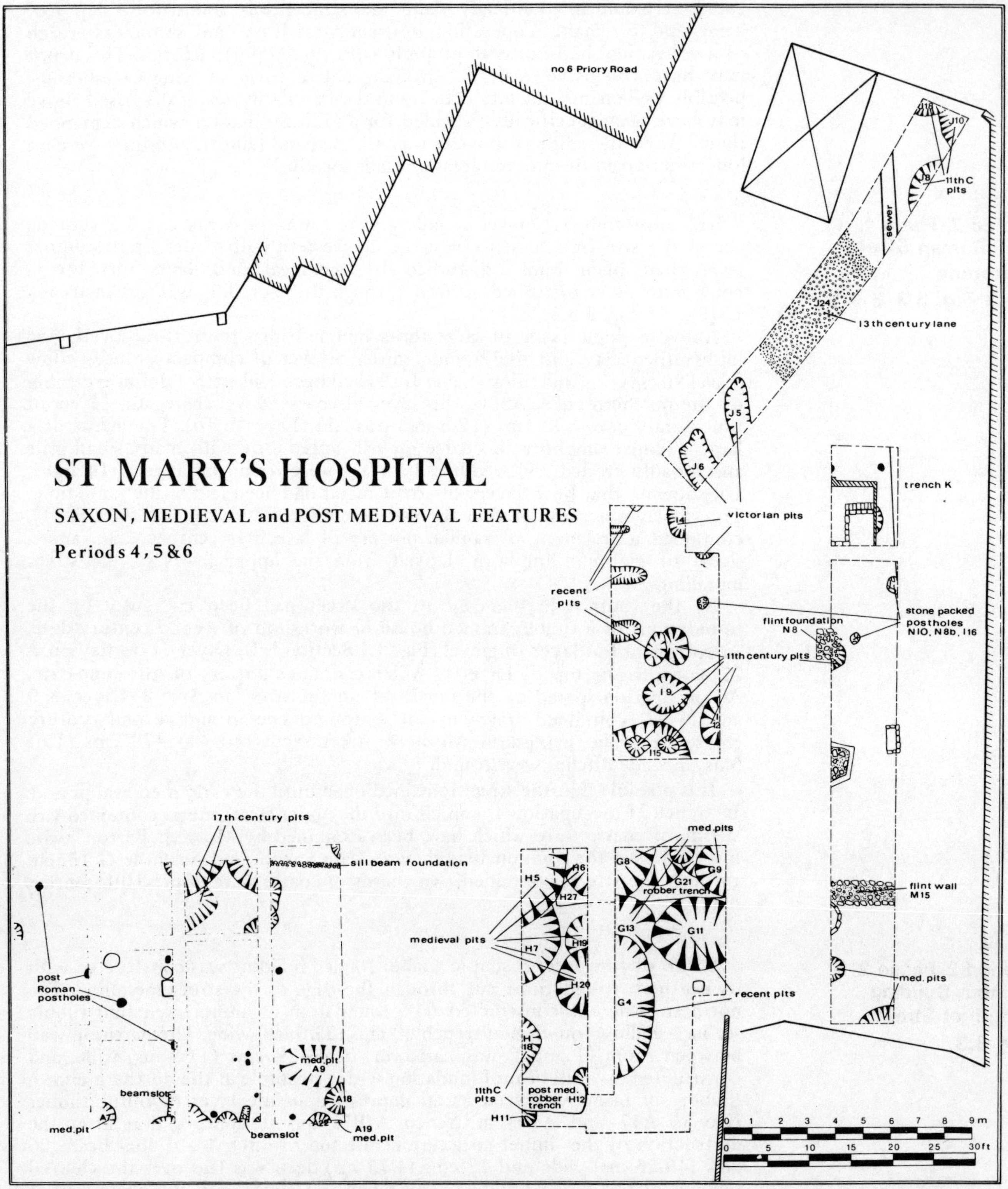
ST MARY'S HOSPITAL
SAXON, MEDIEVAL and POST MEDIEVAL FEATURES
Periods 4, 5&6
no 6 Priory Road
11th C pits
sewer
13th century lane
victorian pits
trench K
recent pits
stone packed postholes N10, N8b, I16
flint foundation N8
11th century pits
17th century pits
sill beam foundation
med. pits
robber trench
flint wall M15
medieval pits
post
Roman postholes
recent pits
med. pits
beamslot
med. pit
11th C pits
post med. robber trench
beamslot
med. pit
A19 med. pit
0 1 2 3 4 5 6 7 8 9 m
0 5 10 15 20 25 30 ft

Fig. 3.6

it may be the foundation of an 'outhouse' or shed aligned along the road frontage.

The floor levels in room 2 had been completely destroyed by medieval and later pits, but in room 1 traces of a mortar floor remained (Layer G 32a). Below the creamy buff mortar floor the natural clay had baked hard in the vicinity of an oven, constructed with walls of puddled clay reinforced with a few flints and a fragment of amphora. A subsidiary open hearth, filled with a sooty black ash, had been built in a shallow depression with a flat tile floor. Between the open hearth and the oven the floor had been reinforced with a single layer of rammed flints. The whole room was sealed by a layer of black loam (Layer G 17) 5 – 7 cms (2 – 2.75ins) thick containing nondescript Roman coarseware and nothing of post-Roman date. The northern foundation trench contained nine sherds of samian pottery of mid-second century date. Excavation of this building was never completed owing to the circumstances outlined in the introduction.

Discussion.

No conclusive dating evidence was found for this building, but the absence of any post-Roman pottery in the occupation material within the building, and the significance of its alignment with the slot cut into the burnt timber layers in A/B7 (Period 1, phase 3), suggests strongly that it belongs in the Roman period. The slot in A/B7 is demonstrably Roman, the fill above it being of Antonine date at the latest.

The building was cut through the street at a point where it was flat, and in the absence of a complete section across the street it was not possible to ascertain whether the house buildings had destroyed the southern camber, if there was one, or whether the street was only drained to the northern side. Perhaps the most likely explanation is that it represents an encroachment on a side street which may indeed have been constructed to serve as an access to buildings of minor importance, like storehouses, workshops and artisans' dwellings.

Period 3,
c.3rd-4th Century A.D.
Fig 3.3

No structures can be assigned to this period and the only evidence of occupation on the site comes from a group of pits on the south-west corner of Area 1 (Pits 1, 2, 3, 6 and 8). These contained large amounts of building material; roofing tiles, large fragments of painted wall plaster and much domestic rubbish. These pits were dug through Ditches 1 and 2 at their juction, and the backfilled material included pottery which ranged from pre-Flavian to New Forest purple gloss wares of the late 3rd to 4th century. It is likely that there was a structure of this latter period just outside the area available for excavation and that the pits were the cesspits dug by the occupants.

Period 4,
10-11th Century
Fig 3.6

A number of pits (I 15, I 15A, I 12, I 9 and N14b) and stone-packed postholes (N8b, N10 and I 16) contained sherds of flint gritted, oxidised, hand-made pottery considered by Mr. K.J. Barton to date from the late Saxon/early Norman period. No contemporary hearths or floors were found but a spread of occupation north of the stone packed postholes (layers N7 and I 14) 10-15 cms (4-6ins) thick, contained animal bones, clay daub and pottery of similar type and fabric. In Trench H, Pit 18 cut through the gravel of the Roman street contained similar pottery, as did Pit 11, which cut into the top of the Roman ditch H 22. At the northern edge of the site in Trench J, three pits (J8, J10, and J18) cut through the earlier Roman features and contained sherds of 'Saxo-Norman' coarseware. A thin spread of occupation in Trench J (layers 7 and 9) contained many fragments of clay daub, animal bone, abraded Roman greyware and sherds of hand-made pottery of 'Saxo-Norman' character. A large circular pit (I 9), cut to a depth of 99 cms (39ins) below the top of natural brick earth contained quantities of abraded Roman pottery together with large sherds of hand-made pottery of similar late Saxon type, and several fragments of bun-shaped loom weights.

Period 5, Medieval, 12–14th Century Fig 3.6

Medieval occupation in Area 1 is attested only by the presence in certain pits (A7, A9, A18 and A19) of sherds of medieval ware, ranging from the 12th to the 14th century in date, together with some tile fragments of the 13th-14th century. All the sherds were badly abraded and they are not good dating evidence for the pits which may well be later.

In the south-east corner of Area 2 a series of large medieval pits (G7, G8, G9, G13, H5, H6, H7, H14, H19, H20 and L7) cut through all the earlier levels and contained fragments of pottery, roofing tile and slate of 13th-14th century.

A wall foundation of flints set in cream coloured mortar (layer M15) cut through the Roman levels in Trench M. The clay beneath the foundation contained only a few fragments of abraded Roman grey ware, and there was no direct dating evidence for the structure as all the associated floor levels had been destroyed by the construction of a modern drain and soakaway. In Trenches G and H a large robber trench was found on the same alignment as the flint wall foundation (layers G21 and H27). This robber trench contained fragments of medieval pottery of 13th-14th century, including sherds of similar fabric to that produced in the Orchard Street kiln[7]. This robber trench turned northwards in Trench H but no similar robber trench could be found in Trenches I and J to the north.

A foundation of flints set in clay (layer N8), overlaying a pit containing Saxo-Norman pottery and cut through a layer of occupation containing nothing later than Saxo-Norman potsherds, is probably the foundation for a vertical roof support. The absence of 13th and 14th century pits north of the wall foundation and the robber trench, would be explained if the area was within a building, and the mass of building debris, tiles and slate found in the later pits could have derived from the destruction of such a building.

A cambered gravel lane or path (layer J24) 20 cms, (7.8 ins) thick and 525 cms (17.25 ft) wide was sectioned at a depth of 50 cms, (19.6 ins), running obliquely north-west south-east across Trench J. A spread of occupation (layer J3) partially overlay the southern camber and dates the period of its use.

Much of the stratigraphy in Area 2 had been destroyed down to Roman levels by the foundations of 19th century outbuildings and the construction of soakaways with their connecting pipes. Recent concrete foundations in trench H cut down to the natural clay and it was considered unprofitable to complete excavation of this trench.

Discussion of the post-Roman occupation on the site.

The scatter of late Saxon and early medieval pottery, stone-packed postholes, clay daub and occupation debris found on the north-east portion of the site suggests the presence of rather squalid occupation in timber buildings, but a complete excavation of the area would be necessary to determine its exact nature. The construction of the castle within the north east angle of the city wall by Roger de Montgomery in the late 11th century[8] would have necessitated huts for workmen and servants in the area, and the occupation found would fit into this general picture. In the first half of the 13th century the land was granted to the Franciscan or Grey Friars[9] who must have cleared the site of existing buildings and erected new ones more suited to their particular use, as by 1253, 26 friars were housed in the conventual buildings[10]. The flint wall foundation and its corresponding robber wall foundation discovered in trenches M, G and H, (Fig. 3.6) are tentatively interpreted as part of the foundations of one of the conventual buildings constructed by the Greyfriars on the site in the mid-13th century, and demolished after the site was given to St. Mary's Hospital some thirty years later[11]. South of the building the only evidence for medieval occupation is the presence of a series of pits containing sherds of green glazed pottery of 13th and 14th century date.

In 1290 a licence was granted to the Master of St. Mary's Hospital to close a lane running eastwards from St. Martin's Chapel[12], provided that he made as good a path on his own ground. The closure of this path would have been necessary before the present St. Mary's Hospital could have been built.

The gravel path sectioned in Trench J dates from this period, as occupation debris containing 13-14th century pottery was found partially overlaying the southern camber of the lane. The comparative absence of late medieval and post-medieval occupation on the site supports the limited documentary evidence, which suggests that after 1285, when the land was given by Henry de Chikehull to the warden and brethren of St. Mary's Hospital the site remained open as arable land and gardens attached to the Hospital. (See Speed Map of 1610, Fig. 2.2)

Period 6, Post-Medieval

A straight-sided feature (H 12) cut into the top of the Period 1 Roman ditch (H 21) (Fig. 3.6) contained a fragment of late 16th century painted ware together with a quantity of heavily gritted tile fragments. This feature, 80 cms (31.5 ins) wide and cut to a depth of 112 cms (44.1 ins) below the medieval ground level, had the appearance of a robber trench but was unrelated to any other structure found on the site. However, its position is appropriate for a boundary wall dividing the land immediately north of St. Mary's Hospital from plots of land belonging to the houses in Priory Road.

In Area 1 a number of pits excavated in Trench C 5 and C 7 contained pottery ranging from the 15th to the 18th century. A small sleeper-wall foundation running east to west across the north end of C 7 partly overlaid a layer producing 18th century pottery, and is therefore quite modern.

A number of postholes were found cutting into the yellow clay, and seen only as stains and areas of softer fill. They form no coherent pattern. One (ph 5, B3) contained pottery of the 17th – 18th centuries. Most were truncated and not likely to pre-date the pits.

Notes and References

1 Excavations in the Central Car Park (David Greig site), 1959-63, forthcoming.

2 The authors are grateful to Mr. David Sadler who was able to indicate the spot where his father had dug, and to Mr. Peter Flowers, Mr. Fred Sadler's nephew, who confirmed the site quite independently some years later.

3 Private correspondence.

4 This volume, p. 70.

5 *S.A.C.* 106, 115. Excavations in progress in Chapel Street (1969).

6 Pottery of a similar character has already been described from the excavations in East Pallant House garden in 1950 (*S.A.C.* 91, 145, fig. 3.) but a new appraisal of this ware has recently been made by Mr. K.J. Barton F.S.A. and will be the subject of a forthcoming paper.

7 This volume pp. 153-164.

8 *V.C.H. Sx.* 3, 79.

9 Dugdale, *Monasticum* Poland, *The Friars in Sussex.*, p. 65.

10 Calendar Patent Rolls, 37. Hen. 3 26. Dec 1253.

11 Patent Rolls 13. Ed. 1, 1285. m2. 'Licence for the Prior and brethren of the Hospital of St. Mary Cicestre to retain a plot in the City of Cicestre where the Friars Minor of Cicestre used to dwell, which Henry de Chikehull lately gave them in franc almoin before his death'.

12 Patent Roll 13, Edl. 1290 m.29. 'Licence after inquisition *ad quod damnum* by the Sheriff of Sussex, for the Master of the hospital of St. Mary Cicestre to stop a path in Cicestre running eastward from the Chapel provided that he make as good a path on his own ground.'

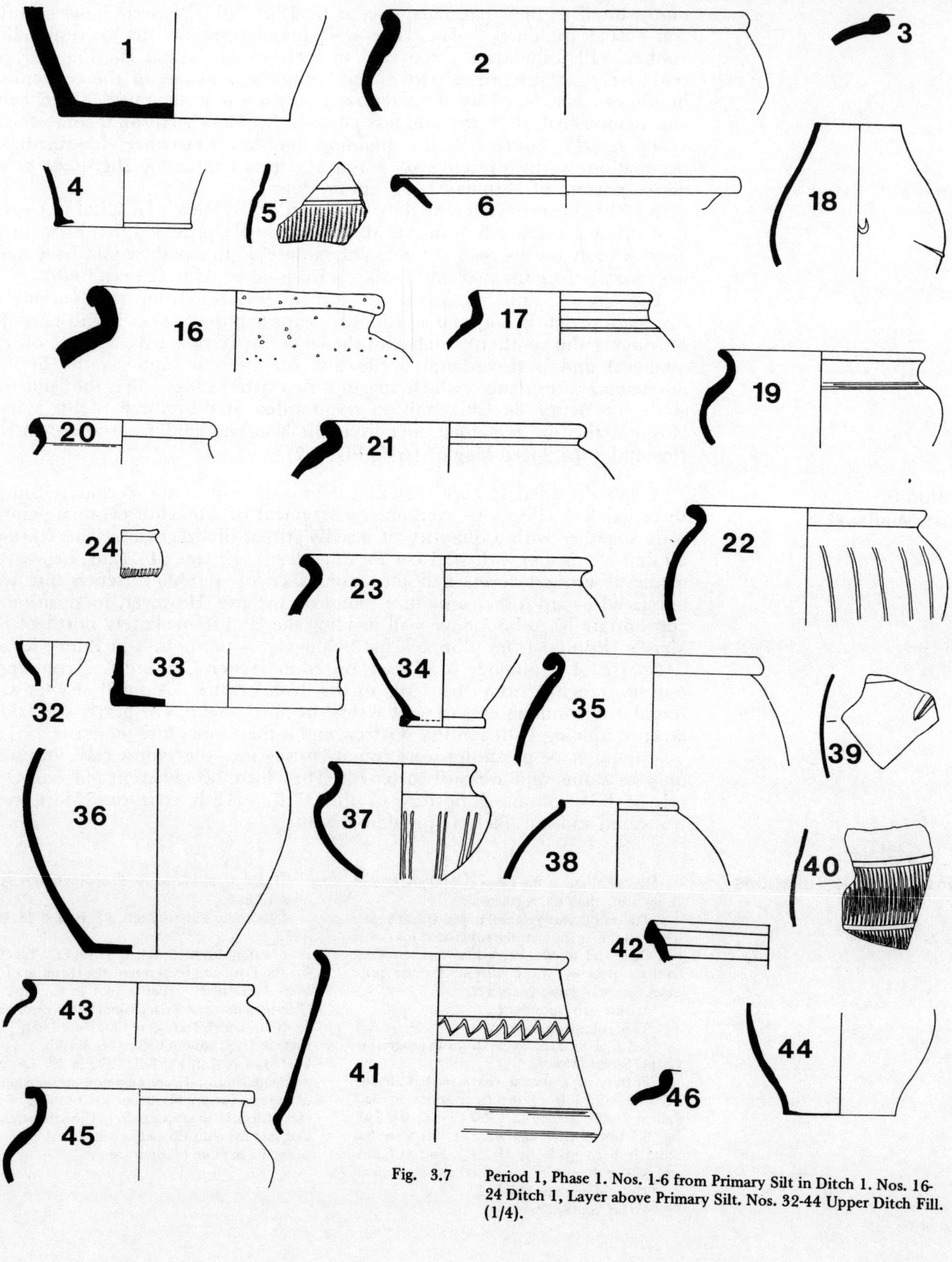

Fig. 3.7 Period 1, Phase 1. Nos. 1-6 from Primary Silt in Ditch 1. Nos. 16-24 Ditch 1, Layer above Primary Silt. Nos. 32-44 Upper Ditch Fill. (1/4).

The Pottery

Period 1, Phase 1

Period 1, Phase 1 (Area 1, B7. 20. Area 2 L.17) (from the primary silt in Ditch 1.).
1. Base of large storage jar; zone of burnishing immediately above base.
2. Bead-rimmed jar in flint gritted grey ware.
3. Bead-rimmed jar in grey sandy fabric with small black flecks; traces of red oxide coating on exterior.
4. Base of imitation Gallo-Belgic butt beaker with dark grey core oxidised to a pale buff colour.
5. Sherd from a butt beaker in hard whitish fabric.
6. Rim of Terra Nigra platter, or possibly an imitation. *Camulodunum* Pl. XLIX No. 3.

The following sherds are not illustrated:

7 & 8. Sherds from rouletted butt beakers in fine grey paste with dirty cream coloured exterior.

9. Bead-rimmed jar in grey ware.
10. Body sherd from flagon in fine grey paste almost completely oxidised to a pink/red colour, with a white slip exterior coating. The ware is hard and well fired, normally found in association with Gallo-Belgic or native imitation wares.
11. Rim of jar in sandy grey fabric; smoothed exterior, with traces of applied red oxide coating.
12. Narrow-mouthed bead-rimmed jar in grey ware.
13. Body sherd from flagon in thin white ware.
14. Wide-mouthed necked jar in hard pale grey fabric.
15. Wide-mouthed jar with rolled over rim above short upstanding neck; in light grey sandy paste.

Associated with the above sherds were the following samian sherds: 1 Ritterling 9, Claudius-Nero; 1 Ritterling 8, pre-Flavian, probably Claudius-Nero; and 1 sherd of 1st century date.

Ditch 1; clay above primary silt. (Area 1. 15 and Area 2. L.19)

16. Heavily flint gritted cooking pot in hard sandy fabric.
17. Jar in fine brick red fabric, grogged with tile fragments, smoothed exterior.
18. Beaker in fine orange paste with whitish/pink slip coating externally.
19. Bowl in hard grey paste burnished on rim and shoulder.
20. Rim of vessel in fine grey paste. The surface is well burnished inside and out and is pale orange in colour with dark orange flecks.
21. Jar in sandy grey oxidised fabric, lightly gritted. Traces of applied exterior red oxide coating.
22. Bowl in sandy grey ware; black reduced fabric.
23. Bowl in sandy grey ware, reduced fabric.
24. Sherd in fine grey ware oxidised to a pale orange; white paint over band of incised decoration.

The following sherds are not illustrated:

25. Bead-rimmed jar in grey ware.
26. Fragment of large storage jar, hand-made in sandy buff fabric with large flint grits. This type of ware is most frequently found in the earliest layers in association with pre-Flavian wares.
27. Small bead-rimmed jar, narrow mouthed with tooling on outside of body, similar to No. 42.
28. Base of vessel in fine grey paste, small bead around base; probably from a flagon.
29. Rim of jar in sandy grey fabric.
30. Small-necked jar in pinkish sandy fabric with rolled over slightly flattened rim.
31. Sandy fragment in pale buff reduced fabric; wide angled lattice decoration, horizontally crossed by zones of tooled burnished double lines.

Associated with these sherds was 1 sherd of samian, a Dr.27 of Flavian date.

Ditch 1; humus stained clay, upper ditchfill. (Area 1. B13; Area 2. L18).

32. Vessel in fine orange paste, external mica dusting.

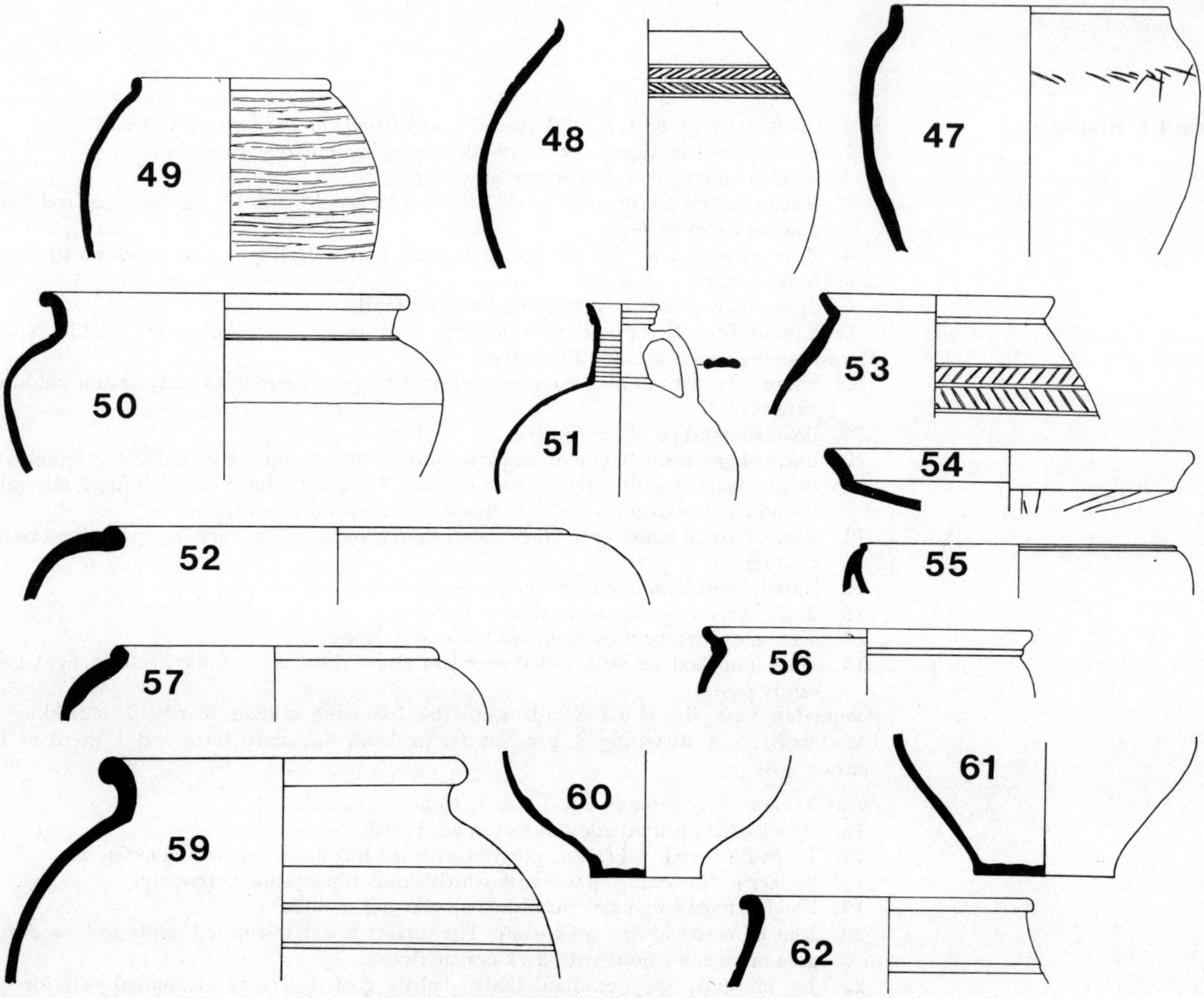

Fig. 3.8

Roman Pottery, Period 1, Phase 1, Upper Ditch Fill. (No. 51 1/8, remainder 1/4).

33. Base of vessel in fine orange fabric; very fine burnished exterior.
34. Base of vessel, probably flagon, in fine orange paste; external micaceous slip.
35. Narrow-mouthed jar with rolled over rim; hard grey fabric, flint gritted.
36. Base of jar in hard grey reduced fabric.
37. Bowl in hard, whitish grey reduced fabric with small black grits.
38. Narrow-mouthed jar in hard grey ware.
39. Sherd in sandy grey paste oxidised red, with traces of white external slip below zone of burnishing and with applied decoration *en barbotine.*
40. Sherd from butt beaker in hard whitish grey ware.
41. Vessel in hard grey paste with small smears of carbon.
42. Terra Nigra dish or lid. Variant of Camulodunum p. 216. Fig 46. No. 7 (Form 6).
43. Rim of small jar in hard fine grey paste.
44. Base of jar in fine grey paste with black flecks. Black tool-burnished externally.
45. Jar in hard grey paste.
46. Narrow-mouthed bead-rimmed jar in hard whitish/grey paste; external applied red oxide coating.
47. Jar in hard grey paste; random tool marks on shoulder.
48. Narrow-mouthed jar in hard light-grey fabric. Zone of burnishing above herringbone decoration.
49. Narrow-mouthed grey ware jar; some flint gritting. External tool burnishing.

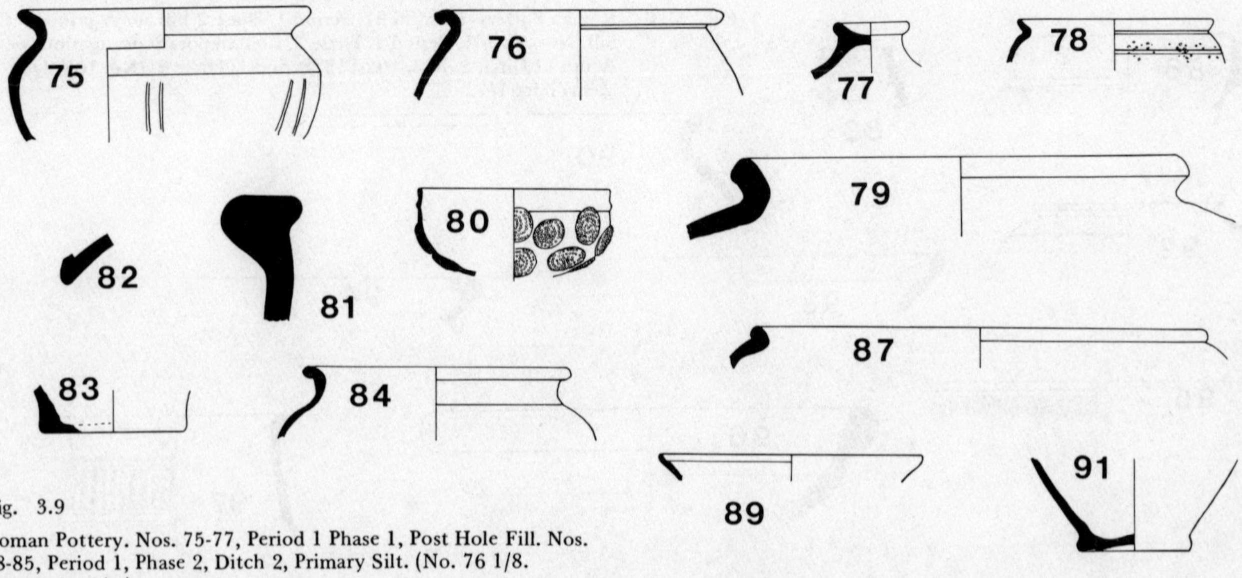

Fig. 3.9

Roman Pottery. Nos. 75-77, Period 1 Phase 1, Post Hole Fill. Nos. 78-85, Period 1, Phase 2, Ditch 2, Primary Silt. (No. 76 1/8. Remainder 1/4.)

50. Jar in hard light grey ware burnished on shoulder.
51. Flagon in pale buff ware.
52. Bead-rimmed jar in hard grey ware with carbon flecks; red oxide coating applied externally.
53. Narrow-mouthed jar in hard light grey fabric, burnished on inside of rim and exterior.
54. Dish or lid in hard light grey ware, smoothed internally.
55. Vessel in fine grey ware with creamy buff micaceous slip coating inside and out.
56. Rim in dark grey ware, burnished black.
57. Bead-rimmed jar in grey ware.
58. Sherd, probably from flagon in fine orange paste, similar to No. 18., with internal mica rich slip in darker colour, not illustrated.
59. Necked jar in grey ware.
60. Base in hard light grey ware reduced black.
61. Base of jar in dark grey fabric.
62. Rim of jar in hard grey paste.

The following sherds are not illustrated:

63. Base of large storage jar in grey ware.
64. Necked jar with wide mouth in hard pale grey fabric.
65. Necked bowl in pale grey reduced paste, burnished on shoulder.
66. Wide-mouthed jar in grey ware, with everted rim.
67. Necked jar, similar to No. 64.
68. Wide-mouthed jar, similar in form and paste to No. 66 but with slight internal flattening on rim.
69. Bowl in grey ware, variant of No. 37.
70. Small narrow-mouthed bead-rimmed jar, tooled on outside of body, similar to No. 49.
71. Imitation Terra Nigra platter or lid in whitish/buff paste.
72. Rim of amphora in sandy oxidised fabric.
73. Fragment of very large hand-made storage jar in reduced grey fabric with large flint grits, (see remarks on No. 26 above).
74. Wide-mouthed jar in grey ware with everted rim.

Period 1, Phase 1, Posthole fill. (H. 25).

75. Grey ware bowl, hard fine light paste, reduced; burnished below rim.
76. Rim in hard grey paste; some flint grits.
77. Lid in fine grey paste; reduced.

Fig. 3.10 Roman Pottery, Nos. 86-97, Period 1, Phase 2 Fill above primary Silt. Nos. 98-101, Period 1, Phase 2, Contemporary occupation South of Ditch 2. Nos. 102-113, Period 1, Phase 3. (No. 105, 1/8. Remainder 1/4.)

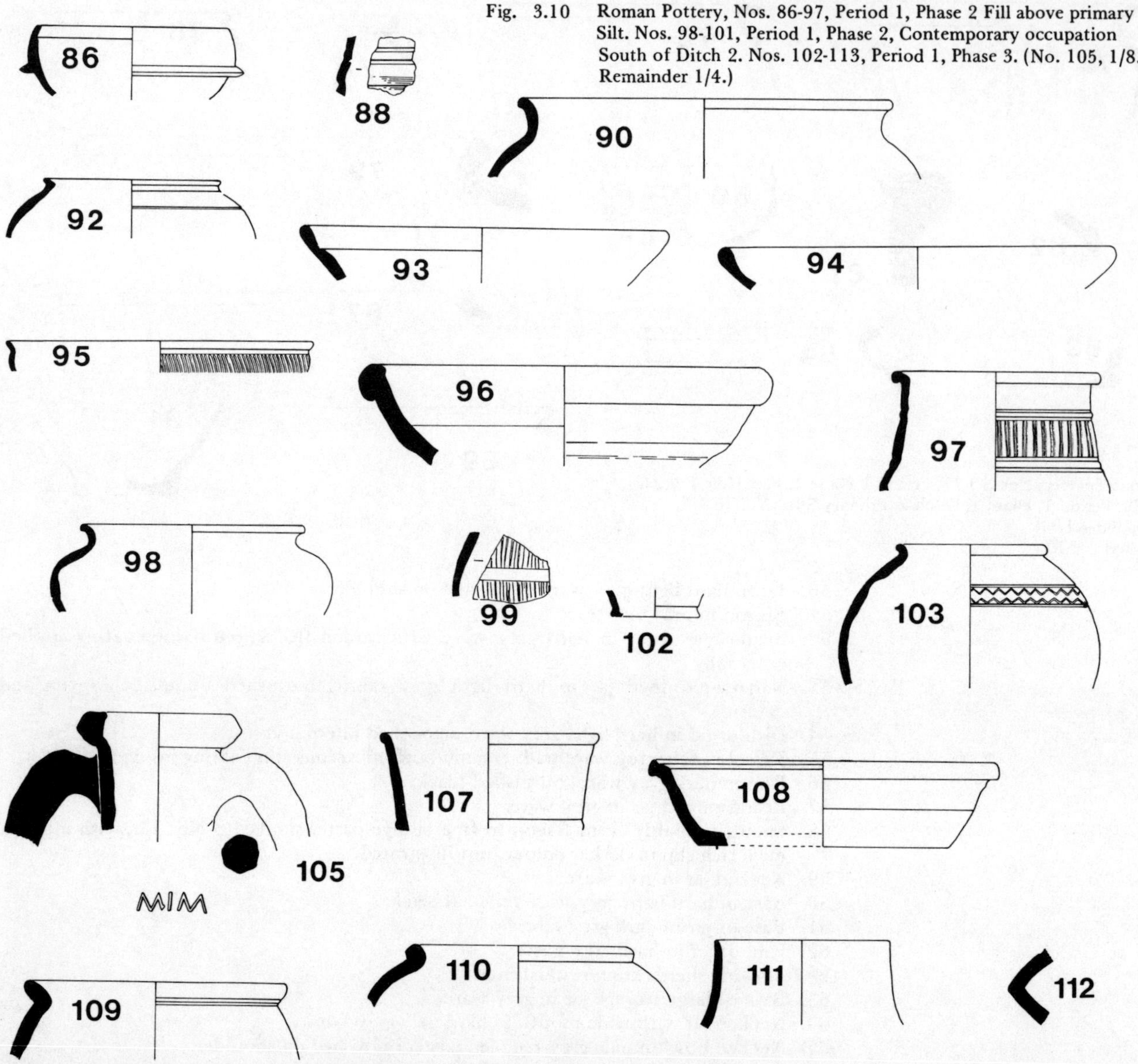

Period 1, Phase 2

Period 1, Phase 2, Ditch 2. Primary silt. (A. 16).

78. Rim of beaker in yellow paste with minute black flecks. Yellowish brown varnish inside and out; applied rustication on body.
79. Rim of storage jar; hard light grey, flint gritted paste.
80. Bowl in creamy yellow smooth fabric with dark brown varnish inside and out. *Camulodunum* Pl. LIII 62 Ba, variant and p. 228.
81. Rim of amphora in hard sandy grey paste oxidised to pale orange.
82. Rim of lid; sandy grey fabric reduced to black externally.
83. Base of vessel in identical fabric to No. 50.
84. Rim in hard light grey ware.
85. Fragment of flagon in hard white paste. Not illustrated.

Associated with the above were the following samian sherds:— 2 Dr 18, pre Flavian.

Period 1, Phase 2. Ditch 2. Fill above primary silt (A. 13).

86. Flanged bowl in imitation Terra Nigra ware. *Camulodunum*, Pl. LIII, No. 58b.
87. Bead-rimmed jar in grey ware.
88. Sherd in imitation Terra Nigra, possibly beaker, sandy fabric, burnished inside and out.

89. Imitation Terra Nigra platter. *Camulodunum*, p. 218, Fig. 47, No. 6.
90. Rim in micaceous dark grey ware, burnished on lip and exterior.
91. Base of flagon or beaker in fine micaceous sandy ware; burnished.
92. Small bowl in identical fabric to No. 66.
93. Dish in micaceous grey ware, burnished inside and out. Imitation of Terra Nigra platter, see No. 89 above.
94. Dish, in similar fabric to No. 93, but with bulbous lip.
95. Rim of imitation Dr 29 in fine whitish grey paste, *S.A.C.* **106**, 123, Fig. 6, No. 1.
96. Mortar in fine grey ware oxidised to a creamy buff colour; pink interior slip coating. *Camulodunum*, p. 255, Fig. 53, No. 8.
97. Rim of butt or girth beaker. Reddish sandy fabric, burnished exterior with black slip coating.

Associated with the above pottery was the following samian ware: 1 Dr 15/17 pre Flavian; 3 Dr 27 pre Flavian; 2 Dr 18 pre Flavian.

Period 1, Phase 2. Contemporary Occupation South of Ditch 2. (A5.8).

98. Small jar in sandy grey fabric.
99. Sherd in hard sandy grey fabric, oxidised to buff colour.
100. Bulbous rim sherd of shallow dish/lid in reduced fabric. Not illustrated.
101. Sherd from large hand-made, flint gritted storage jar; grey fabric. Not illustrated.

Period 1, Phase 3

Period 1, Phase 3.
From burnt timber in the excavation in Ditch 1. (A/B7. 18.)

102. Base of vessel, probably flagon, in orange fabric with burnished exterior.

Pottery from dirty clay fill above burnt timber (A/B14 and 9c).
The native grey wares recovered from these layers were featureless and are not illustrated here. With them were sherds from fourteen samian vessels, of which five were 2nd century and one was of Antonine (East Gaulish) date.

From the occupation layer (yellow clay) on north side of Ditch 1. (B.9).

103. Narrow-mouthed jar in sandy fabric reduced black, burnished below rim.

Associated with this sherd was 1 sherd from a Dr 18 dish, pre Flavian.

From flinty layer above occupation layer. (B7).

104. Bead-rimmed jar in light grey fabric, reduced black. Not illustrated.

From the yellow clay layer above Ditch 2 (A.11.)

105. Amphora in hard sandy buff ware, stamped on handle M.I.M. *Camulodunum* Fig. 45 No. 10, pp. 214-5, there dated as Claudian.
106. Rim of amphora in similar fabric to 101. Not illustrated.
107. Rim of large beaker in grey ware burnished over lip and on exterior.
108. Dish in grey ware with black grits; zone of burnishing above base.
109. Jar in sandy ware reduced black.
110. Bead-rimmed jar in grey ware with black burnished exterior.

Also in this layer were sherds from nine samian vessels of which the latest were two Dr 30's and one Dr 18, all late 1st century.

From turf line sealing ditch L17, 18 & 19. (Layer L. 15)

111. Rim of vessel in pale grey fabric with small black grits; burnished externally.

Clay sealing posthole H 25. (Layer H.24).

112. Sharply carinated bowl in hard grey paste fired orange.
113. Jar with small "pulled out" base and double lines of vertical burnished decoration on body; tooled cross on base. Hard grey paste. Not illustrated.
    Associated samian; 1 sherd Dr 36, 1st century.

Period 2, Phase 1

Period 2, Phase 1. Street metalling. (Layers L10, L11 and L14)

114. Fragments of large globular amphora in coarse pale greyish buff fabric with many small grits; pinkish orange inside and out. External surface very eroded. Not illustrated.
115. Two ribbed handles of large flagon. Smooth pale orange paste with many small flecks of mica. Not illustrated.
116. Base of flagon with small, square-sectioned foot ring. In grey paste, fired orange, external white slip. Not illustrated.
    With these sherds was 1 sherd Dr 27, late 1st century.

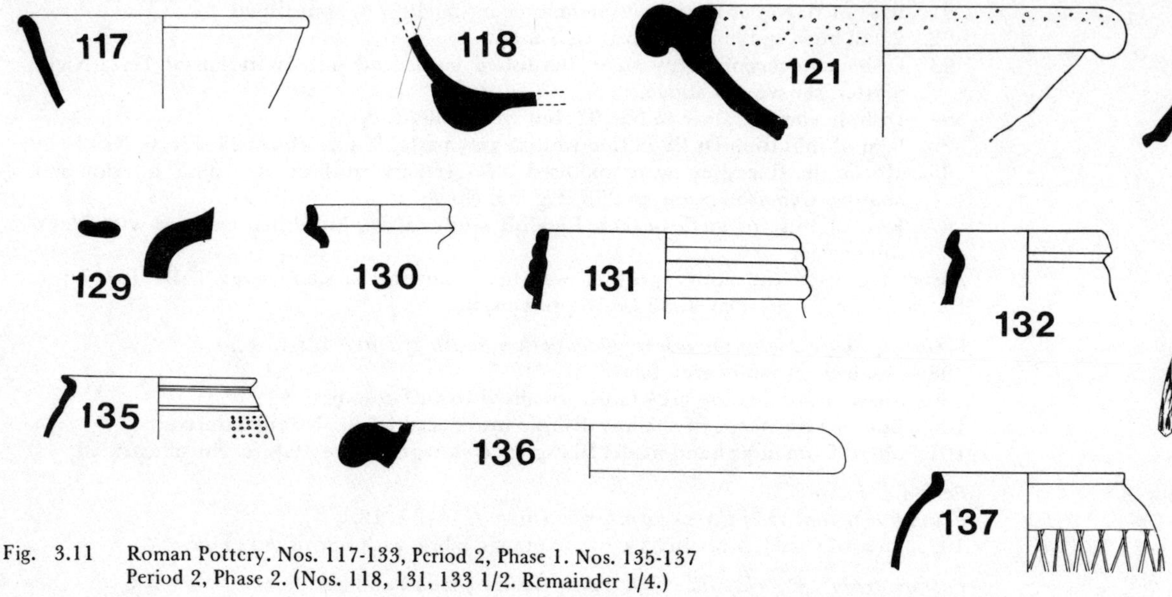

Fig. 3.11 Roman Pottery. Nos. 117-133, Period 2, Phase 1. Nos. 135-137 Period 2, Phase 2. (Nos. 118, 131, 133 1/2. Remainder 1/4.)

Occupation layer contemporary with street. Layers N9 and N9A

117. Bowl in fine grey paste; external red oxide slip.
118. Base in fine smooth pale orange fabric.
119. Bowl with everted rim in slightly vesicular pale grey paste, diagonal burnished decoration below rim.
    See No. 2 from Westgate, (Fig. 7.3). Not illustrated.
120. Jar in pale grey paste with everted rim and random vertical and diagonal burnished lines below rim. Not illustrated.
    With this layer were 2 sherds samian Dr 31 Antonine and 1 Dr 24/25 Claudius/Nero.

Ditch/Pit (M 20, 24 and G22).

The relationship of this feature to the street is uncertain, but the material in the silt is contemporary with the early period of the street, (nothing later than Antonine) and it is cut from the same level as the street makeup.

121. Mortar with light flint gritting inside and carried over rim; pale creamy white paste.
122. Lid with upward projecting rim, flattened on outer edge. Oxidised grey paste blackened inside and out. *S.A.C.* 100, Fig. 7 No. 30. Not illustrated.
    Associated samian; sherds from 4 vessels of which the latest was a Dr 37 Quintilianus style *c.* 120 – 140 A.D.

M 22. Occupation trampled into natural (Layer M 22)

1 samian sherd Dr 24/25 of Neronian date.

Pit 1

123. Dish/lid in grey fabric, black burnished outside.
    Associated with this sherd was a sherd from an imitation Terra Nigra dish and 1 Dr 15/17 sherd, Neronian and 1 Dr 27 of pre Flavian date.

From complex of stakeholes (Layer I 23)

124. Beaker in pale grey paste with carbon flecks, burnished externally. Variant of type 102b from cemetery. Not illustrated.

G3. Occupation trampled into natural. (Layer G.3).

125. Carinated bowl with small everted rim in pale grey paste, burnished over lip and down to shoulder. Not illustrated.

J.22. Ditch (Layer J.22)

126. Lid in black fabric with flattened rim section. Not illustrated.

127. Jar in fine grey paste blackened on the outside; everted rim. Not illustrated.
128. Flagon fragments in fine grey ware, pale pink inside and out. Not illustrated.
With these sherds was 1 Dr 18/31 samian sherd of Hadrianic date, East Gaulish.

Ditch/Pit (Layer J.11)
129. Cup or flagon handle in grey paste; heavy black burnished exterior.
130. Flagon rim in grey ware.
Eight sherds of samian were found of which the latest were a Dr 27 1st century and a Dr 18 early Flavian.

J.20. Lower level Ditch/Pit
131. Flagon rim in red paste; external white slip.

I.3. Occupation trampled into natural (Layer I.3)
132. Conical neck of flagon in grey ware, with vertical tooling below rim. Similar to flagon from cemetery type 59C.
133. Fragment of beaker in hard fired orange paste.

Period 2, Phase 2

Period 2 Phase 2 – Roman timber building south of the street.
134. Vessel in yellowish buff paste with brownish purple colour coat inside and out. Sand dusted externally beneath colour coat. Not illustrated.
135. Beaker in reddish brown paste with black external colour coat.
136. Mortar in pink paste, buff colour externally.
137. Jar, burnished below rim to shoulder level.
138. Jar, grey paste, fired orange with small flecks of mica.
139. Mortar in pale grey paste, buff exterior.
140. Poppy-head beaker in fine hard grey paste with blackish grey external slip. Not illustrated.
141. Bead-rimmed jar in pale grey paste burnished to shoulder level. Not illustrated.
142. *From hearth.* Dish/lid in hard grey paste, black slip inside and out; heavily burnished externally.
Nine samian sherds from these layers of which the latest was a Dr 35/36, probably mid 2nd century.

Pit M.12, postdates and cuts pit/ditch M.24, M.26. Mid – late 2nd century.
143. Cup in pale grey paste with black burnished slip.
144. Jar in grey fabric with small flint grits.
145. Mortar in pinkish paste with small black flecks, gritted internally with calcined flints.
146. Jar with tooled burnish below rim and burnished lattice decoration on body. Small everted rim, pale grey paste fired pale orange. Not illustrated.
147. Large poppy-head beaker with smooth thin everted rim in grey paste, with black burnish inside and out. Not illustrated.
148. Beaker in hard grey paste, variant of type 116b from the cemetery (Fig. 5.23) but base is kicked upwards. Not illustrated.
149. Carinated bowl with everted rim and burnished shoulder. *S.A.C.* 100, Fig. 6, No. 5. Not illustrated.
150. Jar with small everted rim in hard pale grey paste with carbon flecks; applied red oxide slip. Variant of type 18a from cemetery. Not illustrated.
151. Fragment of colour coated ware, orange paste with shiny orange slip. Not illustrated.
152. Handle of lid in grey fabric, oxidised externally and blackened on the inside surface. Not illustrated.
Fourteen sherds of samian were associated, of which the latest were a Dr 31 mid- to late 2nd century, a Dr 33, 2nd century and a Dr 42 variant (with handles) Antonine.

Pit M.8 2nd century
153. Large everted rimmed storage jar in grey paste with carbon flecks; incised tally mark 111. Not illustrated.
154. Poppy-head beaker in fine greyish/buff paste, smooth black external burnish with micaceous flecks. Variant of 26b from the cemetery. Not illustrated.
155. Narrow-mouthed jar in grey paste with small flint grits and small everted rim. Not illustrated.
156. Bowl in slightly vesicular grey paste with black external slip and small rolled-over rim. Variant of type 97b from the cemetery (Fig. 5.23). Not illustrated.

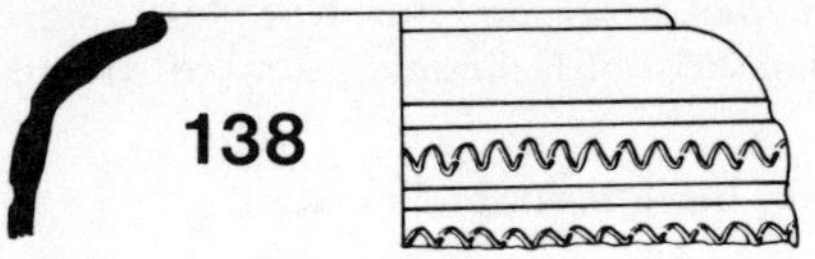

Fig. 3.12 Roman Pottery. Nos. 138-145, Period 2, Phase 2. No. 157, Pit M8, 2nd Cent. Nos. 158-161 Pit M6, Antonine No. 166, Pit A11 Antonine. Nos. 168-171, Pit A3, Antonine. Nos. 173-176, Pit A6, 4th Cent. Nos. 177-178 Pit A8, 4th Cent. Nos. 180-189 from Post-Roman Layer. (No. 143 1/2. No. 169 1/3. Remainder 1/4.)

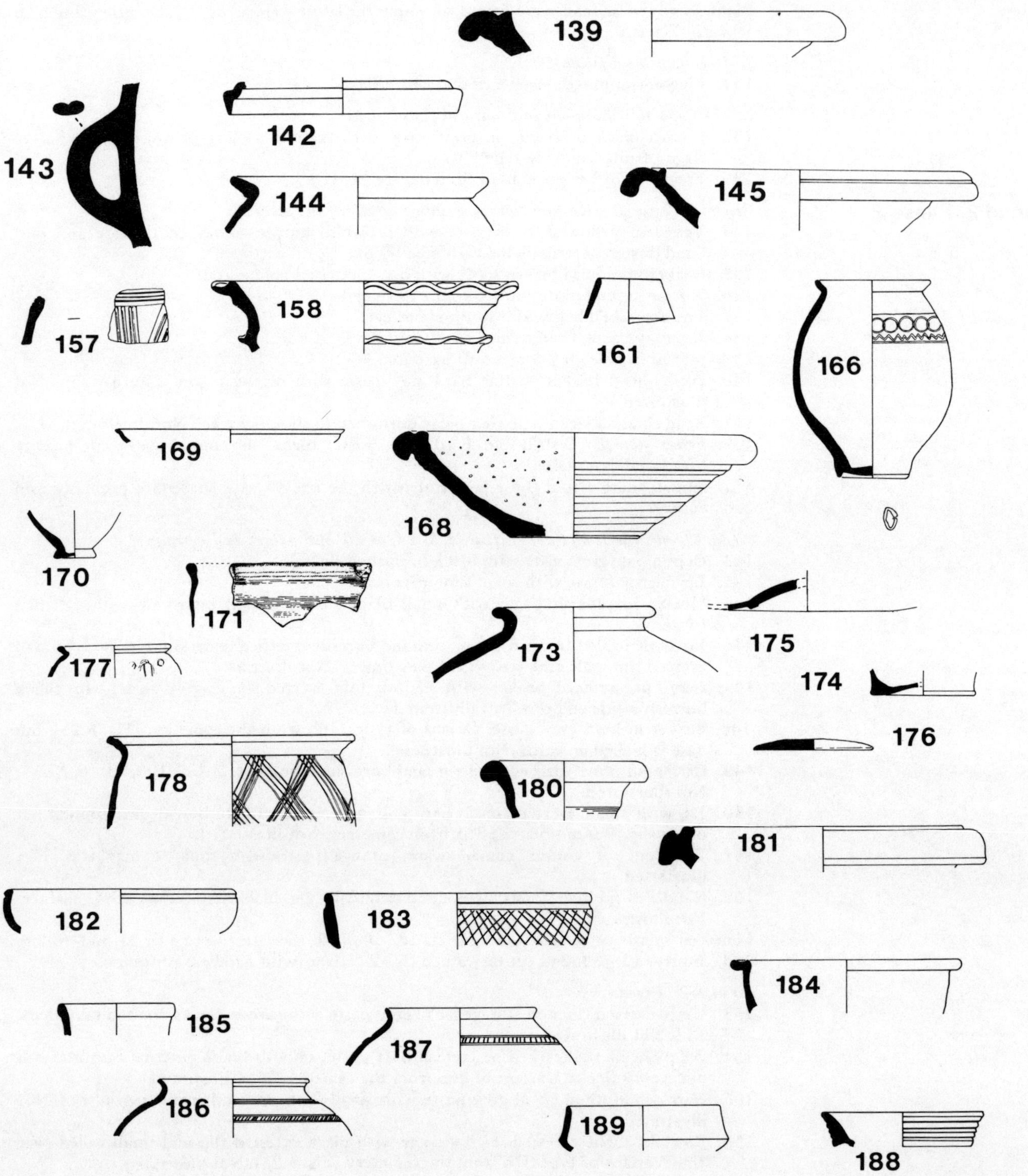

157. Sherd in sandy grey paste.

Eight samian vessels were represented in this pit; the latest being a Dr 18/31, late 1st to early 2nd century, and a Dr 33 of 2nd century date.

Pit N.6. Antonine.

158. Tazza in grey paste with heavily oxodised orange core; pale buff colour inside and out.
159. Dish/Lid in hard grey paste burnished inside and out. Not illustrated.
160. Fragment of Caistor ware with leaf decoration *en barbotine.* Not illustrated.
161. Fragment of beaker in fine grey paste with black external burnish.
162. Necked jar heavily burnished below rim to shoulder level and inside rim. Similar to sherd No. 11 from Westgate (Fig. 7.3). Not illustrated.
163. Bead-rimmed narrow-necked jar in hard grey paste. Not illustrated.

18 sherds of samian were associated; all Antonine.

Pit I.19.

164. Jar with heavily tooled lattice decoration. Not illustrated.

Pit M.16.

165. Sherd of Rhenish ware, not illustrated.

Pit A.11. Antonine.

166. Complete beaker in fine grey paste, burnished over lip to just above zone of decoration.

One sherd of a Dr 33 of Antonine date was found associated.

Pit A.1. 4th century

This pit contained large amounts of Roman building material associated with pottery ranging from 1st to 4th centuries. Latest sherds were New Forest purple colour coated wares. The partially burnt top of a human skull was with the rubbish.

Pit A.2. 4th century.

167. Body sherd of grey ware flagon with conical neck; cemetery type 59c. Not illustrated.

Pit A.3. 4th century

This pit also contained large amounts of Roman building material and the fill was similar to that in Pit A.1 e.g., 4th century New Forest wares.

168. Large mortar in creamy fabric, flint gritting carried over rim.
169. Rim of imitation Terra Nigra dish in hard pale grey fabric burnished black inside and out.
170. Base of small vessel in imitation Terra Nigra; black glossy exterior burnish.
171. Rim fragment from a glass beaker.

Pit A.6. 4th century

172. Rope-rimmed storage jar in pinky buff fabric with large flint grits. Not illustrated.
173. Narrow-mouthed jar in grey ware.
174. Base of vessel in fine light grey fabric oxidised pale buff; traces of orange slip inside.
175. Base of imitation Terra Nigra platter in whitish grey fabric.
176. Amphora seal in soft whitish buff fabric.

Pit A.8. 4th century

177. Beaker in creamy, paste, similar to No. 78 (Fig. 3.9) varnished inside and out.
178. Large grey ware storage vessel.
179. Body sherd of vessel in fine creamy/pink paste, reddish brown slip coating. Not illustrated.

Roman Pottery from Post-Roman Layers

From 15th/16th century layers above Ditch 2, Area 1

180. Rim of small amphora in pink fabric, oxidised buff.

From Pit A.9, medieval or later

181. Rim of mortar in fine light grey paste fired buff.
182. Small bowl in hard grey ware, burnished inside and with applied black slip.
183. Bowl in sandy grey ware with some black grits, burnished black exterior.

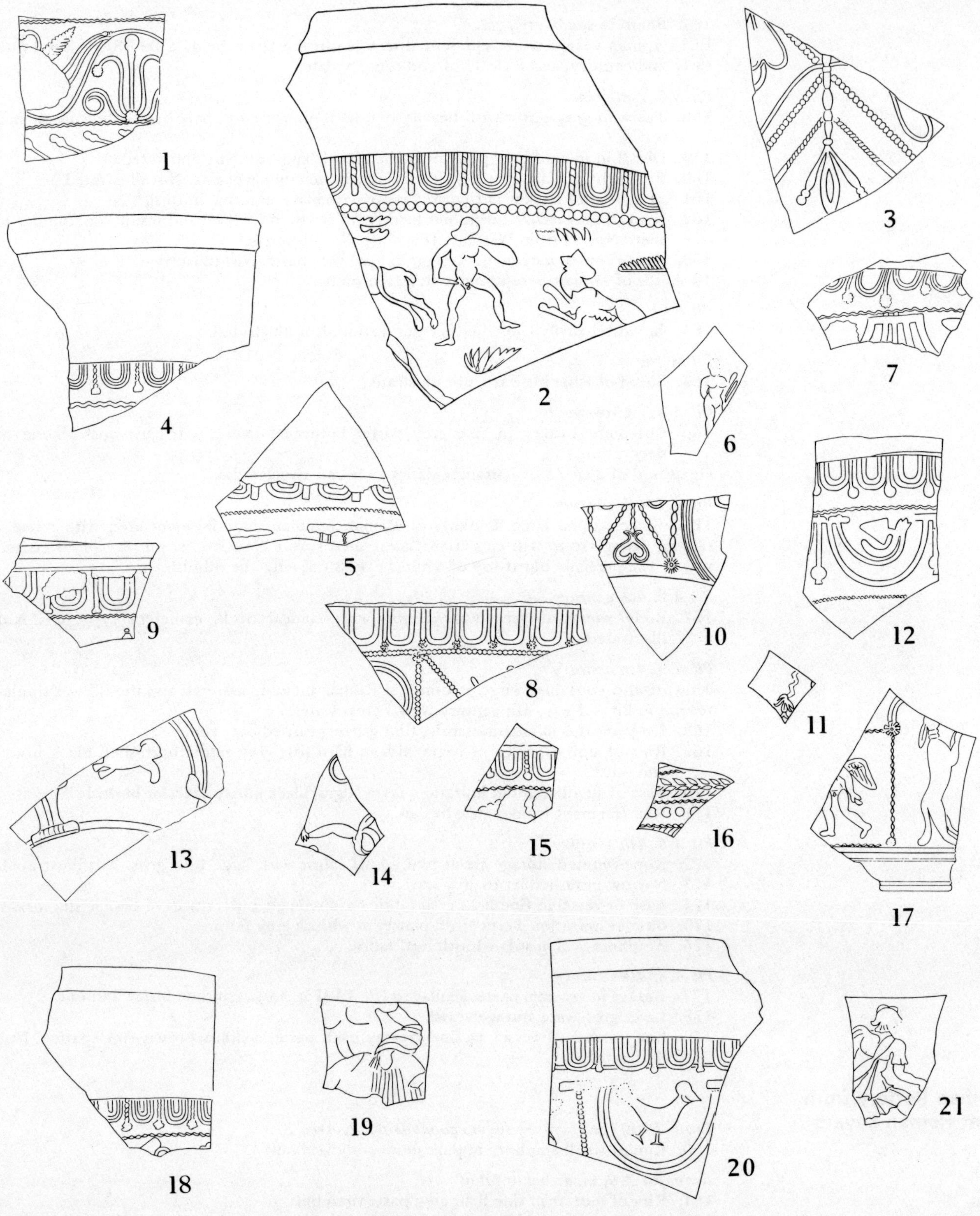

Fig. 3.13 Figured Samian Ware. (1/1.)

184. Small bowl in light grey paste.
185. Rim of small beaker; fine sandy grey ware oxidised reddish buff. Lip and exterior burnished.

From Pit A.23 (Post-medieval).
186. Jar in micaceous fine grey paste burnished black over lip and exterior.

From Pit A.26, medieval or later
187. Beaker in very fine light grey paste, well burnished inside lip and on exterior.
188. Rim of flagon in pale orange paste.
189. Rim of bowl in hard light grey fabric, slightly micaceous; burnished exterior.

The Figured Samian Ware. Fig 3.13 by G. Dannel F.S.A.

1. (A.1, Pit A.3). Form 37. Transitional design in the "Pompeii" style. A winding scroll ending in fern leaves and rosettes, over a "candelabrum" ornament. The leaf is similar to K.19 Taf.69, detail 22 by RVFINVS, and see its use on Taf.69E. Similar designs appear at Pompeii (Atkinson, Pl VI No. 34, and Wheeler, *BRECON*, Fig. 71 S. 52). The careless use of the small tendril binding can also be seen in the work of RVFINVS from Rottweil, K.19 Taf.68A. Date, *c* A.D. 70–85.
2. (N.6). Form 37. Free style design. The ovolo is close to IVLLINVS, C.G.P. Fig 36 No. 1, as is the twist of rope, Pl 127, No. 24. The figures are a stag O. 1781, a lioness, O. 1533 and a warrior O. 1056. Reference should also be made to SEVERVS, a related potter making free style designs, as probably IVSTVS, cf. *C.G.P.*, p. 199. The warrior particularly gives the impression of connection with the Trajanic potters whose figures habitually exhibited the curious roll of hair at the nape. Date, probably early Antonine.
3. (M.12). Form 29. Complex St. Andrew's Cross motif, with long twisted rods flanking poppy-heads with a blade-shaped leaf. Two lanceolate leaves are used as swag-ends, cf. K.52, Taf. 67B on form 30, also Hermet, Pl. 35 No. 47 for similar motifs. The fabric suggests Montans, or even Rozier and the date is *c.* A.D. 60–75.
4. (I.2). Form 30. The ovolo is similar to one ascribed in *C.G.P.* to QVINTILLIANVS but the tongue is corded, cf. Fig. 17, No. 2. The so-called copy by LAXTVCISSA, *C.G.P.* Fig 27, No. 1 is corded, but the present example has not got the "hammer-head" tip. Date, Hadrianic?
5. (I.10). Form 37. Burnt sherd; truncated ovolo, with double border and straight tongue. Below a bead-row, a festoon with two astragali, Perhaps the ovolo of DOECCVS, and if so the date is Antonine.
6. (I.16). Form 30. Very fine product with "orange peel" surface and smooth glossy interior. The figure is O. 350, Dechelette Inv. 44, by LIBERTVS. Date, Hadrianic.
7. Form 37. Double-bordered ovolo with long tongue ending in a rosette attached to the right, the tip itself being bent to the right. Below a wavy line is a festoon. The ovolo could be that of PAVLLVS, K 52 Taf. 50B. Date, later Flavian.
8. (M.6). Form 37, Style of ADVOCISUS. His ovolo *C.G.P.* Fig. 33 No. 2. Bead-row borders with four petalled rosettes, cf. *C.G.P.* Pl.114, No. 37, Date, Antonine.
9. (I.2). Form 30. Very smudged and badly finished. Bold square double-bordered ovolo with straight tongue attached to the left, ending in a "hammer head". The ovolo of LAXTVCISSA, *C.G.P.* Fig. 27, No. 1. Date, Antonine.
10. (L.18). Form 29. Fine, clean piece, with smooth brown-red slip, glossy and pink fabric. A St. Andrew's Cross motif, dangling an unusual pendant, usually associated with festoon ornaments, from unusual wavy lines. To the right, the remains of a medallion. Both pendant and wavy line occur in the Claudian work ascribed to INGENVVS, cf. K.19. Taf. 41L.
11. Form 30. Tiny fragment showing wavy line border with bud or leaves. *C.G.P.* detail 3, Fig. 15 of GEMINVS would fit for size, and from the fabric, date also, but too small for definite identification.
12. (J.15). Form 37. Burnt sherd, blurred, double-bordered ovolo ending in rosette. The upper zone of decoration survives, showing festoons of stipulated cordate buds with large poppy-heads as pendants. Transitional style again, similar to Atkinson, Pl. XI, No. 57 for design. Large poppy-heads were used in the Flavian period, e.g. K.19 Taf 63C, by PASSIENVS. Date, *c.* A.D. 70–90.

13. (G.8). Form 37. Rheinzabern ware. Arcade containing a dog, Ludowici T 79 or 80, probably the latter, sprung from ribbed stone, Ludowici O.47. Date, late Antonine.
14. (I.2). Form 37. The decoration is not clear. Perhaps a small bow or wreath. Probably Antonine.
15. (A.3 2.). Form 37, burnt. Neat double-bordered ovolo with a straight, beaded tongue ending in a rosette. Probably the ovolo of DRSVS, cf. *C.G.P.* Pl.88. Date, basically Hadrianic.
16. (A.1.2). Form 29. Three narrow bands of decoration, with leaf wreaths either side of a row of large beads. A very similar design is from La Graufesenque, without the wavy borders, (Hermet, Pl. 46, No. 23).
17. (A.3.11). Form 30. Panel decoration; to the left a winged figure O. 436; to the right, an upright collared hound O. 1920 in an arcade. It is possible that this is the work of the second-century potter GRATVS. The fabric is similar to his, and both figure-types can be seen in the London vessel, K.52, Taf. 29A. Date by no means certain. It is not impossible that Knorr's potter is the same as the man who worked to produce the bowls in the style of the QVINTILLIANVS group, the styles are not dissimilar. Trajanic-Hadrianic?
18. (A.3.11). Form 37. Ovolo only, style of AVSTRVS, although the tongue is a bit long. Date, Hadrianic.
19. (I.2). Form 30. The nearest to the figure-type is Dechelette 513, but the relief is bolder and the complete type must have been much larger. Stylistically Trajanic-Hadrianic, probably Lezoux work.
20. (Pit A.3). Form 37. Small bowl much accreted with lime. Double bordered ovolo with straight tongue to right. In a semi-circular festoon, a cock O. 2342, and as Oswald suggests, the potter is probably PAVLLVS, cf. *C.G.P.* pp. 276–7. PAVLLVS had connections with potters like CINNAMVS and AVSTRVS, who were working around A.D. 140 plus, but the terminal dates are not fixed.
21. (Pit A.3). Form 30. Figure of a warrior, Dechelette 626A. Oswald's rendition is purely coincidental, the clear superiority of Dechelette's hand and interpretation make identification certain, cf. the figure on *C.G.P.* Pl 69 No. 14, ascribed to IANVARIS/QVINTILLIANVS, and on Pl. 70 No. 19 and Pl. 72 No. 34, ascribed to PATERCLVS. Date, Hadrianic.

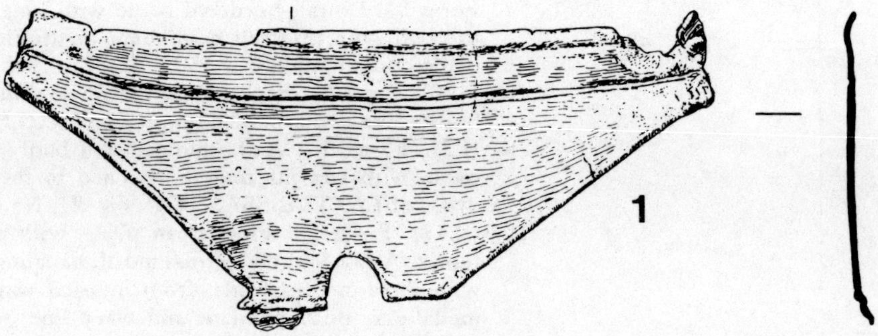

Fig. 3.14 Small Finds. (1/1.)

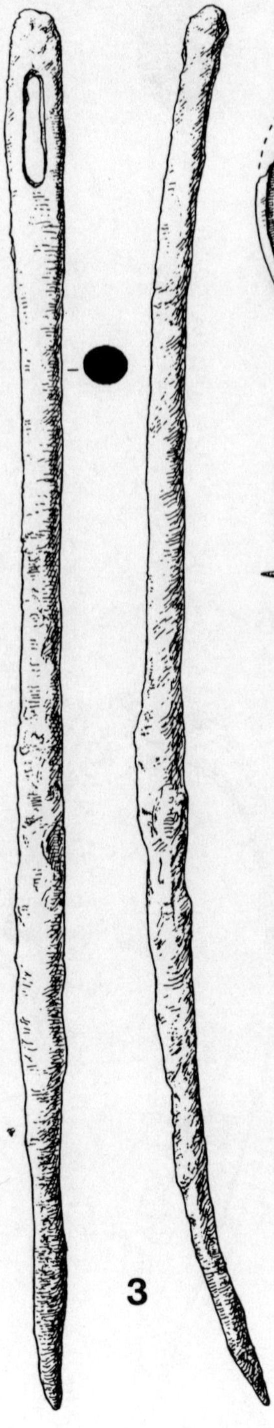

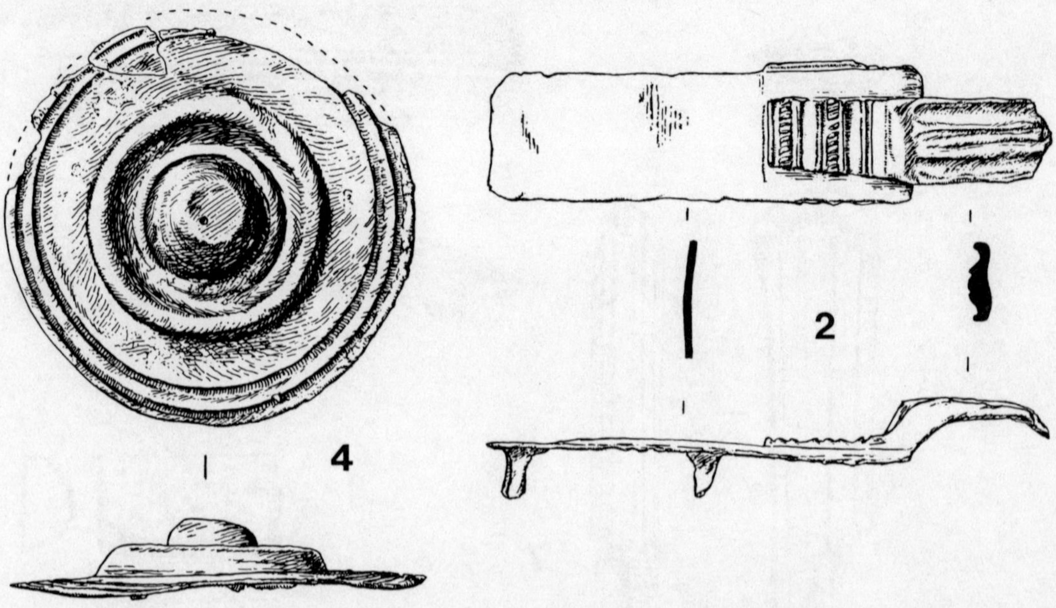

Fig. 3.15 Small Finds (1/1)

Roman Small Finds

Period 1, Phase 1. From the upper fill of ditch 1, (B.14).

1. Fragment of bronze sheet, pierced in two places, the holes being torn when the sheet was detached from its mounting.

From the beam slot, (G.38).

2. Clip for leather strap. Bronze with silver wash. A common mid-first century form as at:

Hofheim Taf. XIII, no. 34; Lincoln, *J.R.S.* 39 (1949) Pl Xa; *Newstead,* Pl LXXIV; *Hod Hill* I, Fig. 2, A.30; Mainz, *M.Z.*, 7 (1912), Abb. 3 Nos. 5 & 6; Brecon, *Y. Cymmrodor,* 37 (1926), Fig. 57; The Lunt, Baginton near Coventry, report forthcoming.

Period 1, Phase 2. From Posthole H.25.

3. Bronze needle.

Period 1, Phase 3.

From occupation layer north of ditch 1 (B.9).

4. Bronze boss.
5. Part of a shale ring 24.5 cms. diameter. This is too large to be a bangle, and unless it was hinged would not function as a neck ring. Two sections were found of which one is illustrated. There is a slight ledge on the inside, and it may be the rim of a large shale tazza made by the assembly of carefully graduated rings.

From fill of period 1, phase 2, ditch/latrine pit. (J.11).

6. Bronze mount.

From the occupation layer above ditch 1. (B.5).

7. Bone knife handle.

From Roman Pits.

From pit N.6, Antonine.

8. Bronze knife handle with lozenge pattern inlays in green and blue enamel. Trace of the iron knife tang is still visible in the base. *Wroxeter 1914,* Pl. XVI, No. 17; *Richborough IV*, Pl. XL, No. 152; A. Hands, *Excavaions at Shakenoak I,* 1968, Fig. 29, No. 11; *R.L.O.*, Wurzberg, Taf. I, Fig. 8.
9. Pipeclay figurine of Venus.

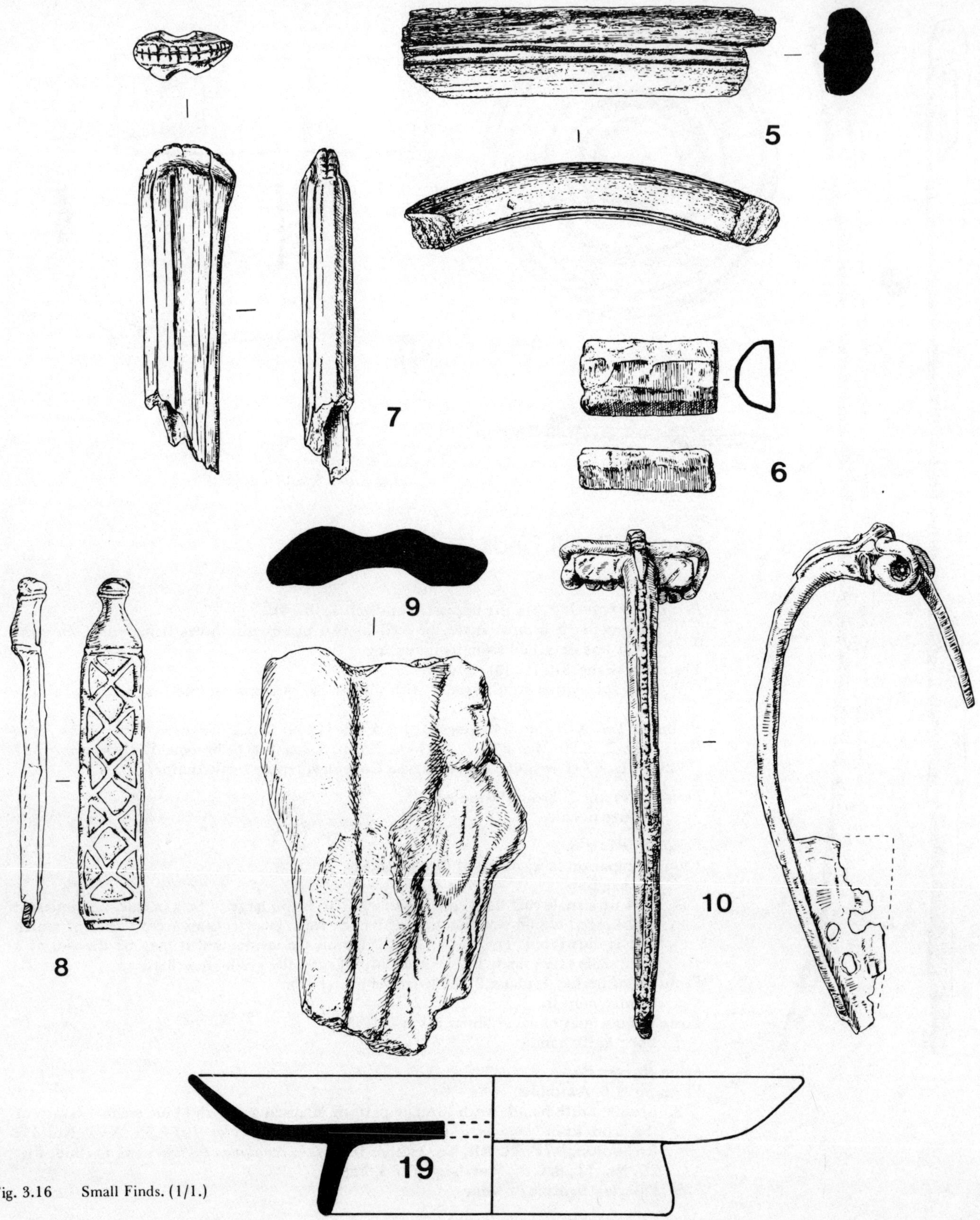

Fig. 3.16 Small Finds. (1/1.)

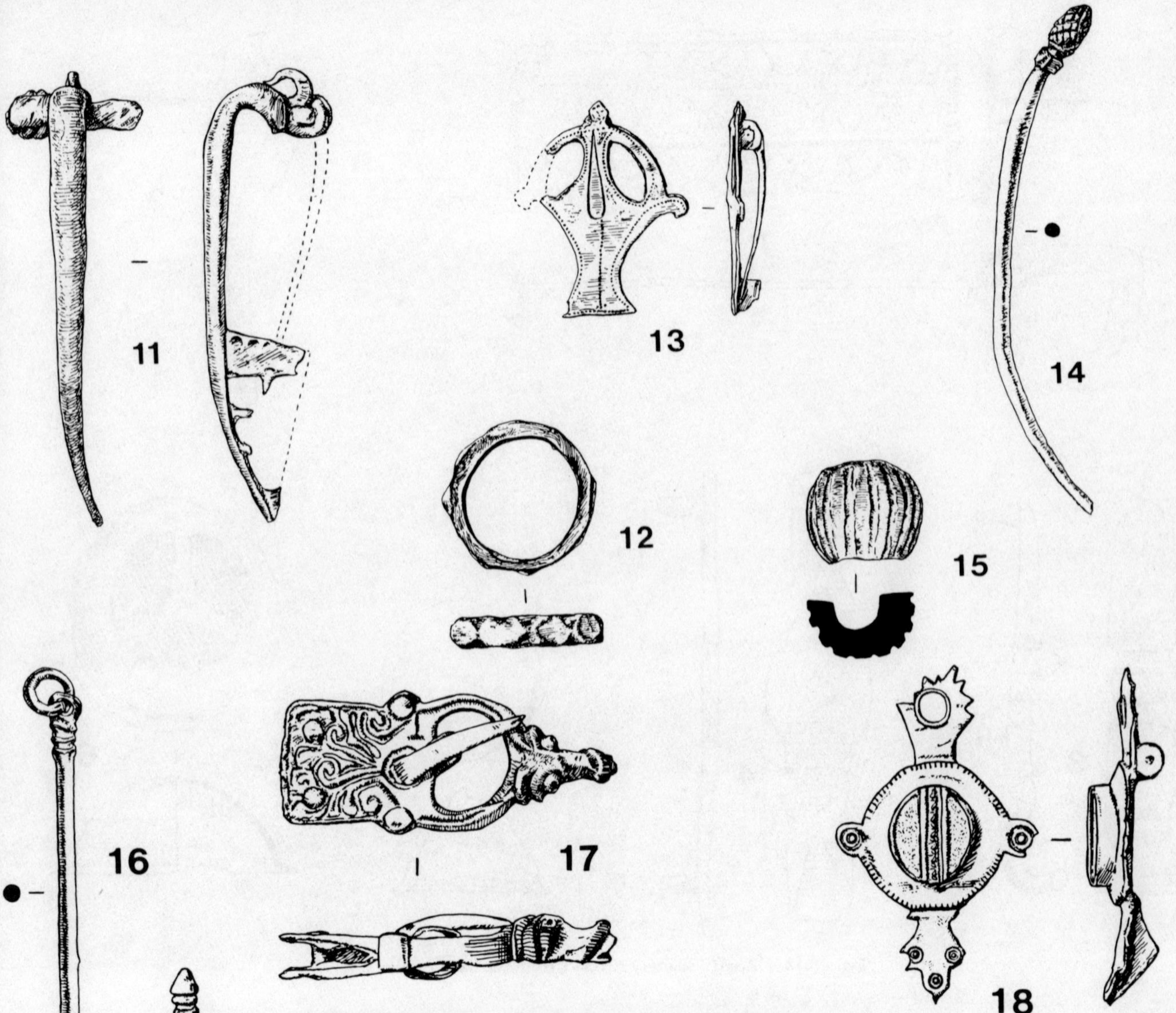

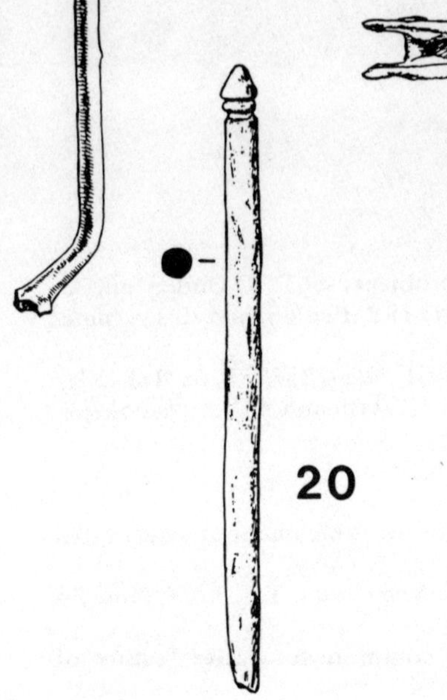

From Post-Roman Pits and Occupation Levels.

10. Bronze fibula, *Camulodunum* Pl. LXXXIX, Type 111. (Pit A. 18).
11. Bronze fibula, *op.cit.* Type 111 (Pit B.3).
12. Chip-carved bronze finger ring. (Pit A.9).
13. Bronze brooch, tinned on face. (Medieval layer in A.5).
14. Bronze pin. (post-Roman layer in A.5).
15. Melon Bead. (medieval layer in A.5.).
16. Fragment of Bronze toilet article. (medieval level H. 26).
17. Bronze buckle with zoomorphic terminal. (Medieval level H.26).
18. Bronze brooch. (Recent occupation level I.2).
19. Glass bowl. (10–11th century pit I. 15). Fragment of fine bowl in pale green tinted glass. *Camulodunum* Pl. LXXXVIII, Type 60.
20. Bone pin. (Recent occupation level M.6).

10–11th century occupation levels Not illustrated.

21. Pottery Counter. (From occupation spread I.14). Half a roughly cut disc, perforated in the centre. Cut from a sherd of Roman grey coarseware.
22. Bronze needle. (From occupation spread J.7).

Fig. 3.17. Small Finds. (1/1.) approx.)

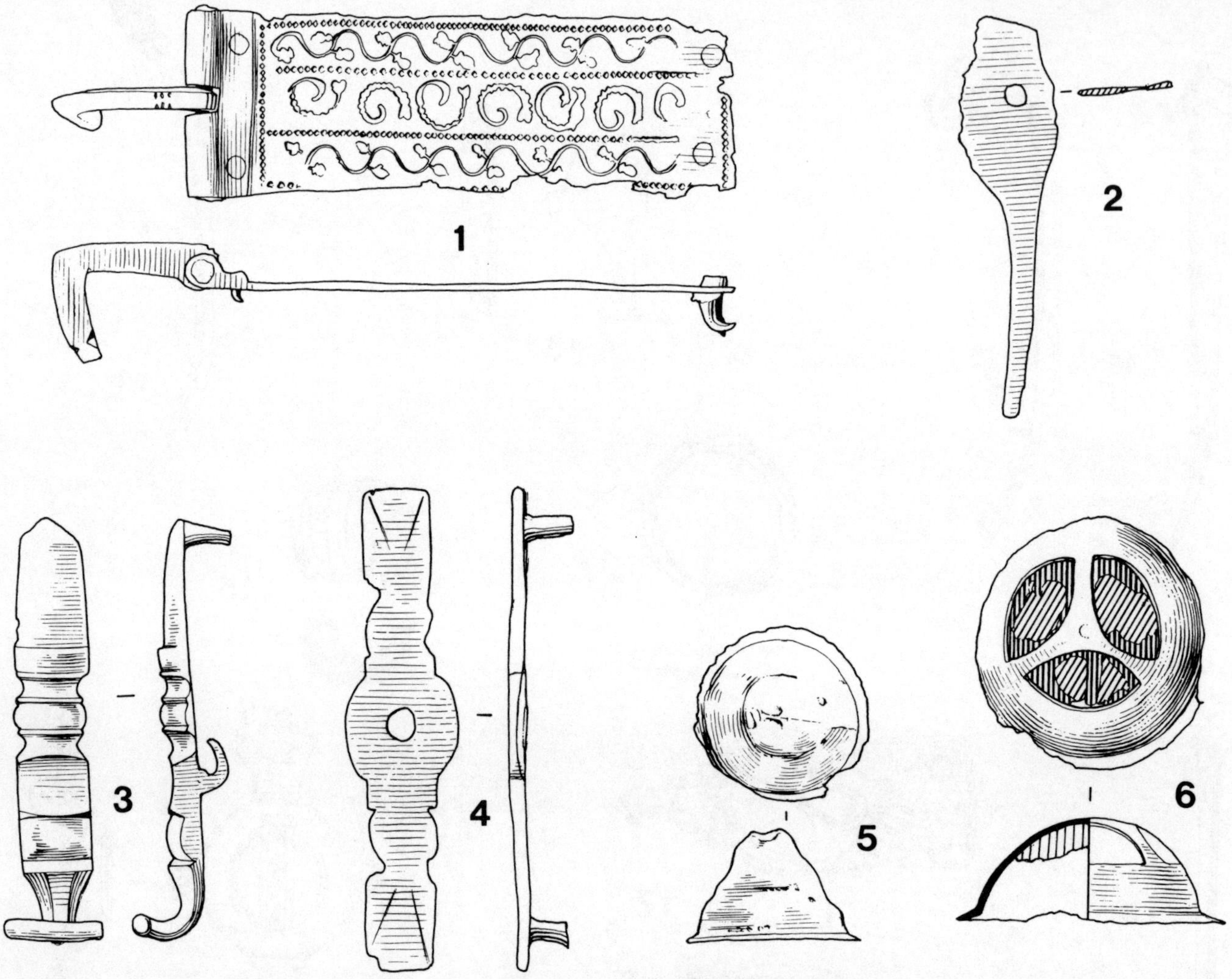

Fig. 3.18 Roman Military Bronzes from the Sadler Collection.

For a discussion of the significance of the Sadler bronze objects see D.R. Dudley and G. Webster, *The Roman Conquest of Britain, A.D. 43–57*. **61**, 192, Fig. 48, and this volume, p. 26.

1. Belt-plate with hook, cf. *Richborough IV* Pl. XXXIII, No. 72; *Hofheim* Taf. XII, Nos. 1–7; Mainz *M.Z.* VII, (1912) 4 Nos. 23 & 24.; "Verulamium", *Archaeologia* **90**, Fig. 4, No. 11.
2. Fragment of flattened cuirass-hook, cf. *R.L.O.*, 2, Fig. 24.
3. Silvered toggle-end of belt or baldric.
4. Belt-plate. The rivet-hole in the centre was probably for the attachment of a decorated stud.
5. Small domed stud with trace of mask ornament, cf. *Novaesium*, Taf. XXX, Nos. 24 & 26.
6. Small domed stud with traces of niello inlay. A common decorative feature of legionary belts or aprons, cf. *Hofheim*, Taf. XII, Nos. 40–44.

The Coins

Period 1, Phase 2. A.3, 14, upper fill of Ditch 2.

1. VESPASIAN, *dupondius*, (R.I.C. 478) A.D. 71.

Period 1, Phase 3, B.7, 14, upper fill above burnt timber (Antonine).

2. NERO *As*, (R.I.C. 342) with obverse legend C, attributed to A.D. 66–68.

Post-Roman pit (A.9)

3. AE 18 mm.,? Radiate late 3rd century.
4. DOMITIAN, *dupondius.* (R.I.C. 351) A.D. 87.

Post-Roman pit (J.10), cut into top of ditch/latrine pit J.20, (Period 1, phase 2)

5. TIBERIUS, *As*, of Lugdunum, (R.I.C. 11).

Post-Roman pit (I.15, I.15a), containing Saxo-Norman potsherds.

6. CLAUDIUS 11 (R.I.C. 261) 268–70 A.D.
7. AE, 3rd or 4th century, worn.
8. CONSTANTINOPOLIS, (H.K. 66) 330–335 A.D.
9. House of Constantine. (copy as H.K. 226), 335–345 A.D.
10. CONSTANTINE 11 (copy as H.K. 48). 330–345 A.D.
11. CONSTANS, (H.K. 244), 337–341 A.D.
12. CONSTANS, (as H.K. 117 but PTR ?), 337–341 A.D.

Post-Roman pit (I.9).

13. TETRICUS 11. Antoninianus (R.I.C. 272) 270–273 A.D.
14. ? POSTUMUS. 359–368 A.D.
15. VALENTINIAN 1. (C.K. 506), 367–375 A.D.

Post-Medieval Occupation

16. Ancient British, probably TINCOMMIUS. Reverse, Medusa head. (M.6).
17. DOMITIAN?, *dupondius*, 81–96 A.D., reverse illegible. (I.2).
18. DOMITIAN, *sestertius*, (R.I.C. 401) 89-90 A.D. (I.2).
19. TRAJAN, *sestertius*, 101-111 A.D., reverse illegible. (I.2).
20. HADRIAN, *sestertius*, (R.K. 637), 124-138 A.D. (I.2).
21. HADRIAN, *As*, (R.I.C. 617) 117–124 A.D. (K.2).
22. Barbarous radiate. Reverse for SALUS. 270–290 A.D. (I.8).

References

Atkinson, D. "A hoard of samian ware from Pompeii" J.R.S. 4 1914.

C.G.P. Stanfield J.A. and Simpson G, *Central Gaulish Potters* Oxford 1958.

Hawkes, C.F.C. & Hull M.R., *Camulodunum*, Soc. of Antiquaries, 1948.

Hermet, F. *La Graufesenque*, Paris, 1934.

Knorr, R. *Topfer und Fabriken verzierter Terra Sigillata des ersten Jahrhunderts*, (Referred to as K.19). Stuttgart, 1952.

Lukowici, W. *Rheinzabien* Vols 1–11, 1901–5.

Oswald, F. *Index of figure-types on Terra Sigillata*, Liverpool 1937.

Dechelette, J. *Les vases ceramiques ornes de la Gaule Romaine*, Paris, 1914.

Wheeler, R.E.M. *The Roman fort near Brecon*, Y Cymmrodor Soc., 1926.

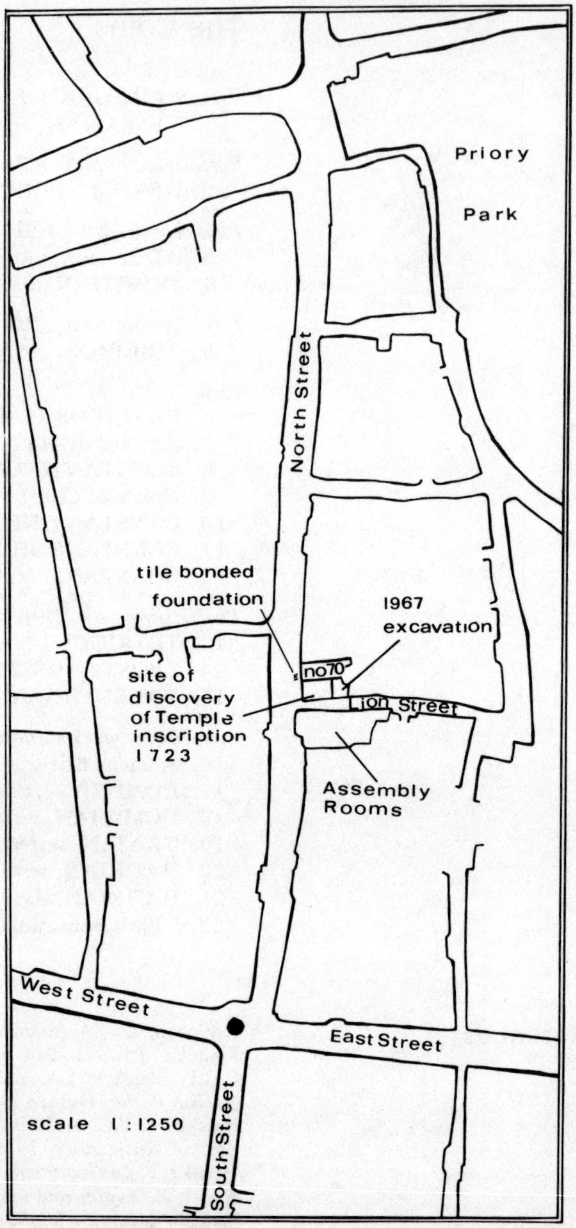

Fig. 4. The Temple of Neptune and Minerva

4

Lion St., Temple of Neptune and Minerva

One of the most important and perplexing inscriptions ever discovered in Britain is the one found in North Street in 1723 (plate 8).[1]

The well-cut inscription, with fine lettering and punctuation records the dedication of a Temple to Neptune and Minerva by a guild of workmen with the authority of Tiberius Claudius Cogidubnus, King and Legate.

The reference to Cogidubnus, known to have been alive in the first century,[2] and the high standard of lettering indicate that somewhere in Chichester or the surrounding countryside a classical temple dedicated to purely Roman gods was built early in the Roman period.

Stukely[3] and Gale[4] record that the inscription was found face uppermost at a depth of four feet when the cellars of the house at the north corner of Lion Street and North Street were constructed. Although Gale records two walls, each 3 feet thick, being found nearby, it is by no means certain that the inscription was found in a primary context associated with the walls.

Professor Jocelyn Toynbee[5] has suggested that the stone might have arrived in Chichester as part of the material robbed from Fishbourne Palace, one and a half miles away to the west, in the second or third century. But no part of the Fishbourne complex so far excavated has been interpreted as a classical Temple, and in the absence of inscriptions from Fishbourne, the connection between King Cogidubnus, Fishbourne and Chichester, although logical, remains conjectural.

In 1967 the rebuilding of the Liberal Party Headquarters on the site immediately east of the house where the inscription was found (Fig. 4) afforded a brief opportunity to excavate a limited area.[6]

If the inscription was in a primary context when it was discovered in 1723, it was possible that judicious excavation would reveal part of the *podium* of a classical Temple of first century date. Certainly the frontage on to a major street of Noviomagus, the tribal capital of a Romanised client King, is one of the few appropriate positions for a classical Temple at this early period.

Summary

The archaeological levels on the northern two thirds of the site had been totally destroyed by cellar foundations cut down into the subsoil. Excavation of the southern third of the site revealed a spread of third century occupation, below medieval rubbish pits and occupation spread.

While the excavation was being carried out in February 1967, watch was kept on a shallow service trench cut along the east side of North Street. Part of a foundation of Roman tiles, *tegula,* set in creamy buff mortar was seen at a depth of 58.4 cms (23 ins) below the modern street makeup in front of 70, North Street (Fig. 4). It was not possible to determine the depth of the feature and it was badly cut away on the north and south side by modern service trenches, but it is just possible that this tile-bonded structure was part of the foundation for a flight of steps approaching the *podium* of the Temple from North Street.

The Excavation

A trench 76 cms (2 ft 6 ins) wide[7] was dug by a mechanical excavator across the northern two-thirds of the site. The entire area was found to be a complex of cellars filled with rubble and wine bottles, going beyond the limits of the site. It was hoped that the cellar foundations would be above the Roman levels, but limited excavation in the central area of the site showed that brick foundations had penetrated the natural subsoil at a depth of 213 cms (7 ft). The northern part of the site was immediately backfilled and a trench 76 cms (2 ft 6 ins) wide was dug by hand across the southern third of the site. A spread of medieval occupation, (layer LS 3) 83.8 cms (2 ft 9 ins) thick was found at a depth of 106.7 cms (3 ft 6 ins) below the present ground level. It was cut by a large medieval pit, (layer LS 5) circa 91.4 cms (3 ft 0 ins) wide and 83.8 cms (2 ft 9 ins) deep containing pottery of late thirteenth and fourteenth century date.[8] Below the medieval level a spread of occupation (layer LS 7) 31 cms (1 ft 0 ins) thick contained only Roman material, oyster shell, tile (*tegula* and *imbrex*) animal bone and a few sherds of grey ware.

A large circular pit (layer LS 6) contained grey coarseware sherds of nondescript character and two sherds of purple gloss New Forest pottery together with animal bone and oyster shell. The pit cut through the occupation level to a depth of 259 cms (8 ft 6 ins) below the modern ground level. Natural, undisturbed brickearth was found at a depth of 198 cms (6 ft 6 ins) below present ground level.

As there was imminent danger of the narrow trench collapsing, the Roman pit was not completely excavated.

Detail of Finds

Roman Occupation. 2nd Century. (Layer LS 7).

1. Jar in pale grey paste with small everted rim. Tooled burnish below rim and burnished lattice decoration on body.
2. Jar with everted rim in pale grey fabric with small flint grits.

Roman Pit. 3rd Century. (Layer LS 6).

Two fragments of folded beaker in purple gloss New Forest ware.

Medieval Occupation. Circa 1300 A.D. (Layer LS 3).

Fragment of chimney pot. Slashed around top edge.

Cooking pot. Rim in grey fabric oxidised to yellow buff outside, darker pinky buff inside. Light, thin green glaze in angle of neck and inside rim.

Jug. Sagging base with continuous light frilling at the basal angle.

Jug. Strap handle and body sherd of same jug. Inner surface yellowish pink, external overall green glaze with darker green streaks.

Medieval Pit. Circa 1300 A.D. (Layer LS 5).

Two fragments of tile with heavy flint gritting.

Jug in light brown fabric, reddish brown outside. Splashes of light green lustrous glaze.

Two sherd unglazed ware in harsh sandy fabric with sparse angular flint grits.

Conclusion

The results of the excavation were negative in the sense that no first century structure of any sort was found on the site. However, a temple fronting onto North Street need not have been large enough to reach the Liberal Party headquarters site in Lion Street, and the area immediately adjacent to a temple would almost certainly have been kept clear of other structures at least for a time when the temple was newly built.

The foundation seen in the service trench in front of 70, North Street appeared to be Roman, and excavation beneath the pavement could reveal more of this structure. In the meantime it is essential that any public works excavation or redevelopment in the area is done under archaeological supervision. This particularly applies to public works trenches which for reasons of public convenience are often literally 'dug overnight'.

Notes and References

[1] *Corpus Inscriptionum Latinarum* vii, noll.

[2] Tacitus. 97-98 A.D., *Agricola*, 14.

[3] Stukely. *Itinerarium Curiosum*, 1776.

[4] Gale. *Transactions of the Philosophical Society*, 1723, 32, 391-401.

[5] Toynbee. 1964. *Art in Britain Under the Romans*, p. 46.

[6] The writer wishes to express her thanks to the Chairman of the Chichester branch of the Liberal Party, and Douglas Newman Ltd., the site contractors for courtesy and co-operation throughout the excavation.

[7] Owing to the collapse of the sides of this trench, the final width was in excess of 5 feet.

[8] The author wishes to thank Mr. G. Dunning F.S.A., for assistance in dating the medieval finds from this site.

5

The Roman Cemetery at St. Pancras

The location of the Roman Cemetery outside the East Gate at Chichester has been known since 1895, and the excavations reported here are the third to disturb the ground. The site lies on the north side of St. Pancras (Stane Street, some 315 metres (350 yards) outside the East Gate of the City. (Fig. 2.1). To the west of the main excavation area is the land known as the Litten which was a burial ground from the 12th to the 19th centuries, and it is certain that a part of the Roman cremation cemetery occupied this area also.

In 1895-6 Councillor Butler, who owned a number of cottages fronting on to the east side of Alexandra Road, excavated under the floors of some of them and recovered approximately 150 vessels,[1] which he later presented to the Chichester Museum of that time. No grave groups were recorded.

Between the years 1934 and 1937 Messrs. Carlyon Britton and Llewellyn White excavated on the site of the Butler cottages, which by that time had been demolished, and also in the gardens and orchard to the rear. A total of 65 burials were recorded and these were reported by Mrs. Grahame Clark (Miss G.M. White) in *Sussex Archeological Collections.*[2]

Other burials have been reported from time to time when workmen have dug service trenches in Alexandra Road and New Park Road,[3] but with one exception (see below) it has proved impossible to trace any of the finds.

The demolition by the City Council of Nos. 16 to 21 St. Pancras in 1965 provided a further opportunity to investigate the cemetery. No stratification had been recorded in the previous excavations, and it was hoped to establish the relationship of Stane Street to the cemetery, and to obtain the largest possible sample of samian ware in association with native wares so as to establish reliable dating criteria for the first two centuries A.D.

Five periods of occupation were noted during the excavations. Of these only the first four are of immediate significance, and are discussed below:-

Period 1. Roman c. 43 A.D. (Fig. 5.10 and P14)

Running approximately north-west across Area 1 was a deep defensive ditch probably of military origin. It was not open for very long; the fill above the rapid silt contained only pre-Flavian samian and imitation Gallo-Belgic wares and associated coarse wares, together with a mass of food bones. Some 1.83 metres (6 feet) to the east was another smaller ditch which was filled with rammed clay and in which there were a number of soft areas which may have contained posts. It is likely that this was a palisade trench, and implies a defensive work to the east of the present City. A possible explanation is that these features formed part of a military camp or depot perhaps for the Second Legion.

Period 2 c. 60 - 70 A.D.

At some time after the Period 1 ditch was filled in, quarrying for gravel and clay along the western lip of the ditch was commenced. This quarrying was not confined to Area 1, but was noted in Area 4 (Recreation Ground), and was probably for material to metal Stane Street and areas within the City.

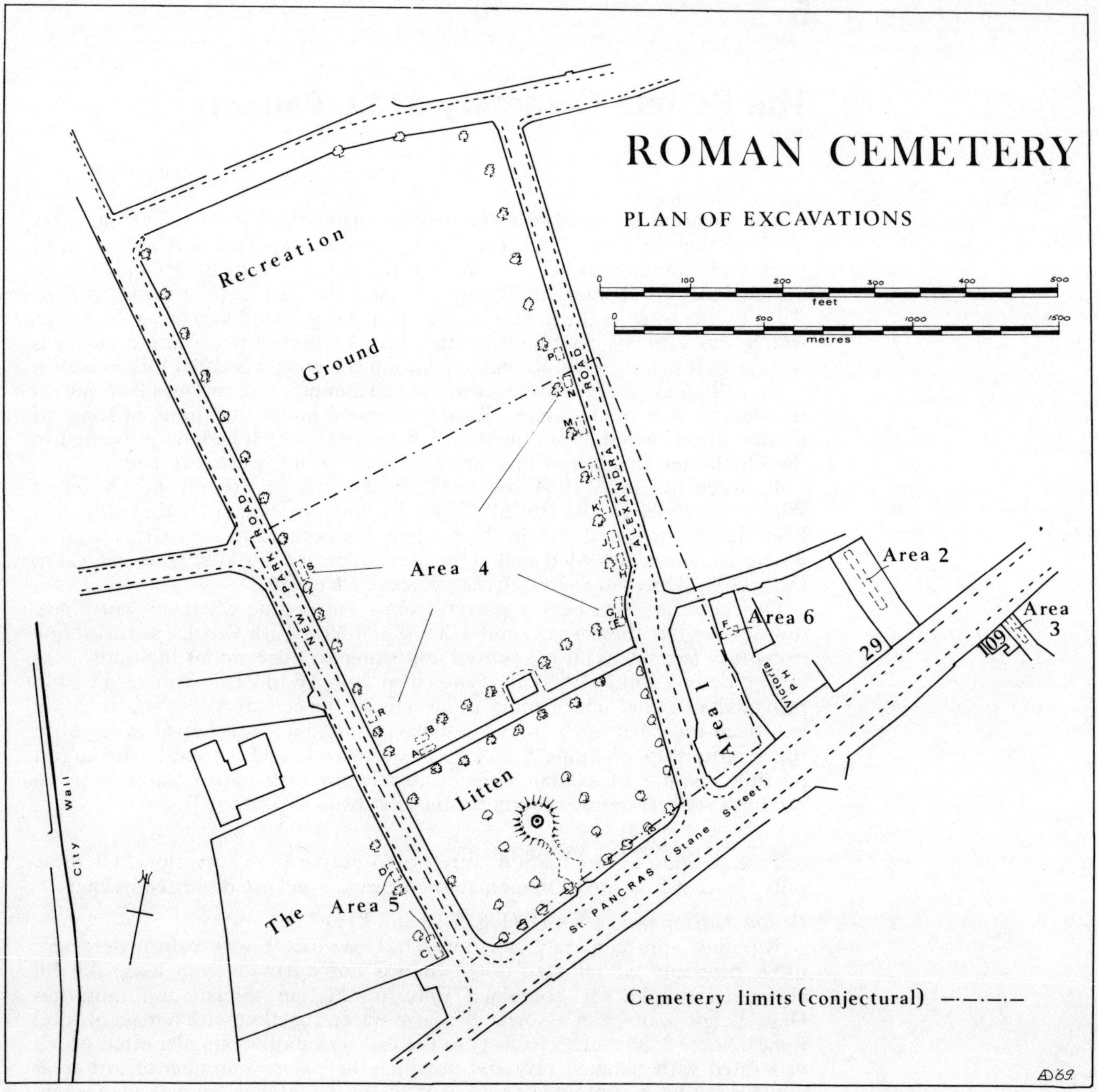
ROMAN CEMETERY
PLAN OF EXCAVATIONS
0 100 200 300 400 500
feet
0 500 1000 1500
metres
Recreation
Ground
NEW PARK ROAD
ALEXANDRA ROAD
Area 4
Area 2
Area 6
Area 3
Area 1
Area 5
The
Litten
Victoria P H
29
109
St. PANCRAS (Stane Street)
City Wall
Cemetery limits (conjectural)
AD69

Fig. 5.1

Photos: G. R. Claridge

PLATE 4. *Top:* St. Pancras Roman Cemetery, Area 1. Burials 193 & 194.
Bottom: St. Pancras, Area 1, Period 1, defensive ditch.

Photo: G. R. Claridge

PLATE 5. St. Pancras Roman Cemetery. Burials in Trench G, Area 2.

Period 3. c. 70/80 A.D. to 3rd/4th century. Areas 1 and 4.

At some time in the early Flavian period the Roman cremation cemetery was set out, the cremations spreading across the area formerly occupied by the defensive ditch and gravel pits. This cemetery continued in general use until late Antonine times at least and probably until the turn of the 2nd century. Thereafter it fell into disuse apart from a few inhumations which were placed there from time to time during the 3rd and possibly 4th centuries. The total area of the cemetery was approximately 4.3 acres.

Period 4. c. late 4th century or later. Areas 1 and 4.

At some time after the cemetery went out of use a further phase of gravel digging took place, disturbing parts of the cremation cemetery in Areas 1 and 4. There is no direct evidence that this phase of activity took place during the Roman period, but the absence of any post Roman material in the slow silt suggests a late Roman date, c. 4th century, as a possibility.

Period 5. c. 13th - 15th centuries (Areas 1 and 2)

Medieval occupation alongside the road (St. Pancras) is represented by an area of metalling and oyster shells, possibly a yard, and a deep ditch containing medieval pottery and tiles running east-west across the north side of the site.

Site History

According to the *Victoria County History of Sussex,*[5] the burial ground now known as "the Litten" was in use both in Roman and Saxon times. Its description in Domesday Book is as follows: 'In the same Hundred, (Estocbridge, or Stockbridge) Chetel holds land for one plough. It has never been set out in hides. King William granted him this land. There he has one mill of 5 shillings and one bordar and 5 acres of meadow. Worth 25 shillings'.[6] Chetel later exchanged this land, or part of it, with the Earl of Arundel, and by 1098 it had been given by Hugh, Earl of Arundel and his brother Henry to Ralph de Luffa, Bishop of Chichester. The gift was confirmed by Henry 1. In the year 1212 the king is said to have had a garden on part of the land formerly held by Ketel Esterman and this garden was committed to the charge of the Bishop of Chichester in 1226. In the following year the king granted to the bishop his garden without the walls of Chichester, with the chapel built therein and the place where the bodies of the dead were buried, the bishop agreeing to place two chaplains in the chapel to pray for the souls of the king and his father. This chapel, of which all traces were later lost, was dedicated to St. Michael.

In 1331, John Stubbe, a wool merchant and future Mayor of Chichester, and his Wife Mabel founded a chantry in the chapel, at the altar of St. Mary, called the 'chantry of the Charnell.'.

By the 17th century the burial ground was known as 'Michaels Lytton' to distinguish it from the 'High Church Lyten', or 'the Lighten called Paradise' within the precincts of the Cathedral.

St. Pancras Church and a few houses to the north west of it are marked on John Speed's map of Chichester, 1610, (Fig. 2.2) but apart from this, the parish of St. Pancras (in which the site of the excavations lie) is shown as open country. During the seige of Chichester in 1642 the suburb of St. Pancras was almost completely destroyed, and the Litten therefore probably suffered some damage. The effects of this destruction were long lasting, the re-building of the church being delayed until 1750-1751.

The cemetery was still in use in 1815,[7] and was sometimes known as 'the Litten' and sometimes as the 'Bishops Garden'. It was the custom for the dead of all Chichester parishes except Subdeanery to be buried there, and this custom continued until the opening of the present Chichester cemetery in 1859.[8]

The Excavations

Area 1 (Fig. 5.11).

Prior to demolition by the city council of the houses fronting on to St. Pancras, trial trenches were dug in the gardens of Nos. 17 and 18 (Trenches A and C; Fig. 5.2) and eleven burials recovered.

Trenches D and E (Figs. 5.3 and 5.11) were cut alongside the road to examine the relationship of the cemetery to Stane Street. As a result of what was found, a further grid of trenches were cut on the same alignment at the northern end of the site, (Trenches S, T and U. Figs. 5.8 and 5.11). The remainder of the trenches (V to Z) were cut by machine to a depth of 0.46 metres (1 ft 6 ins) and deepened by hand digging. This was necessary in order to examine as much of the ground as possible before the time limit for excavation expired.

Area 2 (Fig. 5.1).

To test the extent of the cemetery eastwards and to look for traces of military occupation a trial cutting was made on waste ground to the East of No. 29 St. Pancras. No Roman features were found, but a ditch was sectioned at the north end of the site (see discussion under Period 4).

Area 3 (Fig. 5.1).

A further cutting was made at the South end of St. Pancras to the East of No. 109. The cut was made from North to South as close as possible to the south pavement to look for the side ditch alongside Stane Street. Results were negative, and were confirmed by a contractor's trench cut a few yards to the East. The undisturbed subsoil, which was within a few inches of ground level was yellow clay-with-flints overlaying coombe rock.

Areas 4 and 5 (Fig. 5.1).

In order to answer outstanding questions arising from the excavations in Area 1 a further series of trenches were dug on the Litten on the west side of New Park Road[9] before it was made into a car park, and also on the south, east and west sides of the Recreation Ground.[10] The objects were two-fold. It was hoped that although the Litten would have been disturbed many times by medieval and later burials it might be possible to identify pre-Flavian Roman pottery in the disturbed grave fill and this would give some indication as to whether or not the early part of the cemetery lay near to the city limits. It was also hoped that the northern boundary of the cemetery could be fixed. Trenches C and D (Area 5) were dug immediately to the west of New Park Road to a depth of 1.22 metres (4 ft.).

Trenches G to S were dug around 3 sides of the Recreation Ground and produced a further 89 burials. (See discussion under Periods 3 and 4).

Area 6 (Fig. 5.1).

The demolition of the St. Pancras Community Hut on the east side of Area 1 in 1968 afforded an opportinuty to define the eastern boundary of the cemetery. By kind permission of Messrs. Tamplins a trench was cut east to west across the site, linking up with Area 1. No burials were found, natural gravel being reached at a depth of 0.61 metres (2 ft.).

Period 1

Period 1 c. 43 A.D. (Figs. 5.9 and 5.10).

At the eastern end of Trench D a deep ditch was sectioned. Although the lips of the ditch on both sides had been cut away by later excavations it must have been originally about 4.57 - 4.88 metres (15 to 16 ft.) wide and probably about 2.14 metres (7 ft.) deep. It was 0.92 metres (3 ft.) wide at the bottom and cut into coombe rock with a precision which suggested that it was of military origin. This ditch was sectioned again in Trenches S, T and

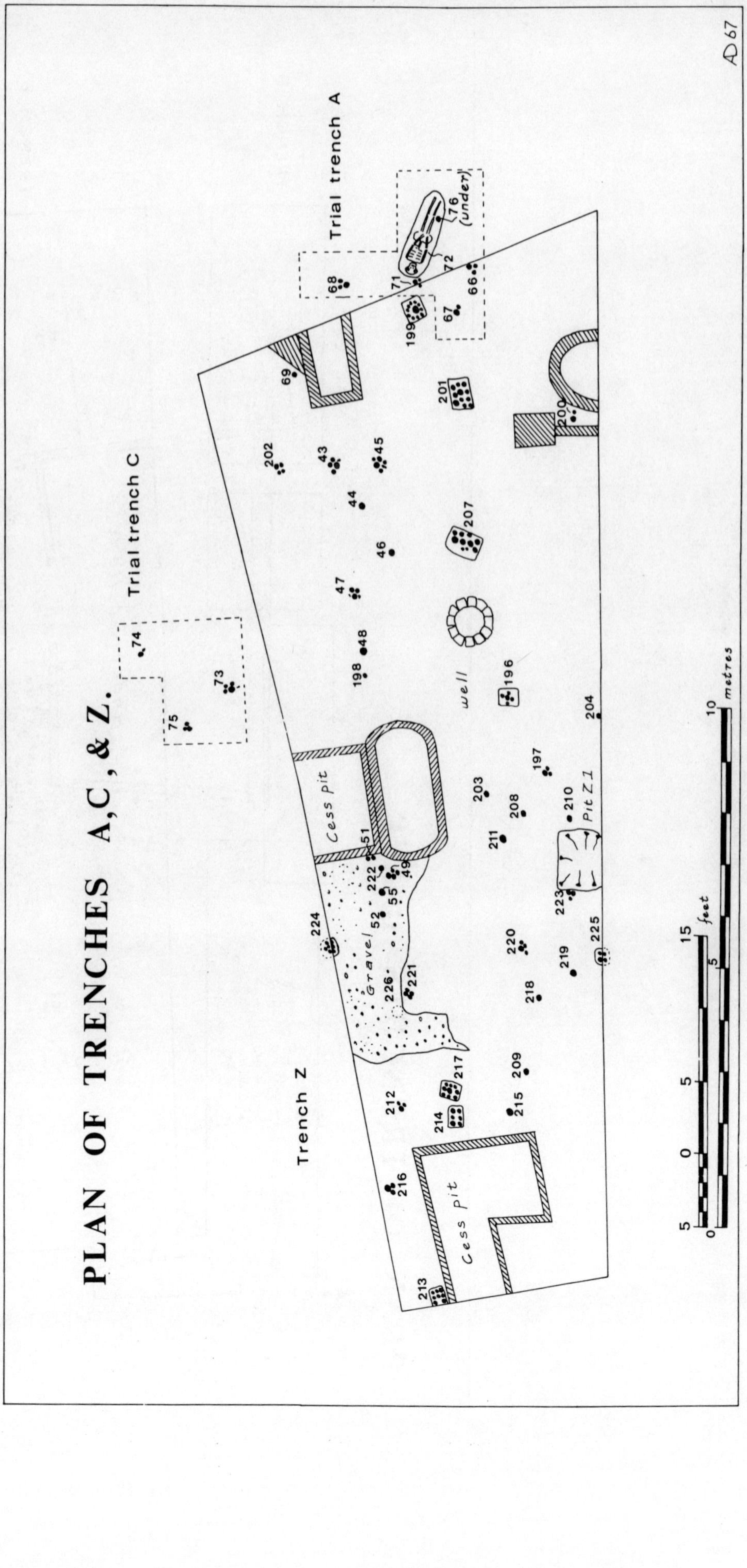
PLAN OF TRENCHES A,C, & Z.
D67
Trial trench A
Trial trench C
Trench Z
Cess pit
Cess pit
Gravel
well
Pit Z1
76 (under)
66
67
68
69
71
72
73
74
75
43
44
45
46
47
48
49
51
52
55
196
197
198
199
200
201
202
203
204
207
208
209
210
211
212
213
214
215
216
217
218
219
220
221
222
223
224
225
226
feet
metres
15
10
5
0
5

Fig. 5.2

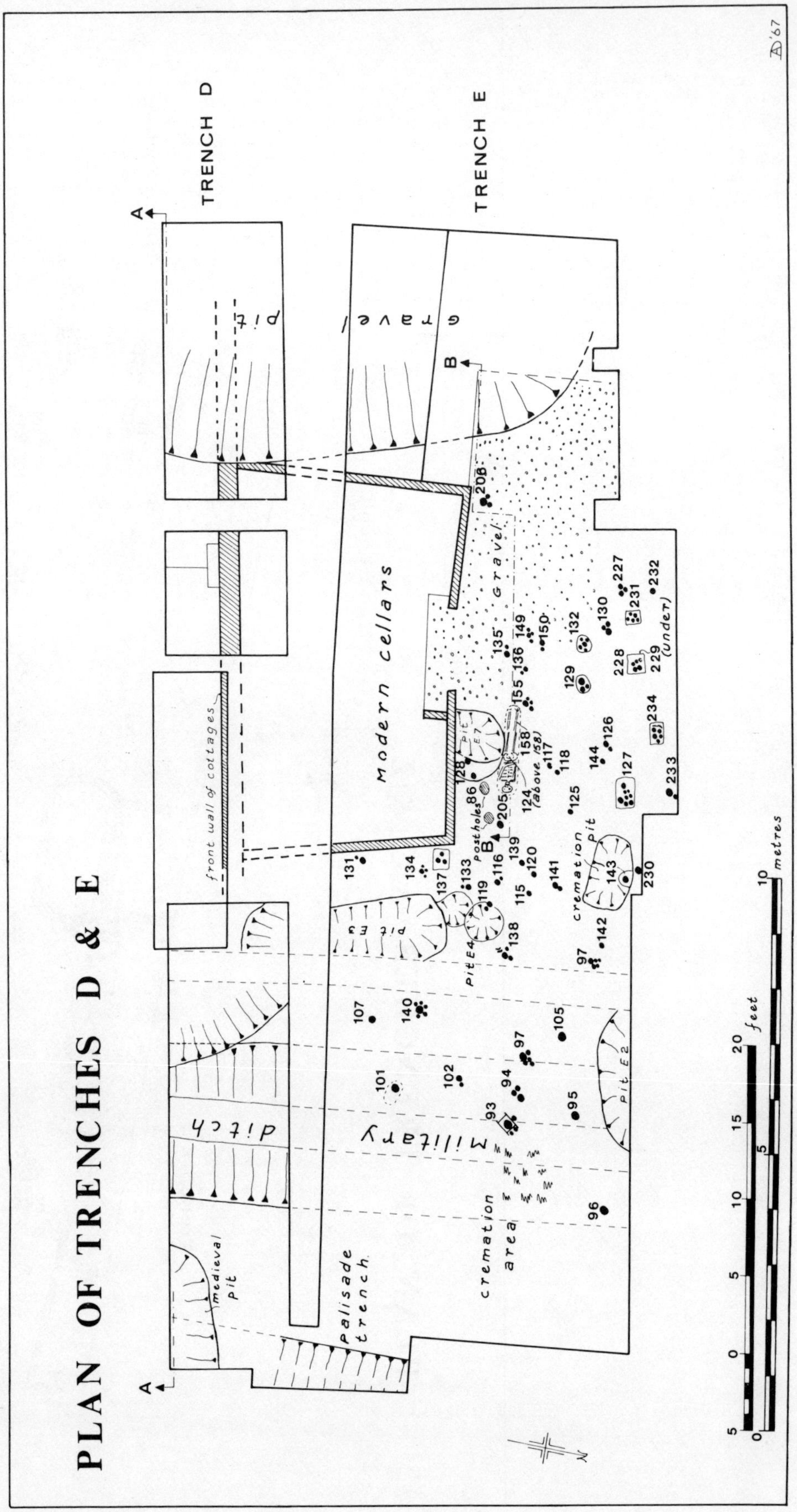

PLAN OF TRENCHES D & E
TRENCH D
TRENCH E
front wall of cottages
Modern cellars
pit
gravel
Gravel
ditch
Military
medieval pit
palisade trench
cremation area
cremation pit
pit E2
pit E3
pit E4
pit E7
postholes
(above 158)
(under)
A
B
feet
metres
5 0 5 10 15 20
0 5 10

Fig. 5.3

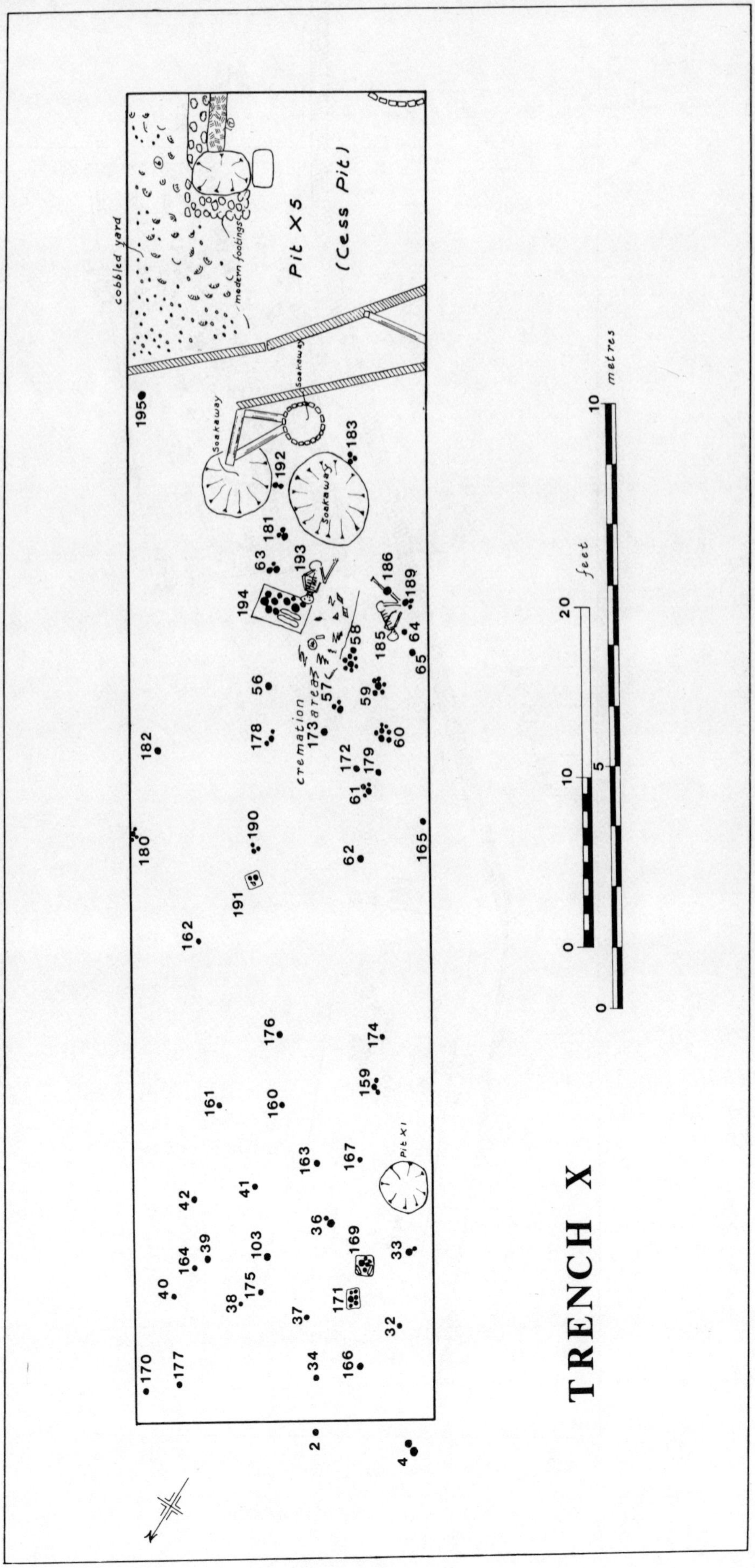
TRENCH X
Pit X5
(Cess Pit)
cobbled yard
modern footings
Soakaway
Soakaway
Soakaway
Soakaway
cremation area
Pit X1
feet
0
10
20
metres
0
5
10
195
183
192
181
63
193
186
189
194
58
185
64
65
56
57
59
178
173
60
182
172
179
61
180
190
165
62
191
162
176
174
161
160
159
163
167
42
41
36
169
33
164
39
103
40
175
38
171
37
32
170
177
34
166
2
4

Fig. 5.4

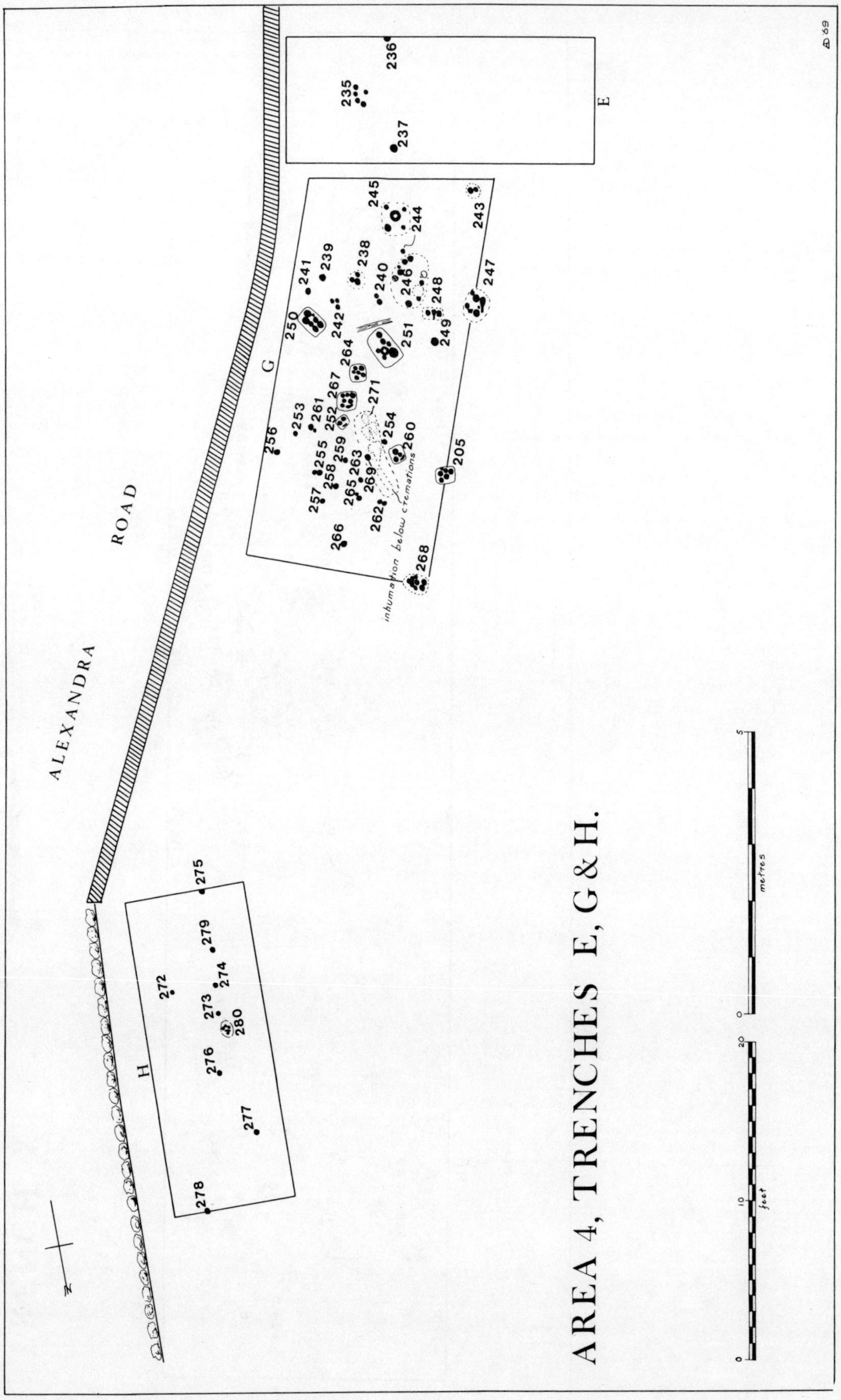
AREA 4, TRENCHES E, G & H.
ALEXANDRA ROAD
E
G
H
235
236
237
238
239
240
241
242
243
244
245
246
247
248
249
250
251
252
253
254
255
256
257
258
259
260
261
262
263
264
265
266
267
268
269
271
205
272
273
274
275
276
277
278
279
280
inhumation below cremations
metres
feet
0
5
0
10
20

Fig. 5.5

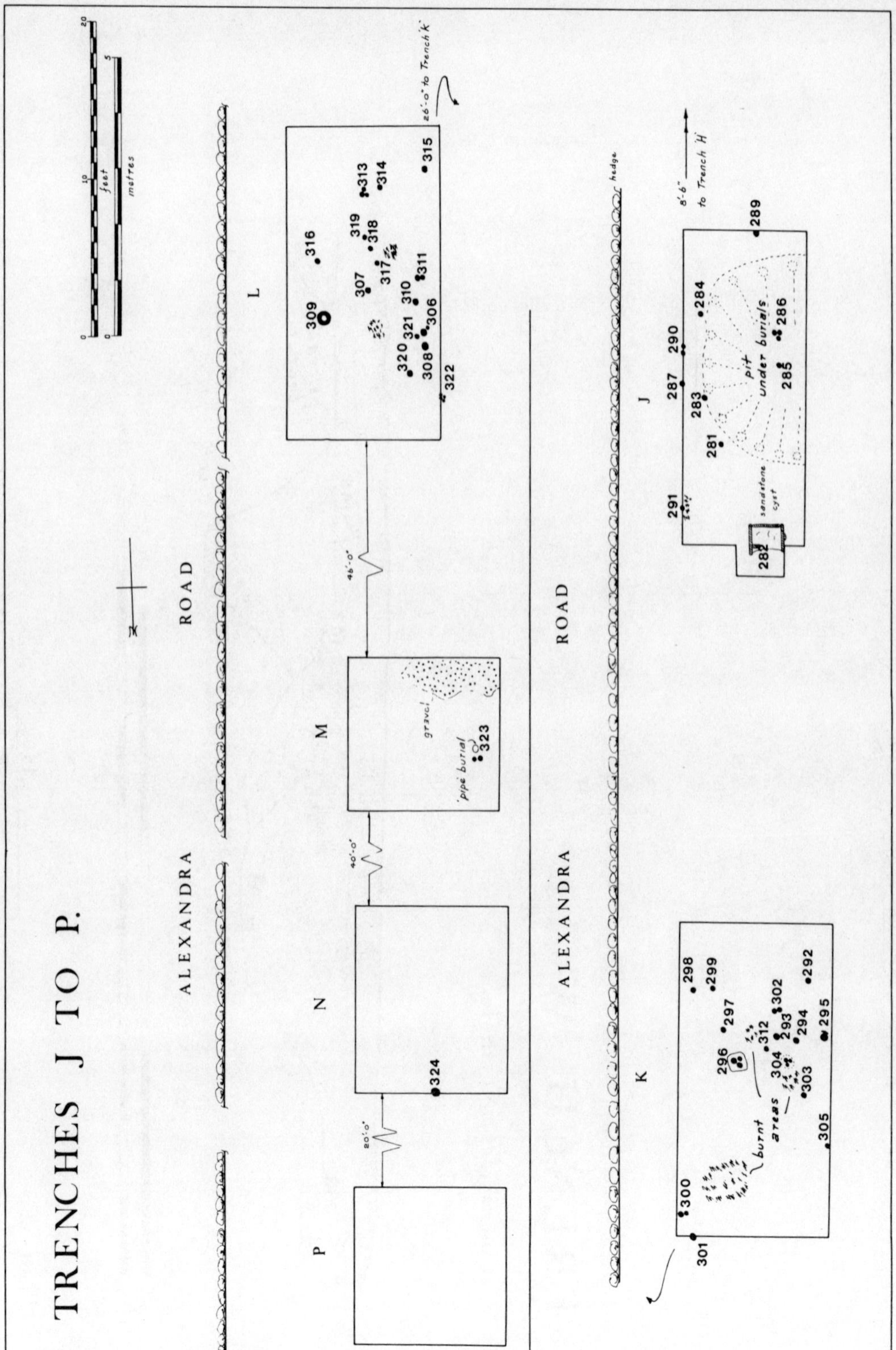

AREA 4, TRENCHES J TO P.
ALEXANDRA ROAD
ALEXANDRA ROAD
feet
metres
L
M
N
P
J
K
hedge
gravel
'pipe' burial
pit under burials
sandstone cyst
burnt areas
26'-0" to Trench 'K'
8'-6" to Trench 'H'
46'-0"
40'-0"
20'-0"

Fig. 5.6

TRENCH W

Section across North face

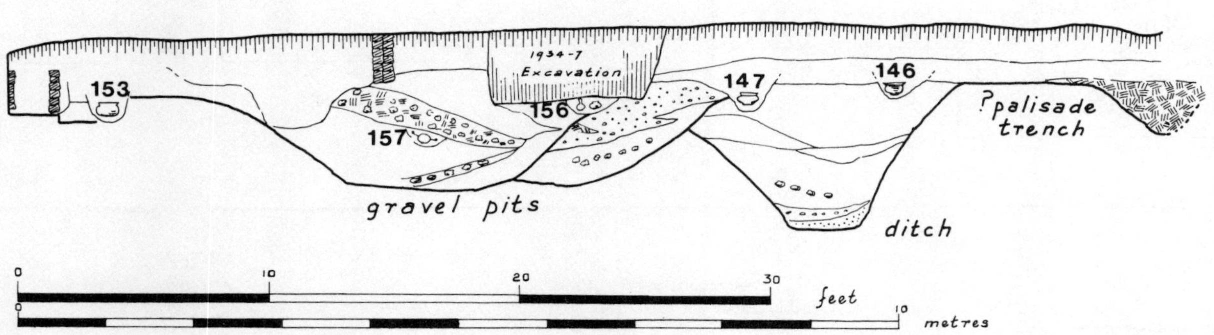

Plan

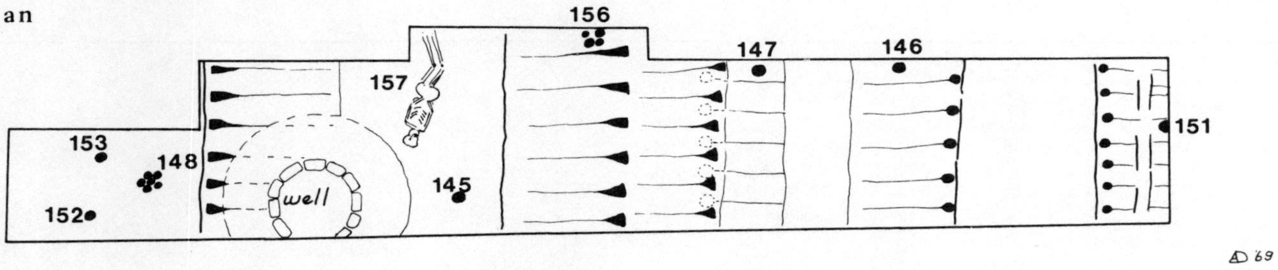

Fig. 5.7

Fig. 5.8

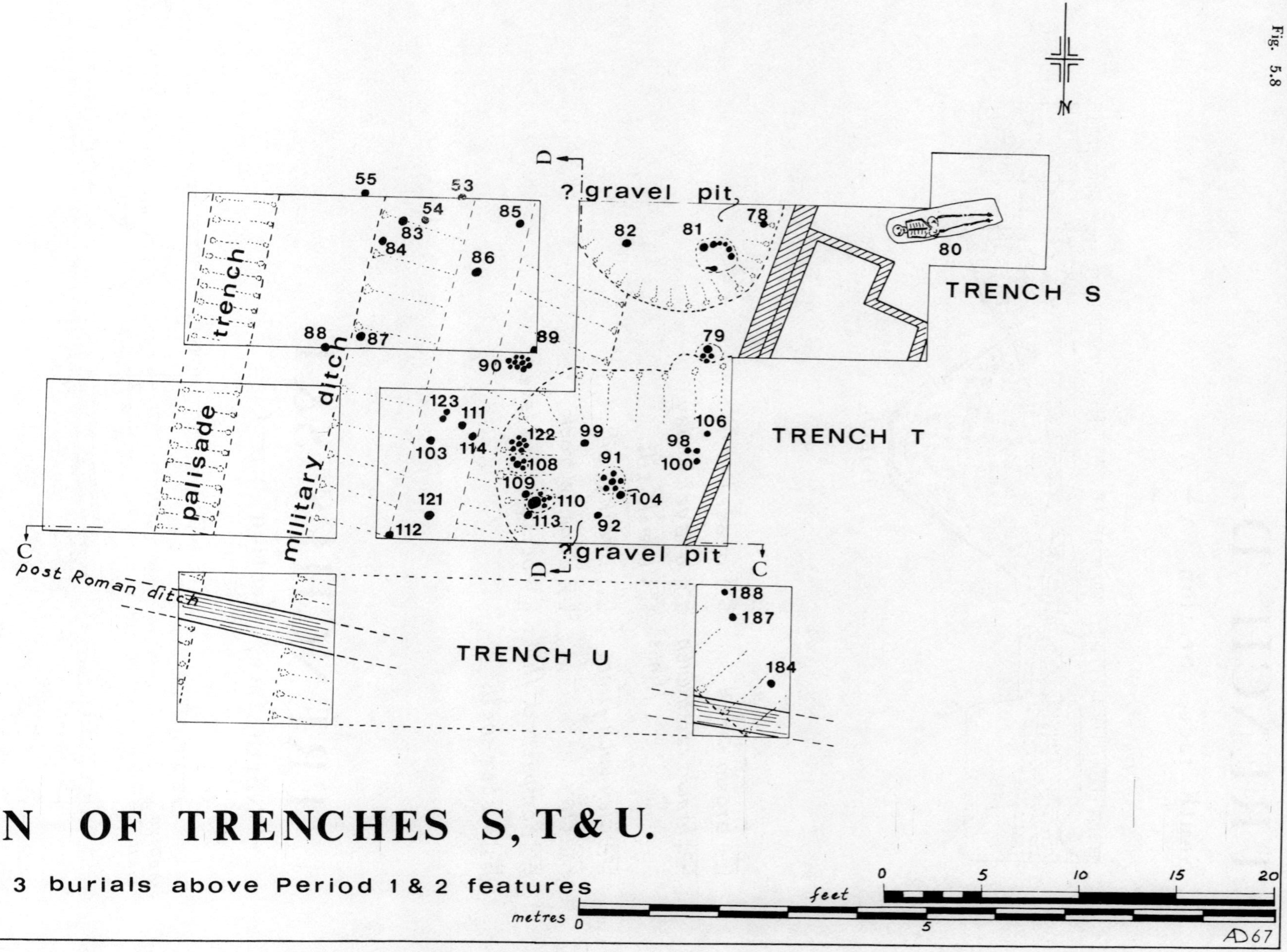

PLAN OF TRENCHES S, T & U.

Period 3 burials above Period 1 & 2 features

TRENCH D

South face, Section A – A

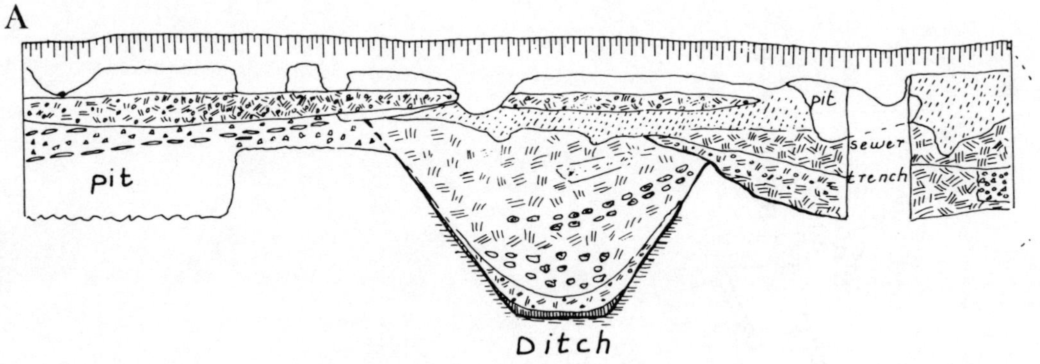

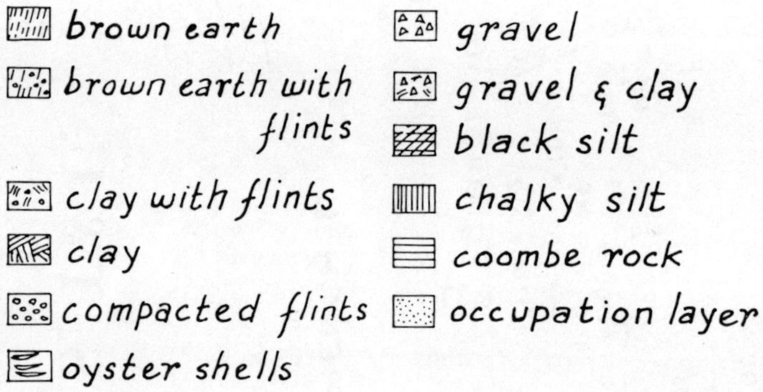

TRENCHES S&T

North face, Section C – C

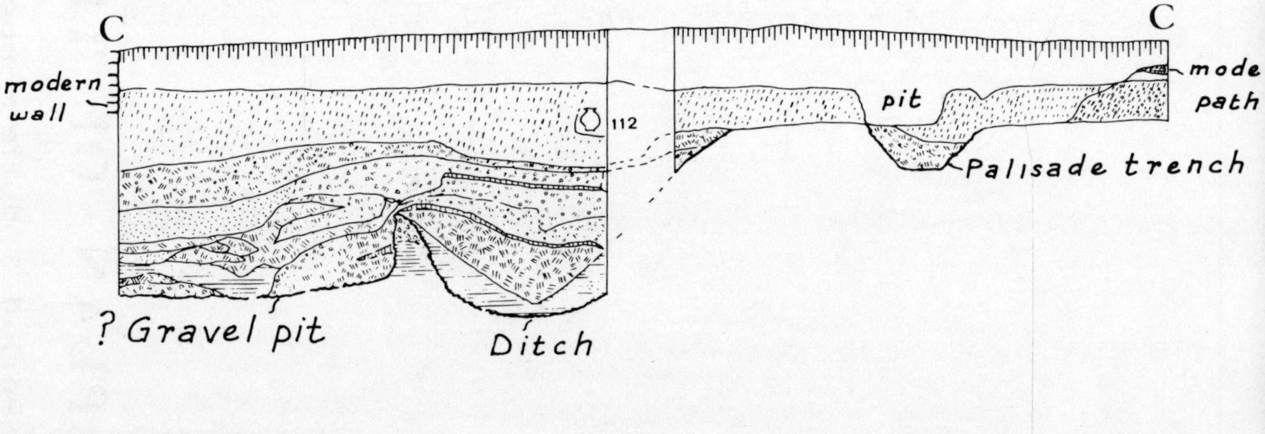

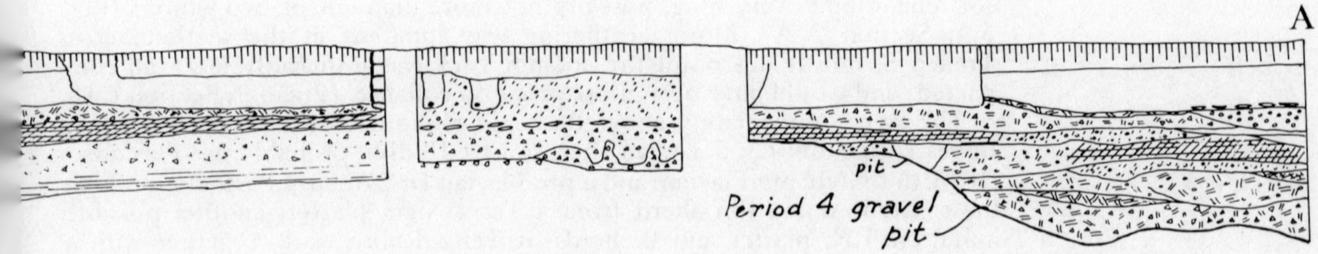

RENCH E

h face, Section B – B

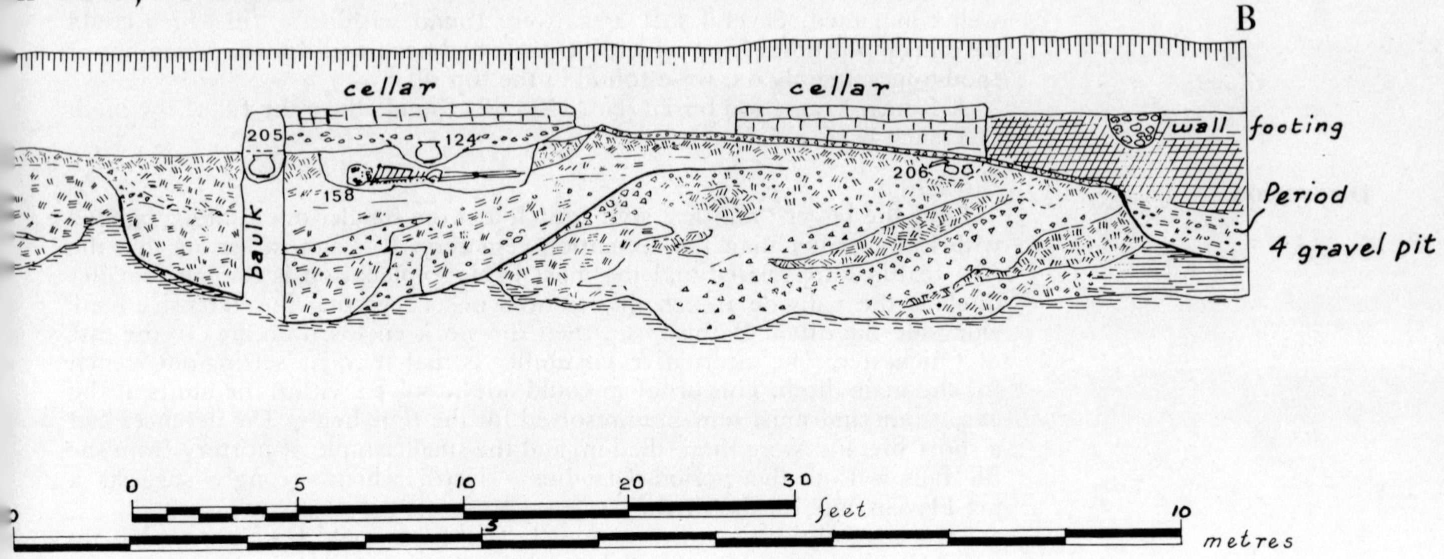

East face, Section D – D

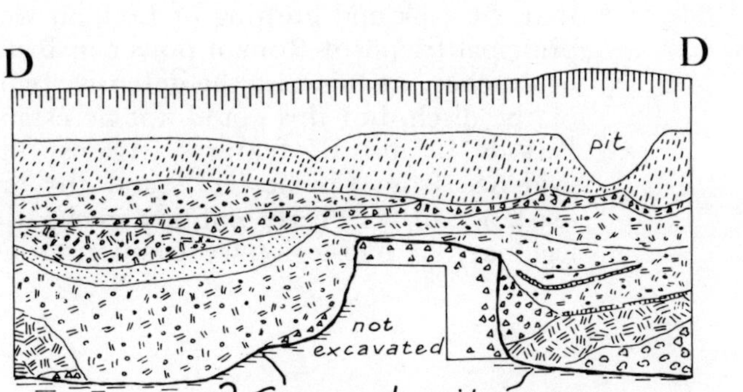

Fig. 5.9

W, and although in Trench U most of the top part had been cut away by medieval pits, enough remained to show that it was continuing in a northerly direction under Alexandra Terrace.

The sides of the ditch in Trench D showed very little signs of weathering, and the fill above the rapid silt was mainly clean clay and clay-with-flints. No evidence of a turf line was seen and it may be concluded that the ditch did not remain open very long, possibly not more than one or two winters (Fig. 5.9; Section A-A). More weathering was apparent in the section across Trench S, but at this point the coombe rock was noticeably less well compacted, and would have been more prone to collapse. (Fig. 5.9; Section C-C).

The layers immediately above the rapid silt contained a number of animal bones (Appendix C); 3 samian sherds; a Dr 18 dish, probably pre-Flavian; a Dr 18, definitely pre-Flavian; and a pre-Flavian Dr 27 cup. In association with these sherds was a rim sherd from a Terra Nigra platter, another possible imitation T.N. platter and 2 sherds of Terra Rubra ware, together with a "lug" from an amphora, a bell-mouthed flagon of "early" type and part of a flagon in fine creamy ware (Fig. 5.12). The rapid silt was barren except for part of a human skull.

To the east of the ditch and at a distance which varied from 1.83 - 2.44 metres (6 to 8 ft.) was another smaller ditch (Figs. 5.8 and 5.9) Section C-C). This feature was sectioned in four places and although the top part had been cut away by modern disturbances it is likely that it would not have been more than .92 - 1.07 metres (3 to 3 ft 6 ins) deep when dug. The fill was quite distinctive, consisting of either yellow clay-with-flints or yellow clay well compacted. Several soft areas were found within the fill which could have been postholes from which the posts had been withdrawn. A number of food bones, mainly ox, were found in the top fill.

A Roman cremation burial (No. 151) was found above the fill of the ditch in Trench W (Fig. 5.7).

Discussion

Discussion

Both the larger "military style" ditch and the smaller one running parallel with it are earlier than the cremation cemetery. It is almost certain that the two features are related and the most likely explanation is that the smaller ditch is the palisade trench dug to hold posts revetting the defensive bank alongside the ditch. If this is so, then the work enclosed an area to the east of Chichester. The alternative possibility is that it was a setting-out trench for the main ditch. This problem could not be solved within the limits of the excavation and must remain unresolved for the time being. The defences had a short life and were then filled in, and the small sample of pottery from the fill falls within the period Claudius - Nero, which strongly suggests a pre-Flavian date for the ditch.

Two possibilities must be examined. The ditch could have been a hastily constructed defence organised by the pro-Roman client King Cogidubnus during the Boudiccan uprising. Although there is no historical evidence for Boudicca penetrating farther south than London, there is a possibility that the revolt may have involved Winchester.[11] In any event, there is no doubt that the sack and burning of London would be a powerful incentive for the principal friend of Roman power in Britain to put his new town into a state of defence. In this case the defensive bank would have been on the west side of the ditch, but this could not be established due to later disturbances by Periods II and III features. Against this theory is the growing mass of evidence from Chichester[12] and the area around the harbour[13] for the existence of very early military occupation which would make a temporary legionary or half-legionary camp a strong possibility. The precise nature of

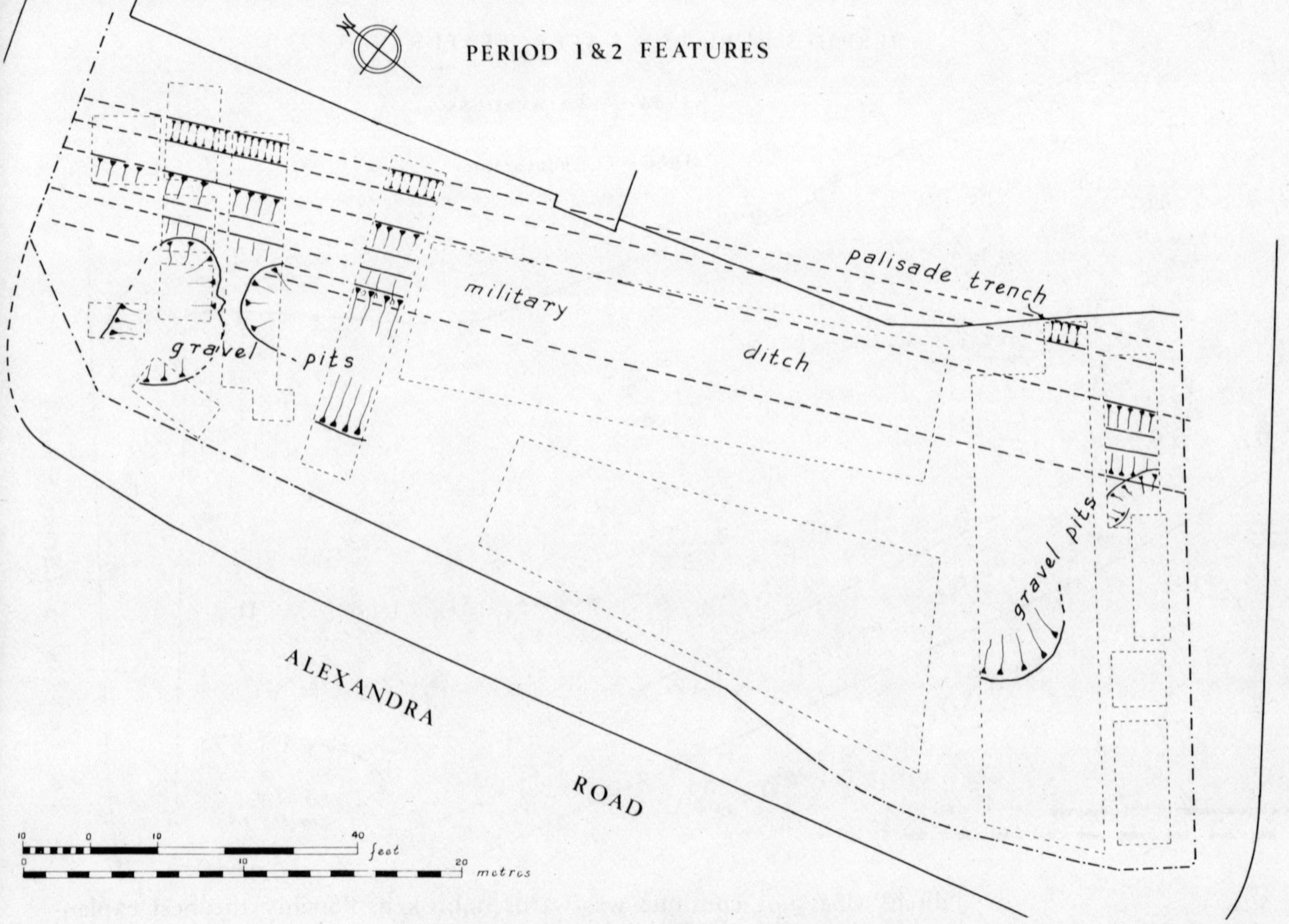

Fig. 5.10

the cutting indicates a military origin and it is a reasonable assumption that the area enclosed by the ditch formed part of a Roman military base camp or depot set up in the latter part of A.D. 43 as a preliminary to the campaign in the west. Such a camp would not have been needed for long. The advance westward, and the resulting strain on supply lines would make it imperative for other base camps to be established nearer the scene of operations, and it is likely that by the end of A.D. 44 the Chichester camp was no longer in use by Vespasian on the same scale as in A.D. 43, although the possibility of some sort of base in friendly territory for a much longer period should be considered, especially in view of recent finds elsewhere in the City.[14]

The relationship of the ditch to Stane Street could not be established within the limits of the excavation as the Roman street must lie under the centre of St. Pancras, which at this point is 18.29 metres (60 ft.) wide, including the pavements, but it is certainly earlier if the date of 70 A.D.[15] for the street is reliable.

Period 2

Period II. c. 60-70 A.D. (Figs. 5.8 and 5.10) (Area 1)

At some time after the military ditch was filled in a number of deep excavations were cut on the west side of the ditch, cutting away the west bank in places. When first noted in Trenches S, T and W it was considered that these excavations represented a second period of ditch digging, and, indeed, the section across Trench W (Fig. 5.7) considered in isolation suggests a second and third ditch sequence, but this proved to be misleading as the

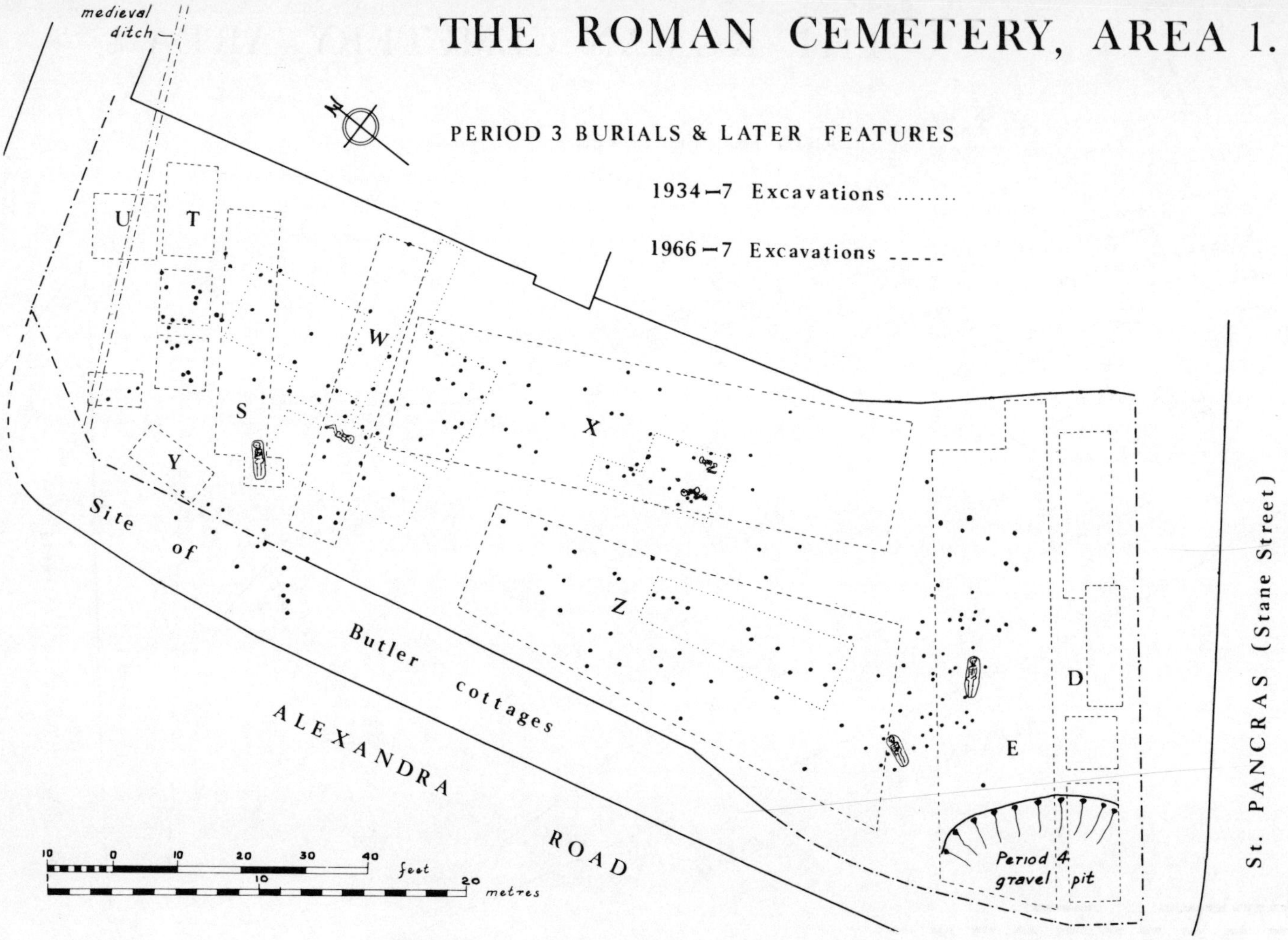

Fig. 5.11

"ditch" does not continue westwards unbroken. Possibly the best explanation of these features is that they may represent quarrying along the western lip of the military ditch for gravel and clay, and this activity may be linked with the construction of Stane Street a few feet away. These pits or quarries may have stayed open for some time, probably until the ground was required for the extension eastwards of the new cremation cemetery. The pit in Trenches S and T (Fig. 5.9; Sections C-C and D-D) remained open long enough for a spread of occupation material to accumulate, and during the backfilling of the pit sectioned in Trench W (Fig. 5.7) a body (Burial 157) was rolled into the partially backfilled hole and a layer of gravel thrown over it.

Period 3. c. 70 A.D. to late 3rd/early 4th century. Areas 1 & 4

From *c.* 70 A.D. until the late 3rd or early 4th century the area formed part of the Roman cemetery (See Fig. 5.11 and Appendix A). The cemetery certainly extended westwards towards the city and the precise boundary will never be known, owing to the cemetery which has occupied the ground since medieval times; but it is unlikely that it extended much farther west than New Park Road.[16] The eastern limits of the Roman burial ground fall just short of the boundary between the site owned by the City Council (Area 1) and the land immediately to the east (Area 6), while to the north the burials do not extend beyond trench N in Area 4 (Fig. 5.1). There is no record of any burials having been found on the South side of St. Pancras.

The number of burials excavated during the period covered by the report was 260 of which 9 were inhumations. The total number recovered from

Areas 1 and 4 is therefore 326 if the 65 burials excavated between 1934 and 1937 are included, and a detailed report of these is contained in Appendix A. The figure of 326 burials excludes the vessels recovered by Councillor Butler who kept no record of individual burials. Any attempt to date the commencement of the cemetery must lean very heavily on the dates ascribed to the samian vessels in the burials, and in doing so the possibility of "heirloom survivals" over quite long periods must be considered. In no instance was there a pre-Flavian samian vessel directly associated with a burial. Some pre-Flavian sherds were found in disturbed modern grave fill in Area 5 (The Litten– and others in Area 4. These latter sherds were almost certainly from disturbed graves, but they were few in number and it is most likely that they were survivals. It may be regarded as highly unlikely that any of the burials in Areas 1 and 4 were placed there before c. 70 to 80 A.D., and nearer 80 than 70. It is possible that there may be an earlier part of the cemetery farther west towards the East Gate, under what is now the Litten, but it will not be possible to prove this. If the cemetery had started nearer to the City limits and spread eastwards one would expect the latest burials to be at the east end of the site. In fact six of the burials with Flavian samian are near to the eastern boundary, and the only firm evidence to come from the west side of Area 4 is of 3rd/4th century inhumations. Possibly the explanation is that the cemetery was developed in a uniform manner with plots distributed evenly across the site and the density thickened up as time went on. If this pattern of development was followed a date of c.70 to 80 A.D. for the eastern end might fit the whole of the cemetery. This hypothesis is supported by evidence of a negative character. No Gallo-Belgic ware or its native imitations was found with a burial, nor were any burials found with the type of bead-rimmed coarse ware which, in Chichester, is usually found with Gallo-Balgic ware in a pre-Flavian context.[17] (For an illustration of this type of bead rim, see Fig. 5.12, No. 38).

A date of c. 70 A.D. as the earliest possible date for the cemetery supports the date given for Stane Street. The road it is assumed would come before the cemetery, and the road would not have been built unless there was a Roman town at the starting point. It has been shown elsewhere[18] that all the evidence for the development of Chichester as a Roman planned town points to the years between 70 and 80 A.D., and Mrs. Grahame Clark's date[19] of the last quarter of the 1st century for the establishment of the cemetery is amply confirmed by the additional evidence. No such firm evidence can be adduced for the terminal date. The samian ware does not take us past the Antonine period and insuffcent is known of the colour-coated wares to provide a good basis for dating the coarse ware. Mrs. Grahame Clark had put forward a date of c. 3rd to 4th century for the end of the cemetry, based on two conical neckèd flagons from Burials 49 and 59, which she thought were from the New Forest kilns, although Burial 59 contained a Flavian samian vessel, which could hardly have survived as an heirloom for over 200 years. Dr. A.E. Wilson[20] in a re-assessment of the evidence, pointed out that these conical necked jugs can well be earlier, and implied a date of c. late 2nd century for the cemetery based on the absence of colour-coated wares from the burials. The recent series of excavations have produced Castor ware and some inhumations including one from Area 4 with bangles, and a bronze gilt crossbow brooch from a disturbed burial. It appears that whilst a date of c. early 3rd century might be supported by the ceramic evidence, the inhumations suggest that the cemetery was in use for some time later.

It seems therefore that the cemetery commenced as a cremation cemetery no earlier than 70 A.D., and continued in general use until late 2nd century.

From then on the use of the ground became more sporadic, a few inhumations and cremations being placed there, (probably the continued use of earlier family plots) and these occasional burials went on into the 4th century. By this time other cemeteries must have existed, and one was certainly outside the South Gate, where in 1819 a cremation burial and a skeleton were discovered during the digging of the canal basin.[21] Nothing has so far been discovered outside the North and West Gates of the City although there has been information of a cinerary urn being found during the recent public street works in 1968.[22] One important question remains unresolved. Where were the inhabitants of Cogidubnus's native town buried? If we accept that between 70 and 80 A.D. the town was laid out with a street grid and a forum, and that the cemetery under discussion was started then, we must look elsewhere for the cemetery of the earlier town, if indeed one existed. We do not know when Cogidubnus set up his capital at Chichester. It is possible that it was within 10 years of the conquest and he may have moved from an earlier site at Selsey. We know that between 58 and 60 A.D. his guild of stonemasons were cutting an inscription to Nero[23] and at about the same time or a little later were sufficiently wealthy to dedicate a temple to Neptune and Minerva[24], but there is no really firm evidence that these inscriptions came from buildings within the City limits; they may well have come from Fishbourne. Recent excavations have shown that sealed below the Forum and streets are occupation layers of pre-Flavian date[25], and these can be equated to the early military occupation of the site and *possibly* a native town which grew up alongside it. On the other hand the native "town" of this period may have been more than an agglomeration of fairly squalid huts representing the shelters of the camp followers who set up shop around any fairly permanent military establishment. In any event, if this picture of pre-Flavian Chichester is correct there should be both a military and a non-military cemetery of earlier date than the one reported here, and these should contain cremation burials with the pre-Flavian types of coarse ware and Gallo-Belgic ware which are conspicuously absent from the St. Pancras cemetery. These cemeteries would not necessarily be outside the present city limits, but placed outside the limits of the military establishment, and there, for lack of evidence, the problem must be left for the time being.

Burial Types (Table 1)

During the years the cemetery was in use it may be fairly considered that the tribal customs of the people who initially formed part of Cogidubnus's kingdom would become modified by outside influences, and that these would be reflected in variations in the burial rites. In an attempt to test this, various types of burials have been isolated and are discussed below:

Type 1. Single vessel cremations with the bones placed in the urn.

Type 2. Burials with food and drink vessels. These may be divided into 6 sub-types, as follows:-

Type 2a Box burials. Rich burials containing a number of food and drink vessels and placed in, or covered by, a wooden box. In some cases the bones were scattered inside the box and not placed in the urn. Boots or sandals, and sometimes lamps or lampholders (but never both together) were included. Objects of value; (jewellery, tools of trade, and trinkets) were relatively rare.

TABLE 1

ANALYSIS OF BURIAL TYPES

TYPE 1 (single vessel cremations)				TYPE 2 (Food vessel cremations)																														TYPE 3 (Inhumations)				
				Sub-Types							Other Characteristics													Drinking vessels				Glass						Sub Types				
Trinkets & jewellery	Bones in pot	Bones scattered	Total of type	2a Box burials	2b Cyst burials	2c No box or Cyst	2d Crescentic	2e Inverted Pots	2f Coin with burial	2g "pipe" burial	Bones in pot	Bones scattered	Jewellery & trinkets	Boots	Tools of trade	Lamps & Lampstands	Samian	Imitation Samian	Lead Glazed ware	mirrors	Shale platters	Gaming counters & dice	casket fittings	Flagons	Flasks & bottles	Cups & beakers	Infant feeding bottles	Flasks	Unguentaria	Beakers & Jars	Eating utensils	meals	Total of Type	3a Extended	3b Crouched	with pots	with jewellery	Total of type
3	143	4	147	33	3	64	3	9	6	1	96	8	14	10	1	36	36	16	3	5	1	2	3	82	15	88	3	1	7	3	7	11	104	7	2	1	2	9
			56.5% App.																														(40%)					(3.5%) App.

Type 2b, Tiled cyst burials. These may be regarded as a variation of Type 2a (3 found).

Type 2c – Food vessel burials, but not in boxes or cysts.

Type 2d – Crescentic burials. Vessels arranged in a semi-circle with a flagon or dish opposite and the bones scattered between, (3 found).

Type 2e Burials where one or more of the vessels were inverted (5 found).

Type 2f. Coin burials, where the coin was placed in the urn or associated with the burial in some other way, i.e., beneath one of the vessels. (6 found).

Type 2g. Pipe burials. (One found)

Type 3. Inhumations. (9 found) These may be further subdivided:

Type 3a Crouched burials.

Type 3b. Fully extended burials.

Discussion

Type 1 (single vessel) cremations are the largest group but they may not necessarily represent a variation in burial customs from the Type 2 burials. The absence of food and drink vessels may indicate poverty. On the other hand Burial 87 which was a single vessel burial had a bronze tinned mirror with a wooden frame and leather case, together with a fine bronze bangle and a large bronze needle. This was undoubtedly the grave of a woman, and hardly the grave of a pauper. Burial 59 also had a ring and a brooch with it. The type 2 burials may represent the continuance of the rich Belgic style burials of the late Iron Age and the variations in the number and quality of the grave goods reflects the amount the relatives were able or willing to pay for the funeral rites. A careful examination of the nails in some undisturbed burials seems to indicate that most boxes had a centre batten across the lid. No corresponding batten seems to have been present across the bottom of the box as no nails were ever found sticking upwards under the funerary vessels. It seems that the box, possibly with one or more divisions in it, could have been without a bottom and the vessels placed in the compartments in a similar manner to the tiled cyst burial No. 93 which was also without a base. The lid may have been removable to allow the pouring of libations. In some burials the dishes were stacked on edge in order to fit into the box. It could not be firmly established whether the ritual meal placed in the food vessels was complete or whether part of it had been eaten by the mourners, but the condition of some of the bird bones found with Burial 93 suggests that the latter might have been the case (See Appendix C).

The lamp burials are of great interest. Most of the lamps had been used, but there was very little soot on the spouts and they were unlikely to have been used more than once, possibly for some form of purification rite. It seems likely that they were specially purchased for funerary or votive purposes. Placed with a burial they would serve to light the deceased on the journey through the underworld, and where a lamp was not available a lampstand was an acceptable substitute. The number of lamp/lampstand burials was small, representing only 11% of the total, and this may indicate that only a small minority believed that the dead needed a light. On the other hand, the number of lamps in use in Britain for lighting purposes at any time must have been relatively small. Oil was expensive and had to be imported, and torches and candles would have been the usual method of lighting, as well as being more effective. These could have been deposited with burials and would have left no trace.

The Type 2e burials with the inverted vessels seem to have some ritual significance, but it is difficult to determine what it might be. The practice of inverting a pot with a burial is as old as the Bronze Age, and the ones noted here may perhaps represent an earlier tradition lingering on long after it had been discarded by the majority. It may have been a variation of the ritual "killing" of the grave goods, whereby they were removed from the use of the living to that of the dead, the vessels being inverted instead of broken.

The Type 2f coin burials were in all cases food vessel burials also. They show an awareness of the early Roman belief that the souls of the dead were ferried across the Styx by Charon, and may be the graves of natives who had grafted a little classical tradition on to their burial customs. There were only six out of a total of 326 burials examined, and this seems to indicate a certain conservatism in burial customs among the local population.

The Type 2g (pipe burial) was the only example found, and it was fortunate that later disturbance of the top soil had not completely destroyed the evidence. Here a pipe had been formed by placing 2 imbrices together and this was placed vertically above one of the vessels so as to communicate to the ground surface, to facilitate the pouring of libations. As it was, only the bottom part of the imbrices which formed the pipe were present, but from these the position of ground level in Roman times could be established as 42 cms (1 ft 4 ins) above the urn, and 34 cms (1 ft 1.5 ins) below present ground level. Sections of imbrices had been noted before in association with disturbed burials, and it may well be that this practice was more common than the single example noted here suggests. Pipe burials have been noted elsewhere, at Caerleon[26] and Colchester[27] in connection with inhumations and cremations, and a similar custom of providing regular ritual food and drink for the dead is still practised today in South Africa by hunters of the Lunda Tribe[28]. There the dead hunter is buried in a sitting position with a forked peeled stick between his hands, touching his lips and his brow and emerging from the ground surface. When a hunter relative makes a kill he must pour some of the blood down the stick to feed the shade of the dead man.

Little can be said about the Type 5 burials (inhumations). Two of these were crouched in the foetal position, and one of these, Burial 193 certainly dates after the mid-2nd century as the head was above Burial 194. Of the extended burials, one, (No. 158) was earlier than the cremation burial above it, but no date can be assigned to it. The scarcity of inhumations is further support for the view that the cemetery was not in general use by late 3rd century as by that time inhumation had practically superseded cremation as a custom.

There was very little destruction of earlier burials by later ones and this implies some system of marking the graves or plots. No tombstones were found, and this is not surprising since they would have been rare in any case, due to shortage of suitable local stone and those which had been erected would have been robbed for use as building stone later on. It is possible that marker posts were used and in Trench E (Fig. 5.3) two postholes were found adjacent to cremation burials which may have served this purpose; Burial 181 in Area 4 (p. 109) certainly had a wooden post associated with it.

In many instances the mouth of the flagon would have protruded from the ground, as in the cemetery at Ostia,[29] and while it would facilitate the pouring of libations it also explains why so many of the flagons had the neck missing or damaged. The cremation of the bodies must have taken place in certain defined areas as there were few traces of extensive burning which could be expected if each burial was burnt in situ. Certain areas could be identified (Figs. 5.3 and 5.4) and the Period 4 excavation in Trenches D and E may have destroyed others, as the fill contained large amounts of charcoal and disturbed burial material. The presence of many nails with the cremated bones indicate that the dead were cremated on wooden biers. Boot studs in many of the urns show that some were cremated with their boots on, while in other cases the footgear was placed in the grave with the urn.

Large numbers of the vessels with burials were wasters, and this could well be another example of using a "killed" object for funerary purposes.

Cemetery Population

The total number of stratified burials recorded during the excavations was 326 including the 65 reported on by Mrs Grahame Clark. Many of the burials were badly disturbed by later foundations, tree roots and gravel digging, and it is estimated that a further 20% were unrecognisable as burials on this account. This "disturbance factor" added to the burials found gives a figure of 391 for the total surface area of the cemetery excavated (839 square yards), or an average density per acre of 2,280. The estimated surface area of the cemetery is 4.3 acres, and as the sample excavated gave a fair average of high and low density burial areas, a reasonable estimate of the total cemetery population accumulating over the years from c. 70 to c. 250 A.D. (allowing the largest time bracket likely) would be between 9,500 and 10,000.

Period 4

Period 4. c. mid 3rd to late 4th century A.D. (Areas 1 & 4)

At the western end of Trenches D and E in Area 1 (See Figs. 5.9 and 5.11) was a deep ditch like feature which extended westwards under Alexandra Road. This contained in the upper layers a series of deposits of dark gritty silt, and below this, clay and gravel, (Fig. 5.9, Section B-B). The fill contained nothing but Roman sherds, and the samian ware ranged in date from the last quarter of the 1st century to Antonine.

Fragments of calcined bone were found in the yellow clay at the bottom of this feature, suggesting a disturbed cremation burial. There were also a number of lumps of iron slag and carbon distributed throughout the layers.

The disturbed top layer of the pit or ditch contained medieval and late Roman sherds, together with 2 coins of the 4th century date (p. 88).

No firm explanation can be offered for this feature. It turned westwards within the limits of Trench E and may be a very large excavation for gravel, although it would be very close to the street. It was certainly cut through part of the Roman cemetery, and the majority of the pottery recovered is contemporary with that found in the cemetery, and may be considered to be from disturbed burials. It appears to have remained open for a long time, during which about 1.05 metres (3 ft 6 ins) of dark silt was laid down. It is unlikely to have been dug during the period that the cemetery was in use and is provisionally dated 4th century or later.

A similar feature was observed in Area 4 in Trench B, which was dug immediately north of the lines of trees now known to mark the original boundary of the Christian cemetery. This pit could not be fully excavated owing to the presence of a large tree and post-medieval burials a few feet away, but in the half section excavated there was 3 feet of slow silt in the bottom and calcined bones and boot studs from a redeposited Roman burial. The extent of the feature was plotted by resisivity meter[30] and was seen to be roughly circular in plan. Other deep distrubances which were probably gravel pits, and which had destroyed burials were noted in Trenches J and S.

Discussion

These deep pits cannot be dated with any certainty. All that can be said is that they were dug through the Roman cemetery, and their size and number suggests that clay and gravel were again being sought. The whole area seems

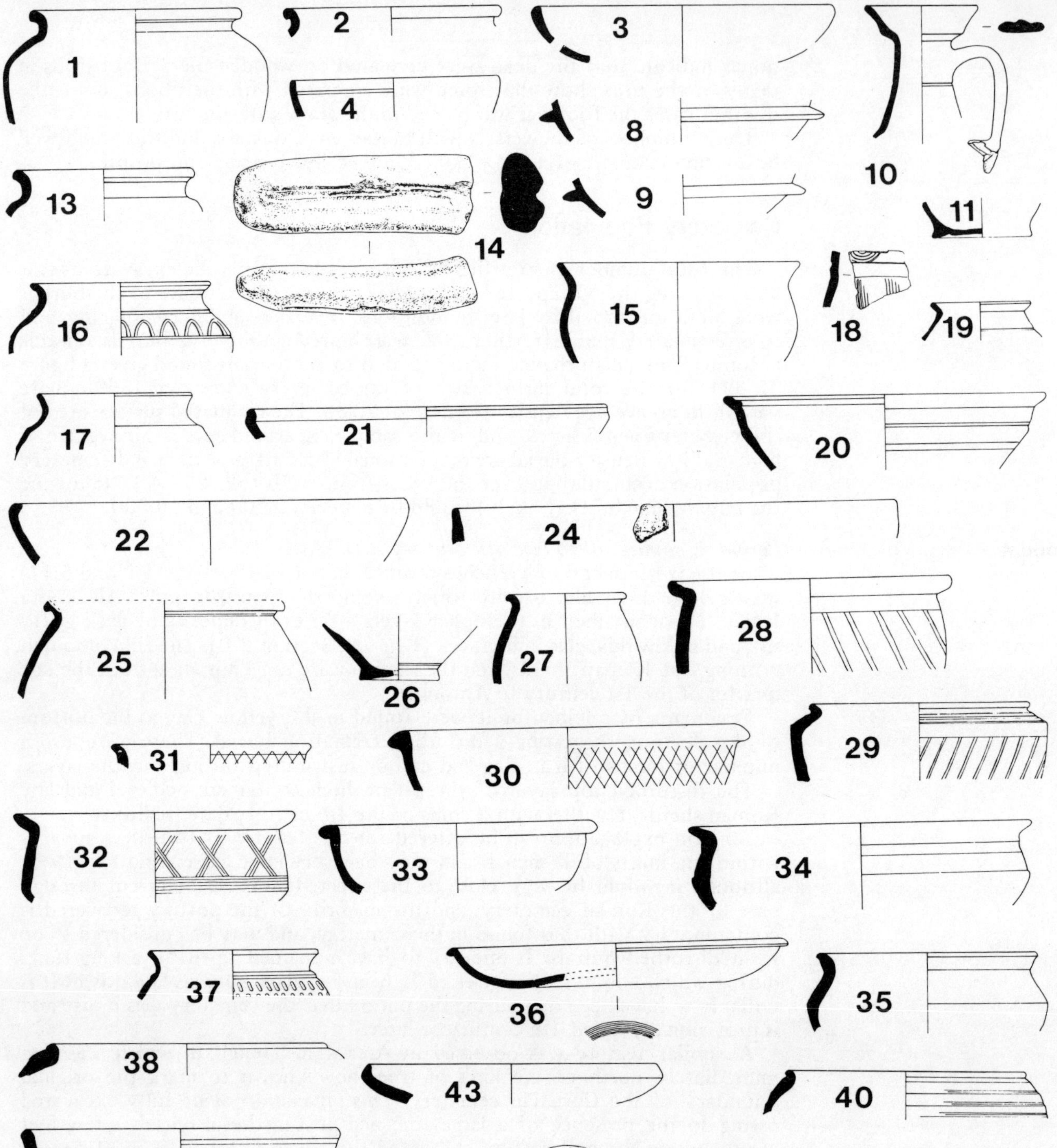

Fig. 5.12 Roman Pottery. Nos. 1-14 Period 1, Pre-Flavian Pottery from Military Ditch. Nos. 15-24 from Period 2 Gravel Pit. Nos. 25-40 from Period 4. Nos. 41-49 Miscellaneous. (Nos. 2 and 25 1/8. No. 49 2/1. Remainder 1/4.)

to have provided a handy quarry for these materials, and it may be that the two ponds shown on the Gardner Map (Fig. 2.5) were originally large quarries and also belong to this period. The absence of any post-Roman evidence in the slow silt in the two features discussed above suggests that they were dug during the Roman period and this suggests a date of c. 4th century.

Period 5

Period 5 - c. 13th - 15th Centuries. (Areas 1 and 2).

Occupation on the site during the 13th to 15th centuries is attested by pottery from rubbish pits and in disturbed modern layers. Alongside the road, in Trench D (Fig. 5.3) was a layer of compacted gravel with a thick layer of oyster shells on top. This may represent a yard in front of houses fronting on to St. Pancras. It was most evident below the front gardens of Nos. 16 and 17 St. Pancras, but traces of it were discernable further east in front of Nos. 20 and 21. The foundations of the 18th-century houses along Alexandra Road and St. Pancras had completely destroyed any earlier structures.

A deep ditch containing medieval pottery and tiles runs roughly east – west across the north side of Area 1, cutting away the Period 1 ditch and presumed palisade trench. This was again traced in Area 3, and may have been intended to carry away flood water from the River Lavant.

The Pottery

Area 1

Period 1; the pre-Flavian pottery from the military ditch (Fig. 5.12)

1. Necked bowl in grey ware.
2. Rim of bowl in sandy buff ware, flint tempered.
3. Rim of shallow bowl or plate in imitation Terra Nigra.
4. Rim of shallow bowl or plate in imitation Terra Nigra, recessed for a lid.

5,6 & 7. Body and base sherds of a vessel similar to 4, but in imitation Terra Rubra; in fine grey fabric with pink colour coat. This vessel is the well-known type with omphalos base and a functionless footring (see *Camulodunum.* Fig. 47, No. 22, p. 218). Not illustrated here.

8. Flanged bowl in hard white ware.
9. Flanged bowl in pinky white ware with traces of pink colour coat, (See *Camulodunum* Pl. LIII, 58A and 58B).
10. Flagon in grey ware.
11. Base of a jar in grey ware with smooth dark grey slip on exterior.
12. Body sherd, probably from same vessel as 11; not illustrated.
13. Necked bowl in hard grey ware.
14. Lug from amphora in sandy buff fabric.

Associated with this group were the following samian sherds:–

1 Dr 18 dish, probably pre-Flavian,
1 Dr 18 dish, definitely pre-Flavian,
1 Dr 27 cup, pre-Flavian.

Period 2: Pottery from the occupation layer in Trench T (Fig. 5.9, Section C-C)

15. Bowl in hard whitish grey ware, smooth black exterior.
16. Necked bowl in reddish sandy ware.
17. Necked bowl in fine grey ware with micaceous black slip coating.
18. Sherd in fine grey ware, micaceous black slip on exterior.
19. Vessel in fine grey ware, oxidised fabric.
20. Dish in coarse dark grey ware, reduced fabric.
21. Rim of shallow plate in soft gritty black ware.
22. Rim sherd, possibly a lid, in buff ware.
23. Sherd from a colour coated "rough cast" beaker; fine cream paste with red/brown slip. Not illustrated.
24. Small fragment of rim sherd from an Early Iron Age bowl. The ware is soft, brown and heavily gritted. A second fragment from the same vessel was also found.

Period 4: Pottery from Gravel Pit (Figs. 5.12 and 5.9, Section B-B)

25. Large jar in grey ware, flint tempered.
26. Base of vessel in fine grey paste with dark grey colour coat, identical ware to type 235B and 250A (Fig. 5.25).
27. Grey ware beaker.
28. Bowl in dark grey ware, burnished exterior.
29. Carinated bowl in hard grey ware.
30. Bowl in grey ware, fine glossy burnish inside and out.
31. Small grey ware bowl, burnished on exterior.
32. Bowl in sandy grey ware.
33. Bowl in whitish grey ware.
34. Bowl in sandy grey ware.
35. Grey ware bowl.
36. Dish in fine grey ware with dark micaceous slip coating.
37. Necked jar in fine grey ware.
38. Vessel in sandy white paste, grey exterior.
39. Two sherds of black glossy "eggshell ware"; not illustrated.
40. Bowl in sandy grey ware burnished on exterior.

Miscellaneous Roman pottery. (Fig. 5.12)

41. Sherd in whitish grey fabric, thin and well fired with external dark grey slip.
42. Shallow bowl in dark grey ware.
43. Shallow bowl in grey ware.

(These three sherds from the pit cutting away the west lip of the military ditch in Trench D (Fig. 5.9, Section A-A).

From Trench X, Pit X.1 (Fig. 5.4)

44. "Belgic type" bead-rimmed bowl in hard grey ware.

45 & 46. Two lead glazed vessels from modern rubbish pits. For a discussion of these two vessels and other lead glazed wares from the cemetery, see below and also Fig. 5.12 and pls. 14 and 15.

Two vessels from New Park Road (Fig. 5.12)

Of the finds reported to have been found by workmen digging service trenches in Alexandra Road and New Park Road, it has only been possible to trace two.[31] These were unearthed by a workman some 60 years ago when the sewer trench was laid in New Park Road. They are therefore the most easterly recorded finds, and in view of the fact that later excavation west of New Park Road [32] when the defences of the City were examined did not disturb any burials, it is possible that the cemetery's western limit does not extend much beyond the point where these vessels were found.

47. Small glass flagon with an infolded rim, broad neck expanding into a conical body and "crested" handle. This glass is a pale green. (See Morin – Jean. *la verreria en Gaule sous l'Empire romaine,* Type 59). This vessel would fit into a late 2nd century context.[33]
48. Small beaker in fine light grey ware with a dark grey slip coating. These vessels are difficult to date without other associations, but this one could possibly be late 3rd century.

No further details are known of the two vessels, nor is it certain that they were dug up from the same spot or were part of the same burial. The former owner understood from the finder that they were dug up "from down towards the Litten end of the road".

49. (from Area 2 Trench J, Layer 5). A very small rim sherd from a vessel, possibly a bottle with a flared rim, but more likely a small cup or lid. The paste is a very fine hard fired buff colour and is coated with a very hard glossy blood-red slip for which the writer has not been able to find a parellel. Comparison with T.R. fabrics in Colchester Museum shows that it is not the same, the gloss being much superior and the colour lighter. Approximate diameter of the vessel would be 5 cms (2 ins). The layer in which it was found contained nothing other than Roman burials.

The Lead-Glazed Wares. Plts: 14 - 16

Seven lead-glazed wares were found during the course of the excavations. Of these, five were stratified with burials, the other two being recovered from post-Roman layers. Until the discovery of these vessels in an indisputably Roman context it is likely that isolated body sherds in a reddish orange fabric with a brown or green glaze would have been regarded as intrusive post-medieval ware in spite of the Romano-British decorative styles. Excavations by the late Mr Fred Sadler in his garden at Little London, Chichester produced some sherds of glazed ware which were discussed by Professor Jope.[34] These have not been seen by the writer, nor was their existence known to the present generation of excavators in Chichester as Mr Sadler did not publish his findings, but nevertheless did correspond with the archaeologists of his day. It appears from the description given these sherds by Jope that the Sadler finds were in a "bricky red paste", a description which does not strictly equate with the examples discussed here. More recently at Chapel Street, Chichester[35], the writer has found some brown glazed sherds in a coarser red fabric which may well be similar to the ones found by Mr Sadler, but a direct comparison is not possible as the whereabouts of the Sadler material is unknown.

Other glazed wares have been found at Armsley in Hampshire by Mr John Musty[36], and although the form of the footrings illustrated is slightly different from the Chichester examples, his description of the wares, ("orange paste, heavy treacly glaze with poor adhesion to the fabric"), is very similar to that of the cemetery vessels.

Lead glazed sherds have also been found at Fishbourne[37], but of the four types found, only one, (Type B (b), sherd 595) which had a smooth red paste with a green glaze, of Flavian date, bears any resemblance to the cemetery wares. The remainder found by Professor Cunliffe were pre-75 A.D., types A and B being beakers in a hard white paste with an apple-green glaze; much superior in fabric and glaze, and probably imported from Gaul.

The distribution of these lead glazed vessels is much wider than originally thought. Excluding the Fishbourne examples and the wares from St. Remy and Holt, it appears that there was a considerable area of southern Britain, from South Wales to Sussex where they were used. While the forms are generally either in imitation of Gallo-Belgic or samian wares, the decoration is undoubtedly native and this, plus the poor glazing technique employed suggests that these pots were produced in a number of centres throughout southern Britain, probably in an attempt to capture the samian market. It is possible that a kiln existed somewhere in the Chichester area in view of the relatively large number of vessels found, and the fact that beaker No. 81f discussed below was so fragile that it could hardly have travelled very far without falling to pieces.

With the exception of No. 81f all the wares are in a fine pale orange paste.

No. 45 (from post Roman layer in Area 1) (Fig. 5.12) (Pl. 14).
Imitation Dr 30 bowl with lines of wavy combed decoration below a double cordon; rouletting below carination. The glaze is heavy and varies in colour from dark olive green to light brown in patches. Blobs of glaze on the rim indicate that it was fired upside down.

No. 46. (from post Roman layer in Area 1) (Fig. 5.12) (Pl. 15).
Only fragments of this vessel were discovered and a complete reconstruction was not possible. It was an imitation butt beaker with a glaze which varied from light green to light brown, rouletted on body.

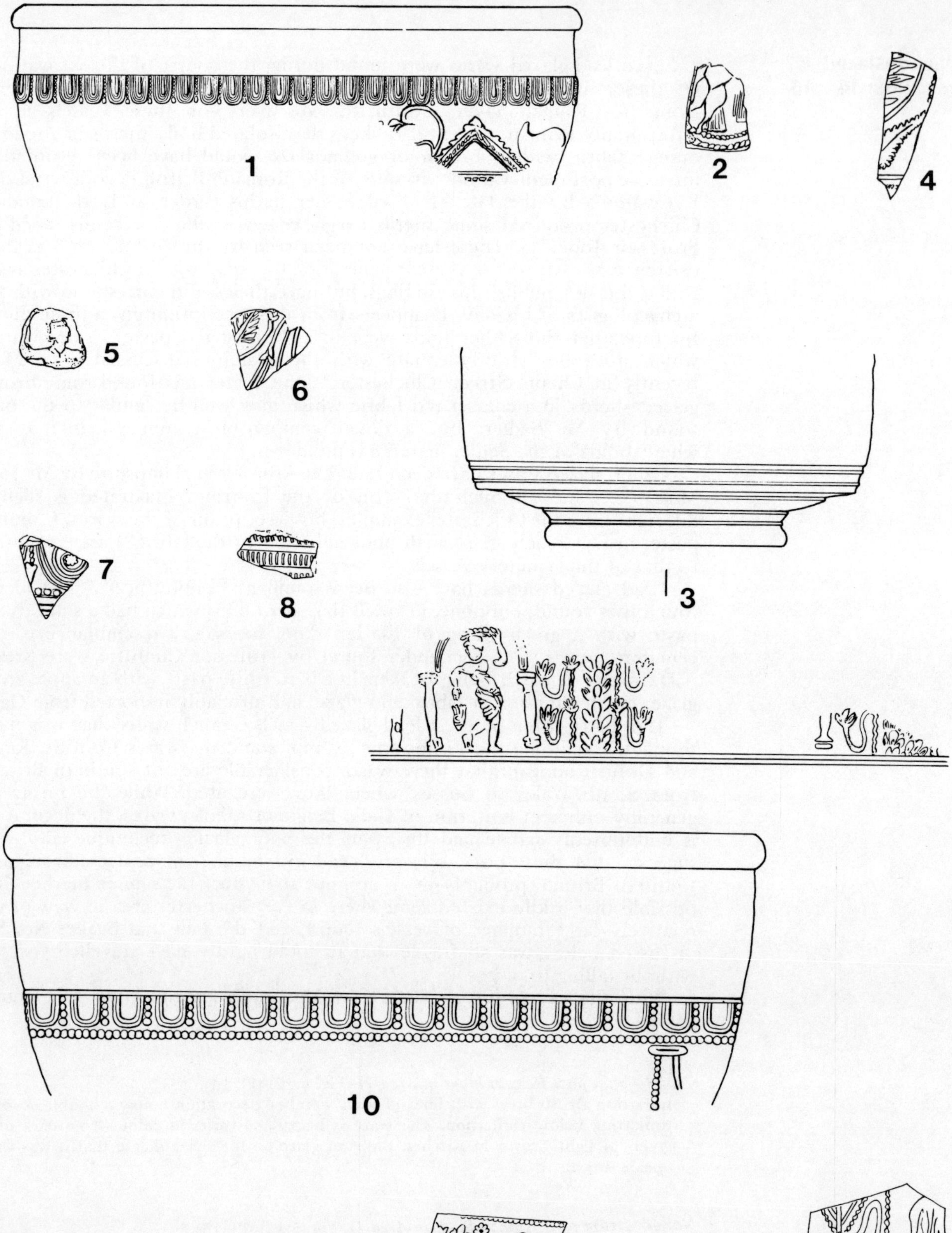

Fig. 5.13
Figured Samian Ware. Unstratified Material. (1/1.)

No. 81f (Fig. 5.22)
Beaker in dirty buff paste, very friable and badly underfired; decorated with diagonal lines of combing below a cordon, and with a carination low down on body. All the glaze had shelled off the vessel excepting small blobs, of mid-brown colour which remained in the bottom of the combing. Probably a waster or second and unlikely to have travelled far from the source of manufacture.

No. 171f. (Fig. 5.24) (Pl. 15)
Imitation Dr 37 rouletted below a plain zone at the top of the vessel, the rouletting being almost completely filled by the heavy light brown glaze. This vessel has a plain footring, the rest of the group having grooved bases.

No. 171g. (Fig. 5.24) (Pl. 14)
Ovoid beaker, rim missing but probably a simple everted type although it could be a bead rim. There is a band of wavy combed decoration below the rim, and the body of the vessel is decorated with fourteen lines of vertical stripes of white slip. The glaze is a pale brown, and there is a zone of rouletting above the foot.

No. 247c. (Fig. 5.26) (Pl. 16)
Dish with wavy combed decoration on rim and a thin patchy light brown flaze.

No. 247g. (Fig. 5.26) (Pl. 16)
Imitation Dr 30 bowl with similar decoration to No 81f and with rouletting below carination. In an olive green glaze, lighter than that on No. 45 and applied less thickly. Slight thickening of the glaze on the rim shows that it, too, was fired in the inverted position.

The Figured Samian Ware (Fig 5.13)

1. Form 37; style of CETTVS of Central Gaul. His triangular motif, cf *Central Gaulish Potters*, Pl. 143, No. 41, and decorative details, ibid. p. 245, Nos. 5 and ovolo 3.
2. Form 37; shows part of an eagle, *Oswald*, 2163, there ascribed to the East Gaulish potteries.
3. Form 30. Bacchus, *Oswald* 597 under arcade which springs from columns. Typical work of the later Flavian period from the South Gaulish potteries, c. 85–110 A.D.
4. Form 37, showing saw-edged leaf, and part of circle with leaf-tip infilling. Similar to the designs of the "Pompeii" 37's. c. 75–90 A.D.
5. Form 37, showing head only of male figure facing right. The characteristic lock of hair at the nape, and the soft flaked slip, indicates one of the Trajanic Martres-de-Veyre potters, probably IGOCATVS, cf. his Perseus, *C.G.P.* Plates XVII/XIX, Nos. 223, 224, etc.
6. Form 29, showing part of scroll and half of a thin-lobed palmate leaf. A light-brown/orange slip, smoothly applied, suggests an early date. Claudius/Nero.
7. Form 29, scrap from upper frieze, with conventional swag motif, e.g. Knorr, 1919 Taf. 83D or 67K. c. A.D. 70–85.
8. Form 29, pre-Flavian.
9. Form 29, upper frieze showing grass tuft, cf. Knorr, 1919, Taf. 36B. c. A.D. 70–85, Not illustrated.
10. Form 37, probably ovolo 1 of CASVRIVS (*C.G.P.* Fig. 40). Late Antonine.
11. Form 37. St. Andrews Cross motif. To the right a figure, too indistinct for identification. Date, c. A.D. 80–100.
12. Form 37. In the style of DOECCVS. He uses the beaded medallion (*C.G.P.* Pl. CXLVIII, No. 19) and the leaf, too, is his. (*C.G.P.* Fig. 44 No. 22). Against this, the frond is not known to be his, and is of the type used by CINNAMVS, (cf. *C.G.P.* Pl. CLX, No. 45). Date, Antonine, and probably after A.D. 150.

Index of Samian Potters' Stamps

a) Stratified with burials.

Stamp	*Form*	*Provenance*
AGEDILLVS. F	27	Area 1, Grave 58.
ALBINVS	33	Area 4, Grave 245
ADVOCIS. OF (ADVOCISVS)	33	Area 1, Grave 231
BIGA. FEC	18/31	Area 1, Grave 45
∴ BONOXVSt∴ (BONOXVS)	27	Area 1, Grave 224
BRICCVS F	33	Area 4, Grave 250
CANVVS (CANNVVS)	31 & 18/31	Area 1, Grave 225
CARRILLVS. F	18/31	Area 1, (Butler Collection).
CVCC. ILL IM (CVCCILLVS)	35	Area 1, Grave 194
IIMOꓷ (retro) (DOMITVS)	27	Area 1, Grave 194
DONNAVC. F	18	Area 1, Grave 59
EL VILLI	18/31	Area 1, (Butler Collection).
FELIX. F.	33	Area 4, Grave 245
IVLLINI FE (IVLLINVS)	31	Area 1, Grave 228
LIBERALIS	31	Area 4, Grave 270
LITTERA. F	18	Area 1, Grave 60
LUCC. ILL. I.M.	33	Area 1, Grave 228
L. LLI. M.	18/31	Area 1, (Butler Collection).
MACELLVS	27	Area 1, Grave 58
PATERCLO FEC	18	Area 1, Grave 35
PATERNI	31	Area 4, Grave 250
ATERN (PATERNVS)	33	Area 1, Grave 214
PEREGRINI (PEREGRINVS)	18	Area 1, Grave 190
PATNA. F.	18/31	Area 1, (Butler Collection).
REGINI. M	27	Area 4, Grave 251
ROPPVS F (ROPPVS)	27	Area 1, Grave 171
SACIRO. M.	33	Area 4, Grave 270
SACRAPO F	33	Area 1, (Butler Collection).
SILVI. OF (SILVIVS)	42	Area 1, Grave 73
TITVRONIS	Lud. Ob 6.	Area 1, (Butler Collection).
///NIC ///RVS F (VENICARVS)	31	Area 1, Grave 227

b) Not stratified with burials

ADVOCIS. OF	27	Area 1, Trench E
ANNIVS. F	31	Area 1, Trench X
CETTVS	37	Area 1, Trench E
CIITTIM	18/31	Area 1, Trench E
]N. T. VSSA (CINTVSSA)	33	Area 1, Trench E
CAMVLIXSVS	18	Area 4, Trench H
[RE ---I.M]	27	Area 4, Trench H.

Summary of Small Finds from Grave Groups

Grave No.	
66d	Bronze finger ring. Not illustrated.
66f	23 bone gaming counters, (Fig. 5.15 and below).
87b	Bronze needle.
87c	Rectangular bronze mirror, tinned, in a wooden frame secured by iron studs to a wooden back. Traces of a leather case were found on the back.
87d	Bronze bangle.
124b	Bronze serpent ring.
124c	Bronze plate brooch.
171i	Bone spoon.

171k Bronze lock assembly.
171 1. Bronze disc.
171n Iron object
195b Circular bronze mirror.
213 1, Slate pallette for grinding cosmetics or ointments.
228h. Glass cup handle with yellow slip decoration.
228i. A group of 8 bone needles, broken in antiquity (ritually "killed"). Not illustrated.
228j. Bronze needle, eye end broken.
228k. Bronze brooch with red enamel inlay.
228 1 Blue melon bead.
228m Worn bronze coin of Nero with hole pierced. Not illustrated.
228n. Dog tooth with hole drilled through.
228 o. Green glass bead.
228p Glass bead.
228q. Blue "eye" bead (*Arch.* 90 (1964) p. 165)
228r Amber bead.
228s Bronze ring.
228u Bronze brooch with silver embossing on face.
228v and w. Bronze barnacle pendants.[38]
228 Bone toilet instrument
228y. Bone toggle
250 i. Set of bone gaming counters (25 or 26). The exact number not determinable due to the extreme friability of the bone. (See below for discussion and Fig. 5.15 for those illustrated).
250k. Lead disc, 1.6 ins diameter and 0.2 in thick. Not illustrated.
250 m. Small sandstone rubber, broken in antiquity. Not illustrated.
250 n. Two bone dice; very friable, not illustrated.
250 o. Small flat pebble, not illustrated.
250 p. Glass disc, 2 ins diameter, not illustrated.
251. (See Fig. 5.18 for the objects listed below)
Two bronze pendants, probably j & k terminals for thin leather cords.
l Bronze knife, much corroded with two small holes in the top end of the blade on either side of the central spine.
m. A thin half cylinder of bronze. When found it was wrapped around the blade of 1. It is possible that there were originally two of these and that they formed the reinforcement for the sides of a leather case for the knife.
n. Small bronze stud recessed for enamel inlay.
o. Part of a thin sheet of bronze with serrated decoration, folded at an angle of approximately 120 degrees. One end has been rivetted, the rivet remaining in the sheet. It is possible that this could have formed part of some sort of lid for a leather or bronze receptacle.
p. Bronze buckle and six bronze plate fittings for a leather belt. All the plates are recessed for enamel inlay, which has disappeared, and two of them have toggle ends, making it difficult to envisage the true function of the assemblage. One of the plates has an eyelet hole, shown here at the top, but this is conjectural.
q. Part of a bronze tube, D shaped in section, with a swivel joint soldered on to one end.

Discussion – These bronze fittings were placed under, around and in a Dr 27 samian cup. Viewed as a complete assemblage they seem to be a ceremonial regalia for some kind of minor official. The bronze knife, which could have been used for trimming quills, and the scrap of serrated bronze with the rivet, which might have formed part of a lid for an inkwell, suggests perhaps some minor scribe holding a public appointment.

302d Bone spoon, not illustrated.
302 e and f. A pair of identical bronze penannular brooches, one illustrated here.
302 g and h. Remains of 2 fibulae, very corroded, the coiled springs only surviving. Not illustrated.

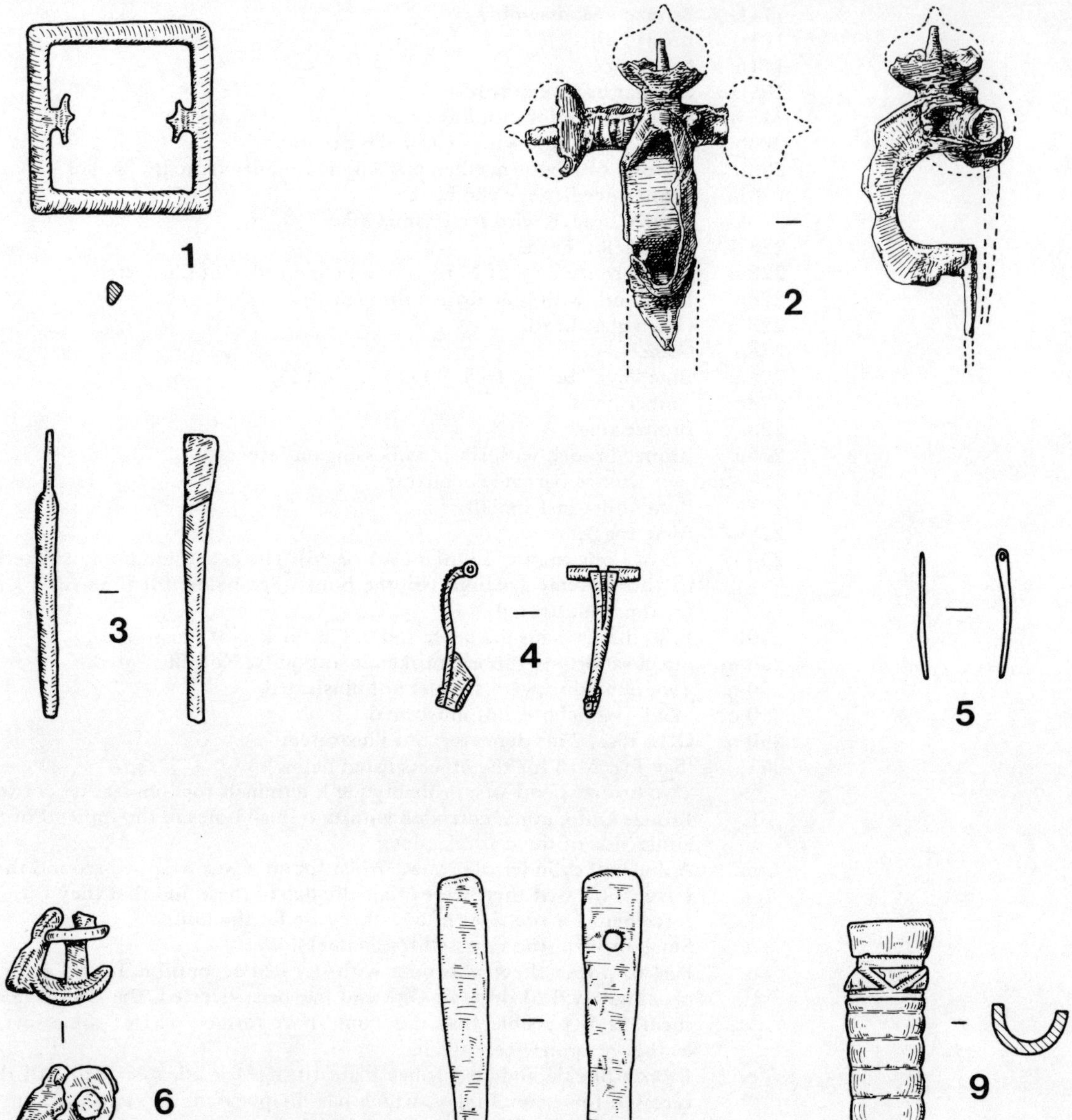

Fig. 5.14 Small Finds. Nos. 1-9 Miscellaneous. No. 302e, one of a Pair of Pennannular Brooches in Grave 302. Nos. 2 and 5 1/1, Remainder 1/2.

Small Finds other than from Burials

Objects of metal

1. Tinned bronze brooch which had been subjected to fire. From the cremation pit in Trench E, (Fig. 5.14).
2. Gilded bronze Crossbow brooch. From the gravel pit in Area 4, Trench S. (see *Colchester Museum. Joslin Collection.* there dated 3rd to 4th century).
3. Bronze stylus. From Trial Trench A (Fig. 5.14), in a disturbed Roman layer.
4. Bronze brooch. From the Period 4 gravel pit in Area 1. (Fig. 5.14).
5. Bronze needle. From Trench D, Area 1, in the top layer of the ditchfill.
6. Bronze object, use uncertain, but probably a fitting for a leather strap.

Objects of stone

7. Whetstone with hole pierced for carrying cord. From disturbed burial layer in Area 1.
8. Slate palette, half only; identical to the one from Burial 213 (see Fig. 5.17). From the Period 4 gravel pit in Area 1 (Fig. 5.11). Not illustrated.

Object of bone

9. Part of a carved bone toggle. From Trench E, Area 1.

Gaming Counters. (Fig. 5.15).

, Mr. R. P. Wright, F.S.A., kindly examined the bone gaming counters found in Burial Groups 66 and 250, and his notes are re-produced below:—

Burial Group 66. (p. 97).

23 counters were found. 6 of these, Nos. 1, 12, 15, 16, 17 and 20 had no marks at all. As the burial was disturbed it is fairly certain that a complete set was not present. All the counters were countersunk on the obverse face and varied in diameter from 2.4 cms (0.9 in) to 1.6 cms (0.6̄ in).

2: *rim*; V11. *obverse*; 3 holes, probably to indicate 3. *reverse*, 6 pointed star, 3 drilled holes, 2 bevels.
3: *obverse*, incision resembling D, but perhaps casual. *reverse*: X (10), not illustrated.
4: *reverse*, 6 pointed star.
5: *reverse*, 6 pointed star and 2 casual cuts.
6: *reverse*, V̄ Ì, probably 6 with superscript bars.
7: *Rim*, XII, / XXIIII XV (12 casual stroke, 24, 15).
8: *reverse*, M I N I
P R
9: *reverse*, 2 bevels, X with several scorings, *rim*, IV, V, I, IIIΛ, IIIIΛ, (4, 5, 1, 8 inverted and lightly scored, 9 inverted and deeply scored).
10: *rim*, ΛIII, X, VI (5 inverted, 4, 10, 6).
11: *reverse* ΛT, (and not IV) presumably 2 letters.
13: *rim*, I III (1, 3,) not illustrated.
14: *reverse*. X, probably X (10) with a stroke above and below *rim*, II ΛV (2, 5 and inverted 5).
18: *reverse*, 6 pointed star, not illustrated.
19: *reverse*, RÎ or RV̂. not illustrated.
21: *reverse*, Grid pattern, 3 digits, 6 drilled holes.
22: *obverse*, 6 pointed star *reverse*, X with cross scorings, *rim*, 6 digits with 6 lightly cut digits between the 2nd and 3rd digits. The 6th digit flanked by 3 and 3 lightly cut digits.
23: *reverse*, X, (10) *rim*, XI, XII, XIII, XIIII, XV, (11, 12, 13, 14, 15,).

Burial Group 250. (Fig. 5.15 and p. 117).

At least 24 counters were present with this group, but the exact number could not be determined easily as some of the counters were so decomposed as to be virtually unrecognisable. A total of 12 were able to be cleaned sufficiently to examine the markings, and these are detailed below. The diameter of the counters varied between 1.9 cms (0.8 in) and 2.4 cms (0.9 in).

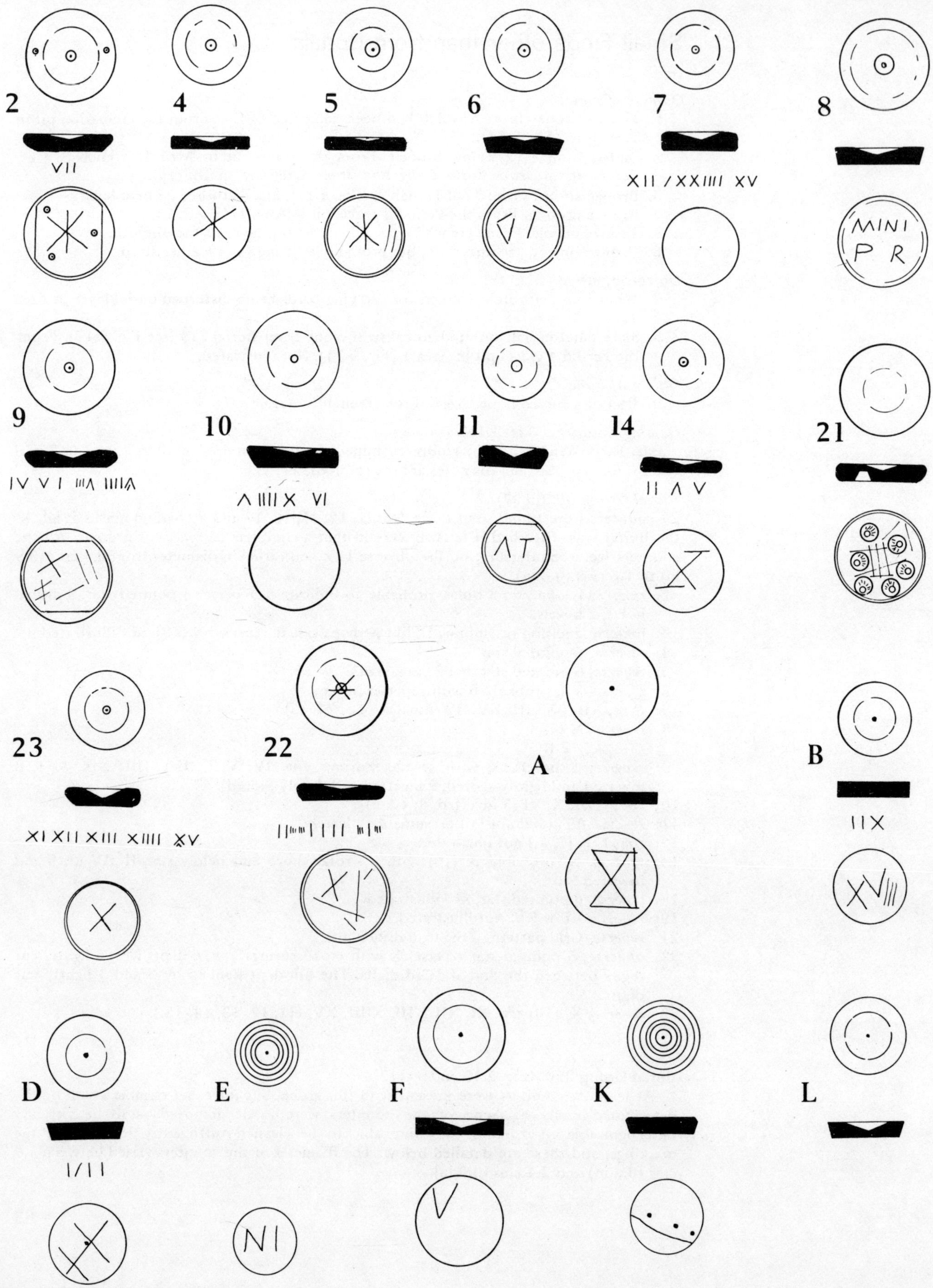

Fig. 5.15 Bone Gaming Counters. Nos. 1-22 Burial Group 66, A-L Burial Group 250. (2/3.)

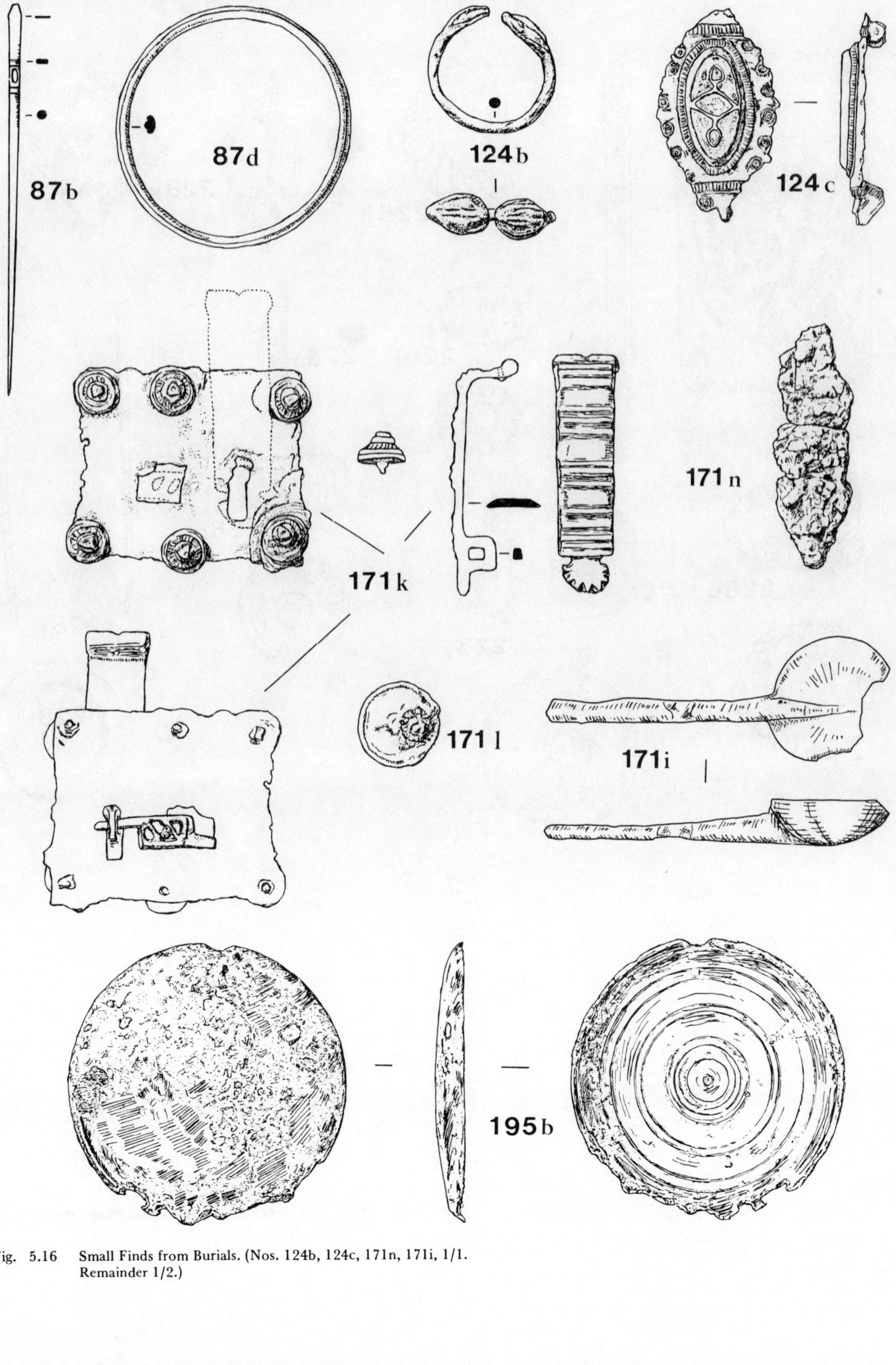

Fig. 5.16 Small Finds from Burials. (Nos. 124b, 124c, 171n, 171i, 1/1. Remainder 1/2.)

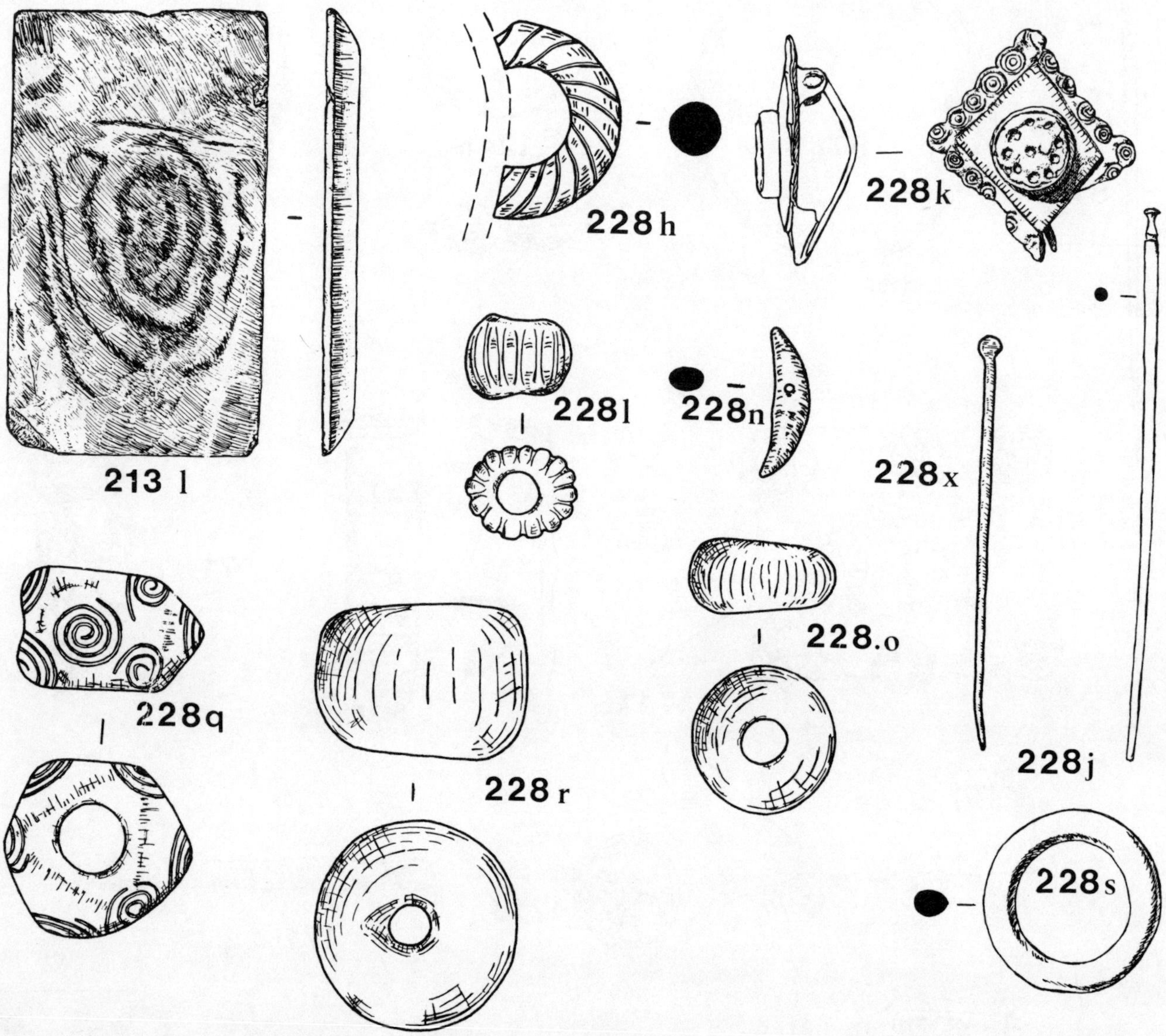

Fig. 5.17 Small Finds from Burials. (Nos. 213l, 228m, 228x, 228y, ½. Remainder 1/1.)

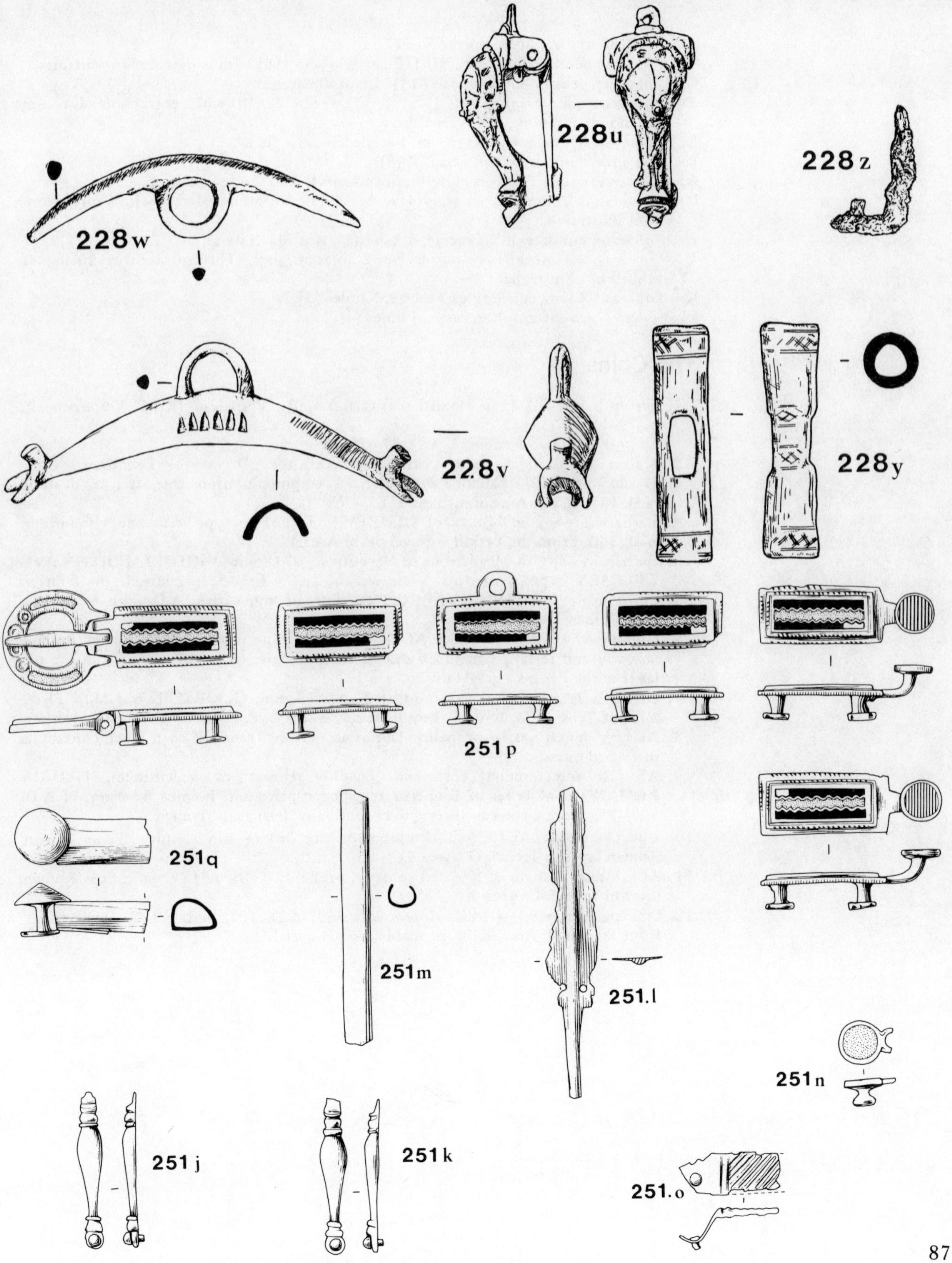

Fig. 5.18 Bronze from Burial Group 251. (1/1.) Drawn by D. S. Neal.

A: *obverse* central hole, *reverse* XI (11).
B: *obverse* countersunk, *rim*, XII (12), *reverse*, Xv (15) with earlier shallow cuttings.
C: *obverse*, central hole, *reverse* Xl (11), not illustrated.
D: *obverse*, countersunk. *rim*, 1 1 1 1 (4), *reverse* X (10) with central hole, also some shallower incisions. XX is less likely.
E: *obverse*, 5 concentric rings, *rim*, bevelled, *reverse*, N I.
F: *obverse*, countersunk, *reverse*, V (5).
G: *obverse*, countersunk, *reverse* M; not illustrated.
H: *obverse*, 5 concentric rings, *reverse*, MV (M beside an inverted 5, with a dot below), not illustrated.
I: *obverse*, countersunk, *reverse*, 1 hole (1), not illustrated.
J: *obverse*, 3 concentric rings, *reverse*, 2 holes or more. (This counter was missing one third) not illustrated.
K: *obverse*, 4 concentric rings, *reverse*, 3 holes (3).
L: *obverse*, countersunk, *reverse*, 4 holes (4).

The Coins

1. (From burial 76).As of Domitian as Caesar, under Vespasian. (R.I.C. *Vespasian* 723 or 791).
   R. type of Spes advancing l. A.D. 77–78.
2. (From Burial 217) As, much corroded, 1st century A.D., possibly Domitian.
3. (From Burial 251) Faustina the Elder, As; commemoration issue after her death in A.D. 141 (R.I.C. Antoninus Pius 1162 – obv (a)).
4. Barbarous copy in bronze of GLORIA EXERCITVS type with one standard. *c.* A.D. 340. From the Period 4 gravel pit in Area 1.
5. Barbarous copy of Magnentius or Decentius. AE 18 mm. VICTORIAEDD NN AVG ET CAES type with two Victories, of A.D. 351–3, overstruck on coin of Constantine 1 (GLORIA EXERCITVS type, of mint Arles) A.D. 330–5. From a post-Roman layer in Trench E.
6. Gratian AE16 mm GLORIA NOVI SAECVLI type with Emperor facing, holding *labarum* and resting 1 hand on shield. Mint of Arles, A.D. 367–75. From the top layer in the Period 4 gravel pit in Area 1.
7. URBS ROMA type of Constantine 1. AE 18 mm. (L.R.B.C. 1. 65) M.m TR.P. Mint of Trier. A.D. 330–5. From Trench X in a layer containing disturbed burials.
8. As very much worn, probably Domitian. From Trench Z in a layer containing disturbed burials.
9. AE 18 mm, much corroded. Possibly House of Valentinian, GLORIA ROMANORUM type, of Emperor dragging captive and holding *labarum*, of A.D. 367–78. From a layer of dirty gravel containing burials, in Trench Z.
10. Undecipherable AE15 mm. Presumably late 3rd or 4th century. From a post Roman layer in Trench G (Area 4).
11. AE 18 mm Radiate of late 3rd century, probably Tetricus 1. From a post Roman layer in Trench L. Area 4.
12. Crispina, *sestertius*, (R.I.C. *Commodus* 669) A.D. 177, before 192. Unstratified from Trench M, Area 4, but probably from a burial.

Appendix A

The Burials

In *S.A.C.* **80** (1939) Mrs Grahame Clark reported in detail on the 65 grave groups excavated between 1934 and 1937 by her father, Mr. Llewellyn White, and Mr. Carlyon Britton. She also reported on eight vessels from the Butler Collection which were not paralleled in the later excavations. For the sake of the reader, it has been found convenient to re-publish this material, and to follow the same method of reporting used by Mrs Clark. The burials excavated between 1966 and 1969 have been added on to the end and the numbers altered accordingly. Our No. 1 burial is, therefore, No. 66 in this context. I am deeply grateful to Mrs. Grahame Clark for permission to reproduce this section of her report, and to the Sx. Arch. Soc. for permission to reproduce the line drawings.

Since 1939 the considerable amount of Roman material excavated from Chichester has added to our knowledge of pottery types, and advances in samian dating technique have required that some of the dates suggested for the samian ware from the cemetery require amendment. Mrs. Clark's dates for some of the ware have therefore been omitted or amended in the light of present knowledge.

Butler Collection: Numbers refer to Museum Catalogue existing in 1939 (Fig. 5.21)

108. Very small example of the olla, in fine grey ware with black surface.
124. Child's feeding bottle in hard grey ware, black/red surface.
152. Large poppy-head beaker in fine grey ware, burnished black surface.
163. Flagon with alphabet graffiti in soft pink ware.
(This flagon had been seen by Professor R.G. Collingwood who reported that above the shoulder the graffiti read A X B X C X, followed by some small meaningless signs; below the shoulder III O P H O I A N and a large K N).
171. Bell-mouthed flagon in soft pink ware with cream slip. (cf. *Col*, Pl. L. No. 220).
179. Globular urn in hard sandy grey ware, burnt pinky red by double firing, burnished on lip and shoulder, cross on base. The type is related to Mr. Ward Perkins South-Eastern B pottery (see the Sussex examples, *Proc. Prehis. Soc.*, 4 (1938), 164, Fig. 10, 3, and p. 165, Fig. 11, No. 2) and probably belongs to the late first or early second century.
183. Ovoid beaker in red-brown sandy ware and black burnished surface. Tooling on shoulder.
220. Wide-mouthed bowl in grey ware.

Burial Group 1 (Fig. 5.19)

A: Pear-shaped urn in grey ware with cross on base.

B: Carinated beaker in soft fine grey ware. Traces of black coating (cf *Col.* Pl. V, Nos 48-55).

Burial 2. Grey ware urn, type 1A.

Burial 3. Urn in red ware with black surface, type 1A.

Burial Group 4.

A: Urn, type 1A with red slip and cross on base.

B: Urn, type 1A.

Burial 5. (Fig. 5.19). With-mouthed vessel in dark grey ware, with red surface, tooled on shoulder.

Burial 6. Single urn, type 1A.

Burial Group 7.

A: Carinated vessel, type 5A, red ware with black surface.

B: Similar vessel in grey ware with cross on base.

Both contained cremated bones.

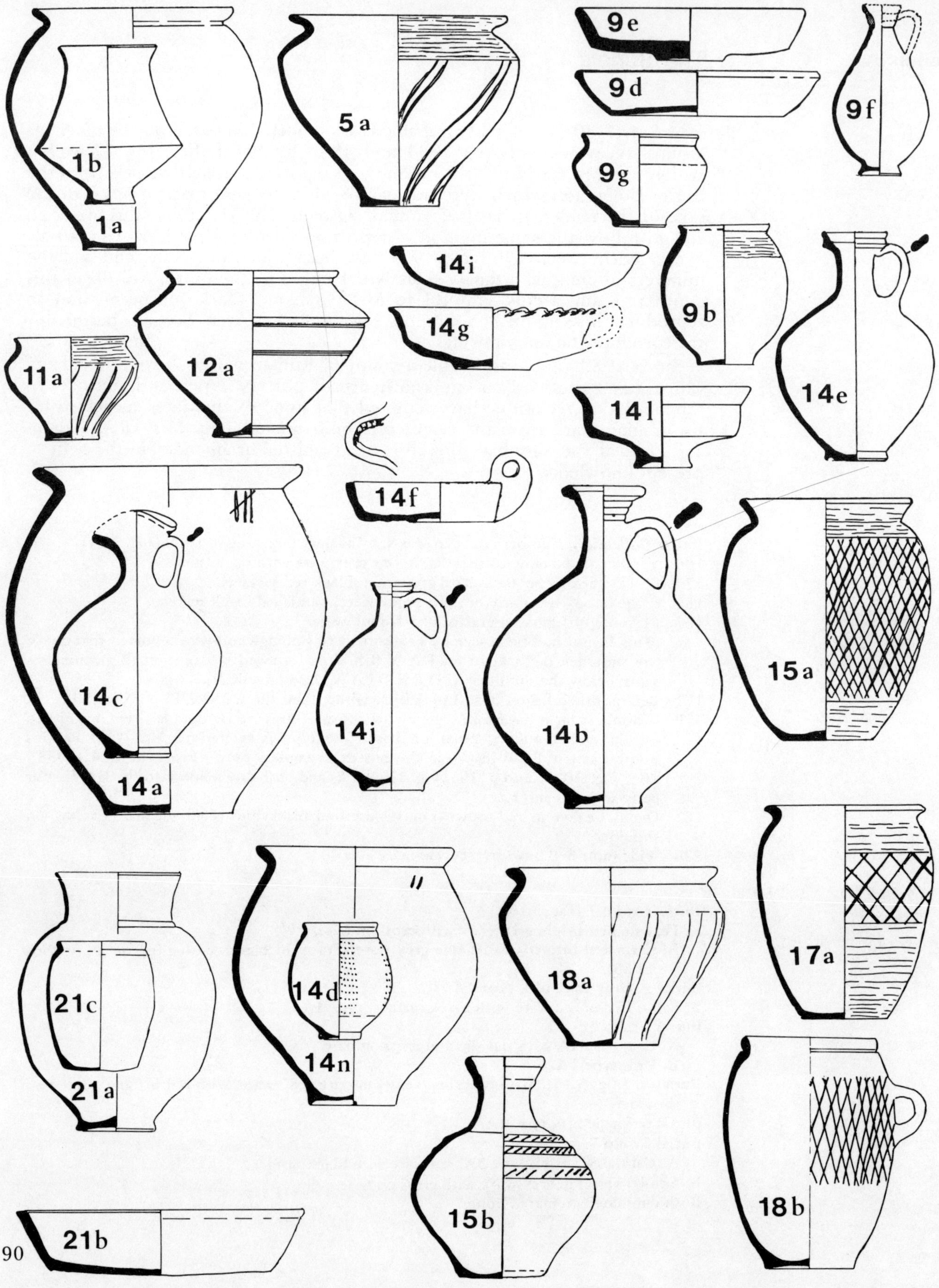

Fig. 5.19 Burials 1, 5, 9, 11, 12, 14, 15, 17, 18, 21. (1/¼ approx.)

Burial 8. Grey ware vessel, type 5A.
Burial Group 9. (Fig. 5.19).
A: Urn, type 1A, with red slip.
B: Beaker in grey ware, red slip, tooling on shoulder, cross on base.
C: Plate in red ware.
D: Plate in soft red ware mica-dusted.
E: Plate in hard grey ware with black tooled surface.
F: Small flagon in soft buff ware, white slip, neck missing.
G: Wide-mouthed bowl in grey ware.
Burial Group 10.
A: Urn, type 1A, in grey ware with red slip, tally mark, /// under lip.
B: Fragmentary buff flagon.
Burial Group 11 (Fig. 5.19)
A: Carinated bowl, red slip, cross on base.
B: Spherical flint pebble.
C: Iron bell, of simple form with rectangular mouth.
The clapper is attached to the ring forming the handle. This was the grave of a child and the pebble and bell were evidently play-things.
Burial Group 12. (Fig. 5.19)
A: Wide-mouthed vessel in soft, thin brownish ware, black surface. This is a Belgic type which survives into second half of the 1st century. Weaker copies of a later date may be seen in Groups 63A and 59A (cf. *Ver.*, Fig. 15, Nos. 38 and 39). A bowl of similar type was found by Mr. S. Winbolt at Greatham, Sussex. (*A. J.* 7, 516).
B: Similar vessel, slightly smaller, also contained burnt bones.
C: Buff ware flagon with lighter slip, neck and handle missing.
D: Samian dish Dr 35; Flavian.
Burial 13. Grey ware vessel, type 5A.
Burial Group 14. (Fig. 5.19)
A: Pear-shaped urn in hard grey ware with light red slip.
B: Flagon in gritty pink ware, paler slip.
C: Flagon with pinched mouth soft pink ware, paler slip. (cf. *Rich. III*, Pl. XXXIII, No. 207).
D: Beaker in soft grey ware, white slip over greater part of body. Five panels of applied dots.
E: Flagon in soft cream ware, orange red slip.
F: Lamp-holder in coarse red ware, cream slip, burnt round nozzle.
G, H, and K: Shallow bowls or cups with frilled rim, in soft pink ware, lighter slip. The frilled rim is usually found on the pedestalled tazza or incense cup (cf. a bronze patera in the Guildhall Museum, *Catalogue of the Guildhall Museum*, 2nd edition 1908, p. 10, No. 106, Pl. V, 5).
I: Plate in soft pink ware, lighter slip.
J: Flagon in gritty buff ware with lighter slip.
K & M: Bowls in coarse grey ware and black tooled surface.
N: Urn, similar to 14A, tally mark below lip, also contained burnt bones.
Burial Group 15. (Fig. 5.19)
A: Olla with cross incised on base, in soft grey ware with white slip on upper part of body.
B: Bottle in sandy red ware.
Burial 16. Grey ware urn, type 14A.
Burial 17. (Fig. 5.19). Single olla in coarse reddish ware, black surface.
Burial Group 18. (Fig. 5.19).
A: Wide-mouthed vessel in hard grey ware with lighter slip, probably a waster.
B: Handled beaker with undercut lip in smooth grey ware with white slip (cf. *Rich. III.* Pl. XL, No. 322).
Burial 19. Single olla, type 15A, cross on base.
Burial 20. Single urn, type 14A, in hard grey ware, red slip.
Burial Group 21. (Fig. 5.19)
A: Beaker of poppy-head type with hollow base, thin grey ware.
B: Dish with straight side cross tooled on base inside and out, sandy ware, black surface.

C: Beaker with bead rim, black burnished surface.

Burial 22. Single beaker, type 25K.

Burial Group 23. (Fig. 5.20).

A: Thin-walled olla with wide band of lattice pattern in sandy grey ware, black surface.

B: Pear-shaped beaker with wide mouth and scribbling on base.

C: Bag-shaped beaker in soft grey ware, white slip on upper two-thirds of body.

D: Poppy-head beaker in soft grey ware, white slip on upper two-thirds of body.

E: Samian cup Drag. 46 poor glaze, date Trajan-Hadrian.

Burial Group 24. (Fig. 5.20)

A: Globular urn with bead rim and zone of lattice-pattern in coarse grey ware, black tooled surface.

B: Lead lamp-holder.

C: Cup, imitation Samian Dr 27, in soft pink ware, darker slip, (cf. *Rich. III*, Pl. XXXIV, Nos. 225–7).

D: Flagon in sandy ware, cream slip.

E: Cup, imitation Dr 27, but without foot-ring.

F: Plate in soft pink ware, darker slip.

Burial Group 25. (Fig. 5.20)

A: Pear-shaped urn.

B: Flagon in coarse brown ware, black surface.

C: Small olla, fragmentary.

D: Unguent pot, roughly made, in sandy buff ware.

G: Plate in grey ware tooled inside and out, chevrons on base, cross in foot-ring, (cf. *Ver.*, Fig. 22, No. 15).

H: Flint tool, of type known as fabricator, 2.8 in. long, triangular in section, much worn on one end, probably a strike-a-light, lying close by G.

I: Urn, fragmentary.

J: Urn, fragmentary, containing K.

K: Beaker with tooling on shoulder, traces of red slip.

L: Indeterminate iron object inside K.

M: Bowl similar to E, without cross.

N: Flagon similar to F.

O: Nail-studded sole of shoe.

P: Bronze spoon inside G., tinned and reeded handle.

Burial Group 26. (Fig. 5.20)

A: Olla, fragmentary, of gritty red ware with black grey surface and wide zone of lattice pattern on body.

B: Poppy-head beaker in soft red ware, grey surface, white slip on upper part of body, five panels of applied dots.

C: Bowl in coarse grey ware, black burnished surface, chevrons tooled on side, cross on inside and outside of base. Contained lamp and bottle.

D: Lamp in pink ware, darker slip, stamp FORTIS on base. Lamps bearing the name FORTIS are known from sites dating before A.D. 80 and continue into the second century.

E: Bronze mirror tinned on one surface adhering to the side of A.

F: Flagon, biconical body with foot-ring, neck and handle missing, in sandy cream ware.

G: Jug in soft pink ware, cream surface (cf. *Rich. III*, Pl. XXIII, No. 206, which dates from the middle of the first century).

H: Dish with foot-ring and rising base in soft red ware.

I: Glass bottle.

J: Bowl with straight side and out-curved lip;

K: Iron object, possibly a knife. With this burial, which was much disturbed, were found traces of a wooden casket with bronze fittings (N–O) and a fragment of lead sheeting (M) with squared shoulder, which may have enclosed the whole burial).

L: Iron hinge.

N: Three bronze rings, 0.9 in. diameter, with iron attachments, and one bronze ring, 3.8 cms (1.5 in) diameter, hanging from two iron loops.

O: Hasp, ending in a palmette, of tinned bronze, with broken iron rivet.

P: Three lion's mask mounts of very thin bronze, secured by bronze pin through centre.

Burial 27. Single urn, fragmentary.

Burial Group 28.

A: Urn, type 1A.

B, C, D, E, F and H: Saucers, type 25G.

G: Bowl, type 11A.

This burial was enclosed in a cist of six red tiles, the cinerary urn being supported on a rib bone.

Burial Group 29.

A: Urn, fragmentary.

B: Beaker, fragmentary.

Burial Group 30.

A: Olla with drooping body in sandy ware.

B: Beaker, fragmentary.

C: Flagon with saucer mouth and two-ribbed handle in soft cream ware.

D: Flint 'ball'.

E: Flagon straight-sided in soft pink ware, cream slip.

This uncommon type resembles a more barrel-shaped flagon from the camp at Niederbieder, A.D. 190–260 (Oelmann, *Die Keramik des Kastells Niederbieder,* Pl. III, No. 63).

F: Lamp-holder in gritty red ware, type 14F.

Burial Group 31.

Much disturbed; all that remained of this burial were traces of a wooden casket (A) with three bronze lion-mask mounts and three bronze rings, 2.4 cms (0.9 in) diameter, and a lamp (B), similar to 45C, two lugs on rim and mask on disk, in red ware with black slip.

Burial Group 32. (Fig. 5.20)

A: Single urn with the upper part of the body decorated with applied clay *en barbotine* in sandy grey ware and traces of black burnished surface. The mouth was sealed with a thin plate of tinned bronze, probably a mirror. Among the bones were pellets of molten glass. This burial, together with the similar urns 37 and 39, was overlaid by a spread of gravel, on the upper surface of which lay a coin of Hadrian (A.D. 119) in fresh condition bearing the figure of Britannia on the reverse (R.I.C. 577 (a) R^2.). The use of exactly similar urns for the three burials would suggest a family connection. For the type, see Burial Group 50, Pl. II (cf. *Wroxeter,* Fig. 18, No. 52 dated A.D. 80–120).

Burial Group 33.

A: Urn, type 1A.

B: Small olla with zone of lattice-pattern.

Burial 34. Single urn, type 1A.

Burial Group 35. Second half second century. (Fig. 5.21)

A: Olla with zone of lattice-pattern in soft grey ware with darker slip on neck and shoulder, running down over body.

B: Samian dish, form 31, bright orange glaze, band of rouletting on floor; Antonine. (cf. *Ter. Sig.*, Pl. LXXV, No. 2).

C: Beaker, type 30A.

D: Beaker with drooping body in sandy grey ware with vertical lines of darker slip.

E: Samian plate, form 18, stamp probably PATERCLO FEC (Domitian-Trajan).

F: Flagon with saucer mouth in pink ware, lighter slip.

Burial Group 36.

A: Urn, type 1A, much broken.

B: Cup with down-curved rim, similar to 60F.

Burial 37. Late first to early second century. Urn decorated *en barbotine,* type 32A (see remarks under Burial 32).

Burial 38. Single carinated urn, type 5A, crushed.

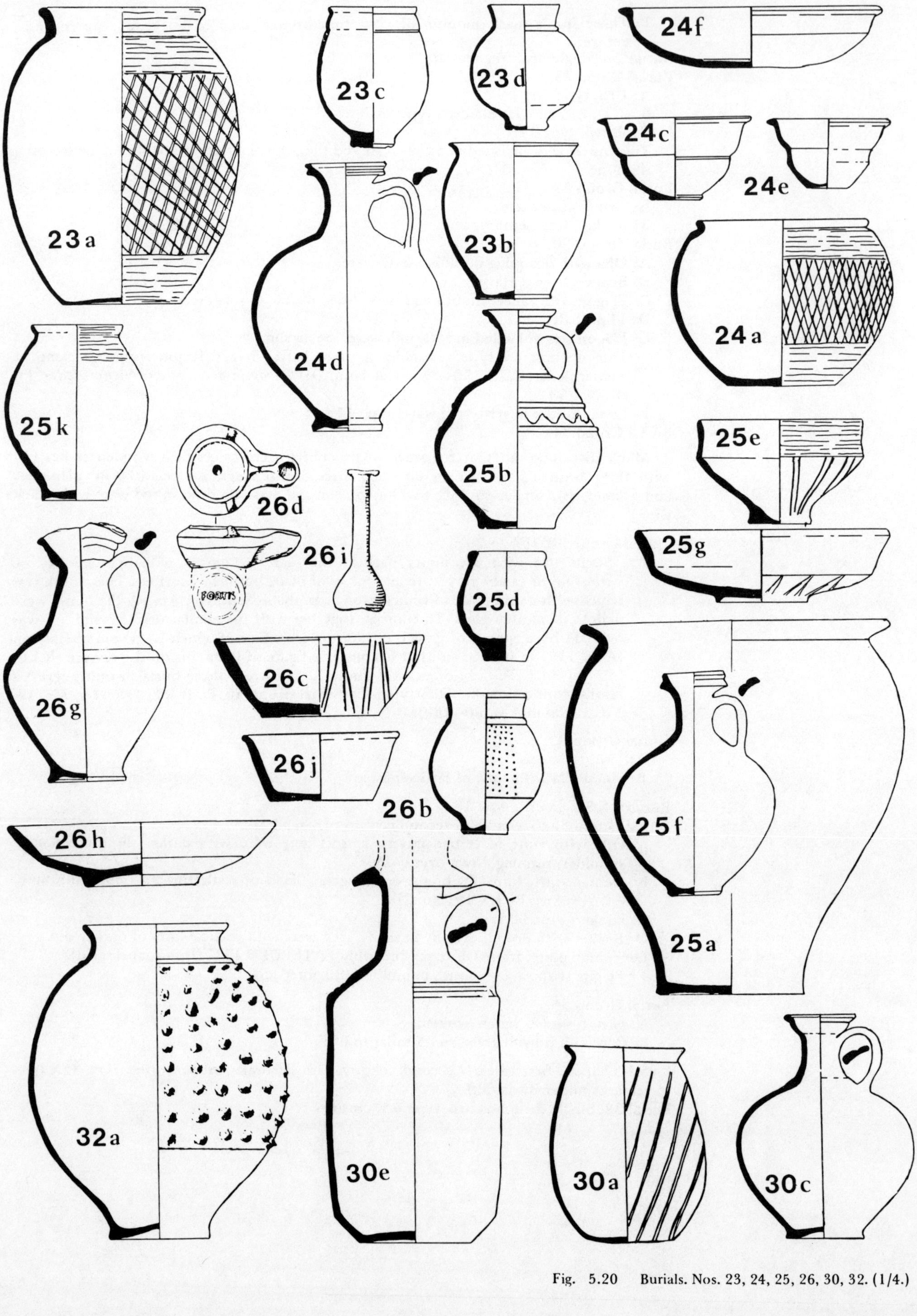

Fig. 5.20 Burials. Nos. 23, 24, 25, 26, 30, 32. (1/4.)

Burial 39. Late first to early second century. Single urn decorated *en barbotine*, type 32A (see remarks under Burial 32).
Burial 40. Single urn, fragmentary.
Burial 41. Single urn, fragmentary.
Burial 42. Single urn, fragmentary.
Burial Group 43. (Fig. 5.21)
A: Carinated urn, type 5A, in sandy red ware burnished black, chevrons tooled on body.
B: Rough-cast beaker in white ware with red/brown slip.
C: Lamp in fine white ware, orange slip.
D: Glass tear-bottle, type 26I, placed in urn.
E: Flagon with stopper neck and two-ribbed handle in soft cream ware.
Burial 44. Single urn, fragmentary.
Burial Group 45. Late first to early second century.
A: Olla with zone of lattice-pattern, type 23A, in white slip.
B: Samian plate, form 18/31, stamp BIGA FEC (Domitian-Trajan).
C: Lamp with lugs on rim in soft white ware, red/brown slip.
D: Pear-shaped urn in hard grey ware, red slip, potter's mark / / / below lip.
E: Poppy-head beaker in grey ware white slip on upper two-thirds of body, foūr panels of applied dots.
F: Flagon in hard sandy buff ware.
Burial 46. Single urn, fragmentary.
Burial Group 47. (Fig. 5.21)
A: Carinated urn, type 5A.
B: Bowl with high rounded shoulder and rolled lip in sandy dark grey ware, black burnished surface, tooled chevrons on body.
C: Flagon with saucer lip and two-ribbed handle in sandy cream ware.
D: Iron knife.
E: Iron lamp stand.
Burial 48. Single urn, fragmentary.
Burial Group 49.
A: Pear-shaped urn, type 1A.
B: Beaker, derived poppy-head type with weak shoulder.
C: Flagon in hard grey ware, tooling on neck, tooled chevrons on shoulder.
D: Flagon with double-ring lip in gritty buff ware.
Burial Group 50.
A: Rusticated urn, type 32A.
B: Pear-shaped urn, type 1A.
C: Poppy head beaker, with slip on upper two-thirds of body, four panels of applied dots.
D: Flagon with double-ring lip, soft cream ware.
E: Lead lamp-holder, placed in cinerary urn.
Burial Group 51.
A: Pear-shaped urn, type 1A.
B: Dish, type 25G.
Burial 52. Single urn, fragmentary.
Burial 53. Single urn, fragmentary.
Burial 54. Single urn, fragmentary.
Burial 55. (Fig. 5.21). Single urn with wide mouth and high rounded shoulder in hard grey ware, chevrons tooled on body; the Romanized form of similar bowls from the Iron Age site at Selsey. (*A. J.* 14, 49, Fig. 5, No. 12).
Burial 56. Single pear-shaped urn, type 1A, contained no bones. This burial and the following were much disturbed and the assocation is not certain.
Burial Group 57. Last quarter of first century.
A: Small ovoid beaker with everted lip in red ware, black surface, burnished on shoulder and base, zone of lattice-pattern on body.
B: Samian cup, form 35, decorated *en barbotine* on rim (Flavian). (cf. *Ter. Sig.* Pl. LIII, Fig. 3).
C: Samian dish, form 36, decorated *en barbotine* on rim (Flavian).

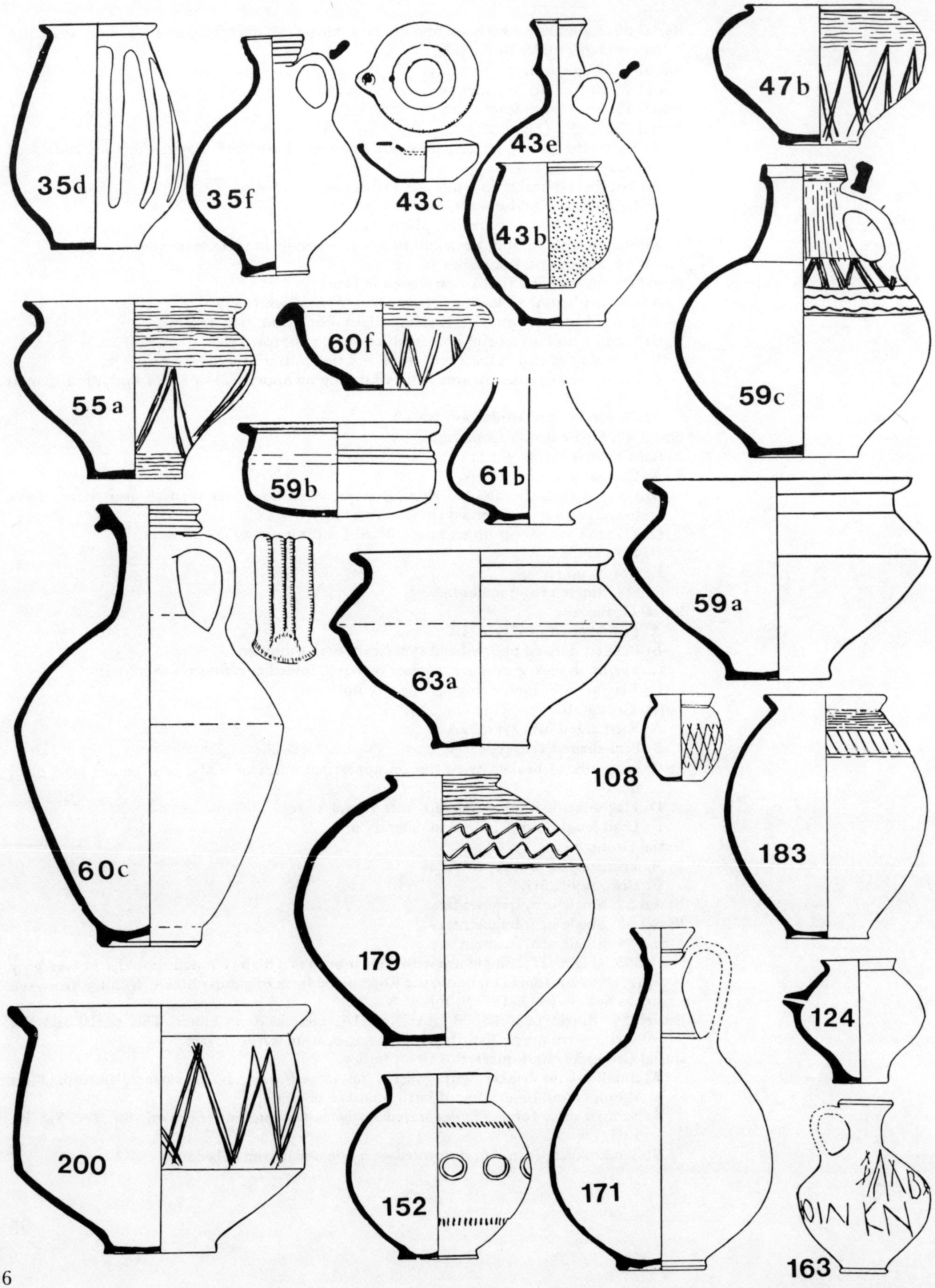

Fig. 5.21 Burials. Nos. 35, 43, 47, 55, 59, 60, 61, 63. Butler Collection, Nos. 108, 124, 152, 163, 171, 179, 183, 200. (1/4.)

Burial Group 58. A.D. 90–110
A: Pear-shaped urn, type 1A.
B: Flagon in cream ware.
C: Samian plate, form 18, stamp illegible, late first century.
D: Samian cup, form 27, stamp MACELLVS, (Trajanic).
E: Small olla with zone of lattice-pattern, black ware.
F: Poppy-head beaker with small lip, white slip on body, five panels of applied dots.
G: Samian cup, form 27, stamp AGEDILLVS F, (Trajanic).
H: Coin of Domitian (A.D. 81–96) among bones in cinerary urn; As, much corroded.

Burial Group 59. (Fig. 5.21)
A: Sharply carinated bowl with wide mouth and narrow foot in sandy grey ware.
B: Round-bottomed bowl with reeded lip and cordon on body in sandy pink ware with lighter slip; compare a 1st century bowl from Colchester with flat base, *Col.*, Pl. LVII, No. 253.
C: Flagon with squat body and conical neck, flanged handle, in sandy grey ware with white slip, chevrons and wavy band drawn through slip to show grey body.
D: Samian plate, form 18, stamp DONNAVC. F. (Hadrianic).
E: Samian cup, form 33, no stamp, much burnt, possibly an imitation of East Gaullish ware, 2nd or early 3rd century.
F: Bowl similar to B but smaller.

Burial Group 60. A.D. 80–100 (Fig. 5.21)
A: Carinated urn, type 1A.
B: Small olla in black burnished ware with lattice pattern on body.
C: Flagon in sandy cream ware with pink slip.
D: Samian dish, form 36, ? Flavian.
E: Carinated cup with pedestal foot, type 25E, in hard grey ware.
F: Bowl in heavy turned-down lip in sandy ware with tooled chevrons on body, (cf. *Col.*, Pl. LVII, No. 259, "probably Flavian").
G: Carinated cup, type 25E.
H: Samian plate, form 18, stamp LITTERA. F (Flavian).
I: Coin of Titus (A.D. 79–81) (*Brit. Mus. Cat.* No. 866, Pl. 42, No. 2, *rev.* Altar, PROVIDENT).
J: Bronze brooch in one piece with coiled spring and solid catch-plate, 1st century type.
K: Bone point, 14 cms (5.5 ins) long.
L: Rectangular bronze mirror with tinned surface, 7 cms x 7.6 cms (2.75 x 3 ins), with traces of wooden cover.
M: Poppy-head beaker, fragmentary.

Burial Group 61. First century.
A: Urn, much disturbed.
B: Flagon with neck missing in reddish ware with black surface.
C: Cup, fragmentary.
D: Samian dish, form 36, ivy leaves *en barbotine* on rim, no stamp, good glaze, 1st century.
E: Small cylindrical bead, black glass, red surface, with bones in cinerary urn.

Burial 62. Single urn, type 5A, cross on base.

Burial Group 63. (Fig. 5.21)
A: Sharply carinated urn in sandy grey ware. This vessel is similar to 12A, but the neck is more pronounced and the ware coarser.
B: Urn, fragmentary.
C: Beaker, fragmentary.

Burial 64. Single pear-shaped urn, type 1A.

Burial 65. Single pear-shaped urn, type 1A.

Burial Group 66. Trial Trench A. Disturbed (Fig. 5.22)
A: Small urn in grey ware with vertical tooled decoration neck missing, type 30A.
B: Remains of (?)Flagon in greyish white ware.
C: Small indented beaker in grey ware.
D: Bronze finger ring.
E: Iron disc, 4.4 cms (1.75 ins) diameter and .5 cm (0.2 in) thick.
F: Group of 23 bone gaming counters (Fig. 5.15) and p. 83.

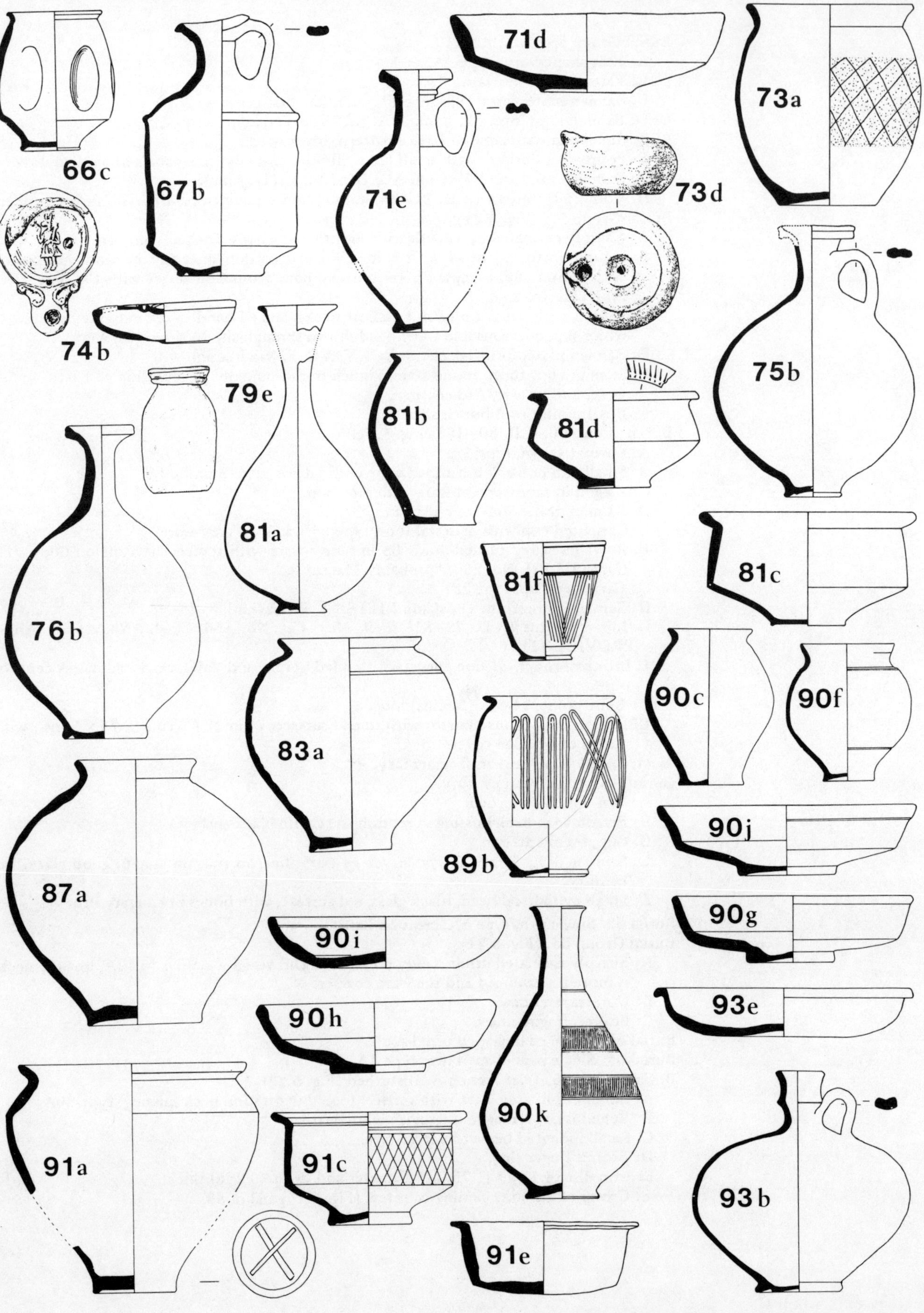

Fig. 5.22 Burials. Nos. 66, 67, 71, 73, 74, 75, 76, 79, 81, 83, 87, 89, 90, 91, 93. (1/4.)

Burial Group 67. Trench A. Disturbed.

A: Remains of large urn in reddish grey ware with lattice decoration, type 23A.

B: Bottle shaped flagon in buff ware (Fig. 5.22)

Burial 68. Trench A. Badly disturbed. Dr 46 samian dish with handles (Antonine).

Burial 69. Trench A. Single burial. Urn in grey ware, type 14N.

Burial 70. Trench A. Large urn with lattice decoration, type 15A.

Burial Group 71. Trench A. (Fig. 5.22)

A: Imitation of Dr 27 in buff ware, type 24C.

B: An identical vessel (half only).

C: Shallow dish in buff ware, probably imitation Dr 18, type 14i.

D: Shallow dish in grey ware.

E: Remains of flagon in fine white paste.

F: Small poppy-head beaker, type 26B.

This group was found beside the head of Burial 72. The absence of a cinerary urn may indicate that these vessels belong to the inhumation, or that the Burial 72 is later and the cinerary urn belonging to Grave 71 was destroyed when the grave was dug.

Burial 72. Trench A. Inhumation, head to N.E. Supine. Two nails found in vertical position, probably buried in a coffin. See Appendix B.

Burial Group 73. Trench C. Mid second century. (Fig. 5.22)

A: Grey ware urn with lattice decoration similar to 17A.

B: Flagon, type 59C, in grey ware. Fragmentary.

C: Flagon in sandy buff ware, variant of type 24D.

D: Lamp in sandy reddish ware.

E: Samian dish, Dr 42 with potters stamp SILVI–OF (SILVIVS c. 125–145 at Lezoux).

F: Small pear-shaped jar, type 11A.

Burial Group 74. Trench C. (Fig. 5.22)

A: Urn, type 5A.

B: Lamp, colour coated, creamy buff paste, grey metallic slip-ware, with moulded figure of Anubis.

Burial Group 75. Trench C.

A: Small urn in grey ware, type 14N.

B: Jug or flagon, neck missing, in hard sandy buff ware.

C: Plate in grey ware, type 25G.

Burial Group 76. This burial was partly disturbed by Grave 72, the urn being below the right knee of the skeleton. Parts of the flagon and dish were re-deposited in the grave backfill.

A: Grey ware poppy-head beaker, type 26B, containing cremated bones and a worn coin of Domitian.

B: Bottle, (fragmentary) in soft creamy buff ware with pink core.

C: Fragment of shallow dish with pinched lip in buff ware with grey core.

Burial 77. Trench D. Grey ware urn, type 25A, fragmentary.

Burial 78. Trench S. Pear-shaped urn, type 5A, fragmentary.

Burial Group 79. Trench S. Box burial, Flavian.

A: Urn in grey ware, type 1A.

B: Flagon, lip missing, in sandy buff ware similar to type 14E.

C: Samian dish, Dr 35 with leaf decoration on rim, *en barbotine* (Flavian).

D: Samian dish, Dr 36 (Flavian).

E: Glass jar. (Fig. 5.22)

Burial 80. Inhumation. Supine, head to east, adult male. See Appendix B.

Burial Group 81. Trench S. Late first – early second century. Burial arranged in the form of a crescent (Fig. 5.22. The cremated bones were scattered within the crescent.

A: Flask in "eggshell" ware, very fine creamy paste with blood red colour coating.

B: Beaker in sandy grey ware.

C: Carinated dish in grey ware, variant of type 14L.

D: Grey ware carinated dish with incised decoration on rim.

E: Similar to 81D, the rim decoration is slightly different.

F: Beaker in dirty cream ware, very soft and friable; combed decoration. Traces of brown lead glaze in the combing (See p. 79).

G: Samian dish, Dr 35, with handles, late first – early second century.

H: Samian dish Dr 36 with handles, late first – early second century.

Burial 82. Narrow-mouthed jar in grey ware, variant of 25K.

Burial 83. Single burial. Jar in buff ware, grooves on shoulder, traces of pink colour coat on exterior (Fig. 5.22).

Burial 84. Fragments of grey ware vessel with tooled decoration.

Burial Group 85. Trench S. Fragments of 3 vessels.

A: Base of vessel in creamy buff ware, with footring.

B: Base of vessel in grey ware probably small jar.

C: Rim of grey ware dish, probably type 9E.

Burial 86: Disturbed cremation. Fragments of fine grey ware jar, type 32A.

Burial Group 87. Trench S. Burial of a woman. (Figs. 5.22 and 5.16).

A: Narrow-mouthed grey ware jar.

B: Bronze needle.

C: Rectangular bronze tinned mirror in a wooden frame with traces of a leather case on the back.

D: Bronze bangle.

Burial 88. Trench S. Grey ware urn, type 14A. Tally marks on shoulder / / /.

Burial Group 89. Trench S.

A: Narrow-mouthed jar in grey ware; fragmentary.

B: Tall beaker in creamy paste with applied decoration *en barbotine*. Grey metallic slip coat. (Fig. 5.22).

Burial Group 90. Trench S. (Fig. 5.22).

A: Urn in grey ware, type 23A (waster).

B: Urn in fine grey ware with traces of black colour coat type 32A.

C: Beaker in grey ware with narrow mouth and base and everted lip.

D: Carinated dish in grey ware, type 194G.

E: Small pear-shaped jar in grey ware, variant of type 11A, but with smaller base.

F: Small beaker in reddish sandy ware.

G: Plate in grey ware.

H: Plate in grey ware, partially reduced fabric (waster).

I: Shallow plate in grey ware (waster).

J: Plate in grey ware.

K: Flask in reddish buff ware and black colour coated micaceous slip. Two zones of rouletted decoration on body.

Burial Group 91. Trench T. (?) Box burial. (Fig. 5.22).

A: Wide-mouthed carinated bowl in grey ware, cross on base, fragmentary.

B: Fragmentary grey ware bowl, type 55A.

C: Carinated bowl with footring, grey ware, reduced black.

D: Shallow flat based bowl in grey ware.

F: Small spouted beaker in grey ware, probably feeding bottle, cf. No. 124 in Butler Collection. (Fig. 5.21).

G: Fragmentary bronze needle.

H: Flat iron object in 1 in. square with nail through centre, possibly a fitting for a box.

Burial 92. Trench T. Single burial. Grey ware vessel, type 5A.

Burial Group 93. Trench E. Tiled cyst burial (Fig. 5.22).

A: Large urn, variant of type 1A.

B: Flagon in creamy buff ware.

C and D: Imitation Dr 27 cups with footring, type 24C. Both cups contained small food bones (See Appendix C.)

E and F: Shallow plates in buff ware imitation Dr 18.

Burial Group 94. Trench E. Fragmentary. (Fig. 5.23).

A: Fragmentary grey ware urn, probably type 1A.

B: Small grey beaker with applied decoration *en barbotine*, type 32A.

C: Shallow straight-walled bowl with flat base in pinkish grey ware.

Burial 95. Trench E. Truncated by cottage foundations. Large grey ware urn, probably type 14A.

Burial Group 96. Trench E.

A: Disturbed remains of a pear-shaped grey ware jar.

B: Fragments of a grey ware jar with groove on shoulder.

Burial Group 97. Trench E. (Fig. 5.23).
A: Disturbed grey ware urn, type 1A.
B: Grey ware platter, reduced fabric, down turned rim.
C: Vessel in creamy buff ware, probably a funnel.
D: Small pear-shaped bowl in grey ware, black exterior, type 9G.
E: Small beaker in sandy buff paste, black slip coating.

Burial Group 98. Trench T. Disturbed by Group 100.
A: Shallow plate in buff ware, type 901.
B: Flagon in sandy buff ware similar to type 24D.

Burial 99. Trench T. Fragmentary, cut away by Pit T2.
A: Grey ware jar, type 23B.

Burial 100. Trench T. Cut through Group 98. A single urn, type 32A.

Burial 101. Trench E. Fragmentary. Large grey ware urn, type 32A.

Burial Group 102. Trench E. Disturbed.
A: Base only of large grey ware vessel.
B: Grey ware beaker with conical neck. (Fig. 5.23).

Burial 103. Trench T; fragmentary. Remains of large grey ware urn, top missing, probably type 5A.

Burial 104. Trench T. Pear-shaped jar in grey ware with tooled decoration on body. Variant of type 5A.

Burial Group 105. Trench E. Fragmentary.
A: Sherds of a grey ware carinated vessel with everted rim, possibly type 5A.
B: Fragments of a vessel, probably flagon, in pinkish buff ware.

Burial 106. Trench T. Fragments of grey ware urn with flat base with a few cremated bones in it.

Burial 107. Trench E. Fragmentary, Remains of a large urn, type 1A, in sandy greyish ware fired black. Heavily scored tally mark / on body.

Burial Group 108. Trench T, fragmentary.
A: Grey ware vessel with everted rim and tooled decoration on body, similar to type 5A.
B: Small jar in grey ware with traces of red slip on exterior, similar to type 9B.
C: Shallow grey ware plate, variant of type 25G.
D: Remains of flagon in white ware.

Burial 109. Trench T. Fragmentary. Remains of grey ware urn with flat base and everted rim, possibly type 14A.

Burial Group 110. Trench T. (Fig. 5.23).
A: Biconical vessel in fine grey ware, variant of type 59A.
B: Shallow plate in sandy buff ware, dark grey colour coat.
C: Large plate with footring and tooled decoration.
D: Fragments of grey ware vessel.
E: Base of vessel, probably flagon, in buff ware.

Burial 111. Trench T. Very disturbed. Flagon in fine creamy ware associated with cremated bones.

Burial 112. Trench T. Small grey ware vessel, type 23B.

Burial 113. Trench T. Fragmentary grey ware urn with flat base and everted rim, (?) type 5A.

Burial 114. Trench T. Urn in sandy grey ware, flat rim. (Fig. 5.23).

Burial 115. Trench E. Remains of large buff ware vessel with footring. Contained cremated bones.

Burial Group 116. Trench E.
A: Grey ware jar with everted rim, type 23B. Traces of pale slip decoration above base.
B: Small beaker in fine grey ware (Fig. 5.23).

Burial 117. Trench E. Disturbed, single burial. Fragments of grey ware urn with flat base.

Burial Group 118. Trench E.
A: Grey ware vessel, fragmentary.
B: Grey ware vessel, fragmentary.

Burial Group 119. Trench E. (Fig. 5.23).
A: Straight-walled bowl with flanged rim and flat base, dark grey ware, fired black.
B: Beaker in fine white paste with grey colour coat.

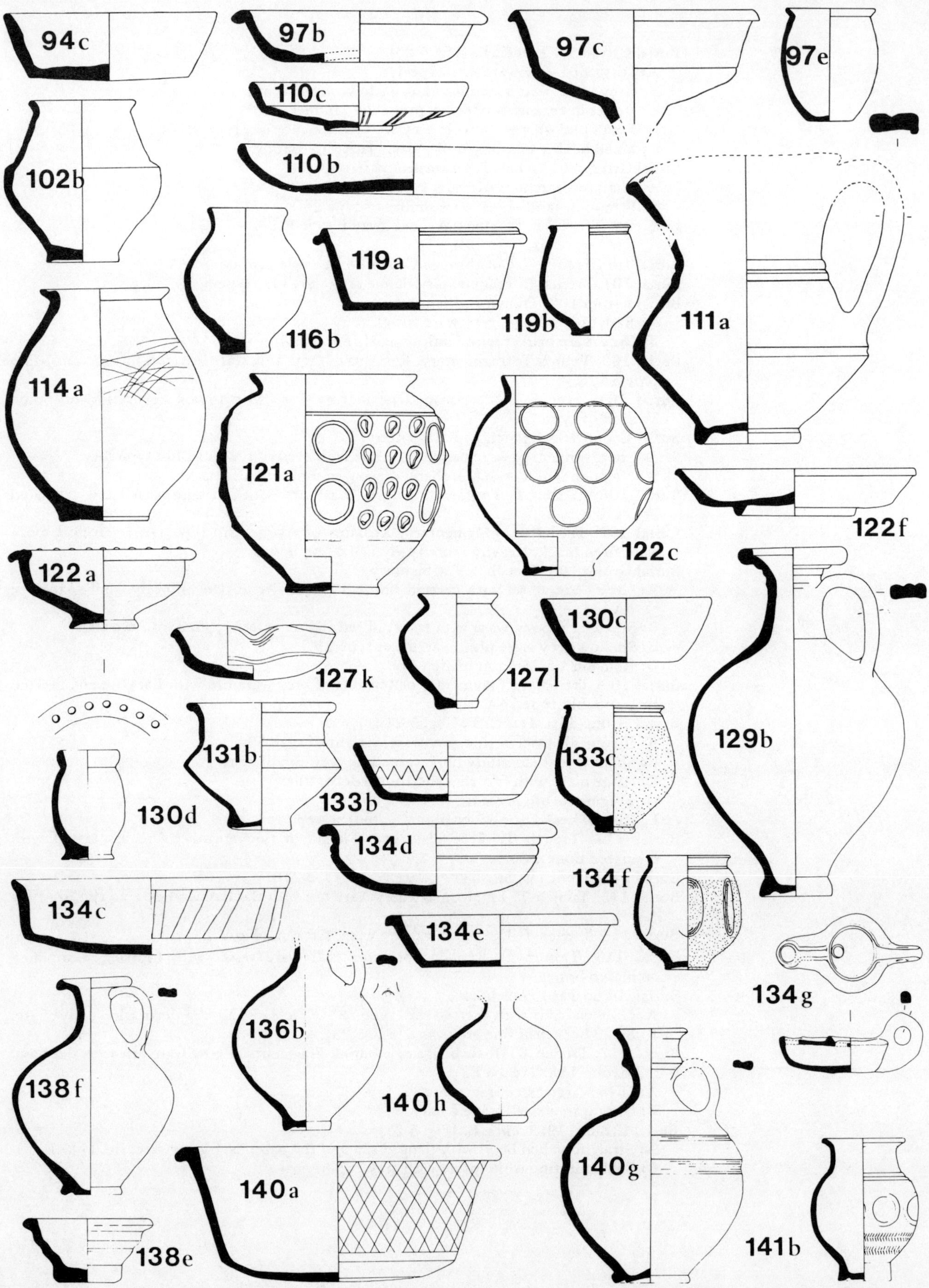

Fig. 5.23 Burials. Nos. 94, 97, 102, 110, 111, 114, 116, 119, 121, 122, 127, 129, 130, 131, 133, 134, 136, 138, 140, 141. (110c, 1/8. Remainder 1/4.)

Burial 120. Trench E. Fragments of a pear-shaped jar similar to type 18A.

Burial 121. Trench T. Urn in fine grey ware with applied decoration *en barbotine* interposed with applied circles. (Fig. 5.23).

Burial Group 122. Trench T. (Fig. 5.23).

A: Grey ware urn, type 25A.

B: Jar in fine grey ware with upstanding rim and applied circle decoration on body, similar to No. 152 in the Butler Collection. (Fig. 5.21).

C: Carinated dish with footring. Smooth burnished finish on exterior, type 194B.

D: Crudely made dish in grey ware with applied blobs on rim.

E: Plate in gritty dark grey ware, type 90I.

F: Plate in fine reddish buff ware, imitation Dr 18.

G: Remains of plate in grey ware, with metallic grey slip coating.

.H: Flagon with saucer mouth, ribbed handle and grooving on body in sandy buff ware, a variant of type 35F.

Burial 123. Trench T. Fragments of grey ware urn, type 63A.

Burial Group 124. Trench E. This group was above grave 158 (inhumation).

A: Fragments of a flat based urn in reddish paste, base only surviving.

B: Bronze ring.

C: Bronze brooch (Fig. 5.16).

Burial 125. Trench E. Grey ware urn, tally mark \\\\ on shoulder, variant of type 14A.

Burial group 126. Trench E.

A: Large grey ware urn, fragmentary, probably type 14A.

B: Remains of grey ware jar, probably type 9B.

Burial Group 127. Trench E. Probably a box burial (Fig. 5.27).

A: Grey ware urn with bones, type 1A.

B: Large grey ware urn, type 1A. This vessel was empty and inverted over a group of smaller vessels.

C: Cup with frilled rim in pinkish buff ware, type 14G
This vessel contained oyster shells.

D, E and F: Shallow plates in soft buff ware, type 14I, one containing small fragments of rib bone and traces of mussel shell.

G, H I and J: Imitation Dr 27 cups in buff ware, type 24C, these appear to be a set. Diameters range from 11.4 cms (4.5 ins), 10.8 cms (4.25 ins), 9.5 cms (3.75 ins), 8.9 cms (3.5 ins).

K: Shallow dish in pink buff ware, with pinched lip.
This vessel contained mussel shells.

N: Poppy-head beaker in grey ware, type 26B.

O: Flagon with pinched mouth in pink buff ware, variant of type 26G.

Burial Group 128. Trench E.

A: Grey ware urn, type 14N.

B: Small jar in grey ware with black slip coating, type 23A but without lattice decoration.

Burial Group 129. Trench E. (Fig. 5.23).

A: Grey ware urn, type 23A, but without decoration.

B: Flagon in fine white ware.

C: Dr 33 cup probably a waster or second, orange paste and orange slip, the paste is not samian and it may be a local imitation. (Antonine).

Burial Group 130. Trench E. (Fig. 5.23).

A: Urn in reddish ware fumed black, type 25A.

B: Carinated dish in grey ware, type 71D, tooled chevron decoration on underside, mark on base D.

C: Flat based bowl in grey ware fumed black outside.
Cross inside and outside on base, tooled decoration on body.

D: Small beaker in coarse buff ware.

Burial Group 131. Trench E. (Fig. 5.23). Disturbed.

A: Olla with lattice pattern, type 13A, burnished on shoulder and below lattice, but no cross on base.

B: Carinated bowl with high neck and pedestal base. In fine grey ware with dark grey slip.

Burial Group 132. Trench E.

A: Large beaker in fine whitish grey ware, type 21A (variant)

B: Small pear-shaped jar in fine grey ware, tooled decoration on body and potter's mark in the form of two interlaced circles on base. A variant of type 9G, but with narrower base.

C: Roughly made carinated dish in grey ware. Probably a 'second', type 81C.

D: Flat based bowl in dark grey ware. Potter's mark in the form of a "scribble" on base, type 26J.

Burial Group 133. Trench E. (Fig. 5.23).

A: Grey ware urn, type 14A.

B: Shallow dish with flat base in grey ware with traces of a dark grey slip. Scribble decoration inside.

C: Colour coated beaker, fine white paste and dark grey metallic slip; "rough cast" body.

Burial Group 134. Trench E. Box burial. (Fig. 5.23).

A: Grey ware urn, type 1A.

B: Grey ware beaker, variant of type 25K.

C: Straight walled shallow dish with slightly sagging base and traces of tooled decoration on sides. A cross is tooled on inside and outside of the base. In dark grey ware, fumed black outside.

D: Shallow bowl in grey ware, with rounded base and turned over rim.

E: Shallow dish in grey ware with scribbled decoration on base and sides.

F: Indented beaker with rough cast body; fine white ware with dark grey colour coat.

G: Pottery lamp, reddish buff ware.

H: Plate in creamy buff ware with food bones in it, type 14I. (See Appendix C).

Burial Group 135. Trench E. fragmentary.

A: Grey ware urn, type 14N.

B: Base only of flagon or jar in white ware.

Burial Group 136. Trench E. (Fig. 5.23).

A: Fragments of grey ware urn, type 17A.

B: Fragments of flagon in grey ware with small pedestal base and traces of cream slip.

Burial Group 137. Trench E. Box burial with sandals and lampholder.

A: Grey ware urn, variant of type 14N.

B: Flagon in sandy buff ware, lip missing, probably type 14B. This vessel was inverted.

C: Crumbled remains of flagon in very soft pink ware.
This vessel was also inverted and crumbled away when lifted.

D: Shallow dish in pink/buff ware with pinched lip which was coated with soot and had evidently been used as a lamp.

Below and around this burial were bones and one sherd of a decorated samian plate.

Burial Group 138. Trench E. (Fig. 5.23).

A: Grey ware urn, traces of red oxide slip, type 1A.

B: Small pear-shaped jar with tooled decoration on body, type 11A.

C: Buff ware plate, type 14I, traces of dark pink slip.

D: Buff ware plate, very badly made, type 14I.

E: Crudely made cup in pink/buff ware; poor imitation of a Dr 27.

F: Flagon in fine white ware.

Burial 139. Trench E. Grey ware urn, type 14N.

Burial Group 140. Trench E. Box burial. (Fig. 5.23).

A: Bowl in coarse flint tempered grey ware. Rounded bottom, carination low down on body; lattice decoration, flat rim. There was an iron knife lying in it.

B and C: Plates in pink buff ware, type 14I.

D and E: Imitation Dr 27 cups in buff ware, type 24C

F: Colour coated beaker in fine white fabric and rough cast body, variant of type 133C.

G: Flagon in white ware.

H: Small bottle in buff ware, neck missing.

I: Child's feeding bottle in hard whitish grey ware with black slip coating, spout missing.

J: Pottery lamp holder, type 14F. Gritty reddish ware with cream slip decoration.

K: Iron knife.

Burial Group 141. Trench E. (Fig. 5.23).
A: Grey ware urn, tally mark / / on shoulder, type 14N.
B: Grey ware beaker with black slip decoration, pedestal base; applied decoration in the form of 9 circles around body with 2 bands of chevron decoration below.
Burial 142. Trench E. (Fig. 5.24). Flagon only in fine buff ware. No sign of any other pots or bones in vicinity.
Burial 143. Trench E. Cut into by Pit E8. Straight walled dish, type 26J.
Burial Group 144. Trench E. Fragmentary. (Fig. 5.24).
A: Colour coated beaker, type 133C, fragmentary.
B: Remains of glass jar.
Burial 145. Trench W. Disturbed. Remains of grey ware urn with flat base and lattice decoration, probably type 15A.
Burial 146. Trench W. Fragmentary. Remains of urn with everted rim in coarse pink ware burned black in patches.
Burial 147. Trench W. Fragmentary. Sandy grey ware pear-shaped jar, traces of white slip coating, variant of type 9G.
Burial Group 148. Trench W. (Fig. 5.24).
A: Grey ware urn, type 1A.
B: Remains of flagon in fine white ware, neck missing, base similar to 14C.
C and D: Imitation Dr 27 cups in pink buff ware, similar to 24C but with more pronounced grooving and finely executed bases.
E: Carinated bowl, type 25E.
F: Small dish in coarse dark grey ware.
G: Pottery lamp in buff ware, traces of burning in spout.
Burial Group 149. Trench E. (Fig. 5.24).
A: Grey ware vessel, type 18A.
B: Indented beaker in fine grey ware with dark grey colour coat.
C, D and E: Coarsely made shallow plates in buff ware with darker slip coating, type 14I.
F: Bottle with pedestal base and grooved lip. Fine grey paste with dense black colour coat.
Burial Group 150. Trench E. Disturbed (Figl 5.24).
A: Large beaker containing bones, in fine grey ware with white slip and applied dot decoration. Variant of type 14D.
B: Flagon in fine white ware with ? disc rim and pedestal base.
Burial 151. Trench W. Most easterly recorded burial (above palisade trench). Fragmentary. Large pear-shaped urn in reddish paste. Cross on base, variant of type 18A.
Burial 152. Trench W. Fragmentary. Wide-mouthed urn in sandy ware, type 18A.
Burial 153. Trench W. Fragmentary. Urn in fine light grey ware, flat base and upstanding rim. (Fig. 5.24).
Burial 154. Trench W. Disturbed. Wide-mouthed vessel in grey ware, type 18A.
Burial Group 155. Trench E. Fragmentary. (Fig. 5.24).
A: Large grey ware urn, type 1A.
B: Small jar with everted lip; sandy grey ware with tooled decoration on body, type 30A.
C: Small flagon, lip missing, in sandy pink ware. Traces of combing on body.
D: Flagon in sandy buff ware, lip missing, type 155C.
E: Vessel with narrow pedestal base, grooved body and double ringed lip, in coarse gritty buff ware.
Burial Group 156. (Fig. 5.24). This burial was discovered during a collapse of part of the side of Trench W, due to 1934/7 excavations. No cremation urn was found, and this was almost certainly found in 1937 and the remainder missed. Probably a box burial.
A: Fine glass phial with flattened rim.
B: Dish in sandy grey ware.
C: Dish in grey ware, variant of type 156B.
D: Fragments (base only) of grey ware dish.
E: Remains of straight-walled plate in grey ware, probably type 25C.
F: Samian jar Dechelette Form 72 with applied leaf decoration *en barbotine*, (Antonine).

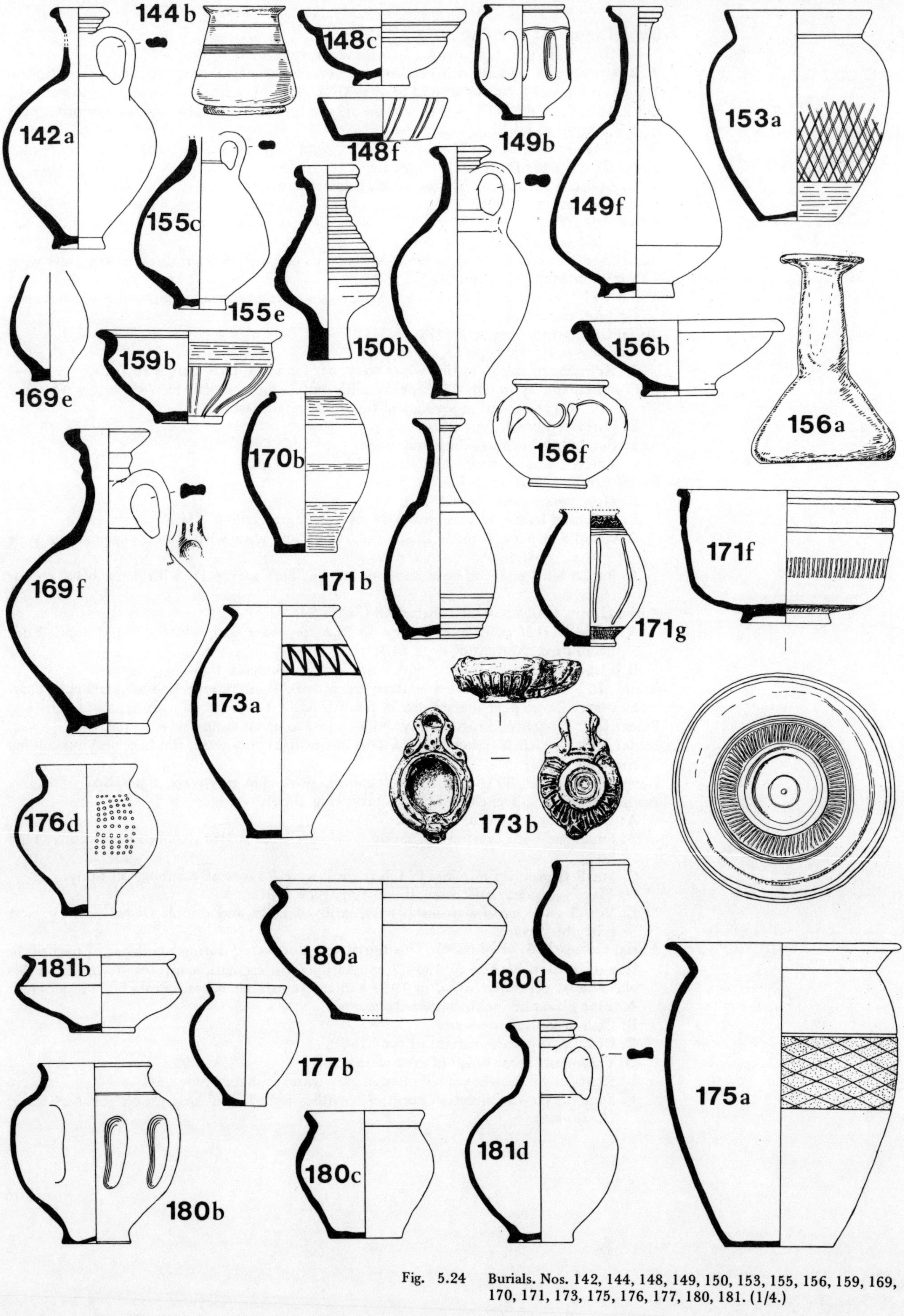

Fig. 5.24 Burials. Nos. 142, 144, 148, 149, 150, 153, 155, 156, 159, 169, 170, 171, 173, 175, 176, 177, 180, 181. (1/4.)

Burial 157. Trench W. Inhumation. See Appendix B.
Skeleton (possibly of a woman) lying just below the western lip of the (?)gravel pit. The skeleton was lying on the right side with knees slightly bent. Layer (6), (Fig. 5.7) covers the body, and it is apparent from the section that it was tipped into the hole when it was backfilled.

Burial 158. Trench E. Below Group 124. Inhumation (Appendix B.)
Skeleton of a young adult woman, fully extended with head to the East. No sign of coffin. Cremated bones from an earlier burial in grave fill, together with one fragment of coarse ware and two fragments of decorated samian from the same vessel.

Burial Group 159. Trench X. Fragmentary. (Fig. 5.24).
A: Wide-mouthed urn in grey ware, variant of type 55A.
B: Wide-mouthed vessel in grey ware.
C: Ovoid beaker with dark grey slip decoration on lip and shoulder, faint traces of lattice decoration on body. In fine dark grey ware, variant of type 73A.

Burial 160. Trench X. Base only of large grey ware vessel with tooled decoration on body, probably type 5A.

Burial 161. Trench X. Disturbed. Bowl in reddish paste, black exterior, type 11A.

Burial 162. Disturbed. Large grey ware pear-shaped vessel, top missing. Tooled decoration on body; probably type 5A. Traces of red oxide coating.

Burial 163. Trench X. Disturbed. Fragments of large jar with applied dots *en barbotine* in panels around body; in fine grey ware.

Burial 164. Trench X. Disturbed. Grey ware vessel, top missing, probably type 1A.

Burial 165. Trench X. Grey ware urn, type 14N.

Burial 166. Trench X. Pear-shaped jar in reddish paste, type 18A.

Burial 167. Trench X. Fragmentary. Remains of pear-shaped jar(?) type 18A.

Burial 168. Trench X. Large grey ware urn, slight carination high up on shoulder, variant of type 5A.

Burial Group 169. Trench X. (Fig. 5.24).
A: Grey ware urn, type 1A.
B: Small pear-shaped jar, coarse pink/grey ware, type 9G.
C and D: Plates in coarse grey ware, type 9E.
E: Small beaker in reddish coarse ware, top missing.
F: Flagon in whitish/buff ware, ringed neck.
G: Pair of sandals or boots; these were resting against the flagon.

Burial Group 170. Very fragmentary. (Fig. 5.24).
A: Grey ware urn, type 1A, flint gritted.
B: Remains of grey ware beaker with pedestal base and bead rim.
C: Base of vessel in grey ware with buff exterior.

Burial Group 171. Trench X. Box burial. (Fig. 5.24).
A: Grey ware urn, type 18A.
B: Bottle in fine grey ware with black slip coating.
C: Glass unguent bottle, type 26I, neck missing.
D: Samian Dr 35 plate, Nero-Vespasian.
E: Samian Dr 36 plate, Nero-Vespasian.
F: Samian imitation Dr 37 bowl in red paste with treacly lead glaze. See below for discussion on these vessels.
G: Small beaker in identical paste to 171F, brown lead glaze.
H: Pottery lamp in reddish ware, type 148G.
I: Bone spoon.
J: Bronze object, much corroded and unidentifiable, app. 3.2 cms x 2.6 cms (1.25 ins x 1 in).
K: Bronze escutcheon plate for lock.
L: Bronze disc.
M: Base of samian vessel stamped "ROPPVS", probably used as a gaming counter, late Flavian in date.
N: Heavily corroded iron object.

Cremated bones were scattered amongst the pots and none were in the urn. Some sherds of 171F were missing, some were in urn and some underneath[39]

Burial 172. Trench X. Grey ware beaker with lattice decoration, type 217. (?) Child burial.

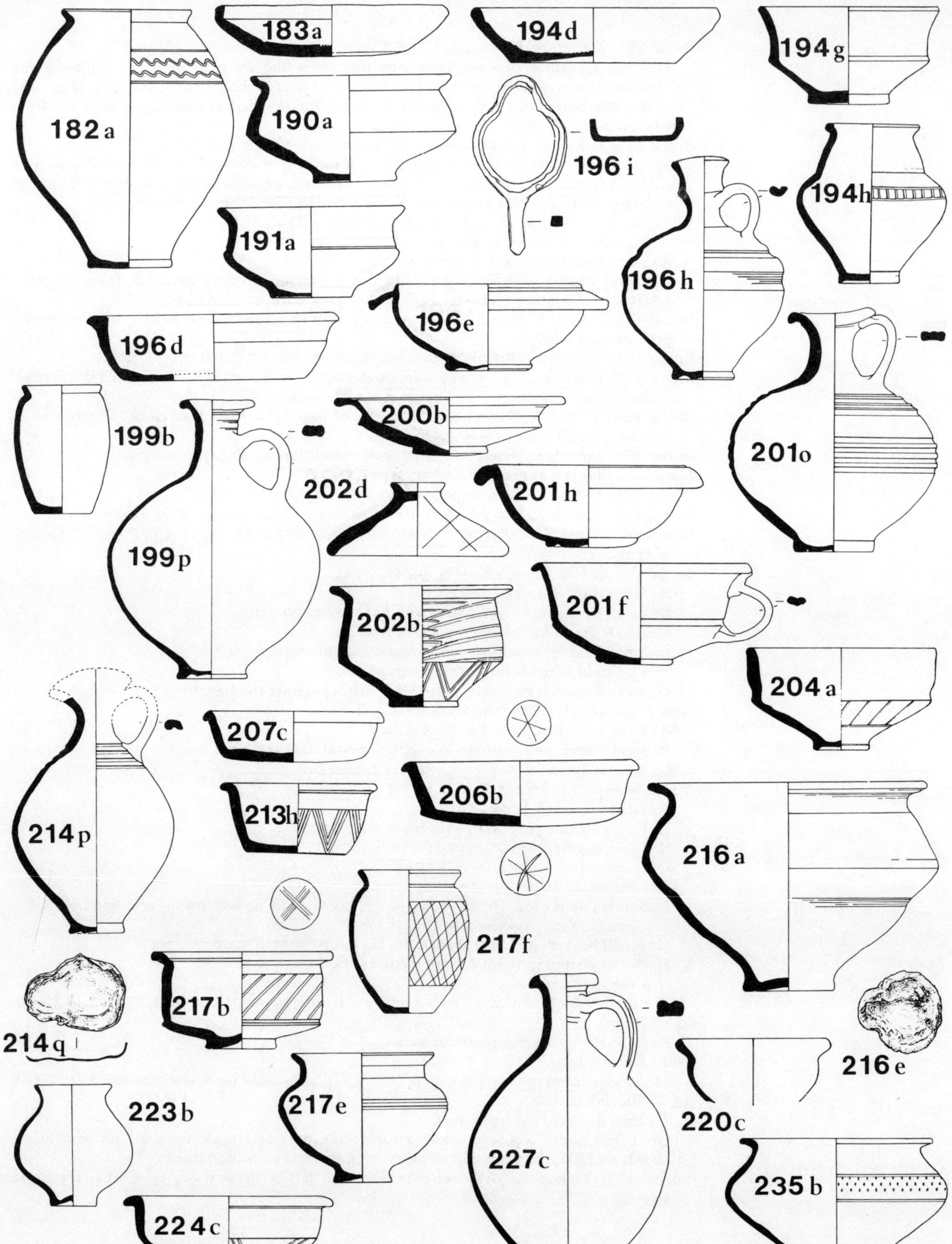

Fig. 5.25 Burials. Nos. 182, 183, 190, 191, 194, 196, 199, 200, 201, 202, 204, 206, 207, 213, 214, 216, 217, 220, 223, 224, 235, 227. (1/4.)

Burial Group 173. Disturbed. (Fig. 5.24).

A: Grey ware vessel with narrow mouth and pedestal base, cross on base.

B: Brownish green glazed St. Remy lamp, handle broken in antiquity.

Burial 174. Trench X. Fragments (base only) of small grey ware beaker with flat base.

Burial 175. Trench X. (Fig. 5.24). Large olla in grey sandy ware, black exterior. Many burnt nails around burial and a scatter of cremated bones around pot.

Burial Group 176. Trench X. (Fig. 5.24).

A: Large grey ware urn, type 5A. In grey ware with traces of red oxide slip. Marked on base ⋇.

B: Jar in dark grey ware with black exterior, variant of type 1A.

C: Pear-shaped vessel in reddish ware. Black exterior, variant of type 5A.

D: Small grey ware beaker with applied dots *en barbotine*.

E: Remains of bronze chain bracelet.

F: A number of unidentifiable iron objects.

Burial Group 177. Trench X. (Fig. 5.24).

A: Grey ware urn, type 1A.

B: Small beaker in soft buff ware, traces of pink slip decoration outside.

Burial Group 178. Trench X. Fragmentary.

A: Remains of large grey ware urn, probably type 1A.

B: Badly made small pear-shaped jar, probably a 'second', containing a small number of food bones. Tooled decoration on body, type 55A.

C: Remains of buff ware flagon, type 25F.

Burial 179. Trench X. Small jar in grey ware, type 11A, but without tooled decoration on body.

Burial Group 180. Trench X. (Fig. 5.24).

A: Pear-shaped vessel in coarse grey ware.

B: Indented beaker, containing bones; fine reddish paste, dark metallic grey slip coating.

C: Small jar in dark grey ware, black exterior.

D: Small beaker (waster) in hard pinky buff ware; much blackened by fire.

Burial Group 181. Trench X. (Fig. 5.24).

A: Large grey ware rusticated urn, type 32A.

B: Small wide-mouthed carinated jar with tooled decoration on body, in grey ware.

C: Samian Dr 36 plate, probably Flavian.

D: Flagon in white ware.

Burial 182. Trench X. Grey ware urn.

Burial Group 183. Trench X. Cut away by soakaway, Pit X 2. (Fig. 5.25).

A: Remains of grey ware platter with flat base and upstanding rim. Potters mark on inside of base.

B: Small beaker with lattice decoration in fine grey paste with dark grey slip, variant of 217F.

C: Flagon in buff ware, variant of type 60C.

Burial 184. Trench U. Sharply carinated vessel in sandy grey ware, type 63A.

Burial 185. Trench X. Inhumation above ditchfill (Ditch 1).

Remains of skeleton, much disturbed by tree roots, lying in a crouched position with the head to the North. Two later cremation burials had partially cut it away.

Burial 186. Trench X. Cuts into 185 and therefore later.

Fragmentary remains of large grey ware urn, associated with cremated bones. Very disturbed.

Burial 187. Trench U. Disturbed, fragments only.

Burial 188. Trench U. Very disturbed, Remains of grey ware vessel with conical neck, probably type 59C.

Burial Group 189. Trench X. Very disturbed, cut away part of 185.

A: Fragments of urn, type 1A.

B: Grey ware beaker, inverted when found, variant of type 23B.

C: Small pear-shaped jar, variant of type 18A. Associated with this burial was the rim of a disc rimmed flagon in coarse buff ware.

Burial Group 190. Trench X. (Fig. 5.25).

A: Sharply carinated bowl in sandy grey ware.

B: Samian dish Dr 18 stamped PEREGRINI (Flavian).

C: Samian dish Dr 46 rosette stamped inside base, (Antonine).
D: Small iron object, unidentifiable.

Burial Group 191. Trench X. Very disturbed. Box burial. (Fig. 5.25).
A: Shallow bowl in dark grey ware; black burnished exterior.
B: Base only of red ware vessel with footring, traces of darker slip coating inside.
C: Pottery lamp in buff ware with dark grey slip, type 148G.

Burial Group 192. Trench X. Disturbed.
A: Thin-walled flat-based urn in reddish sandy grey ware. Lattice decoration, variant of type 17A.
B: Grooved cup in underfired brown ware, badly burnt in cremation, variant of type 24C but with very pronounced footring.

Burial 193. Trench X. Inhumation. Aligned North-South, knees drawn up and on right side. Very fragmentary due to disturbance by tree roots. Head was above lamp-holder in Group 194. (See Pl. 4).

Burial Group 194. Trench X. Box burial. (Fig. 5.25 and Pl. 4).
A: Grey ware urn, type 23H.
B: Large grey ware flagon type 59C.
C: Pair of hobnailed boots, 32 cms. (12.8 ins.) long.
D: Plate in sandy grey ware, scroll decoration in centre of base inside.
E and F: Plates in grey ware type 194D, but without centre scroll.
G: Carinated dish in dark grey ware.
H: Grey ware beaker.
I: Samian Dr 27 stamped IIMO (Retro) DOMITVS) (Trajan-Hadrian.).
J: Samian dish Dr 35 stamped (CVCC ILL.IM) (CVCCILLVS). Early to mid-Antonine.
K: Iron lampholder.
L: Iron object, (?)spike.

Burial Group 195. Trench X. Disturbed.
A: Base only of large grey ware vessel with tooled decoration on body.
B: A circular tinned bronze mirror above bones in pot.

Burial Group 196. Trench Z. Box burial, disturbed. (Fig. 5.25).
A: Grey ware carinated bowl with vertical tooled decoration on body, a variant of type 18A, but this example is more squat.
B: Base only of large grey ware vessel.
C: Crudely made plate in hard gritty dark grey ware, black exterior, tooling on base and body; type 9E.
D: Plate in hard gritty paste, pink exterior.
F: Variant of 196E, in buff ware with traces of pink slip coating.
G: Flagon in fine grey ware, pink/buff exterior, type 138F.
H: Flagon in buff ware with traces of brown slip.
I: Lead lamp holder.

Burial Group 197. Trench Z, fragmentary.
A: Bottom half of grey ware urn, probably type 14A.
B: Remains of grey ware plate, type 25G.
C: Base only of vessel, probably flagon, in fine grey ware with black slip coating on exterior.

Burial 198. Trench Z, fragmentary. Remains of buff ware flagon.

Burial Group 199. Trench Z. Box burial, (Fig. 5.25).
A: Olla, type 23A.
B: Small beaker in hard gritty dark grey ware.
C: Roughcast beaker, type 43B, dark grey paste; black slip coating.
D, E, F and G: Plates in soft pink ware, type 24F. Food bones in one dish.
H, I, J, K, L, M, N and O: Eight imitation Dr 27 cups in buff ware, type 24C. These are graduated in sizes ranging from 11.4 cms (4.5 ins) diameter to 8.6 cms (3.4 ins) across the rim. There are two "sets" of 4 cups, obviously intended to nest into each other.
P: Flagon in sandy buff ware.
Q: Pottery lamp in dark reddish ware; slight traces of soot at spout, type 148G, but larger.

Burial Group 200. Trench Z. Disturbed by pipe trench. (Fig. 5.25).

A: Poppy-head beaker in fine grey ware with 5 panels of applied dots *en barbotine*, variant of type 26B.

B: Dish in pink/buff ware with red slip decoration, imitation Curle 15. A few large grits inside.

Burial Group 201. Trench Z. Box Burial, disturbed, (twin burial). (Fig. 5.25). Food bones in dishes, oyster and mussel shells strewn about burial.

A: Grey ware urn, type 14A, boot studs mixed in with cremated bones.

B: Grey ware urn, also containing bones, top missing, base similar to type 25A.

C: Plate, type 25G, traces of red slip coating.

D: Grey ware bowl, type 26C.

E: Small grey ware beaker with pedestal base; top missing, probably child's feeding bottle, type 140I.

F: Large cup in creamy buff ware.

G: Imitation Dr 27 cup in pink/buff ware, variant of type 24C; rim is round instead of flat.

H: Small bowl in pink/buff ware.

K, L and M: Shallow plates in pink/buff ware, variants of type 14I.

N: Small buff ware flagon, neck missing.

O: Buff ware flagon.

P: Samian dish, Dr 35 Hadrian/Antonine.

Q: Samian dish, Curle 15, Hadrian/Antonine.

R: Pottery lamp, cream paste, orange slip, type 148G, soot on spout.

S: Large iron object, much corroded and fragmentary, possibly lock of box.

Burial Group 202. Disturbed. (Fig. 5.25). Trench Z.

A: Remains of large grey ware urn, probably type 25A.

B: Carinated bowl in sandy grey ware.

C: Dish in grey ware with flat base, cross on base inside and out, tooled decoration on side, type 134C.

D: Grey ware lid, inverted in grave.

Burial 203. Trench Z. Large grey ware urn, type 25A.

Burial 204. Trench Z. Disturbed. Grey ware carinated dish with narrow base. (Fig. 5.25).

Burial 205. Trench E. Grey ware urn with tally marks on shoulder , variant of type 14A but with flattened rim.

Burial Group 206. Trench E. (Fig. 5.25). Box burial, urn lying on side.

A: Grey ware urn, type 14N.

B: Grey ware dish burnished black outside, tooled decoration on base and tool marks on body.

C: Small rough cast beaker with narrow base, variant of type 43B, pink ware with dark grey slip.

Burial Group 207. Trench Z. Box burial. (Fig. 5.25).

A: Fragmentary remains of large grey ware urn with flat base, probably type 23A, but without lattice decoration.

B: Shallow grey ware dish with footring, type 9E.

C, D, E, F, G, H and I: Flat based grey ware dishes with rolled over rims.

J: Dish, variant of type 217B, diagonal tooled decoration on body.

K, L and M: Small beakers in fine grey ware, type 97E.

N: Plate in buff ware, type 24F.

O: Screw-necked flagon in buff ware.

P: Flagon in sandy buff ware, neck missing.

Q: Large grey ware urn, type 14N, containing cremated bones. This pot was immediately below the box burial and may imply a family connection.

Burial 208. Trench Z. Truncated. Base only of large grey ware urn.

Burial Group 209. Badly disturbed. Trench Z.

A: Fragments of grey ware necked jar, possibly type 32A.

B: Base only of vessel in reddish ware.

Burial 210. Trench Z. Badly disturbed. Urn in coarse grey ware containing bones, type 17A.

Burial 211. Trench Z. Fragmentary

Base of large grey ware urn with cremated bones.

Burial Group 212. Trench Z. Badly disturbed.
A: Base only of thin-walled flat-based vessel in grey ware, (?)type 17A.
B: Grey ware plate, probably type 9E.
C: Remains of small beaker in dark grey ware.
D: Base of flagon in reddish ware.

Burial Group 213. Trench Z. Disturbed box burial (Fig. 5.25).
A: Grey ware jar, base only.
B: Jar in reddish ware, fragmentary.
C: Grey ware plate, variant of type 9E.
D: Carinated bowl in grey ware, type 25E.
E: Grey ware bowl, variant of type 26J.
F and G: Variants of grey ware bowl 9G.
H and I: Flat based grey ware bowls, cross on base.
J: Grey ware lid, type 202D.
K: Samian dish, Dr 35/36, probably 2nd century.
L: Slate tablet with chamfered edges (Fig. 5.17) probably a palette for grinding cosmetics; grinding marks visible in centre.
M: Bronze object, much corroded, lying alongside the pallette and probably a palette knife.
N: Iron object, use unknown.

Burial Group 214. Trench Z. (Fig. 5.25). Box burial. Cut through earlier burial. Sherds of 3 vessels and traces of cremated bones in vicinity.
A: Grey ware urn, type 14N.
B: Grey sandy ware beaker, variant of type 23B.
C and D: Small grey ware beakers, variant of 23B.
E: Bowl in grey ware, cross inside on base, variant of 26C.
F and G: Plates in soft buff ware, variants of 14I.
H: Bowl in buff ware with frilled rim, type 14G.
I, J, K and L: Imitation Dr 27 cups in buff ware, type 24C.
M: Small rough cast beaker in thin reddish grey ware, black slip, variant of type 43B.
N: Samian dish Dr 33, stamped P ATERN, probably PATERNUS. Die cut down, (Early Antonine).
O: Flagon in white ware, lip missing.
P: Flagon in buff ware, type 14B.
Q: Small lead lamp holder without handle.
R: Remains of sandals.

Burial Group 215. Trench Z. Very disturbed.
A: Fragments of large grey ware urn with two cordons on upper part of body, rim missing.
B: Fragments of bowl in soft reddish ware.

Burial Group 216. Trench Z. Box burial. (Fig. 5.25).
A: Thin-walled grey ware vessel.
B: Small bowl, type 26C, (waster).
C: Grey ware plate, type 25G.
D: Flagon in sandy buff ware, type 24D.
E: Small iron lamp holder.

Burial Group 217. Trench Z. Box burial beside burial 149. (Fig. 5.25).
A: Grey ware cinerary urn, variant of type 18A.
B, C and D: Straight-walled grey ware carinated bowls with tooled decoration on body.
E: Thin-walled wide-mouthed bowl in sandy grey ware, inverted in box, hole through base.
F, G and H: Small beakers with lattice decoration and everted rim, in fine grey ware with black slip coating.
I and J: Dishes, type 21B.
K: Samian dish Dr 36, (Flavian).
L: Samian dish Dr 35, (Flavian).
M and N: Buff flagons, variants of type 60C.
O: Glass bottle, type 26I.
P: Lead lamp holder, type 196I.

Q: Iron knife.
R: Bronze coin (possibly of Domitian) below flagon.

Burial Group 218. Trench Z. Disturbed.
A: Remains of very large grey ware urn, type 1A.
B: Bowl in dark grey ware, type 159B.

Burial 219. Trench Z. Grey ware urn, type 1A.

Burial Group 220. Trench Z. (Fig. 5.25). Some bones scattered around pot.
A: Grey ware jar with carination high on shoulder and tooled decoration on body, type 5A.
B: Small grey ware jar, type 23B.
C: Remains of cup in thin, flaky pink/buff ware, base missing.
D: Flagon in creamy buff ware, type 24D.

Burial Group 221. Trench Z. Badly disturbed.
A: Remains of grey ware bowl.
B: Base only of grey ware vessel.
C: Base only of flagon in sandy buff ware.
D: Pottery lamp in buff ware with metallic grey slip, type 148G, stamped STROBIII.

Burial 222. Trench Z. Very disturbed. Remains of coarse grey ware jar, type 5A.

Burial Group 223. Trench Z. Disturbed. (Fig. 5.25).
A: Base only of grey ware vessel.
B: Beaker in sandy grey ware.
C: Large flagon in gritty buff ware, neck missing.

Burial Group 224. Trench Z. Very disturbed. (Fig. 5.25).
A: Fragments of grey ware urn.
B: Grey ware jar, type 18A, (variant).
C: Grey ware jar, fragmentary, cross on base.
D: Remains of grey ware vessel with flat base.
E: Fragments of vessel in sandy reddish ware, probably type 15A.
F: Remains of plate in pinkish buff ware.
G: Base only of flagon in pink buff ware.
H: Samian cup Dr 27, stamped ∴ BONOXVS ∴ possibly Les Martre de Veyre fabric, early 2nd century.

Burial Group 225. Trench Z.
A: Rough cast beaker in fine white paste, dark grey slip, type 43B.
B: Dr 18/31 Samian dish stamped CANNUS, Central Gaullish, probably Antonine.
C: Dr 46 Samian bowl with handles, rosette stamped on inside of base; Antonine.

Burial 226. Trench Z. Disturbed by laying down metalled area. Grey ware urn, type 14A.

Burial Group 227. (Fig. 5.25).
A: Grey ware urn, type 1A.
B: Samian dish, Dr 18/31, stamped ≡ NIC /// RVS.F. (VENICARUS) Rheinzarben, late Antonine.
C: Flagon in sandy pink/buff ware.

Burial Group 228. Trench E. Box burial. (Figs. 5.26 and 5.17).
A: Large grey ware urn with diagonal tooled decoration on body; carination low down.
B: Buff ware flagon.
C: Glass beaker, type 144D.
D: Rough cast beaker in reddish grey ware, dark grey slip, type 43B.
E: Samian cup Dr 33 stamped LUCC.ILL.I.M. Antonine.
F: Dr 31 Samian dish stamped IVLLIN FE (I VҤLLINUS), Lezoux, late Antonine.
G: Samian dish Dr 36, Antonine.
H: Glass cup-handle with yellow stripes.
I: A group of 8 bone needles, broken when deposited in grave.
J: Bronze needle, eye end broken in antiquity.
K: Square bronze brooch with red enamel inlay.
L: Blue melon bead.
M: Bronze coin of Nero worn smooth, hole pierced in it.
N: Dog or boar tooth with hole drilled through.
O: Green glass bead.
P: Glass bead.

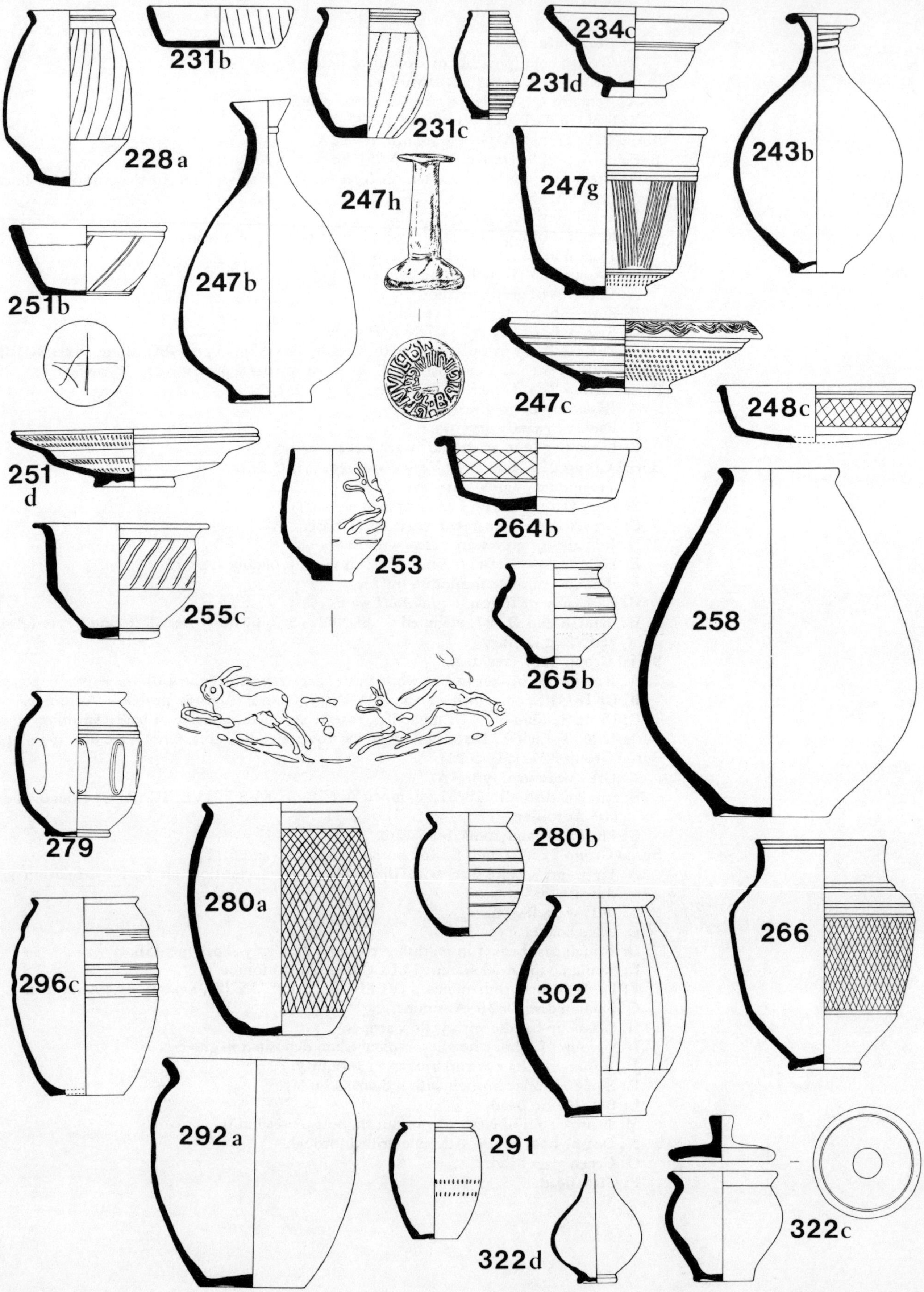

Fig. 5.26 Burials. Nos. 228, 231, 234, 243, 247, 248, 251, 254, 255, 258, 264, 265, 266, 279, 280, 291, 292, 296, 302, 322. (228, 1/8. Remainder 1/4.)

Q: Blue "eye" bead with spiral white decoration, c.f. *Arch* 90, 165.
R: Large amber bead.
(L–R probably formed part of a lucky charm bracelet).
S: Bronze ring.
T: Bronze pin with ornamental head.
U: Bronze brooch.
V and W: Bronze barnacle pendants.
X: Bone toilet instrument.
Y: Carved bone toggle.
Z: Iron bracket.

Burial Group 229. Trench E. Below 163 and to one side, possibly a family connection; disturbed by burial above.
A: Grey ware urn, type 14N.
B: Poppy-head beaker, type 26B; grey ware, black slip.
C: Grey ware dish with sagging base; black exterior, type 134C. Tooled decoration on base.
D: Grey ware dish with sagging base, variant of 134C, cross inside base.
E: Buff ware flagon, type 138F.

Burial 230. Trench E. Disturbed. Grey ware urn, type 1A.

Burial Group 231. Trench E. ? Box burial, arranged in rectangle. (Fig. 5.26).
A: Grey ware urn, tally mark /// on shoulder, type 1A.
B: Small dish in grey ware.
C: Small jar in grey ware.
D: Small beaker in fine grey ware, black slip coating.
E: Samian cup Dr 33 stamped ADVOCISI OF. Lezoux, late Antonine.

Burial 232. Trench E. Fragmentary. Remains of grey ware urn, probably type 1A.

Burial Group 233. Trench E.
A: Large grey ware urn, type 18A.
B: Flagon in buff ware, type 25F.

Burial Group 234. Trench E. Box burial with sandals. (Fig. 5.26).
A: Grey ware urn, type 1A.
B: Grey ware carinated bowl, variant of type 204A; chevron pattern on body.
C: Imitation Dr 27 cup in buff ware, very well made, variant of 24C.
D: Beaker in creamy buff ware; dark metallic grey slip, type 133C, but not rough cast.
E: Buff ware flagon, type 14B.
F: Hob nails from a pair of boots.
Bones from funeral meal scattered around pots.

Burials from Area 4.

Burial Group 235. Trench E.
A: Grey ware urn containing bones, type 14A, tally mark on shoulder.
B: Pear-shaped vessel in fine light grey paste with darker slip. (see also 250A).
C: Small grey ware vessel.
D: Samian dish, Dr 31, stamp illegible, probably early Antonine.
E: Flagon in sandy buff ware with narrow base and double ring lip; variant of type 150B.
The vessels were arranged in a semi-circle, with the samian dish opposite. Food bones were strewn between the vessels, with some in the samian dish.

Burial Group 236. Trench E.
A: Grey ware urn containing bones; type 1A.
B: Bottle in buff ware, neck missing; carination low down on body; variant of type 149F, but in a different paste.

Burial 237. Trench G; truncated by modern pit.
Single urn burial; remains of flat based vessel in reddish ware, with lattice decoration on body. Possibly type 23A.

Burial Group 238. Trench G.
A: Grey ware urn, type 14N.
B: Carinated bowl in grey ware, type 202B, variant.
C: Flagon in cream ware, handle and neck broken in antiquity, probably type 136B.

Burial 239. Trench G.
Single grey ware urn, type 1A.

Burial Group 240. Trench G; fragmentary.

A: Base of grey ware vessel containing bones.

B: Base of grey ware beaker.

Burial 241. Trench G; fragmentary.

Remains of pear-shaped vessel with bones. Variant of type 18A.

Burial Group 242. Trench G; disturbed.

A: Base of grey ware vessel containing bones.

B: Samian dish Dr 36, 1st century, probably Flavian.

C: Buff ware flagon, neck and handle missing in antiquity, variant of type 173C.

Burial Group 243. Trench G. (Fig. 5.26).

A: Grey ware urn, type 14N.

B: Bottle in pink ware, lip broken in antiquity.

Burial 244. Trench G; (child burial).

Small grey ware beaker containing cremated bones; type 14N.

Burial Group 245. Trench G.

A: A very large grey ware urn, type 1A.

B: Carinated bowl in grey ware, type 91C.

C: Flagon in buff ware, type 138F.

D: Samian cup Dr 33, stamped ALBINVS (Antonine).

E: Samian cup Dr 33, stamped FELIX . F, almost certainly Antonine.

Burial 246. Trench G; box burial.

The burial was arranged in a semi-circle with five nails arranged around the edge. The urn containing bones was set off to one side. Some cremated bones were heaped over flagon D, and bones and charcoal were scattered within the central area. On the east side, within a few inches of flagon H was a mass of charcoal in a small posthole which may have been the charred base of a marker post.

A: Poppy-head urn in sandy grey ware containing bones, and decorated with panels of applied dots *en barbotine*; type 21A.

B: Grey ware lid, inverted in grave; waster. Type 202D.

C: Carinated dish in brown sandy ware, type 194G.

D: Flagon with conical neck, handle broken in antiquity, in sandy grey ware; variant of type 59C without body decoration and tooling on neck.

E: Grey ware bowl, cross inside and outside of base; variant of type 26C.

F: Shallow dish in grey ware with cross tooled on base; variant of type 130C.

G: Very small pear-shaped vessel 5.7 cms (2.25 ins) high, type 18A.

H: Flagon in buff ware, variant of type 138F.

I: A circular object laid with the edge partly across the rim of B. It measured 29.2 cms (11.5 ins) in diameter and was little more than a reddish stain in the clay. The feature was slightly thicker in section at the edges and appeared to be made of a crumbly brown material resembling shale. It may have been a platter or trencher. Some of the nails around the burial showed impressions of the wood from the box in the corrosion products.

Burial Group 247. Trench G; box burial. (Fig. 5.26).

A: Grey ware urn, type 228A.

B: Bottle in fine buff ware, laid on its side.

C: Lead glazed dish in reddish paste, potters mark on base. (See Fig. 5.26 and p. 79).

D: Poppy-head beaker in fine grey paste, white slip and applied dots; variant of type 26B.

E: Grey ware carinated bowl, type 202B.

F: Samian dish, Dr 42 with handles, late 1st century, South Gaullish.

G: Green glazed bowl similar paste to C; variant of type 81F, but larger and in different paste and glaze. (See Fig. 5.26 and p. 79).

H: Glass unguent flask, 9.2 cms (3.6 ins) high with base 5.7 cms (2.25 ins) diameter with letters moulded on base. The lettering, moulded in recess, reads: (outer circle) BR [...] NGFNVIL; (inner circle, anti-clockwise) BRIGINI INGENVL. (Product) of Briginius Ingenuil (lus). The 'E' is moulded as an 'F'.

Burial Group 248. Trench G; (?)box burial. (Fig. 5.26).

A: Small urn in sandy grey ware, type 14N.

B: Buff bottle with grey core, neck broken in antiquity, probably variant of type 76B.

C: Grey ware dish burnished inside and out. This vessel was inverted.

Burial 249. Trench G.
Single cremation urn, type 14N.

Burial Group 250. Trench G; box burial.
A: Urn containing bones in identical paste and colour coat to 235B, type 217F.
B: Grey ware dish, type 207G, variant.
C: Flagon in pale buff ware, handle broken in antiquity, type 129B.
D: Glass unguent bottle, type 26I. This had the neck broken off and had been inverted into the mouth of C as a stopper.
E: Grey ware dish type 231B.
F: Samian dish, Dr 31 stamped P A T E R N I, (Antonine). Two marks, X – X had been cut on opposite sides of the footring, presumably the owner's mark.
G: Samian dish, Dr 35 (2nd century).
H: Samian Dr 33 cup stamped B R I C C V S F, (Antonine).
I: A set of 25 or 26 bone gaming counters. These were scattered in and around B, G and H and the exact number could not be determined due to the extreme friability of the bone. (See Fig. 5.15 and p. 83).
J: Small rough cast colour coated beaker, buff paste, dark brown slip, type 43B.
K: Lead disc 4.1 cms (1.6 ins) in diameter and 0.5 cm (0.2 ins) thick, below F.
L: Pottery lamp in reddish buff ware, soot on spout, type 148G. This was placed in E.
M: Part of a small sandstone rubber, broken in antiquity.
N: Two bone dice, very friable, in B.
O: Small flat pebble under E.
P: Glass disc, 5.1 cms (2 ins) in diameter, shaped from the side of a green glass bottle.

Burial Group 251. Trench G; box burial. (Fig. 5.26).
A: Large grey ware urn, type 14A, containing cremated bones and a bronze coin of Faustina the Elder.
B and C: Two flat based dishes in sandy grey ware, variants of type 26J, but with diagonal tooled decoration, cross inside base and potters mark on bottom.

D: Shallow dish in fine grey paste and dark grey slip (see 235B). This was below I and contained food bones.
E: Poppy-head beaker, type 26B.
F: Bottle in buff sandy ware, variant of type 182B.
G: Small buff flagon, variant of type 14J.
H: Samian dish, Dr 36 (Hadrianic).
I: Samian dish, Dr 27, stamped REGINI . M . (Antonine).
J and K: Two bronze pendants (leather strap ends), (Fig. 5.18).
L: Bronze knife, (Fig. 5.18).
M: Cylinder of bronze, slit down one side, probably part of case of L. (Fig. 5.18).
N: Bronze object with stud fitting for leather.
O: Part of a thin sheet of bronze with serrated decoration, possibly part of a lid for a receptacle.
P: Bronze buckle and a number of rectantular bronze fittings for a leather belt, (See Fig. 5.18). The bronze fittings, pendants and the knife were laid over and around I.
Q: Bronze tube 'D' shaped in section, soldered to knuckle joint, function unknown. (Fig. 5.18).
R: Lead lamp holder, type 1961.

Burial Group 252. Trench G; fragmentary.
A group of four vessels, probably in a box.
A: Remains of a vessel in grey ware, probably type 1A.
B: Shallow grey ware dish, variant of type 97B.
C: Flagon, neck broken in antiquity, grey core, buff exterior, traces of pink colour coat. Type 138F.
D: Urn containing bones, below C. Type 30A.

Burial 253. Trench G. (Fig. 5.26).
A Caistor ware beaker with applied decoration (dog and hare). This vessel had a scatter of cremated bones under and around it. Possibly a child burial.

Burial 254. Trench G; disturbed.
A grey ware vessel, bottom part only, probably type 1A.

Burial Group 255. Trench G, very disturbed.

A: Remains of grey ware vessel.

B: Grey ware jar, variant of type 18A.

Burial 256. Trench G; very disturbed.

Remains of necked jar, sandy grey fabric, black exterior.

Burial 257. Trench G.

Single grey ware urn, type 30A.

Burial 258. Trench G.

A single grey ware urn containing bones.

Burial 259. Trench G, fragmentary.

Remains of grey ware vessel with cremated bones. Probably type 1A.

Burial Group 260. Trench G.

A: Urn in sandy grey ware, type 1A.

B: Shallow vessel in gritty buff ware with pinched lip, probably an oil pourer, type 127K.

C: Imitation Dr 27 cup in pink/buff ware, type 24E, but with footring like 24C.

D: Shallow plate in buff ware with light grey core, variant of type 24F.

E: Flagon with grey core and pink/buff exterior, variant of type 138F.

Burial Group 261. Trench G.

A: Urn, type 14N.

B: Grey ware beaker, type 180C with graffito scratched on side after firing.

Burial Group 262. Trench G.

A: Grey ware urn, type 14A.

B: Flagon in cream ware, handle broken in antiquity; dark pink colour coating on exterior. Variant of type 138F.

Burial 263. Trench G.

Single sandy/grey ware urn, variant of type 14N but with a slight neck to the vessel.

Burial Group 264. Trench G. Box burial. (Fig. 5.26).

A: Fragments of grey ware urn, type 30A.

B and C: Straight-walled carinated bowls with lattice decoration inside wall. In brown sandy ware, black exterior.

D: Carinated dish in sandy ware, type 71D.

E: Carinated bowl in grey ware, variant of type 25E.

F: Samian dish Dr 31, stamp not legible (Antonine).

G: Bottle in creamy ware, neck missing. Variant of type 247B.

Burial Group 265. Trench G. (Fig. 5.26).

A: Small urn in sandy grey ware containing bones. Type 30A; tally marks on base.

B: Small vessel in sandy brown ware, black exterior.

Burial 266. Trench G. (Fig. 5.26).

A single urn in fine grey paste and dark grey colour coat, identical fabric to 235 B.

Burial Group 267. Trench G. ? box burial.

A: Fragments of thin-walled urn in brown sandy ware. Probably type 23A.

B: Flagon, inverted in grave beside urn. In fine grey paste with pink/buff exterior; variant of type 138F.

C, D and E: Plates in soft pink/buff ware with grey core, variants of type 24F.

F: Cup with frilled rim in pink/buff ware, type 14G.

G: Oil pourer in buff ware, type 127K.

H: Buff ware flagon, type 14C, variant, inverted in grave.

I: Buff ware imitation Dr 27 cup, variant of type 24E.

J: Small pottery lamp, soot on spout. In buff ware with metallic dark grey slip. Type 148G.

K: Hob nails from a pair of boots laid alongside vessels.

Burial Group 268. Trench G. Box burial.

A: Remains of thin-walled vessel in sandy ware, containing bones, probably type 23A.

B: Flagon in buff ware, type 25F variant.

C: Bowl in hard whitish grey ware.

D, E and F: Bowls in similar form to C, but in sandy ware. These four bowls are variants of 207C but are larger.

G and H: Carinated bowls in grey ware, variants of type 217B.

The remains of the funerary meal were scattered over the vessels.

Burial Group 269. Trench G.

A: Large grey ware urn, type 1A, with cremated bones inside.

B: Flagon, type 199P, in brown sandy ware, lip broken in antiquity. This vessel was inside A.

C: Boot studs below A.

Burial Group 270. Trench G.

A: Flagon in buff ware with grey core, type 138F.

B: Small beaker in fine grey ware, type 217F.

C: Dr 18/31 samian dish, stamp illegible. Hadrian/Antonine. Very badly worn and with a graffito scratched on the inside wall in the shape of a crude five-pointed star.

D: Dr 18/31 samian dish stamped L I B E R A L I S, late Antonine.

E: Dr 33 samian cup stamped S A C I R O, M., late Antonine.

F: Iron lamp holder.

No cinerary urn with this burial. Traces of boot studs under vessels.

Burial 271. Trench G.

Inhumation lying with head to the South, arms folded upwards across breast with hands at shoulders. A bronze ring, very corroded was found amongst finger bones near right shoulder. The bones were very friable, being little better than stains in the clay. This burial was alongside Group 269 and must be earlier.

Burial 272. Trench H.

A single pear-shaped vessel in sandy grey ware; variant of type 18A.

Burial 273. Trench H.

Single grey ware urn, variant of type 1A.

Burial 274. Trench H.

Remains of a single urn burial, probably type 1A.

Burial 275. Trench H.

Very disturbed single urn cremation.

Burial 276. Trench H.

Disturbed single vessel in grey ware, probably type 5A.

Burial 277. Trench H.

Truncated single urn burial, type uncertain.

Burial 278. Trench H.

Very disturbed single urn burial, type uncertain.

Burial 279. Trench H. (Fig. 5.26).

Very disturbed burial which included one almost complete folded beaker in fine brown paste with black slip coating.

Burial 280. Trench H. Box burial. (Fig. 5.26).

A: Thin-walled vessel in fine white/grey fabric with dark grey colour coat, identical in fabric to 235B.

B: Small grey ware beaker with traces of white slip coating. This was lying on its side.

C: "Rough-cast" beaker in thin reddish ware with dark grey exterior and red/brown interior. Variant of type 43B.

D: Flagon in buff ware, type 129B, lying on its side.

Burial 281. Trench J.

Disturbed remains of a single cremation urn, type 1A.

Burial 282. Trench J.

Part of a cyst constructed of thin slabs of sandstone. The cyst had no lid and was cut away on the north side approximately halfway along its length. A few sherds of coarse ware were associated with it together with the neck of a flagon in hard white ware. The average thickness of the sandstone slabs was 5.1 cms (2 ins). It was 55.9 cms (1 ft 10 ins) wide inside, and the estimated length inside would have been 8.13 cms (2 ft 8 ins). Part of a central division wall was still in position.

Burial 283. Trench J.

Fragments of a single urn burial disturbed by a modern pit.

Burial 284. Trench J.

Remains of grey ware vessel with cremated bones.

Burial 285. Trench J.

Disturbed single vessel cremation burial.

Burial Group 286. Trench J. (Fig.).

A: Necked grey ware jar, variant of type 12A.

B: Small beaker in brown sandy fabric, neck missing.

C: Samian dish, Dr 36, probably Hadrian/Antonine.

D: Small lead lamp holder, type 198I. Interior dimensions 4.5 cms (1¾ ins) long by 1.8 cms (15/16 in) wide.

Burial 287. Trench J.

Fragments of a grey ware carinated vessel with a flat base, with a band with two lines of combed decoration on the shoulder. Below the shoulder were oblique lines of tooled decorations. Variant of type 18A.

Burial 289. Trench J.

Remains of a vessel in sandy reddish fabric associated with boot studs and part of a quern.

Burial 290. Trench J; badly damaged by modern pipe trench.

One complete small jar in sandy grey ware, a variant of type 265B. This had a small hole drilled through the side after firing. It was associated with a number of cremated bone fragments and a few sherds of grey ware.

Burial 291. Trench J. (Fig. 5.26).

A small grey ware beaker with a dark grey colour coat. This was associated with a mass of charcoal and cremated bones and the fragments of a small glass vessel which had been subjected to considerable heat.

Burial 292. Trench K. (Fig. 5.26).

Wide-mouthed flat-based vessel with thin walls and in a sandy brown fabric.

Burial 293. Trench K.

Badly disturbed. The vessel containing the bones was in a white paste and the shape of the lower half and the two pieces of rim which were present suggests that it was a wide-mouthed flagon similar to type 111A.

Burial 294. Trench K. Disturbed grey ware urn, type 1A.

Burial 295. Trench K.

Single urn burial; variant of type 17A, but in fine grey ware.

Burial 296. Trench K; box burial. (Fig. 5.26).

A: Plate, variant of type 9E.

B: Imitation Dr 27 in buff ware, type 148C.

C: Beaker in fine grey fabric with dark metallic exterior slip.

Burial 297. Trench K.

Single grey ware vessel, type 5A.

Burial 298. Trench K. Very disturbed.

Remains of grey ware vessel, possibly type 1A.

Burial 299. Trench K.

Badly disturbed urn, type 1A.

Burial Group 300. Trench K.

A: Grey ware urn, type 5A.

B: Base of flagon in cream ware.

Burial 301. Trench K.

Single grey ware urn, type 1A.

Burial Group 302. Trench K. Disturbed box burial. (Fig. 5.26).

A: Large beaker, similar in form to 25K but in reddish sandy fabric and with vertical tooled decoration on body.

B: Remains of a double ring lipped flagon in crumbly reddish fabric.

C: Fragments of a colour coated vessel in soft brown fabric, form unidentifiable.

D: Bone spoon.

E and F: Bronze penannular brooches.

G and H: Remains of two fibulae, very corroded, the coiled springs only surviving.

Burial 303. Trench K.

Disturbed remains of grey ware vessel with cremated bones.

Burial Group 304. Trench K.

A: Small urn, type 1A.

B: Flagon, grey fabric, buff exterior; variant of type 24D.

C: Small flat-bottomed beaker in thin reddish fabric with traces of dark exterior slip coating, variant of type 97E.

Burial 305. Trench K.

Single small urn lying on side. Sandy, soft reddish brown fabric, flint gritted. The form is a variant of type 35D but without the exterior tooled decoration.

Burial Group 306. Trench L.

A: Grey ware, urn, type 1A.

B: Small grey ware "poppy-head" beaker type 26B.

Burial 307. Trench L.

Fragments of vessel in sandy ware associated with cremated bones.

Burial 308. Trench L.

Remains of single urn burial containing cremated bones.

In sandy ware, possibly type 18A.

Burial 309. Trench L.

Very large grey ware urn, 35.5 cms (14 ins) high, girth 34.3 cms (13.5 ins), and 22.2 cms (8.75 ins) across the mouth; type 14N. The top was covered by a pottery lid, type 202D.

Burial 310. Trench L.

Single grey ware urn, type 14N.

Burial Group 311. Trench L. Disturbed.

A: Grey ware vessel, probably type 91A.

B: Small beaker in soft gritty brown ware. Type 280A, but in different fabric.

Burial 312. Trench K.

Truncated remains of vessel in soft thin brown ware, containing cremated bones.

Burial Group 313. Trench L. Disturbed.

A: Remains of grey ware vessel, possibly type 1A.

B: Platter in brown sandy fabric, type 110C.

C: Beaker in fine grey ware and dark metallic exterior slip coating, lattice decoration on body, type 217F.

Burial 314. Trench L.

Single grey ware urn, variant of type 25A.

Burial 315. Trench L. Very disturbed.

Base of grey ware vessel with cremated bones. Type uncertain, possibly 1A.

Burial 316. Trench L; disturbed.

Base of grey ware vessel, type 1A.

Burial 317. Trench L. Very disturbed.

Remains of urn with cremated bones, in grey sandy ware.

Burial 318. Trench L; disturbed.

Remains of single jar in brown sandy ware.

Burial 319. Trench L.

Single vessel in soft gritty black fabric; variant of type 24A, the rim being slightly more upstanding.

Burial 320. Trench L.

Single vessel in dark grey sandy fabric; variant of type 15A in form but without lattice decoration.

Burial 321. Trench L.

Single grey ware vessel, variant of type 9G.

Burial Group 322. Trench L. (Fig. 5.26). This was an infant burial, consisting of four vessels.

A: Ovoid beaker in grey ware, type 302A but without decoration.

B: Child's feeding bottle in grey ware, variant of No. 124 in Butler Collection (Fig. 5.21).

C: Small vessel 7.6 cms (3 ins) high containing the cremated remains of an infant, and sealed with a pottery lid.

D: Small bottle in fine sandy fabric, neck broken in antiquity.

Burial Group 323. Trench M. (See Discussion on p. 72).

This group consisted of 3 vessels, and had been much disturbed by tree roots.

A: A squat biconical vessel, type 1B. Placed above this vessel were two imbrices arranged so as to form a pipe. The top of the imbrices had been broken away during subsequent disturbance of the ground, but there is little doubt that the assembly was intended to form a channel down which libations could be poured.

B: Fragmentary buff flagon with traces of a brown colour coat. It had a double ringed lip and was probably type 14E.

C: Small beaker with everted rim in thin buff ware and a brown colour coating on exterior.

Burial 324. Trench N. (This was the most northerly burial found).

A: Grey ware urn, type 1A.

B: Shallow dish in buff fabric, variant of type 110B, and used as a lid for the cinerary urn.

Burial 325. Trench R.

The badly disturbed remains of a grey ware flagon with flat base and three grooves around the body. Only one small section of rim remained and two small pieces of handle, but not enough to attempt a reconstruction. Near the remains of this vessel were fragments of human leg bones together with a number of boot studs, and these items considered together probably represent the remains of an inhumation with a flagon placed near the feet.

Burial 326. Trench R.

Inhumation, probably a woman, aligned with head to the south west. The bones were in a very friable state, except where they had been in contact with the bronze bangles. The feet were missing, but there was a bronze bangle on the right ankle. The skeleton was fully extended with the arms folded upwards so that the finger tips rested on the shoulders. There was a bracelet of twisted bronze wire on the right forearm and a flat bronze bangle on the left forearm, both in a very corroded state. No coffin nails were seen, and it was noted that the head and shoulders of the skeleton were resting on a layer containing burnt clay and carbon, some of which had also been backfilled into the grave.

Measurements:	From top of skull to top of pelvis	– 73.6 cms
	From top of skull to knees	– 122 cms.
	From top of skull to furthest extremity of remaining bones	– 152 cms.

No coin was found with the burial, but it is unlikely that it could be earlier than mid 3rd century and may well be later.

A Report on the Skeletons found in the Cemetery

Appendix B
by Helena Ginns
M.B.S, L.R.C.P, M.R.C.S.

Burial 72

Consists of fragmented bones though in relatively good condition. This is probably a middle aged male; the bones are heavy, one intact femur being large with well marked muscle attachments. One almost complete innominate bone is heavy with an acute angled greater sciatic notch. The ischial spine is angled inwards.

The skull is heavy with well marked supra orbital ridges. The lower jaw is square. All the teeth are present including third molars in both upper and lower jaw. They are in good condition though very worn down. There are no particular signs of any pathological process. Height was probably about 5 feet 10 inches.

Long bones – right femur (intact).

Length from greater trochanter to lateral condyle, 44.5 cms.

Length from proximal head to medial condyle, 47.6 cms.

Left femur (broken), approximately same length as right. Right tibia (broken, but all pieces present).

Length from lateral condyle to lateral malleolus, 35 cms.

Left tibia, broken. Fibulae, broken. Right humerus almost intact. Length from head to medial epicondyle, 33 cms. Left humerus, almost intact. Length from head to medial epicondyle, 33 cms. Right radius, broken but pieces present; head to styloid process, 24.5 cms.

Right ulna, broken but pieces present. Olecranon process to styloid process, 27 cms. Left radius, broken, pieces present, head to styloid process, 24.5 cms. Left ulna, broken, pieces present, Olecranon process to styloid process, 27 cms. Left clavicle, end to end, 15 cms.

Skull: Bi-parietal diameter, 11.5 cms. Frontal distance just above supra orbital ridges, 9 cms. Lower jaw, distance from angle to mid point, 10 cms. Angle to head, 6.5 cms. Other bones including vertebrae ribs and skull bones present, but not measurable.

Burial 80.

This skeleton is probably male and old. There are marked osteo-arthritic changes of the spine, lipping and osteophytes. It is possible that the left hip had been diseased during life. Some measurements were made on the few bones whole enough to allow it:

Left Radius (intact); Length from head to styloid process, 19.2 cms. Right Femur (broken); Length from fovea to adductor tubercle, 34.3 cms. Length from greater trochanter to lateral condyle, 36 cms.

Left Humerus (head broken); Length from anatomical neck to medial epicondyle, 23 cms.

Right clavicle, (viewed from above); greatest length 11 cms.

Skull: Length from mental tubercle to the angle, 8 cms. Length from the middle of head of mandible to coronoid process, 3.5 cms. Length from tip of styloid process to middle of mastoid process, 5.5 cms.

Teeth: Right lower jaw — 1 incisor, 1 canine, 2 pre-molars, 1 molar. Left lower jar (very disintegrated), 1 incisor, 1 canine, 1 pre-molar only. Upper jaw (left side disintegrated). Only 7 teeth which included 1st right molar.

The right lower jaw shows resorption of bone over the area of missing molars and premolars. They probably therefore were lost some years before death. All the teeth were well worn down but showed no signs of caries.

Burial 157.

The skeleton was badly fragmented; the right ulna and radius and most of the small bones of the hands and feet were missing. Taking into account the eruption and state of the teeth, the comparative shortness and slenderness of the long bones, and the supra-orbital ridges, which are not pronounced, it seems likely that the bones belonged to a middle aged adult, possibly female. Some measurements:

Right Humerus; anatomical neck to medial epicondyle, 25 cms. Left Ulna: tip of styloid process to top of insertion of triceps, 22.5 cms. Right femur; (2 pieces), lesser trochanter to adductor tubercle; 30.5 cms. Right Tibia (2 pieces) Groove on medial condyle to tip of medial malleolus, 29.5 cms. Right clavicle; tip of sternal end to tip of acromial end, 12.5 cms.

Skull: Right to left mastoid processes, 8.4 cms. Junction of sagittal and coronal sutures to junction of sagittal and lamboid sutures, 11.2 cms. Anterior part not present, including upper jaw. Lower jaw (3 pieces). Teeth: Right , 1 molar with large cavity, 2 pre-molars, 1 canine, 1 incisor. Left: 2 molars, 2 pre-molars, 1 canine. The teeth are well worn, but with the exception of the right molar there are no cavities.

Burial 158.

The skeleton consists of fragmented bones, but many are complete and well conserved. It is probably female, young to middle aged. The bones are light and small. One almost complete to innominate bone shows a wide angled greater sciatic notch and sub-pubic angle. The brim is wide and heart shaped and the ala are flat. The ischial spine is not prominent.

A small part of the mandible remains and the ramus slopes markedly back from angle to head, and is very shallow. The few remaining teeth show marked caries. There is very little wear on the grinding surfaces. There appears to be no particular pathological process. Her height was probably just over 5 feet. Measurements:

Right humerus: proximal head to medial trochlear surface, 28.6 cms. Right femur: a) Head to medial condyle 40.6 cms. b) Greater trochanter to lateral condyle, 38.1 cms. Left femur: as right. Right tibia: medial condyle to medial malleolus, 33 cms. Left radius: head to styloid process, 21 cms. Left ulna: Olecranon to styloid process, 22.9 cms. Clavicles: end to end, 12.7 cms. Mandible: angle to condyle, 5.1 cms. Teeth: Lower jaw, no 3rd molars, 2 (left) pre-molars missing, 2 central incisors missing. One pre-molar of upper jaw only present.

Burial 185.

Generally the bones are quite heavy with well-marked muscle attachment notches, supra-orbital ridges and a "square jaw". This, together with the state of the dentition makes it likely that this skeleton is that of a middle aged male, and the general impression is one of average height. The skeleton was fragmented and extremely friable when found. Teeth: left upper jaw: 3 molars and 2 pre-molars (canine and incisors missing on first inspection). Lower jaw: 2 molars and 2 incisors. Right upper jaw: 1 molar, 1 pre-molar, 1 canine, 1 incisor. Lower jaw: 3 molars, 2 pre-molars, 1 canine, 2 incisors. The teeth are all well worn, but no caries present. Left upper incisor and canine found well inside jaw with several phalanges.

Grave 193

Consists of fragmented bones, very few whole and rather decayed. It is probably a male, middle to old age. The bones are heavy with well marked muscle attachments and sharp-angled greater sciatic notches on the pelvis. The vertebrae particularly show signs of osteo-arthritis with lipping. There is a suggestion of an old healed fracture on the mid shaft of the right radius and possibly of the ulna also. The bone is angled at this point and somewhat thickened.

Just over a half mandible is present with other odd fragments, and this shows all the teeth present including a 3rd molar. One incisor is missing on the other half, probably post mortem. The teeth are not in good condition, there is no caries, but most are worn through on their grinding surfaces to the dentine. The enamel is almost completely gone. Some calculus formation (tartar) is present. The skull is very fragmented, and very few bones can be measured.

Right femus: 44.5 cms. Right humerus: head to mid trochlear surface, 31.75 cms. Right radius: head to styloid, 23.5 cms. Skull: lower jaw, angle to head, 7.6 cms. Teeth: lower jaw, left: incisor, left 2nd molar missing, 3rd molars present. Upper jaw: 9 teeth, probably canines, pre-molars and some incisors.

The Animal Bones from Area 1

Appendix C
by Alan Outen

Bones in Palisade Trench (Fig. 5.8).

Cervical vertebrae – 4. Thoracic vertebrae – 15 fragments. Rib – 204 fragments.

The absence of bones showing diagnostic features makes a positive determination impossible. Tentatively the bones can be attributed to immature ox. The 4 cervical vertebrae are in anatomical sequence as also are some of the thoracic vertebrae. The state of growth of all the vertebrae show the same condition, so it is possible, but not certain, that not more than one individual is present. Some of the thoracic vertebrae fragments show chop marks, indicating that the bones are food waste.

Bones from the military ditch. (Trench D, Fig. 5.7; Section A – A).

Ribs – 10 fragments. Caudal vertebrae – 1. Cervical vertebrae – 8 fragments, 1 with chop marks.

Humerus – 3 distal epiphyses and 1 fragment, all with chop marks, from an ox; 4 fragments of proximal epiphyses with chop/cut marks; 1 fragment shows knife cuts.

Femur – 3 fragments of distal epiphyses; 2 have chop marks. 1 fragment of proximal epiphyses and 1 fragment of shaft with cut marks.

Tibia – 3 fragments of distal epiphyses, 2 from right side and with chop/cut marks. 2 fragments of proximal epiphyses.

Radius – 4 shaft fragments, 1 with part of distal epiphyses; 2 of these are from an aged ox.

Calcaneum – 3 fragments, each from different individuals.

Skull – 1 small fragment.

Scapula – 1 small fragment.

Indeterminable – 32 fragments of long bone shaft, 25 with chop or cut marks.

All the bones described above can be tentatively ascribed to ox. At least 5 individuals are present. From the bones examined, 2 are immature, 2 are mature and 1 is aged.

Bones from Pit on west side of military ditch. (Trench D. Fig. 5.7; Section A – A).

66 fragments of animal bones, all tentatively ascribed to ox were examined. These showed the same features as those from the military ditch; all had chop or cut marks and one had been fashioned into a pointed implement, possibly to scrape marrow from the bones.

Discussion

The most striking aspect of the bones examined is the absence of many of the body bones. The main parts of the body which are not represented are pelvis, skull (with the exception of 1 small fragment), scapula (with the exception of 1 small fragment), cannon bone and teeth. One would normally expect these bones to be represented and their absence suggests that the animals were not slaughtered on the spot but brought to the site as joints, i.e. neck, rib cage and limbs. This would account for the bulk of the bones. Others, such such as the skull and scapula fragments, caudal vertebrae, and calcaneum could have been attached to the joints as a result of bad or unskilled butchery. Most of the limb bone shafts have been split, presumably for their marrow content. Several fragments have a smoothed interior which suggests they had been scraped.

Food bones from Type 2 burials,

Burial Group 93, avian bones in imitation Dr 27 cups.

In cup 93C (p. 100).

Femur (right side), distal epiphyses with fragment of shaft, total length 44 mm. Humerus (right side), proximal epiphyses with fragment of shaft, Total length 45 mm. Tibia (right side) – complete, length 84 mm. Fibula (right side), proximal epiphyses with fragment of shaft, total length 24 mm.

Scapula (right side), nearly complete, length 64 mm, this bone had4 cut marks (knife)

Furculum (wishbone), fragment; length 44 mm, with one knife cut mark.

(?)Ischium – irregular fragment approximately 19 mm x 13 mm.

Ribs – 3 fragments. Lengths are: 21 mm, 19 mm, 16 mm.

The femur and tibia articulate. This evidence, together with the proportions of the humerus and scapula suggests there need not be more than one individual present. The long bones indicate an adult bird with a body size slightly smaller than a pheasant. The cut marks on the scapula and furculum indicate that a knife has been used on these two bones at least. It could be that the flesh was consumed and only the bones or fragments deposited with the burial.

In cup 93D.

Femur (right and left) – 2 complete, each 39 mm in length.

Humerus (right and left) – 2, each complete, of proximal epiphyses only. Metatarsus (right and left) 2 distal epiphyses with fragments of shaft. Total length of right, 32 mm, of left, 34 mm. Metacarpus (right and left). The left is complete, 32 mm in length. The right has a fragment of shaft with proximal epiphyses, total length 18 mm. Ulna (right and left) – 2; the left is complete but in 2 fragments. Proximal fragment is 42 mm in length, distal fragment is 19 mm in length. The right ulna has shaft fragment with proximal epiphyses, total length 33 mm, plus a shaft fragment 14 mm in length.

Tibia (right side), proximal epiphyses with fragment of shaft, total length 43 mm.

Radius (right side) – 2 fragments. One fragment of shaft with distal epiphyses is 19 mm total length. The other fragment of shaft only is 15 mm long. (?)Ischium – 1 fragment, length 28 mm. Rib – 1 fragment, 24 mm long.

Only 1 individual is present; the long bones indicate an adult gull. Size consideration suggests a Black Headed Gull.

Burial Group 199, dish contents.

Radius – shaft only (71 mm), no epiphyses, immature. Ulna – fragment with proximal epiphyses, appears to articulate with radius listed above. Pelvis – 1 fragment of *Os Innomatum.* Tarsus – 4 tarsal bones. Calcaneum (right side), 1 incomplete. Skull, 5 small fragments. Teeth – all deciduous; at least 2 are from the upper jaw and 1 from the mandible.

Only 1 individual is present. The bones and teeth are from an immature sheep or goat. All the teeth are deciduous (milk teeth) and indicate an age of under 2 years. Lack of dental attrition makes it probable that the individual was under 1 year at death.

Burial Group 201, dish contents.

Humerus – 2 small fragments of proximal epiphyses. Femur – 1 small fragment of proximal epiphyses. Tibia – 1 fragment of distal epiphyses. Ulna – 1 fragment of proximal epiphyses. Ribs – 2 fragments. Skull, 1 fragment. Oyster (Ostea Edulis) 1 fragment of shell. Sacral vertebrae — a fragment of ankylosed sacral vertebrae, this is avian.

The animal bones suggest that only 1 individual is present and that it is an adult sheep or goat. It is not possible to determine the species of avian from the fragment available. The size would suggest a bird with the body size of a large duck.

Notes and References

[1] *S.A.C.* **41**, 1 - 3.

[2] *S.A.C.* **80**, 171-192.

[3] *S.A.C.* **72**, 275
Gentlemen's Magazine, 1838, p. 303.

[4] I am greatly indebted to Miss Janet Wallace M.A. who undertook the documentary research.

[5] *V.C.H. Sx.*, 3, 82.

[6] Ed. W. D. Parish *Domesday Book in relation to the County of Sussex*, Sussex Archaeological Society, 1886.

[7] Dallaway, *History of Chichester*, Vol. 1

[8] T.G. Willis, *Records of Chichester*, 1928, quoting an extract from Horsefield's *Sussex*, 1835.

[9] I am grateful to the Diocesan authorities for permission to excavate.

[10] Permission to excavate part of the playing field was readily granted by the City Council.

[11] S.S. Frere, *Britannia*, p 90.

[12] "Excavations at St. Mary's Hospital", this volume, pp. 19-49 "Excavations in the Central Car Park (David Greig site)" forthcoming.

[13] *A J* **45**, i.

[14] This volume, p. 26.

[15] *V.C.H. Sx.* 3, 38.

[16] *S.A.C.* **95**, 125.

[17] "Excavations in the Central Car Park (David Greig site)" forthcoming.
S.A.C. **106**, 115.
This volume, p. 26.

[18] Chichester Paper No. 50, p. 19.
S.A.C. **106**, 117.

[19] *S.A.C.* **80**, 174.

[20] *S.A.C.* **95**, 121.

[21] *V.C.H. Sx* 3, 16.
Gentlemen's Magazine 2, 228-9.

[22] Information from Mrs. M.H. Rule F.S.A.

[23] *S.A.C.* **94**, 104.

[24] *S.A.C.* **94**, 100.

[25] Chichester Paper No. 50, pp 17 - 18.
S.A.C. **106**, 115.

[26] R.E.M. Wheeler, "A Roman pipe burial from Caerlyon, Mon", *A J.* **9**.

[27] *Transactions of Essex Arch. Soc.* (New series), **13**, p 273.
A. J. **IX**, p 3.

[28] V.W. Turner, *Lunda Rites and Ceremonies*, the Rhodes-Livingstone Museum, 1953.

[29] R. Meiggs, *Roman Ostia*, p 464.

[30] I am indebted to Mr. Anthony Clarke F.S.A. who surveyed the area.

[31] I am most grateful to Mr. A.H. Riley the present owner of the vessels who kindly loaned them for the purpose of recording, and to Mr. Stanley Hall the former owner who recovered them from the widow of the workman who found them, and through whose good offices I was able to trace them to Devonshire.

[32] *S.A.C.* **95**, 25.

[33] Identification by Miss Dorothy Charlesworth.

[34] E.M. Jope, "Roman Lead Glazed pottery in Britain", *A.N.L.* 12, No. 11 (1950).

[35] "Excavations in Chapel Street, 1969", forthcoming.

[36] "Roman glazed pottery from Armsley, Godshill, Hants". (forthcoming). I am very grateful to Mr. Musty who kindly sent me a copy of his paper in advance of publication.

[37] B.W. Cunliffe, *Excavations at Fishbourne, 1961-68*, Vol 2, forthcoming.

[38] W.H. Bathurst, *Roman Objects from*
Richborough 1, Pl. XV, No. 32
Richborough 4, Pl. XL, No. 156
Richborough 5, Pl. XXXIX, No. 142
R.E.M. Wheeler, *Lydney Park, Glos, 1932*, Fig 18. No. 45.
R.L.O. **15**, Lauriacum, Fig 13, No. 3.

[39] J.R. Collins, "Excavations at Owlesbury, Hants", *A. J.* **40**, VIII, Part 1, p 27. The author also noted that some burials contained incomplete vessels.

PLATE 6. Polychrome mosaic floor in Cathedral Room I, probably of second century date.

PLATE 7. Fragment of mosaic floor in Cathedral Room 6.

PLATE 8. First century temple dedication found in North Street, 1723.

N)EPTVNO ET MINERVAE
TEMPLVM
PR)O SALVTE DO(MVS) DIVINAE
EX)AVCTORITAT(E T) I CLAVD
CO)GIDVBNI R L(EGAT) AVG IN BRIT
COLLE)GIVM FABROR (ET QV)I IN EO
SVNT)DSD DONANTE AREAM
CLEM)ENTE PVDENTINI FIL

Photographs: *Plates 6 & 7 M. H. Rule.*
Plate 8 Chichester Photographic Service Ltd.

Photo: *M. H. Rule*

PLATE 9. Foundations of Cathedral. Norman side-chapel over-lying early graves and second century mosaic floor in Room I.

Photo: *M. H. Rule*

PLATE 10. Apsidal foundations of Norman side-chapel of Cathedral, cut through tenth century graves and Roman mortar floor.

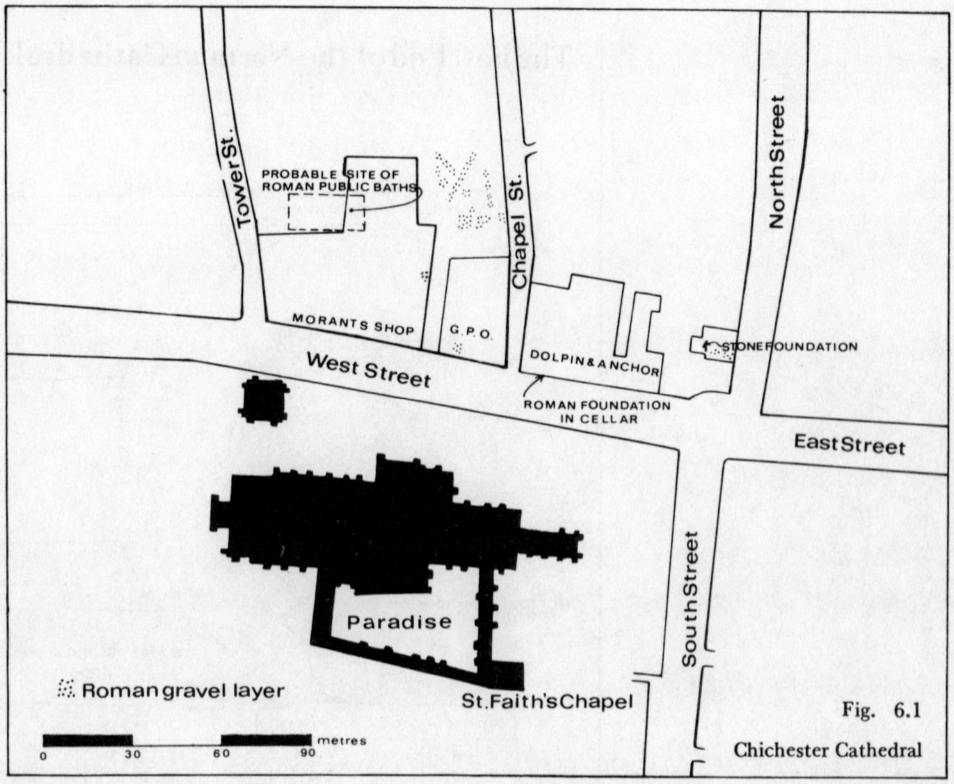

Fig. 6.1

Chichester Cathedral

6
Excavations in Chichester Cathedral

When the decision to girdle the foundations of the buttresses at the east end of the cathedral with reinforced concrete was taken in 1966, it was realised that the necessary excavation would inevitably destroy archaeological evidence of the early history of the site. The Dean and Chapter accordingly invited the Excavation Committee of the Civic Society to sponsor a limited excavation in the north east corner of Paradise (Fig. 6.1) to determine the archaeological potential of the site.

Since the completion of this trial excavation in August 1966, archaeological supervision of work undertaken by the Cathedral Workshop Organisation to underpin the buttress foundations has continued. In July 1968 the area immediately west of buttress 16 was excavated by student volunteers to recover the part plan of a Norman side chapel and examine the underlying Roman structures.

Site History

The earliest cathedral in the diocese was established by St. Wilfrid at Selsey in c. 680 A.D., at a site long since swept away by coastal erosion. The cathedral flourished at Selsey for almost 400 years until 1075, when as part of the Norman re-organisation which followed the Conquest, the see was transferred to Chichester. William of Malmesbury relates that the site chosen for the new cathedral was already occupied by a Saxon nunnery with a church dedicated to St. Peter. As he was writing less than one hundred years after the event, this may be an accurate statement. Certainly part of firstly the nave and later the north transept of the cathedral was used as a parish

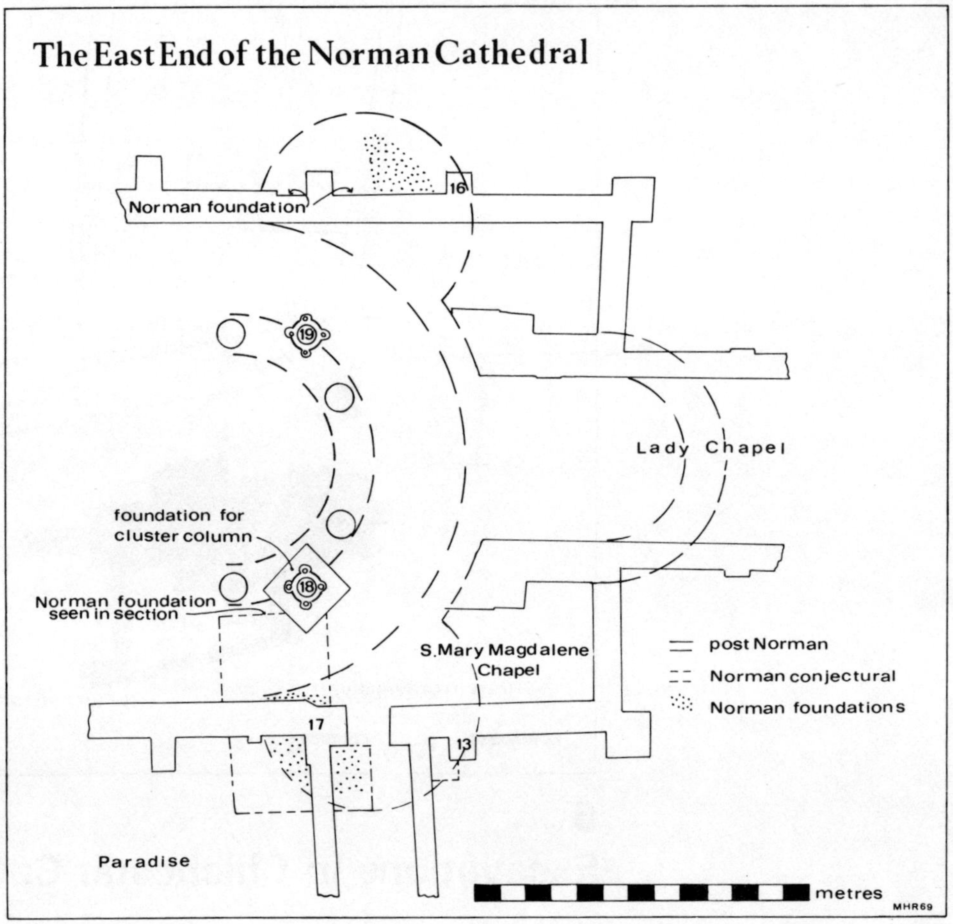

Fig. 6.2

church dedicated to St. Peter up to 1852 when St. Peter's church in West Street was consecrated, and this facility may have been originally granted when the Norman cathedral superseded the Saxon church on the site.

Much of the east end of the cathedral seen today is the result of thirteenth century replanning following the almost total destruction of the roof and superstructure by fire in 1186. It was hoped that the 1966 excavation would determine whether any evidence of the original east end of the cathedral, begun by Bishop Ralph de Luffa in 1091 and consecrated in 1184, still existed, in spite of the continued use of the area as a burial ground since that time.

Site in the Roman Town Plan

Cottrill[1] tentatively identified an extensive area of gravel, discovered on the site of the new post office in West Street in 1934, as the forum. Pottery found in early occupation levels sealed beneath the gravel layer indicated that it had been laid in the second half of the first century. When the telephone exchange was built north of the post office in 1962, it was observed that a gravel layer 2 ft - 3 ft thick continued northwards beyond the limits of the site[2]. Beneath the gravel layer were the foundations of timber framed buildings and occupation debris sealed beneath a layer of charcoal. The indications were that the site had been deliberately cleared of existing buildings and the forum created in the late seventies, possibly as part of the deliberate policy of Romanisation encouraged by Agricola.

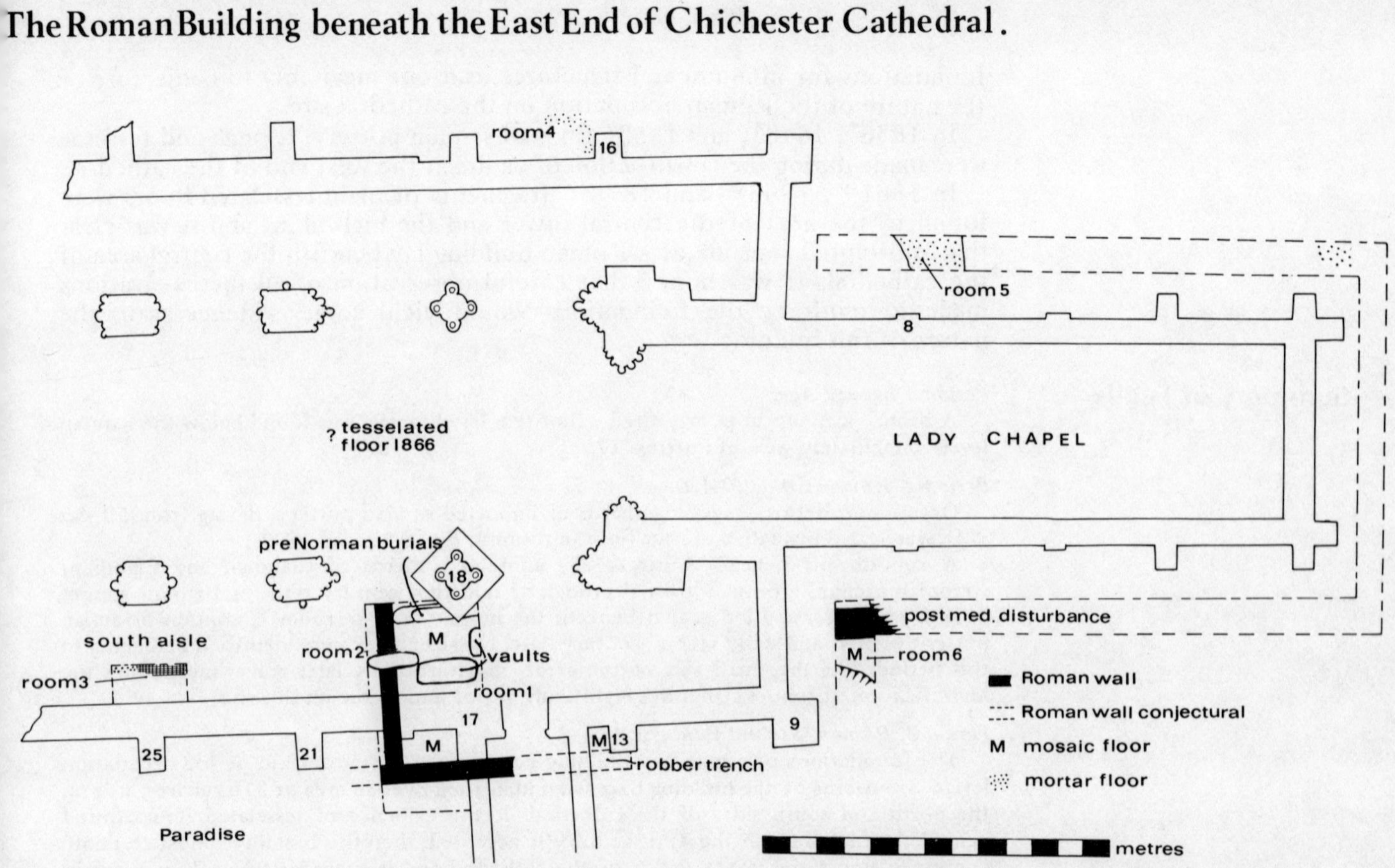

Fig. 6.3

In 1940, the construction of air-raid shelters in the cellars of the 'Dolphin and Anchor' hotel in West Street revealed a massive flint foundation incorporated into the cellar wall "at a depth which is right for the footings of a Roman wall"[3]. This foundation, which ran along the West Street frontage of the hotel, could be the foundation of a colonnade on the south side of the Forum. Its massive thickness, 'at least 6 ft thick', clearly indicates that it was meant to bear a heavy structure.

A column base dedicated to Jupiter[4], found when foundations were dug along the Chapel Street frontage of the post office in 1935, also fits well into the general picture of a forum precinct. In 1967 building development on the site of 3, 4 and 5 North Street[5] showed that the gravel layer continued across this area up to the pavement on the west side of North Street. Several small patches of gravel, up to 2 ft thick were seen at a depth of 3 ft, badly cut away by medieval rubbish pits and later cellars. A corner of a massive foundation built of three courses of water-worn blocks of Eocene Alveolina limestone was seen in one of the holes excavated by the builders for a pier base foundation. Although it was not possible to excavate this structure to determine its extent, it seems likely that it was a foundation for a statue or altar base within the forum precinct.

Development of the site immediately north of Morant's shop in West Street in 1960 and 1962[6] led to the discovery of the foundation of an apsidal plunge bath and a fragment of black and white geometric mosaic floor. The rooms were probably part of the town baths, and although both the mosaic floor and the bath has been dated to the fourth century by the excavator, there was evidence that they overlay earlier masonry structures and were almost certainly part of a replanned bath house complex.

All these architectural splendours, public baths, open forum precinct and foundations for monumental structures lead one inevitably to conjecture on the nature of the Roman occupation on the cathedral site.

In 1836[7], 1848[8], and 1853[9] finds of samian pottery, *tegulae* and tesserae were made during the construction of vaults at the west end of the cathedral.

In 1861[10], 1866[11] and 1878[12] fragments of plain tesselated floors were found in the area of the central tower and the high altar, and it was clear that substantial remains of a Roman building lay beneath the central area of the cathedral. It was hoped that careful observation of all the excavations made to reinforce the foundations would yield some evidence as to the nature of this building.

Summary of Funds

Period 1 Bronze Age.

A bronze age cup in poorly fired, flint tempered fabric, was found below the Roman levels immediately west of buttress 17.

Period 2. Roman 50 - 120 A.D.

Occupation debris, including sherds of imported samian pottery, dating from 50 -85 A.D. was sealed beneath a mortar floor in room 4. Fig. 6.3 (layer 19/9.)

A rubbish pit beneath buttress 25, contained sherds of Claudian and Claudian/Neronian samian, a bronze 'thistle' brooch of mid first century type, and a bone spoon.

A layer of occupation sealed beneath the mosaic floor in room 1, contained samian pottery of first and early second century date. No structures were identified belonging to this period, but the small size of the areas undisturbed by later graves means that the identification of timber structures is difficult, if not impossible on this site.

Period 3, Roman. Second Century. (Fig. 6.3)

The foundations of a masonry building cut through all the second period occupation levels. Six rooms of the building have been identified over an area of 370 square yards on the north and south sides of the cathedral. If the evidence of tesselated floors found behind the high altar in the 19th century is accepted, then this building almost certainly continues across the entire width of the cathedral and it exceeds 1280 square yards in area. Room 1 in the north east corner of Paradise and beneath the south aisle of the retro choir, contained a tesselated floor with a central mosaic panel incorporating an extended polychrome floral motif and a black and white meander pattern. In room 2, immediately west of room 1, medieval and later vaults cut to below the Roman floor level. North of buttress 25, in room 3, part of the room contained the lower floor of a hypocaust, and the eastern half of the room contained a tesselated floor on a solid foundation. Room 4, north of the cathedral and west of buttress 16, contained a fragment of a worn mortar floor; probably the foundation of a mosaic floor. In room 5, north of the Lady Chapel, a fragment of a mortar floor paved with red tiles was found almost totally cut away by later vaults. In room 6, the north wall of a room containing a tesselated floor with a meander pattern was found when drains were laid south of the Lady Chapel.

Period 5. Norman. 12th century.

The foundations of two small side chapels radiating north and south from the east end of the cathedral were found (Fig. 6.2). Constructed as a solid rubble foundation of flints and random greensand fragments in friable sandy mortar, they contained a quantity of re-used Roman architectural material, including four gutter blocks. The realigned thirteenth century walls of the retro choir overlay the chapel foundations on the north and south side of the cathedral, and burials pre-dating the construction of the cloisters cut through the foundations of the southern chapel.

Period 6. Construction of the Eastern Arm of the Cloisters.

Excavation up to the face of the foundation of the wall of the cloister in the north east corner of Paradise (Fig. 6.1) showed that the wall had been constructed on a trench-built foundation of rough chalk blocks in a very hard creamy yellow mortar. This foundation butted onto, and partially overlay the foundation of the southern Norman side chapel and post Norman burials. Documentary evidence suggests that the cloisters were constructed before 1407, and windows in the eastern arm, with four cinquefoiled lights, vertical tracery and two centred heads would support a late fourteenth century date.

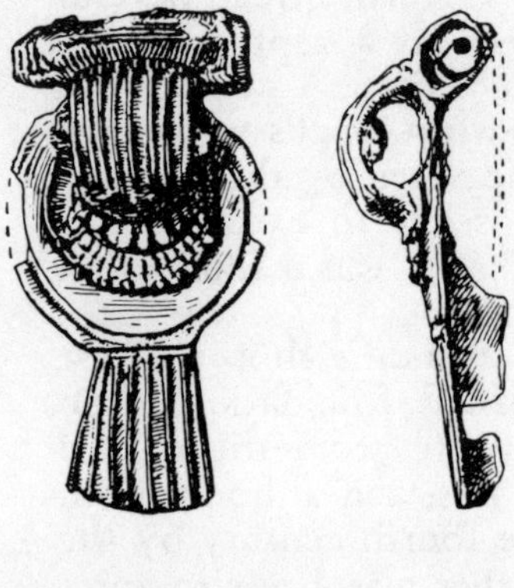

Fig. 6.4 Thistle Brooch. (2/1.)

Fragments of a jug in heavily oxidised fabric were found in the cloister foundation trench. It is just possible that the sherds were derived from an earlier grave cut by the cloister foundation trench, but in view of the near completeness of the vessel and the almost total absence of other medieval pottery from the cathedral site, it seems more likely that the jug was dropped by a careless workman engaged on building the cloister wall. The jug has been studied by Mr. K.J. Barton (see p. 139) and compared with similar jugs from West Sussex of late fourteenth or early fifteenth century date.

Details of Structures and Finds

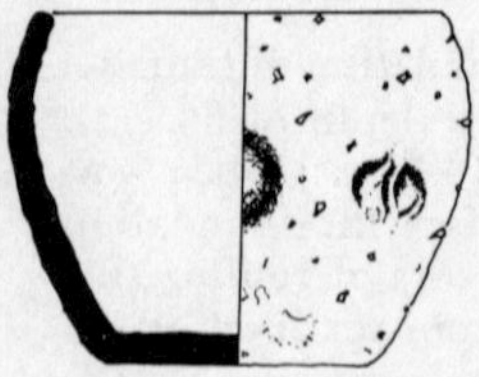

Fig. 6.5

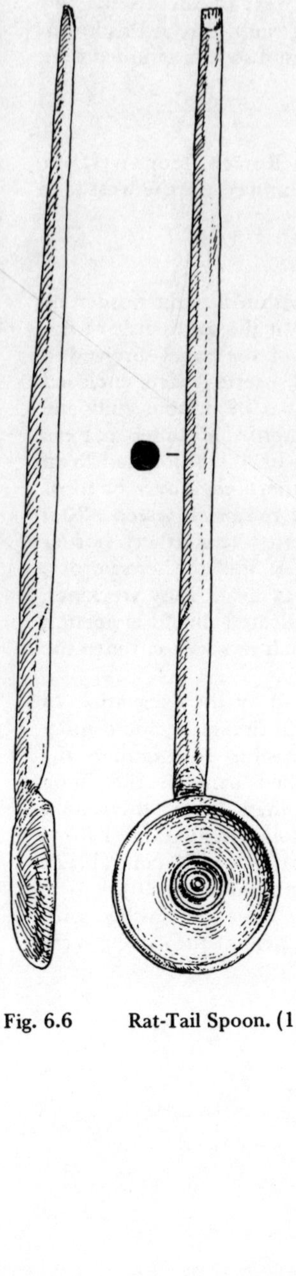

Fig. 6.6 Rat-Tail Spoon. (1/1.)

Period 1 Bronze Age.

A small cup was recovered by workmen from the brickearth at a depth of 193 cms (76 ins) below the thirteenth century wall immediately west of Buttress 17. (Fig. 6.5).

The Bronze Age Cup from the Site of Chichester Cathedral by I.H. Longworth M.A., Ph.D., F.S.A.,.

Diameter of mouth: 5 cms. Height: 4.5 cms. Diameter of base: 4 cms.

Cup of poorly fired paste, tempered with crushed flint, orange-red externally, grey internally. The vessel is undecorated save for the remains of a small, vertically perforated lug. Scars remain of two, possibly three similar lugs round the maximum diameter.

The cup belongs to a type found only in the south and east of England, falling roughtly within a line drawn from Dorset to the Wash. The type seems to represent a miniaturisation of the more common forms of Bucket and perhaps Globular Urns of the Early and Middle Bronze Ages, and is sometimes found in association with them (E.g. Swindon, Wilts. *W.A.M.* XLVIII (1939) 353 - 6.). Similar cups are known from a number of sites in Sussex, listed by R.C. Mussons. *S.A.C.* (1954), 121 fig 6, but none have been found in a context which might reveal their exact function.

Period 2. Roman. 50 - 120 A.D.
Pit 1. Claudian/Neronian.

Excavated by workmen west of buttress 25. A truncated pit cut to a depth of 183 cms (72 ins). The pit was below the level of the Roman masonry building, but the upper levels were badly disturbed by later vaults.

Samian Pottery[13]

Form 18 Claudian; Montans fabric. Form 18; Claudian. Form 15/17; Claudian. Form 18; Lezoux ware; Claudian/Neronian.

Other finds.

Bronze. ':Thistle' fibula. Bronze brooch with high arched reeded bow, central disc and rosette cast in one with reeded footplate. Pierced catch plate and encased spring. (Fig. 6.4). cf. *Cam.* 93, 78 but without reeding on spring cover. Wheeler, *London in Roman Times*, 90, fig 24 No. 5, but the Chichester example has integral disc.

Bone. 'Rat tail' spoon. (Fig. 6.6).

Occupation spread. Flavian. (Layer 19/9)

A spread of occupation, pottery, animal bone and tile fragments in dirty clayey loam. Sealed beneath the mortar floor in Room 4. 11 - 15 cms. (4.3 - 5.9 ins) thick. Lying on undistrubed natural brickearth.

Samian Pottery.

Form 30. Winding scroll with five-lobed leaf and part of an imbricated leaf. For the former cf. K19, Taf. 63, detail 136, SABINVS as an example of the complete motif. On basis of the dark brown/red glossy slip the date is probably Claudius/Nero. (Fig. 6.7 no. 1).

Drag. 29; Probably pre Flavian. Drag. 27; Pre Flavian. Drag. 18; Pre Flavian. Drag. 15/17; Pre Flavian. Drag. 37; c. 70 - 85 A.D. (Fig. 6.7 no. 2). In a fine red brown ware. Legs of 0.565 with the rump of a rabbit to the right. At the bottom, a straight wreath with sharply outturned striated leaves. The Bacchus occurs in the work of GERMANVS, compare particularly the treatment of the grass with HERMET, pl. 102 No. 9. The long leaves of the basal wreath are known in the work of contemporary potters, e.g. PASSIENVS, cf. K.19 Textbild 12, fig. 2.

Occupation spread. Late first/early second century. (Layer 30)

A thick layer of sticky loam with pottery, oyster shell, animal bone and charcoal fragments. Sealed beneath the mosaic floor in room 1 and cut by the foundations of the walls south and west of room 1. Greater than 31 cms. (12.25 ins) thick.

Samian Pottery.

Drag. 30; Probably Trajanic. Drag. 27; First century. Drag. 17; First century. Drag. 37, small, double bordered ovolo with straight tongue attached to the left, above wavy line border. (Fig. 6.7 no. 3).

Coarse ware.

Base wide bellied flagon in sandy orange fabric. (Fig. 6.7 no. 8). Body sherd with raised girth band. Fine dark grey fabric with external burnish above girth band. (Fig. 6.7 no. 9)

Period 3. Second century masonry building.

The fragmentary remains of six rooms of a masonry building were found spread over an area of 370 square yards on the north and south side of the cathedral. (Fig. 6.3).

Wall 1. south of rooms 1 and 2 was constructed on a trench-built foundation of flints set in creamy white mortar 63 cms. (24.75 ins) wide at floor level. At a depth of 50 cms. (19.75 ins) below the floor level an internal offset 37 cms. (14.5 ins) wide was constructed of unmortared flints set in yellow clay. Above the offset the foundation trench was filled with redeposited brickearth containing two fragments of roofing tile. The total depth of the foundation trench was 67 cms. (26.4 ins) from the level of the Roman floor, and it cut through a layer of early second century occupation (layer 30).

Wall 2. between rooms 1 and 2 was similarly constructed of flints in creamy white mortar 63 cms. (24.75 ins) wide at floor level. Two slabs of dressed greensand were bonded into the junction of the wall foundation south of rooms 1 and 2. West of these slabs the foundation of the wall had been destroyed to a lower level by a vault, but at this lower level there was no evidence of a butt joint between the two walls and so it is assumed that rooms 1 and 2 are contempory.

Room 2.

Burial vaults had destroyed the stratigraphy in room 2 below Roman floor level, but traces of painted wall plaster and quarter-round plaster coving survived on the west face and so it must be an internal wall.

Room 1. The mosaic floor. Plate 13 Fig. 6.3

The north west corner of a polychrome mosaic panel set within a plain border of greyish black tesserae 127 cms. (50 ins) wide was found beneath the south aisle of the retro choir at a depth of 130 cms. (51.1 ins) Only a fragment of the panel survived; a corner motif in red, yellow, white and black in an extended floral rosette design, enclosed within a square of double guilloche in the same colours. A bar of double guilloche finished the northern edge of the panel and a black geometric meander pattern filled the white ground east of the rosette. The central area of the floor had been destroyed by vaults. The plain border was finished on the southern edge by a band of seven rows of red brick tesserae 18 cms (7 ins) wide. A panel of red brick tesserae 20.5 cms (8 ins) deep and greater than 112 cms (44 ins) wide set into the southern border probably indicates the position of a doorway. A worn fragment of the southern border, patched with small random fragments of tile was found during excavation by workmen west of buttress 13. The presence of a single row of tesserae indicated that this portion was near the edge of the floor, and the bottom of the robber trench was seen cut into the natural clay beneath the cloister wall.

As the mosaic border south of buttress 17 would be destroyed by the excavation to reinforce the buttress, it was decided to lift the panel, back it with fibreglass, and display it in the Cathedral. Lifting this area of floor made it possible to examine the foundations of wall 1 and recover occupation material sealed beneath the floor. The tesserae were set in a thin slurry of white mortar less than 1 cm. thick on a foundation of pink mortar 5 - 7 cms. (2 - 2.8 ins) thick above a solid foundation of flints set in creamy buff mortar. The total thickness of the floor foundation was 30 cms. (11.75 ins) and it lay directly above a layer of early second century occupation (layer 30).

The junction between the west and south wall and the mosaic floor was finished with plaster quarter-round coving with a red painted surface. Sealed behind the coving were two distinctly different layers of mortar rendering.[14]

The destruction levels in Room 1.

Where undisturbed by later graves two levels of collapsed building material overlay the mosaic floor. The lowest level (layer 18/4) consisted of a dirty mixture of painted wall plaster in soft brownish mortary clay c. 10 cms. (4 ins) thick. The upper level 23 - 25 cms. (9 ins — 9.75 ins) thick (layer 18/5) was much cleaner and contained large flints c. 10 x 12 cms. (4 ins x 4.75 ins), lumps of creamy white mortar, wall plaster fragments and a few snail shells. No pottery was found in the destruction levels. It would seem that the room fell naturally into decay after the roof had been stripped of tiles. No fragments of roofing tile, *tegula* or *imbrex* were found in the destruction levels of the building, but unstratified fragments have been found on the cathedral site. The upper levels of the walls collapsed onto the mosaic floor soon after exposure to weathering, and at a later date the lower walls collapsed or were demolished. There is no difference between decoration on the wall plaster from the primary and secondary rubble levels and wall plaster found in situ on the base of the wall, and the lower level is unlikely to represent a collapsed ceiling.

The presence among the rubble of the land snail, *Helix Aspera*, indicates that the site lay open for a period of time.

The Floor in Room 3. Fig.

Two levels of Roman floor were observed in excavations carried out by workmen north of buttress 25. The upper floor was paved with red brick tesserae circa 2.5 cms. (1 in) square set in a mortar slurry on a foundation of flints in creamy buff mortar 15 - 20 cms. (6 ins - 8 ins) thick, and lying directly on natural brickearth. The lower foundation consisted of a spread of pink mortar 3 - 4 cms. (1.25 ins - 1.5 ins) thick above a poor foundation of flints set into the natural clay. A layer of charcoal fragments and blackish occupation 2.5 cms. (1 ins) thick lay above the mortar floor. Above this, all the upper levels had been destroyed by the construction pit for a brick-built vault, but it was clear that the lower 'floor' continued up to a point directly below the western edge of the upper floor and no wall had ever existed between the two levels of floor. The lower floor must be the foundation for a hypocaust and suitably placed tile *pilae* would have sufficed to support bridging tiles at the junction of the upper floors. Unstratified fragments of box tiles were found nearby in post-medieval vaults.

Room 4.

Patches of worn creamy yellow mortar floor c. 5 cms. (2 ins) thick, lay above a single course of flints set in dirty yellow clay. Sealed beneath the mortar a layer of occupation debris included several sherds of Samian pottery, the latest of which dated to 70 - 80 A.D. Quantities of painted wall plaster and several fragments of a mosaic floor were found in all the later burials in this area.

Room 5.

Fragmentary remains of a mortar floor with a surface of square *pilac* tiles, were seen in section in a drainage trench north of buttress 8. The floor had been almost totally destroyed by post-medieval vaults and no trace of the room could be found to the north in spite of extensive excavation in this area.

Room 6.

Excavation to lay stormwater drains north east of buttress 9, revealed the north wall of a room containing a fragment of a mosaic floor. The floor was decorated with a design incorporating bands, squares and a meander in red tesserae set in a ground of plain grey tesserae. (Plage 7).

Post-medieval vaults had destroyed all the levels down to the mosaic floor and cut through the mosaic floor on the south side.

Period 4 Pre-Norman Burials.

Seven burials, carefully orientated west to east could be shown to predate the Norman Cathedral. One of these, burial 18/11, had been buried in a wooden coffin on a layer of fresh, clean charcoal 15 cms (6 ins) thick. Several burials in secondary positions were also on beds of charcoal. This practice has been noted at Winchester[15] in the New Minster which was founded in 903 and abandoned in 1110. Further excavations at Winchester[16] suggest that the practice there had ceased by 1093. None of the Chichester burials on charcoal is closely dated, and only one can be indisputably shown to predate the Norman Cathedral, but it is clear that the practice of inhumation on a bed of charcoal continued over a period of time coincidently with encoffined burials without charcoal. It is difficult to find an adequate explanation for this practice. The large amount of charcoal used hints at something more than mere ritual. Possibly the charcoal was used as a sanitary measure ; certainly it is an effective deodorant. This would be a distinct advantage in the case of a burial within a church, or if an encoffined body had to be transported a long distance before burial.

Burial 18/11 had been cut through and partially destroyed by a later burial and both were overlain by the foundation of the inner wall of the Norman ambulatory. This suggests that a period of time, (at least two generations?) had elapsed between the deposition of the first burial and the construction of the twelfth century foundations.

Period 7. Norman. Fig. 6.2.

The solid rubble foundation of two small side chapels were found on the north and south side of the cathedral at the eastern end.

Chapel 1. Plate 9.

In the north east corner of Paradise a fragment of a rubble foundation built mainly of flints and random greensand rubble, but incorporating reused Roman architectural fragments, was found just below the present ground level. The upper surface was very eroded and of uneven depth and no indication of the original floor level could be found. Traces of the foundation were found within the south aisle at a depth of 122 cms. (4 ft) below the present south aisle floor. No trace of the foundation could be found in the angle formed between the east wall of the cloister and the Mary Magdalene Chapel, but the area had been disturbed by early medieval burials, and the disturbed levels did contain several fragments of the distinctive sandy mortar used to construct the chapel foundations. Incorporated in the foundation were four Roman sandstone gutter blocks.

Chapel 2. Plate 10.

West of buttress 16, a similar foundation was found. This foundation cut through the Roman mortar floor in room 4 and the overlying burials, 19/4 and 19/4a, to a depth of 290 cms. (98 ft 6 ins)

The foundations of both chapels were overlain by the thirteenth century foundations of the cathedral.

Beneath the floor of the south aisle, the rubble foundation of the inner wall of the ambulatory was found. Constructed of greensand rubble and flints in the same yellow sandy mortar used for the chapel foundations, it incorporated a large fragment of an attic column base. This foundation was cut through by the diamond shaped foundation for the cluster column, 18.

Period 6. The construction of the Eastern Arm of the Cloisters.

The wall of the eastern arm of the cloister was constructed on a trench-built foundation of roughly rectangular blocks of chalk cut to a depth of 96 cms. below the present ground level. The blocks were set in courses in hard creamy yellow mortar, and the surface of the blocks against the face of the foundation trench was covered with a solidified slurry of mortar which had matured to a metallic grey colour. This foundation overlay the foundation of the Norman side chapel, and cut through a burial in a vault of rectangular chalk blocks. (Burial 20)

Included in the foundation trench were several sherds of medieval pottery, including an almost complete jug in a heavily oxidised fabric. This jug has been studied by Mr K.J. Barton and compared with jugs of similar fabric from other sites in Chichester and West Sussex. (see page 139).

Documentary History of the Cloisters

It is difficult to date the construction of the cloisters from documentary evidence as the medieval building records for Chichester cathedral are almost completely nonexistant. This serious loss, which probably dates from the period of the Civil War, leaves us with only the more casual references in wills, visitations and indentures.[17]

The cloister in a church of secular canons did not fulfill the same function as in a monastic foundation. They were never intended as a place of study and meditation, but simply as a thoroughfare between the cathedral church and the buildings of the close. At Chichester this covered way appears to have evolved as convenience dictated, but after the fifteenth century increasing reference to the cloisters is made in wills and indentures and by the sixteenth century it appears that the cloisters were more commonly used for secular transactions than for ecclesiastic use![18]

The earliest reference to the cloisters is in the late twelth century.[19] This clearly refers to an earlier building, possibly a wooden structure, but it is interesting as it shows the earliest of the term in Chichester. In 1373[20] a divinity lecture was delivered in the cloister, 'in clauso lecturus,' and in 1407[21] Dean Maidenhithe's will was proved leaving half his residue;

'ad fabricam domorum pro communitate vicariorum infra clausum construendam'. In 1402,[22] John Paxton was summoned before the Bishop and charged with having made a road through St. Faith's Chapel to his own house. He replied that the Canons Residentiary had 'by ancient custom and from time immemorial been wont to pass through the chapel to the Cathedral church', and he claimed the right to continue to do so. In 1441[23] reference is made to St. Faith's Chapel, 'infra claustrum Ecclesiae Cathedralis.'

The eastern arm of the cloister is clearly aligned on St. Faith's Chapel and the pathway to the Vicar's Close beyond, (Fig. 6.1) and the two western bays of St. Faith's Chapel are incorporated in the cloisters at the south-east corner. It seems logical that the construction of the cloisters in the early fifteenth century was simply to regularise a situation already existing. There is evidence that by 1402,[24] St. Faith's Chapel was used mainly as a store room, and it would not have required a great deal of argument to convince the Dean and Chapter of the advisability of the new arrangement, if only to check the theft of goods stored in the chapel.[25] It seems clear in the absence of direct documentary evidence that whilst the cloisters existed as a recognised area before the fifteenth century, the formal layout as we see it today did not evolve until the beginning of the fifteenth century, and the bequest made by Dean Maidenhithe in 1407 probably marks the first stage of the work.

Conclusion

One of the main reasons for the initial trial excavation in 1966 was to determine whether any archaeological evidence existed to support the theory, first put forward by Willis in 1861,[26] that the original east end of the Norman Cathedral terminated in a great apse enclosing a processional way, or ambulatory, and from which radiated three small apsidal chapels.

The foundations of two of the apsidal side chapels have been found, slightly smaller than Willis conjectured, but in the exact architectural relationship he surmised. Further work is necessary to confirm the junction of the side chapels with the central chapel, and determine the size of the compartments dividing these three chapels, but the foundations for the internal piers of the ambulatory have been found in the south aisle, pierced by the later foundation for the thirteenth century cluster column.

A secondary reason for undertaking the excavation was to ascertain whether additional evidence of the Roman building known to underlie the cathedral might be found. In spite of the comparatively shallow depth of the Roman levels beneath the present ground level, and the high density of Saxon, medieval and post-medival burials, enough of the Roman structure remained to begin to build up a plan of the building. Although few walls have been found and the plan cannot be rationally interpreted without further evidence, we now have a chronological and structural framework on which to add future detail.[27]

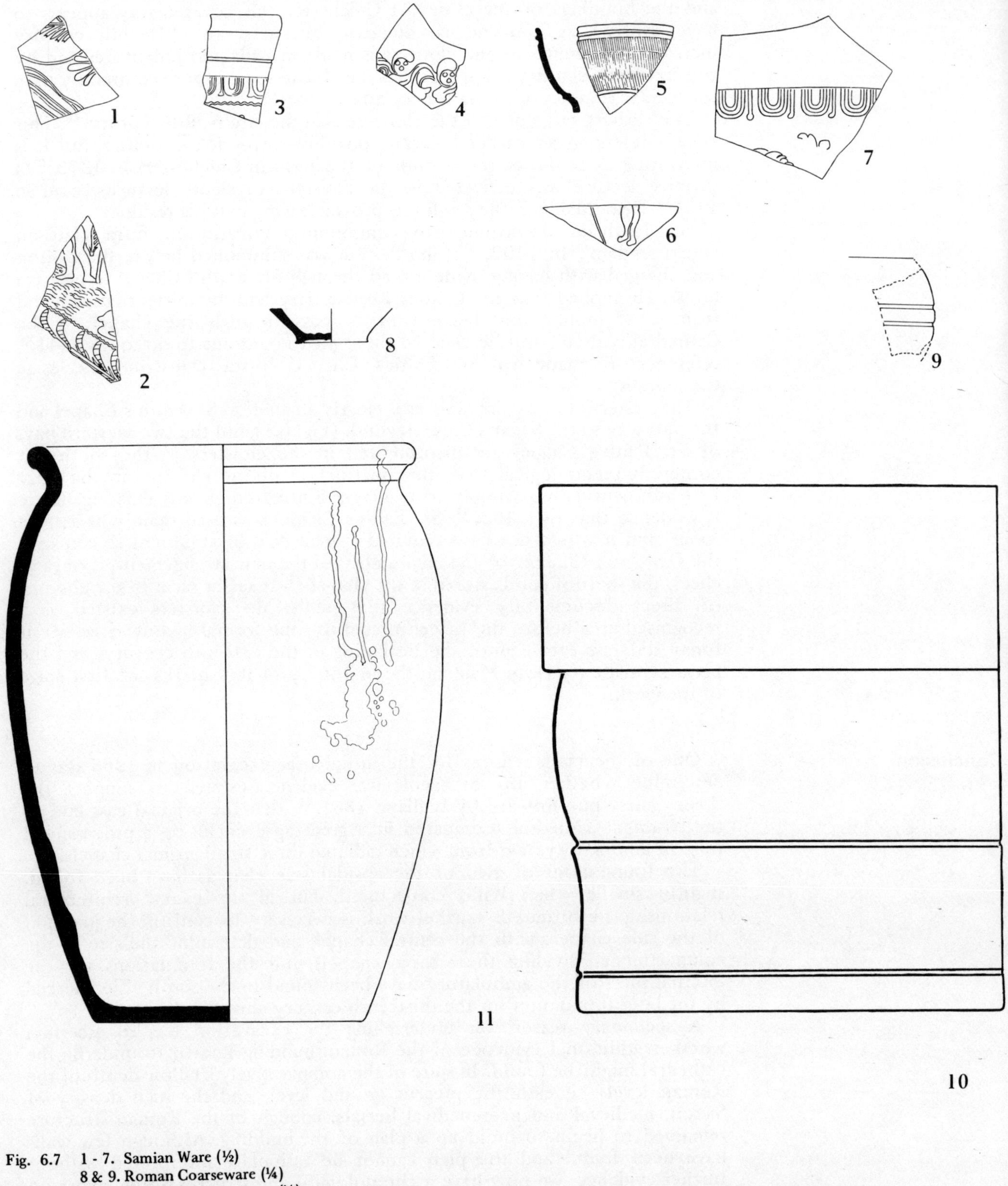

Fig. 6.7 1 - 7. Samian Ware (½)
8 & 9. Roman Coarseware (¼)
10. Engaged Column base (¼)
11. Post Medieval Viscera Jar (¼)

In the light of present evidence the masonry building dates to the second century. The latest occupation sealed beneath the floors is Trajanic, and there is no hint that the site was abandoned and unoccupied between the deposition of the early second-century debris and the construction of the masonry building. The style of the mosaic floor found in room 1 has much in common with two mosaic floors found on the site of the Bank of England in 1933 and 1934[28]. Both of the Bank of England floors overlay occupation of early second century date, but both have been tentatively dated on stylistic grounds to the late second or early third century. Recent discoveries of early mosaic floors at Fishbourne have shown that polychrome mosaic floors incorporating floral motifs and guilloche patterns were laid in the first century alongside black and white geometric floors.[29] It seems perfectly possible for a second century mosaicist in Chichester to have been familiar with both styles.

There is at present no evidence on which to date the destruction of the building, and this problem is a familiar one in Chichester. No sub Roman or early Saxon pottery has been found on the site, and the earliest post-Roman material found consists of four sherds of tenth century pottery associated with burial 16/4, and two fragments of late Saxon 'bun' shaped loomweights found in a disturbed level on the north side of the Cathedral. The mass of Roman masonry used in the Norman foundations indicates the availability of Roman rubble on or near the site in the late eleventh and twelth century. Whether this rubble was obtained from the recently demolished building on the site, or from the Forum immediately to the north, remains conjecture. The clean appearance of the rubble in the secondary destruction levels in Room 1 might perhaps indicate that a substantial standing ruin was demolished before the site was used as a burial ground in the late Saxon period.

To answer the many questions that still remain about the nature of the buildings south of the forum and the subsequent history of the site, it is vital that all future excavation continues under archaeological supervision, and that excavations by public works authorities along the West Street frontage are similarly observed and recorded.

Miscellaneous Finds

Samian Pottery.

Pottery from the disturbed levels around buttress 21.

Drag 17. Two sherds in Montans fabric. Claudian.

Drag 27. Pedestal bowl. Small chip only, in one of the sub Arretine fabrics. The slip is light brown/red and matt; the fabric is light pink and fine. This could be an early Montans fabric and is comparable to the early material from Fishbourne. fig. 6.7, no. 4.

Loeschke 11. Probably Montans ware, but possibly 'provincial Arretine' (cf. Cam. Hawkes and Hull. 186, s 14) A piece from the conquest period. Fig. 6.7, no. 5.

Drag 37. Legs of a(?) bear. Probably Central Gaulish. Antonine. Fig. 6.7, no. 6.

Drag 37. Free style design. The ovolo is CINNAMVS 3. (CGP fig. 47), and similar foliage can be seen there e.g. pl. 163 no. 68. Date, Antonine, Fig. 6.7, no. 7.

Drag 27. First century. Drag 31. Antonine. Ritterling 31. Antonine.

Unstratified in the area of buttress 17.

Drag 36; Probably Trajanic. Ritteling 18; Lezoux. First century. Ritterling 18; Pre Flavian. Drag 27; Probably Nero/Vespasian.

Post-medieval soakaway south of buttress 17.

Ritterling 12. Neronian.

Architectural Fragments.

Dressed stone Gutter Blocks.

Two whole, and two fragmentary, sandstone gutter blocks were found used as rubble in the foundations of the southern Norman side chapel. All were 60 cms wide at the base,

23 – 28 cms deep at the outer edge and 12 cms deep in the centre. Cut with a semi circular channel. One complete block 100 cms long, the other 75 cms long.

Fragment of Attic column Base.

Seen in section in Norman rubble foundations for inner wall of ambulatory. c. 240 mm deep, c. 720 mm diameter.

Engaged column base (?)Quarr Abbey limestone, found in foundation of buttress 16. Possibly derived from the demolition of the Norman side chapel. Fig. 6.7, no. 10.

Pottery vessel

(?)viscera jar of late 16th or early 17th century date. Found upright and empty 79 cms below the floor of the south aisle. Reddish brown fabric with clear brown internal glaze. Splashes of light greenish brown glaze on exterior. Fig. 6.7, no. 11.

The author wishes to acknowledge the invaluable assistance given to her on the site by the Superintendent of Works, Mr. E. Brooks, and all the men of the Cathedral Workshop Organisation. Several student volunteers have assisted with the excavations, often under difficult conditions, and the author is indebted to the Archdeacon of Chichester, the Venerable Lanceolot Mason and Mr. Robert Potter, F.R.I.B.A., F.S.A., for invaluable discussion on the site.

Notes and References

[1] Cottrill. *S.A.C.* 76, 159-171.
[2] *J.R.S.* 53, 156.
[3] Holmes. *Chichester City Papers no. 50.* 'Chichester, The Roman Town'.
[4] *S.A.C.* 95, 131 - 3. *A. J.* 15, 461-4.
[5] Unpublished author's notes. The author is grateful to Messrs. John Snelling and Son, Builders, for permission to observe the excavation for pier base foundations on this site.
[6] Holmes op. cit.
[7] *B.A.A.J.* 35, 94-5.
[8] *V.C.H. Sx.* 3, 13.
[9] *S.A.C.* 8, 291.
[10] *S.A.C.* 19, 197-8.
[11] *S.A.C.* 19,
[12] *B.A.A.J.* 35, 94-5.
[13] All the samian pottery from the Cathedral site has been examined by Mr. G. Dannell B.Sc., F.S.A., and the notes are from his report.
[14] Samples of mortar have been taken from all the periods of building construction on the cathedral site. The results of their analysis will be included in the final report.
[15] Biddle. *A.J.*, 44, 211.
[16] Biddle. *A.J.*, 45, 257.
[17] Extensive search for references to the cloisters in medieval and post-medieval documents has been made by Mrs M. Culver, and the complete abstracts on which these notes are based will be lodged with the excavation records in the West Sussex Record Office.
[18] Chapter Acts. 'The White Book', *S.R.S.* 52, 85.
[19] Dean Mathew (1180 - 93.) *Redes Register* 1402, f 22. MacKenzie Walcott. *The Early Statutes of the Cathedral Church of the Holy Trinity, Chichester.*
[20] MacKenzie Walcott. op cit. *Papal Bull* 1373. Ad. ms. 15, 377, f 328.
[21] MacKenzie Walcott. op cit. *Reg. Arundel,* 242.
[22] *Redes Reg.*, f. XXXIII.
[23] *Reg Praty*, f. 79.
[24] *Redes Reg.*, f XXXIII.
[25] *Redes Reg.*, f XXXIII.
[26] Willis, *The Architectural History of Chichester Cathedral,* 1861.
[27] Copies of the large-scale plans and detailed notes on which this interim report is based will be deposited in the West Sussex County Record Office.
[28] Merrifield, *The Roman City of London,* 1965.
[29] Cunliffe. 1962. *A.J.*

A Jug from the Cloisters and other oxidised Wares from the City

The discovery of this vessel is of considerable importance to the study of the medieval pottery of Chichester as it points the way to the dating of vessels of this form, and provides another sub-type to the already recognised group of West Sussex wares. It also shows how some wares produced in Chichester were fired in an oxidising kiln.

The jug (Fig. 6.8 No. 1) which is made in a red sandy fabric is covered with a thin bright orange glaze. It is decorated with an incised spiral groove around the neck and with light, three-pronged cross-hatched combing on the body. The rim bears no spout, the handle is rod sectioned and slashed, and the base is thumbed with small regular vertical indentations. The vessel is thoroughly and intentionally oxidised. It is almost complete.

In form this jug complies with the standards that define West Sussex ware[1] and although nearest to the Binstead types in this definition, differs from them in quality, this vessel being in every degree coarser, and squatter, with a tendancy to ovoid rather than the globular. The cross-hatching on the body is not typical of Binstead, nor is the coiled groove. Furthermore it is oxidised which all other West Sussex jugs are not. None the less the differences are only in detail and the form of this vessel sets it firmly within the range of West Sussex wares. As the distribution of these wares[2] shows, this should be expected.

The discovery of this vessel in a context which supports its deposition in the late 14th century in a whole condition, is pertinent to the study of these wares. I have stated for some time that such vessels are of late 14th century date with an extension into the middle of the 15th century as shown at Tarring[3] and consistently at other sites in West Sussex. Therefore, this vessel is important in confirming the hitherto theoretical dating.

That this vessel is oxidised is of equal significance. Its general form being so close to that of other West Sussex wares, that a mere fragment of such vessels could be looked upon as a kiln accident and would be ignored. I have seen such fragments from Chichester, but of insufficient size to record them, although one large fragment of an oxidised jug from Chichester is in the Society's Museum at Lewes.

This vessel (fig. 6.8 no. 2) was an exceptionally large jug decorated with three-pronged combing on the body, a wavy line on the shoulder and a spiral groove on the neck. The handle is massive and rod sectioned. The fabric is red and sandy, the glaze is light brown and has two random splashes of copper green in it. Although this is a very large jug, it too, is of West Sussex ware type, and has features which link it directly with the 'Cloister Jug'.

Farther afield, but related, is the fragment of a face jug from Middleton-on-Sea[4] (Fig. 6.8 No. 3) which is West Sussex in character and has a sandy red fabric and a brown glaze.

These three examples all fit into the same date range and all have characteristics which set them within the West Sussex ware group – but at the same time they illustrate sufficient differences to set them apart. Above all they are oxidised and this in itself suggests a separate source from those already known.

[5]The products of a medieval pottery kiln in Orchard Street, Chichester, have been described on page 157 dated to the 13th century and should belong to the phase just prior to these products. What is important is that

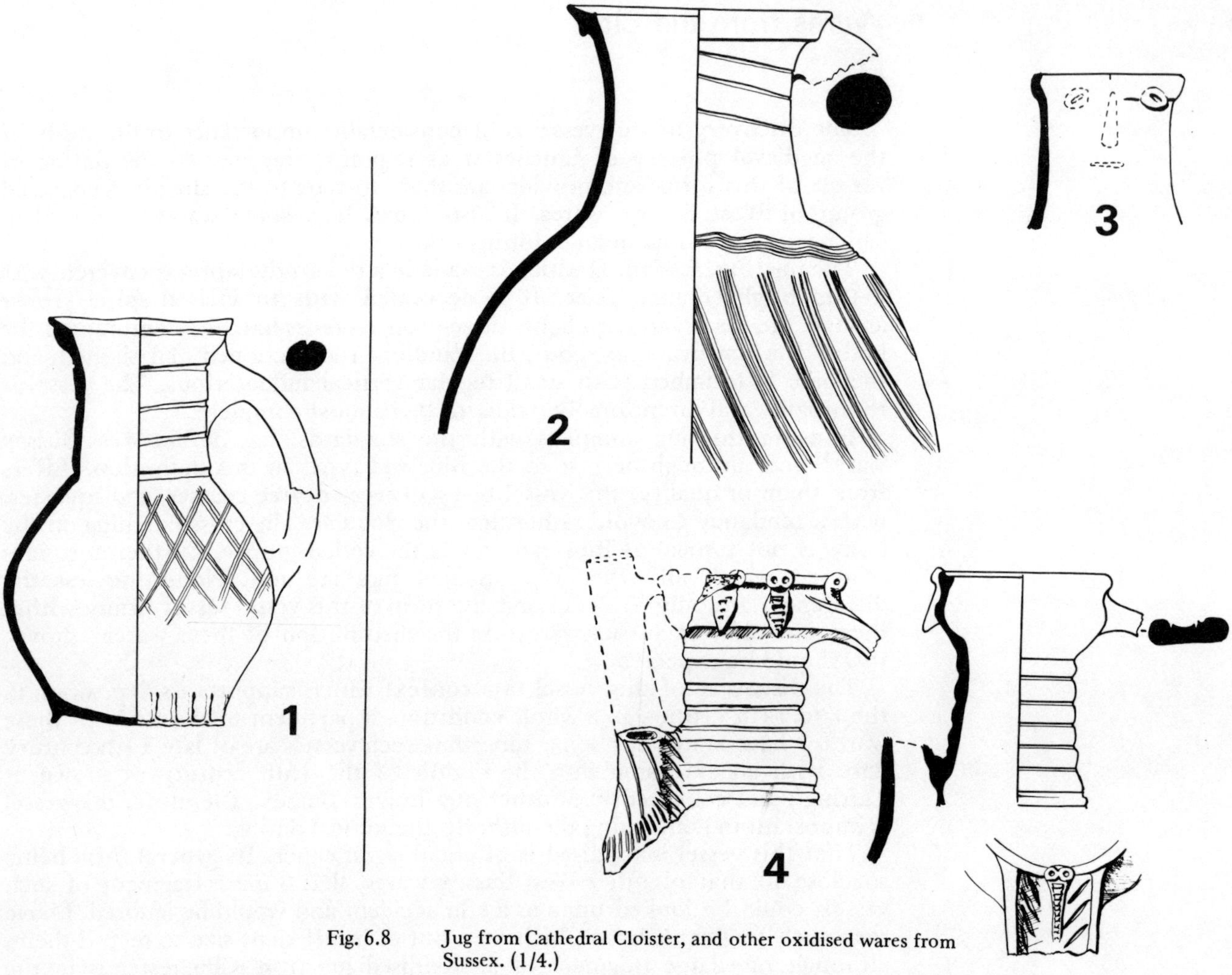

Fig. 6.8 Jug from Cathedral Cloister, and other oxidised wares from Sussex. (1/4.)

the Orchard Street material is all intentionally oxidised.

A vessel in the Chichester City Museum[6] (found in the city) (Fig. 6.8 No. 4) which is typologically similar to the Orchard Street material, although also illustrating some different features than those vessels, is also oxidised. This is the fragment from the upper part of a spouted jug which had a strap handle. The long cylindrical neck is deeply grooved at regular intervals, the spout fixing is slashed and the spout has been grooved. The handle is chevron grooved. Around the neck are pellets which have 'eyes' pierced in the upper part and a pulled-out lozenge shaped piece roughly stabbed across. These motifs could represent bearded faces, although they look more like wasps or bees. The vessel is oxidised, has a sandy brick red fabric and a copper green speckled glaze. The deeply and regularly grooved neck is similar to the Orchard Street material, the tall cylindrical neck and bulbous cup-like rim not dissimilar to other wares from West Sussex, as is the strap handle form which is commonplace. The spout and the decoration are, on the other hand, unusual for Sussex. An unpublished spout from a similar shaped vessel is in the material from the Rye Kiln,[7] another spouted vessel was recently found in Shoreham[8] but the incidence of such vessels is uncommon. The rim decoration likewise is very rare. In Sussex only one other example known comes from Bramber Castle[9] in which the faces are in the form of three piercings to applied pellets on the rim. Such decorations are primarily West Country forms.[10] The "beard" slashing around the base of the spout is not dissimilar to other West Country jugs (*vide* 'Ham Green').[11] This tenuous link with the West rather than to the East of Chichester has already been suggested for the Orchard Street products.[12]

It is proposed, therefore, that the medieval pottery actually produced in Chichester was always fired in oxidising kilns as opposed to the usual reduction firing of other neighbouring kilns. It would appear that the bulk of these localised products were made during the period when "Orchard Street types" were produced but that production continued on a smaller scale in the face of growing competition from the Binstead kilns. It is also probable that in the early phase of production there was more than one potter producing wares, of which one may have been the spouted jug. It must be pointed out that although this note has been written on only four items, these have been the only substantial evidence by virtue of their size or individuality to guarantee some localised form of production. It is hoped that special notice will be taken in the future to save all medieval fragments in order that a statistical analysis of oxidised wares can be made.

Notes and References

[1] Barton. 'Three groups of medieval jugs and their wider significance'. *Hants Field Club,* 24, 62 - 73.

[2] Barton, op cit.

[3] Barton. 'Excavations in the Village of Tarring, Sussex'. *S.A.C.,* 102, 21 - 2.

[4] In Chichester Museum.

[5] Orchard Street Kiln.

[6] Chichester City Museum 49 EP C10/1.

[7] *S.A.C.* 74, 45 - 64 (material in the Ypres Tower, Rye).

[8] In Worthing Museum — to be published by G.C. Dunning, F.S.A.

[9] Excavations at Bramber Castle. Barton and Holden.

[10] K.J. Barton, 'Anthropomorphic decoration on medieval jugs. *Archaeologica Lundensia* 2, 43-53.

[11] K.J. Barton, 'A medieval pottery kiln of Ham Green Bristol'. *Bristol and Glos. Arch. Soc.* Vol. 82 (1963), Fig. 1, No. 22.

[12] Op. cit.

PLATE 11. Westgate: Woodcut by Grimm, 18th century.

7

Westgate 1964

The construction of a new roundabout at the south end of Orchard Street as part of the planning of a new link road around the City in 1964 necessitated the demolition of Nos. 1 and 2 North Walls and Nos. 2 to 10 Westgate (see inset to Plan, Fig. 1).[1] At this bottleneck in the road were two piers which purported to represent the position of medieval Westgate. The pier on the south side remains in position against the front wall of the old Toll House, but the one on the north side was demolished, the stones being stored in the City Museum.

By kind permission of the West Sussex County Council, excavations took place on the site of No. 1 North Walls, as near as possible to the then existing pavement in the hope that the position of the Roman Westgate might be established. The excavations were carried out under the supervision of the writer under the general direction of Mr John Holmes F.S.A., at that time Field Director to the Chichester Excavations Committee.

The Excavations

Two trenches were cut; Trench A was cut alongside the road and Trench B immediately to the north of it to examine further the features which had been revealed in the previous trench.

Immediately below the demolition rubble was found the remains of the Roman town-wall foundations, which must have been just below the floorboards of the houses lately demolished. The west side of the wall had been cut about by cellars, and was only 1.82 metres (6 ft) wide at its widest point. The original width as noted elsewhere[2] must have been 2.13 metres (7 ft) or more.

Below the builder's rubble on the east side of the wall were several layers of clay and gravel to a depth of approximately 1.05 metres (3 ft 6 ins). These layers contained nothing but Roman pottery and represent the bottom layers of the defensive bank thrown up when the first defences were established towards the end of the 2nd century A.D.[3] None of the samian ware found in these layers can be dated later than the Antonine period, and the coarse wares are not demonstrably later. Sealed below the bank was the remains of an occupation layer which contained a large amount of carbon and a number of lumps of iron slag from a forge,[4] indicating the presence of a smithy on the site. Below this layer were a number of postholes and slots which were evident as stains in the yellow clay. The general arrangement of these slots suggest that they were the remains of rectangular timber-framed huts, but the postholes, one of which cuts into the slot aligned north – south, are of different date and may be associated with the smithy. At this level were found several body sherds of a soft heavily gritted vessel which could fit into a pre-Roman, possibly Early Iron Age context, but the absence of any rim or base sherds makes any positive identification impossible.

East of the wall footing (Fig. 2, Section C-C) the bank had been cut away when the wall was built. This was at some time after the town had been enclosed within the defensive perimeter, and the evidence seen here at Westgate reinforces that produced by earlier excavations.[5] The bottom few courses of the wall were unmortared, and droppings of mortar by the wall builders as they worked from inside the cut back can be seen as two successive layers in the section.

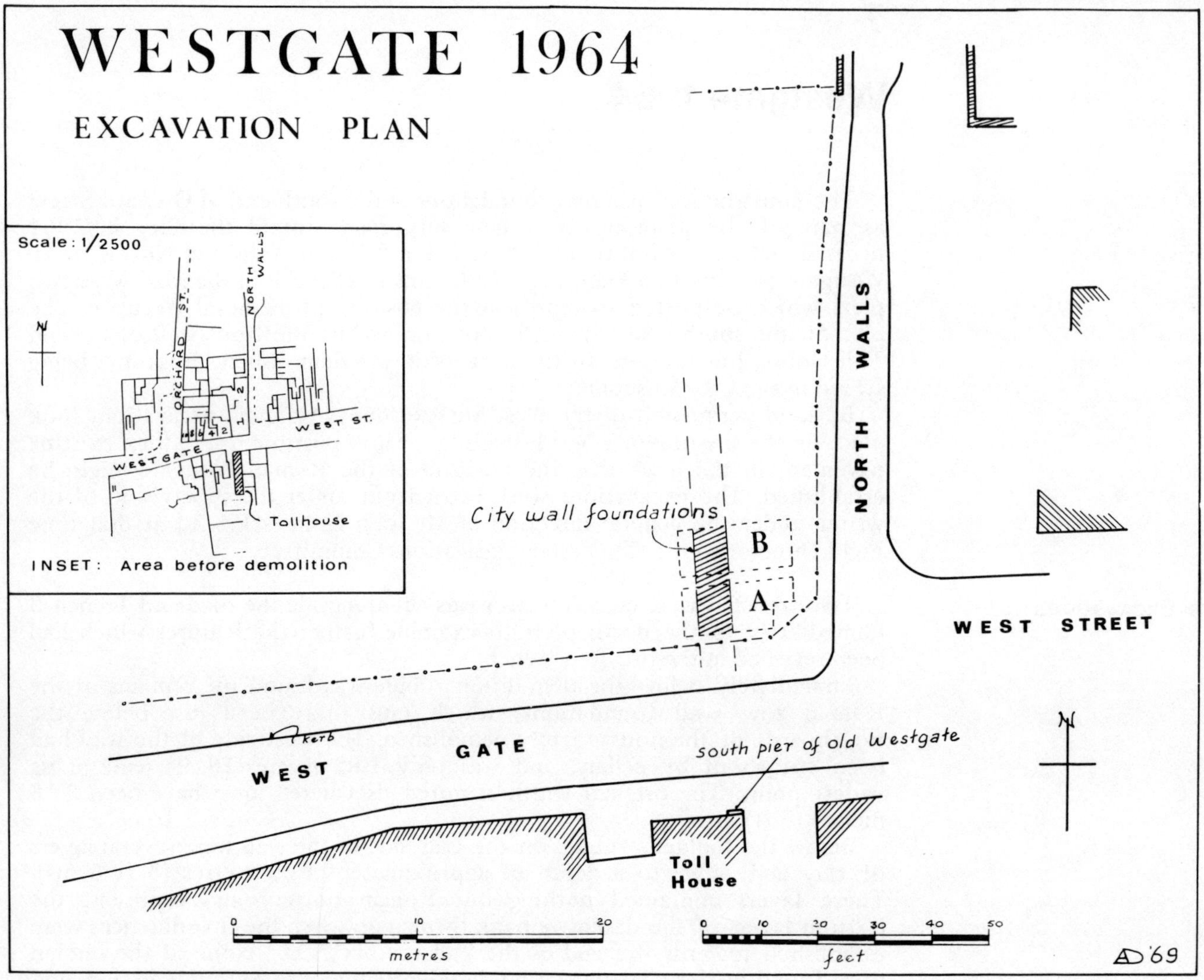

Fig. 7.1

Summary and Discussion

Five periods of activity can be identified from the excavations, and these may be conveniently summarised as follows:—

Period 1. – Pre-Roman occupation, possibly Early Iron Age, as represented by the soft gritty sherds found below the burnt layers.

Period 2a. – Roman. To this period can be assigned the timber-framed huts, and the samian ware found at this level suggest occupation from Neronian times.

Period 2b. – A smithy was erected on or near the site and the postholes and the burnt layers, one of which may be a furnace pit, belong to this phase. Two sherds of samian were found at this level, both of 1st century date.

Fig. 7.2

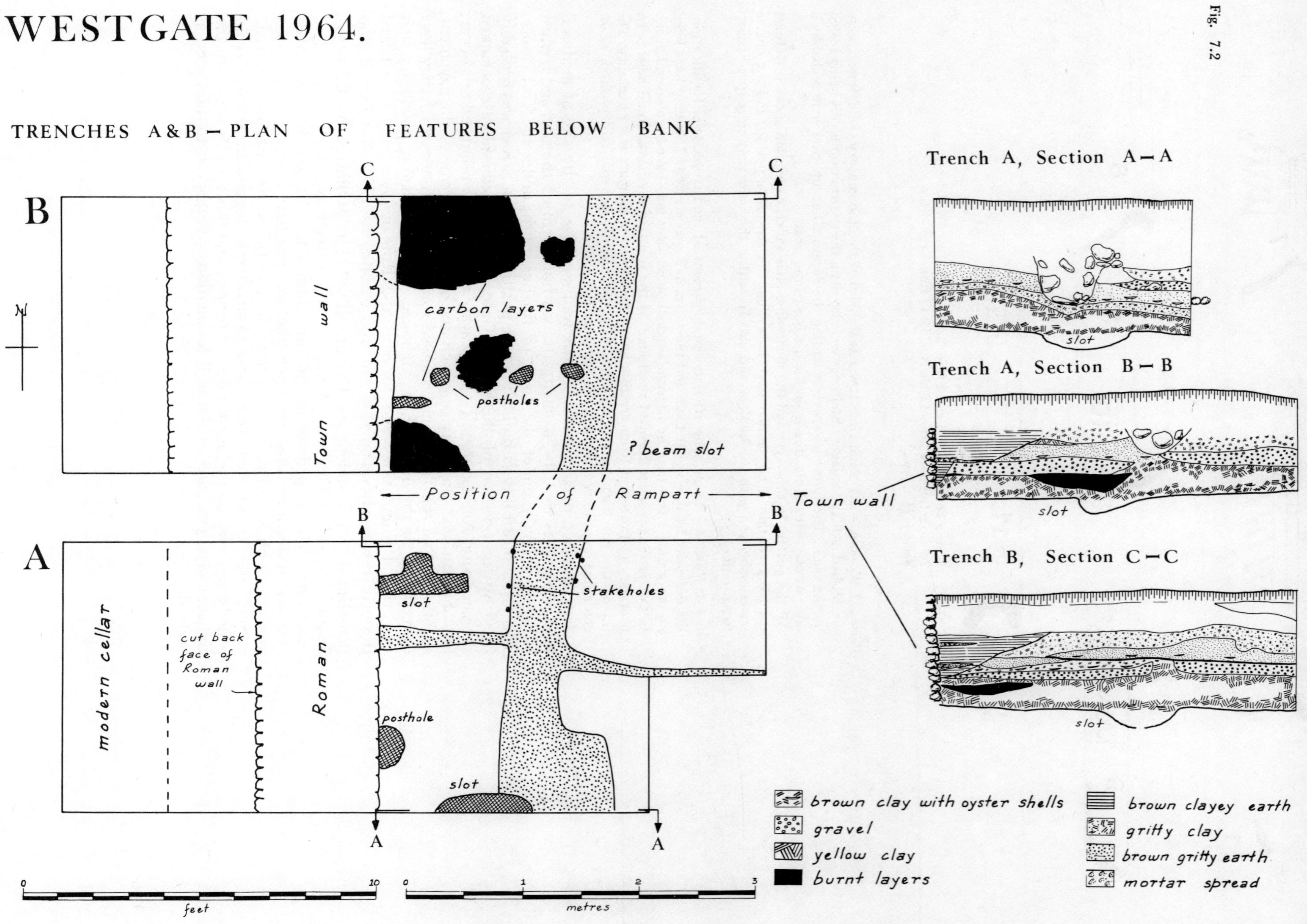
WESTGATE 1964.
TRENCHES A&B – PLAN OF FEATURES BELOW BANK
B
A
C
C
B
B
A
A
Town wall
carbon layers
postholes
? beam slot
Position of Rampart
modern cellar
cut back face of Roman wall
Roman
slot
stakeholes
posthole
slot
Trench A, Section A – A
slot
Trench A, Section B – B
Town wall
slot
Trench B, Section C – C
slot
brown clay with oyster shells
gravel
yellow clay
burnt layers
brown clayey earth
gritty clay
brown gritty earth
mortar spread
0
10
feet
0
1
2
3
metres

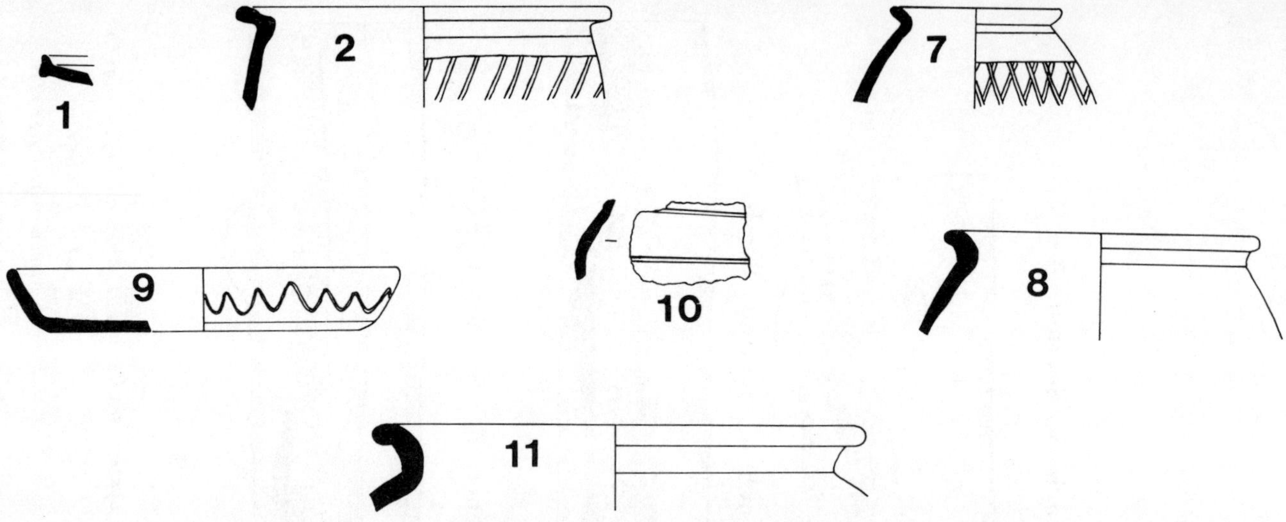

Fig. 7.3 Roman Pottery. Nos. 1 and 2 from Bank behind Town Wall. Nos. 7-9 from Cut-back behind Wall. Nos. 10-11 from Level below Bank. (1/4 approx.)

Period 3. Roman – At some time towards the end of the 2nd century the defences were established. All the adjacent buildings were levelled, the destruction layers being sealed by the bank. The burnt layers representing the Period 2b occupation were sealed by a layer of clay with flints, dug from the ditches to the west.

All the pottery in this layer and the succeeding ones which were piled above it to form the bank contained no samian ware later than the Antonine period, and the coarse wares associated with the bank would also fit within the same time scale (pre-Flavian to Antonine).

Period 4. Roman – Some time after the establishment of the first phase of fortification, the defensive bank was cut back and the town wall was erected. This may have been no more than a few months after the original phase, or it may have been several years. In the latter case some form of revetment of the front of the bank would have been necessary to protect it from erosion; and a turf revetted rampart is a possibility. The fill of the cut back, which was probably the original material re-deposited, again contained no pottery later than the Antonine period.

The presence of the Roman town wall so close to the site of medieval Westgate proves that the Roman gate was not north of the site, and it must either lie directly under the road, or further south, under the Toll House. This latter possibility is unlikely as the position of West Street was probably fixed by the position of the Roman Gate, and the medieval gate occupied the same site. An opportunity to excavate to prove this point did not occur, but observations[6] on a service trench dug on the south side of the pavement, slightly west of the Toll House, showed some dressed stones which may have formed part of the demolished gatehouse. There is a strong possibility that the original foundations and form of the Roman Gate may have lasted through the medieval period up to as late as 1772–3 when it was demolished.[7] A woodcut by Grimm, (Pl. 11) re-published by C. Roach Smith,[8] shows the Chichester Westgate with a single arch for traffic and a small side arch for pedestrians on the south side. The gate has been built over, and it is evident that the superstructure must have been the subject of a number of phases of re-building since Roman times. Nevertheless the basic ground plan could well have survived unaltered. Significantly there is no pedestrian way on the north side of the arch, and this accords well with the archaeological evidence of the wall foundations running out to the street on that side.

The Pottery

Types where quoted refer to cemetery vessels.

From the Bank

1. Rim of shallow platter, burnished internally and over lip. In fine grey ware, form uncertain.
2. Bowl in grey ware with grooved rim and diagonal tooled decoration on body.
3. Rim of bowl in sandy grey ware; reduced fabric, burnished exterior, type 15A. Not illustrated.
4. Lid in sandy grey ware; type 202D. Not illustrated.

Associated with these sherds were 13 samian sherds of which 9 were Antonine in date.

From the cut back behind the town wall.

5. Grey ware carinated jar, type 18A, not illustrated.
6. Neck and rim of flagon in buff ware, variant of type 142A. Not illustrated.
7. Grey ware jar.
8. Grey ware bowl with everted rim, slightly flattened.
9. Shallow dish or platter in hard sandy grey ware, highly burnished inside and out.

2 samian sherds were associated, a Dr 18/31 probably Hadrianic and a Dr 79 of Antonine date.

From the levels below the bank.

10. Sherd from bowl in sandy grey ware, grooved below neck and on shoulder.
11. Vessel in sandy pink fabric.

5 fragments of samian were associated, A Dr 29 of ? Flavian date, a Dr 37 or 29 of 1st century, a Dr 18, 1st century, a Dr 15/17, Neronian, and a Dr 27, pre Flavian.

Notes and References

[1] No plan has been produced to show the existing arrangement of the road and roundabout at the site as this is temporary, and the writer is informed that further work within the next decade will alter the scene even further.

[2] A.E. Wilson, "Roman Chichester" *S.A.C.*, 95, 127.

[3] op cit.

[4] Information from Mr Henry Cleere of the Iron and Steel Institute who kindly examined a sample of slag and confirmed that it was from a forge.

[5] *(i)* J. Holmes, *"The defences of Roman Chichester", S.A.C.* **100**, 88.

(ii) Observations by the writer on a section across the bank in the Bishops Garden, when the wall at the rear of the car park belonging to the Castle Inn collapsed in 1966.

[6] Information from Mr Roger Lintott who watched the site on behalf of the Committee.

[7] *V.C.H. Sx.* 3, 72.

[8] C. Roach Smith, *The Roman Castrum at Pevensey*, London 1858, p. 30.

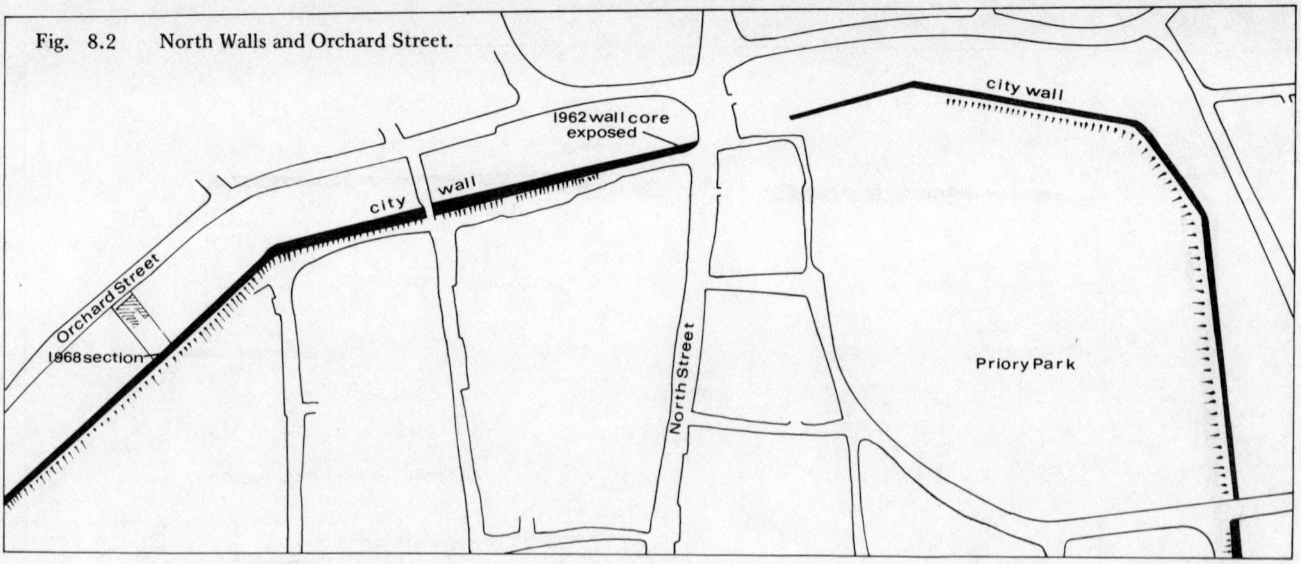

Fig. 8.2 North Walls and Orchard Street.

8

North Walls and Orchard St.

On Boxing Day 1967 part of the face of the North Wall of Chichester collapsed dramatically into the back gardens of numbers 104, 106, 108, Orchard Street. (Fig. 8.2) The repair work undertaken by the City Council the following November provided the opportunity to study the construction, repair and rebuilding of the City Wall at this point.[1] Previous work on the City walls by Hannah,[2] Rae,[3] Collins,[4] Wilson,[5] and Holmes[6], had indicated that a substantial core of Roman work existed behind the 18th and 19th century refacing of the wall.

In 1962, redevelopment of a site west of North Gate (Fig. 8.2) exposed a section of wall core constructed of flints set in creamy buff mortar, with many pockets of air trapped between the stones. Roman work of similar construction had been observed during excavations at Porchester,[7] and Winchester,[8] and in the absence of direct dating evidence the length of masonry core exposed at North Gate was judged to be Roman work.

The new exposure of masonry core in Orchard Street appeared on first examination to be of similar construction, but as work progressed it became necessary for the workmen to demolish much of the flint core in order to reconstruct the new wall on a firm foundation. Eventually it was possible to examine a complete section through the wall to the undisturbed bank behind, and it became clear that only the lower four feet of wall core was the original construction. Several recent patches of repair work using cement mortar could be identified. Behind the garden of 108, Orchard Street, a skin of cement mortar had been applied over the whole surface of the wall from ground level upwards. It was the collapse of this 'skin' and adjacent patchwork repairs that led to the present repair work. Behind the modern casing four major periods of construction were identified.

Period 1

Period 1. Fig. 8.3 Plate 2.

Regular courses of flints set in hard pale orange buff mortar, rising to an average height of 122 cms (4 ft) above ground level (layer 3).

The front face of the wall had been eroded or robbed for building stone, but the inner face was preserved together with the construction trench and bank. The internal face had been dressed with selected flat flints and

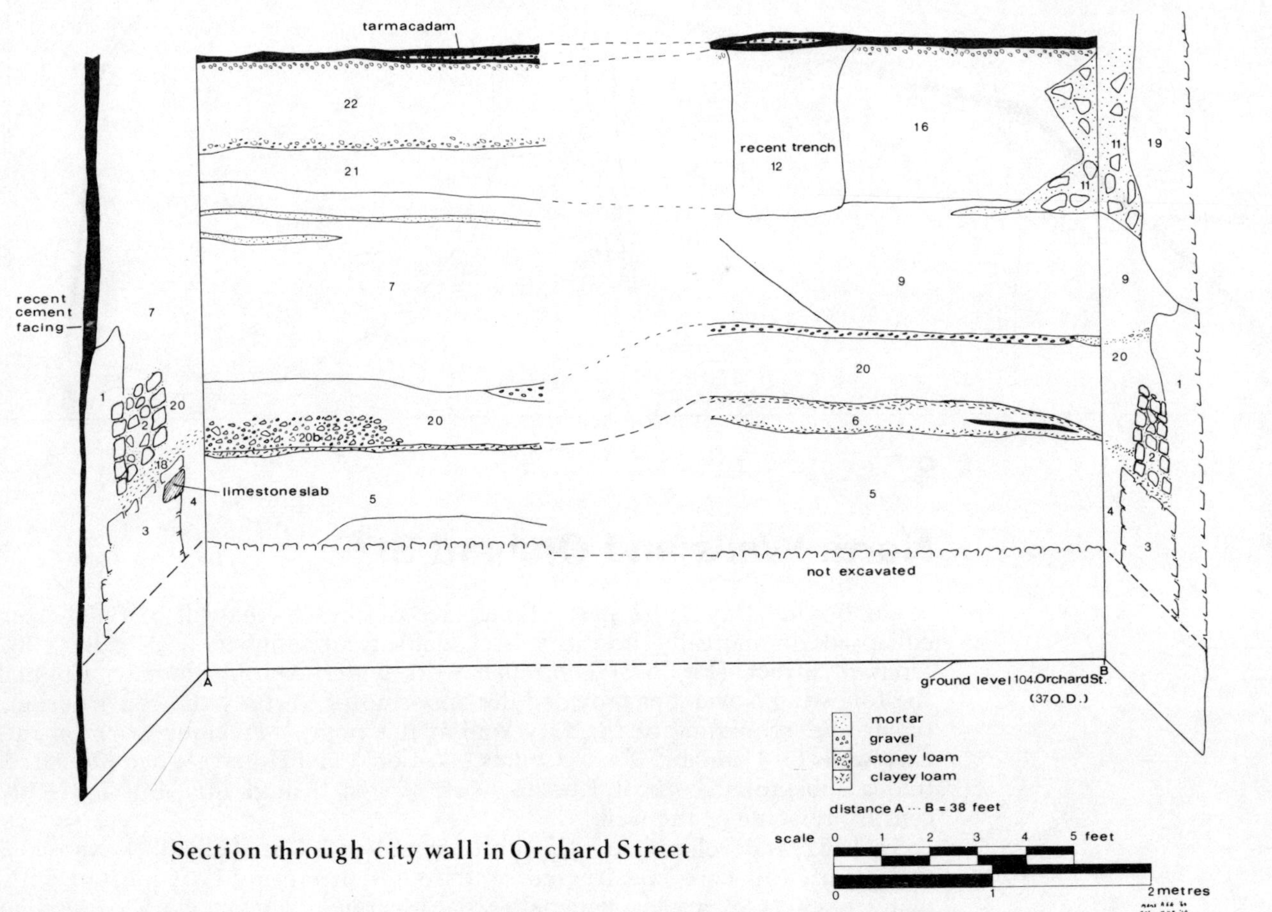

Section through city wall in Orchard Street

Fig. 8.3

incorporated blocks of water-worn limestone (Alveolina limestone) in the lower courses. The compact bank on the south side of the wall (layer 5) clearly showed the tip lines of the organic debris and loam with which it had been constructed. The wall was separated from the bank by a construction trench (layer 4) 13 cms (5.1 ins) wide, filled with soft loose loam and stones, which peeled away easily from the compact bank behind.

The wall, construction trench and bank all contained sherds of samian pottery of first and second century date. Above the period 1 wall, a wedge of dark loam (layer 18) varying in thickness from 15 - 30 cms (6 ins - 12 ins) thick contained two sherds of first century Samian pottery. The bank behind the wall was seen to be constructed of a more clayey loam above this level (layer 6) and a thin line of greyish green clay probably produced by the decay of an ancient turfline sealed the top of the bank above the period 1 level.

Period 2

Period 2.

On the top of the loam sealing wall 1, a new wall (layer 2) of roughly coursed flints set in orange yellow mortar was constructed. The internal face of this wall was set back 15 cms (6 ins) from the vertical face of wall 1 and it contained no limestone blocks. The material of the period 2 bank (layer 20) was piled against the wall face and sealed the turfline over bank 1.

Period 3

Period 3.

Overlying the period 2 wall and completely covering the northern face of walls 1 and 2, there was a skin of flints set in crumbly beige lime mortar (layer 1) varying in thickness from 15 cms - 30 cms (6in - 12 ins).

Period 4

Period 4.

Above the level of the period 3 wall, the wall construction changed again in character and consisted of small flints in smooth pale orange mortar with small fragments of chalk (layer 19). South of the vertical wall core this feature became much wider and in the west section the masonry spread over into the bank (layer 11).

Several minor patches of repair were seen on the outer face of the wall. In the east section a thin skin of grey cement mortar covered the entire face of the wall.

Discussion

Discussion

All the levels of bank examined contained sherds of Roman coarseware and Samian pottery of first and second century date. Layer 9 contained one large sherd of a storage vessel in pinkish red fabric with an outer and inner coat of orange brown glaze streaked with black. This vessel can be dated to the eighteenth century and was probably dropped into the loose fill behind the wall core when the ramparts were repaired in the eighteenth century.[9]

The fourth period of wall construction (layers 11 and 19) dates from this period. Behind the first period wall, the construction trench contained only first and second century occupation material, and the wall must be the original Roman wall built against the cut-back face of an earlier bank. It is difficult to date the second period wall. Clearly it is not of integral construction with the earlier wall as a layer of loam divides the two. It could represent a separate sequence of Roman construction. If the wall was originally built by gangs of workmen who constructed each section of the wall to a certain height and then moved on to the next section, a period of time would elapse before the wall was finally raised to its full height However the Roman labourer would have hardly been permitted to build on top of a layer of loam so this explanation is unlikely.

The change in character of the bank at a point roughly coinciding with the top of the first period wall also indicates that at some time both the bank and wall were much reduced in height.

It is clear from documentary records that in the 13th and 14th centuries a great deal of time and money was spent rebuilding the defences of Chichester. The first grant of murage dates from 1261,[10] but in 1339 King Edward III appointed the Earl of Arundel, Thomas de Braiose and William de Fishbourne to survey the walls and put the city in a state of defence.[11] This work was to be done at the expense of the mayor, baliffs, and citizens, but because of the high cost and the poverty of the citizens of Chichester, the Bishop and the Dean and Chapter agreed to contribute towards the work. In 1341, £27 tax from the fee farm was remitted because of the great expense of enclosing the city,[12] and in 1369[13] and 1377[14] mention is again made of repair and reconstruction of the city walls.

The limited results obtained from observing this new section through the city wall suggests that in the 14th century the wall and bank at this point were reduced in height to a mere four feet or so above the ground level; the wall was covered by collapsed earth from the decayed Roman bank, and that the wall and bank above this level are the result of site clearance and reconstruction undertaken by the command of Edward III.

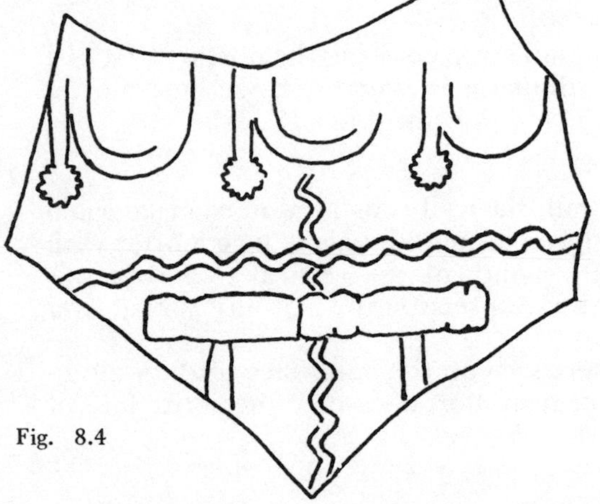

Fig. 8.4

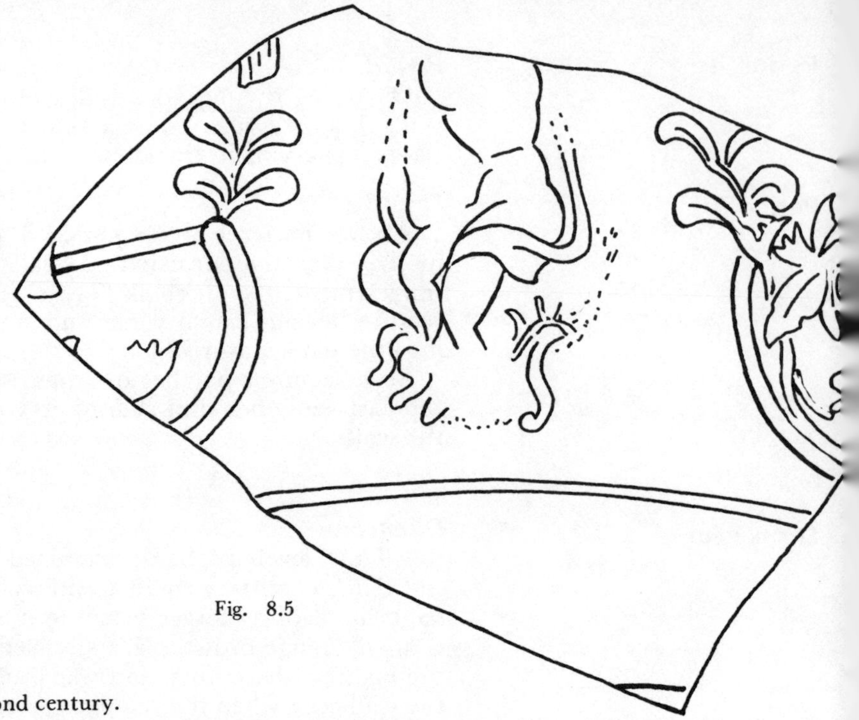

Fig. 8.5

Samian Pottery

Wall (layer 3)
Form 33. Second century.

Construction trench (layer 4).
Form 37. Single-bordered ovolo with straight tongue ending in a rosette attached to the left. Below a wavy line, a festoon. Note the wavy line of the festoon over-ridden by the ovolo border. Very close to the ovolo of DIVIXTVS, CGP Fig. 32 No. 4, but wavy line borders are very rare in his work. Antonine date. (Fig. no. 8.4).
Form 15/17 Pre-Flavian.
Curle 11, late first century.
Form 29. First century.
Form 36. First century (two sherds).
Form 27. Flavian (two sherds).
Form 37. First century.
Form 27. pre Flavian.
Form 18. pre Flavian Lezoux ware.
Form 31. Antonine (two sherds).
Form 37. Trajanic.

Bank (layer 5)
Form 37. Burnt. By COCATVS / IGOCATVS cf. CGP. p. 17 and pl. 17 for design. The figure can be seen there on sherd 208. Date, Trajanic. (Fig. no. 8.5).
Form 31. Had – Antonine.
Form 35. Second century.
Form 18. First century.
Form 24/5. Claud – Nero.
Form 35. First century.

Notes and References

[1]Mrs A.E. Grant supervised the site on behalf of the excavation Committee and this report is compiled from her site notes.
[2]Hannah 1934. *S.A.C.* 75. 107.
[3]Rae 1952. *S.A.C.* 90. 179.
[4]Collins *S.A.C.* 95.
[5]Wilson *Chichester papers No 6.*
[6]Holmes, 1962 *S.A.C.* 100, 80 - 92.
[7]Cunliffe 1963. 'Excavations at Porchester Castle', *Hants. A. J.*, 43, 221.
[8]Cunliffe 1962. 'The Winchester City Wall.' *H.F.C.*, 22, 69.
[9]Hay. *History of Chichester,* 214.
[10]*Cal. Pat R.* 1258 - 66, 189.
[11]*Cal. Pat R.* 1338 - 40, 246.
[12]*Cal. Pat R.* 1340-43, 220.
[13]*Cal. Pat R.* 1367 - 70, 235, 243.
[14]*Cal Pat R.* 1377 - 81, 72.

9

A Medieval Kiln in Orchard Street

Early in November 1967 it was noticed that the large services trench which had been dug along the north side of Orchard Street had sectioned a layer of burnt clay immediately opposite No. 206 and in what had been the back garden of No. 1 St. Pauls Road, which had been demolished prior to the commencement of the street works, (Fig. 1.). Large amounts of medieval tile and pottery recovered from the spoil heap suggested the presence of a kiln or kilns. The West Sussex County Council readily gave permission for excavations to take place, and kindly isolated the area for some months so that work could proceed unhampered by the new street works.

The Excavations. Fig 2

To establish the extent of the kiln and in the hope of finding waster tips, two trenches were dug on the north side of the services trench. The most northerly (Trench B) proved barren, natural clay being reached at a depth of 80 cms (31.5 inches). Trench A, nearest the kiln, produced a pit containing wasters from earlier kilns, and the pipe trench had sectioned a number of pits, (Fig. 4) all of which contained tile fragments and other wasters from earlier and contemporary kilns.

At a depth of 1 metre (39 ins) a layer of yellow brown clay was reached, and on this lay a spread of Roman occupation material together with traces of post and stakeholes consistent with there having been some slight wooden structure on the site. The post and stakeholes were only perceptible in the clay, and need not belong to the Roman period; in fact they may represent temporary shelters erected by the potters working on the site. The Roman pottery found included samian ware of late 1st century to Antonine date and New Forest purple ware of the late 3rd or 4th century.

The Kiln. Pl. 12 Fig. 3.

The services trench had cut through the long axis of the kiln, removing slightly under half, and a complete reconstruction in plan was therefore possible. It was aligned east–west and had been fired from the western end. It was elliptical in shape, overall dimensions being 3.2 metres, (10ft 6 ins) long and 1.8 metres (5 ft 11 ins) across the short axis. The walls of the kiln were built of flints, sandstone, chalk and greensand fragments bound in clay. The base of the outside walls rested on tile fragments bound in clay and laid horizontally, and the interior faces of the flues and the floor of the kiln were coated with a layer of smoothed clay, baked hard.

The flues were choked with debris from the collapsed side walls and it seemed possible that deliberate blocking of parts of the flues had occurred, probably to restrict the circulation of heat and eliminate "hot" or "cold" spots. Amongst the debris within and around the kiln were masses of baked clay re-inforced with tile wasters and these probably represented the material used to construct the upper kiln walls, The flue walls stood to a height of 40 cms (15.75 ins) and the inner faces of the outside walls were recessed at the top to take the kiln bars which supported the wares during firing (see p. 156 below). The actual height of the kiln walls must of necessity be conjectural, but they are not likely to have been higher than 1 metre (39 ins) as the kiln

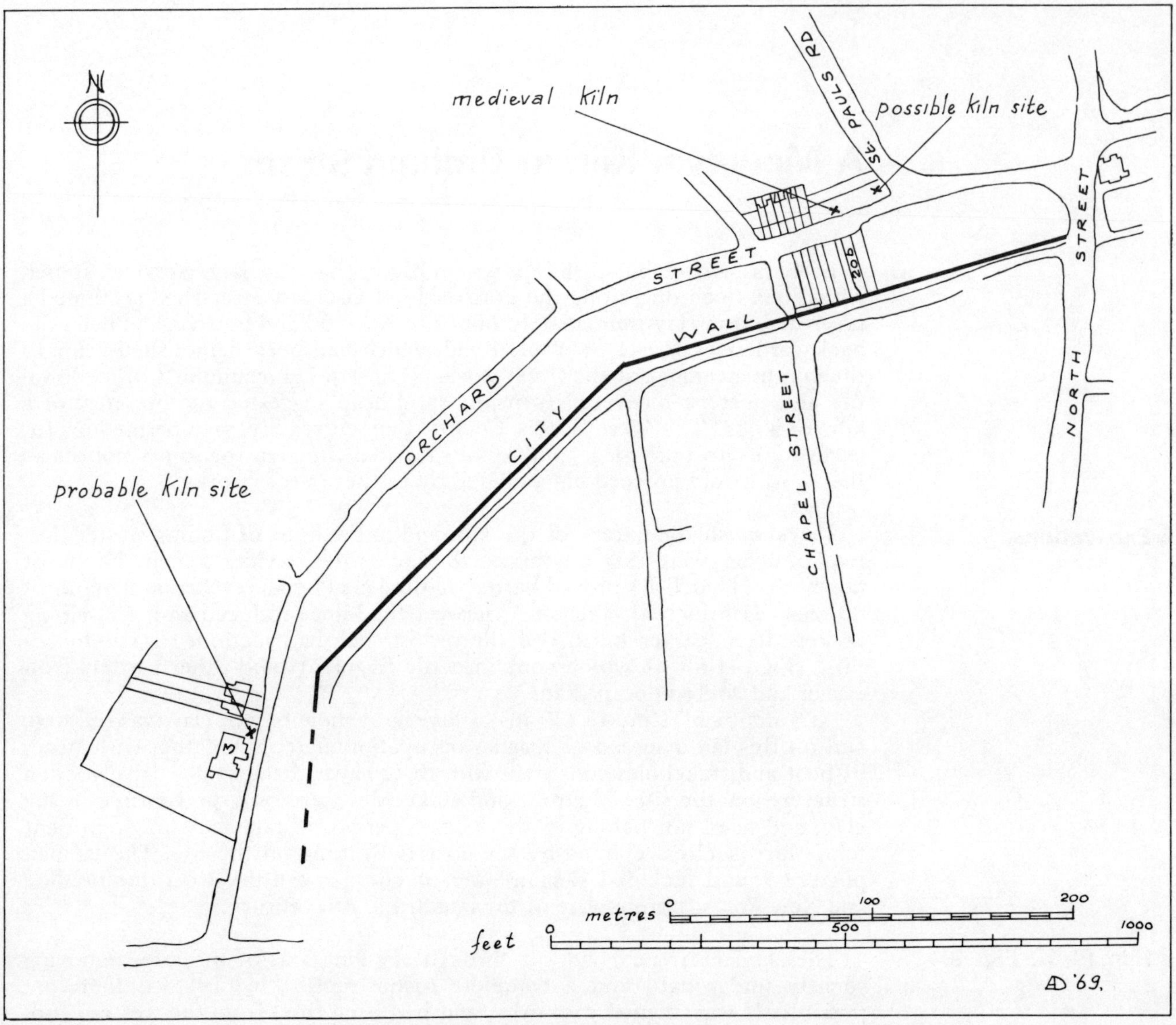

Fig. 9.1 Plan showing medieval kiln site. Based on Ordnance Survey, by permission of the Director General.

would have been loaded from the top. It was built over an earlier pit containing wasters; this was first sealed by throwing down a layer of clay, and the flue walls were then built on top. The ground around the outside of the flue walls was then made up level with the top of the flues, and this would have acted as an additional support for the kiln as well as providing some insulation against heat losses and a convenient loading platform for the wares.

A small amount of soft sticky clay with an admixture of chalk (cob) was found at the bottom of the flues and this is probably from the top seal, which would be demolished after firing. This material has been noted by the writer at the Upmarden Roman Villa[1], where it was used to insulate pilae tiles against the effects of excessive heat, and also at the medieval kiln at Knighton[2], I.O.W. No waster tips were found, the only waste products

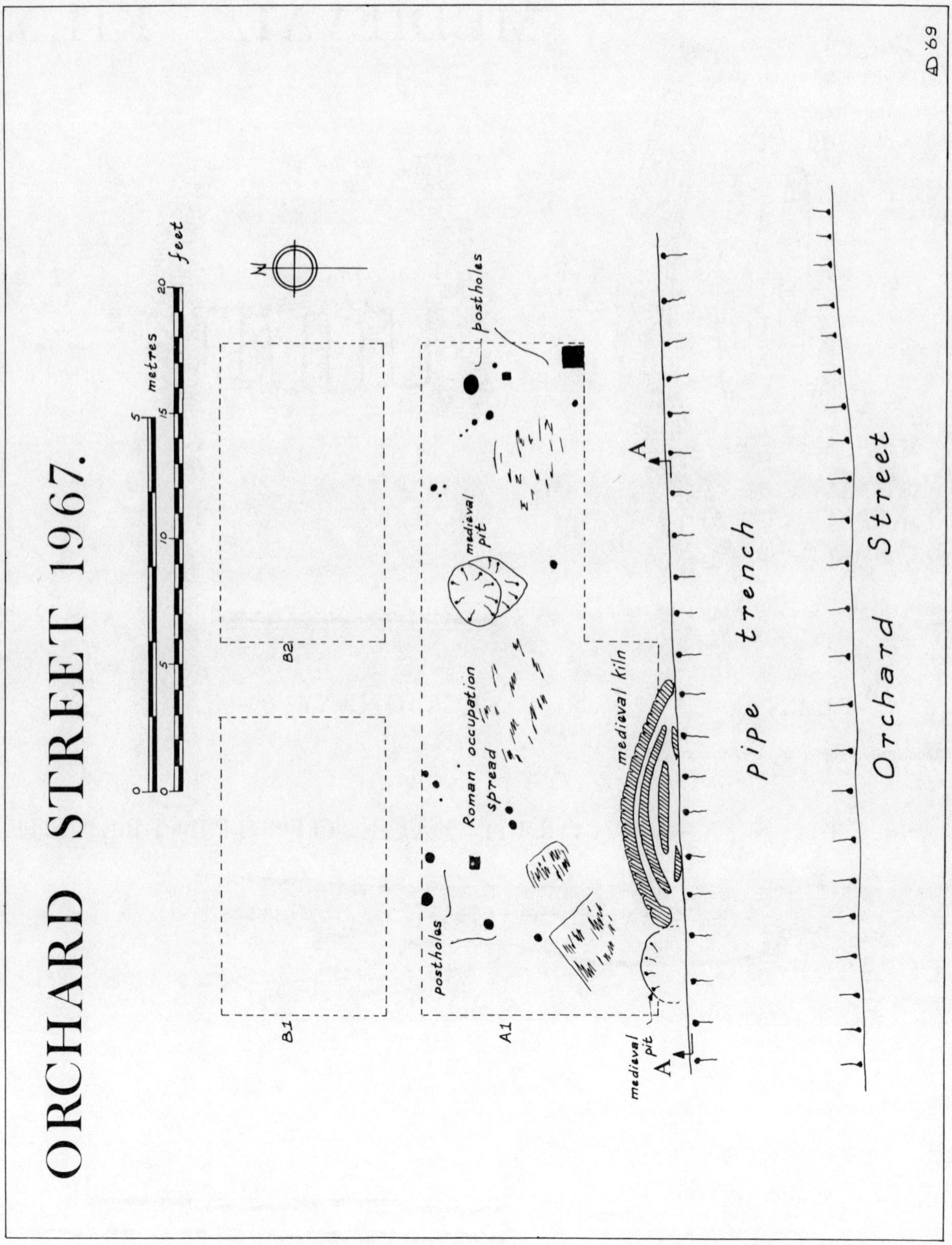

Fig. 9.2 Plan showing Roman and Medieval features.

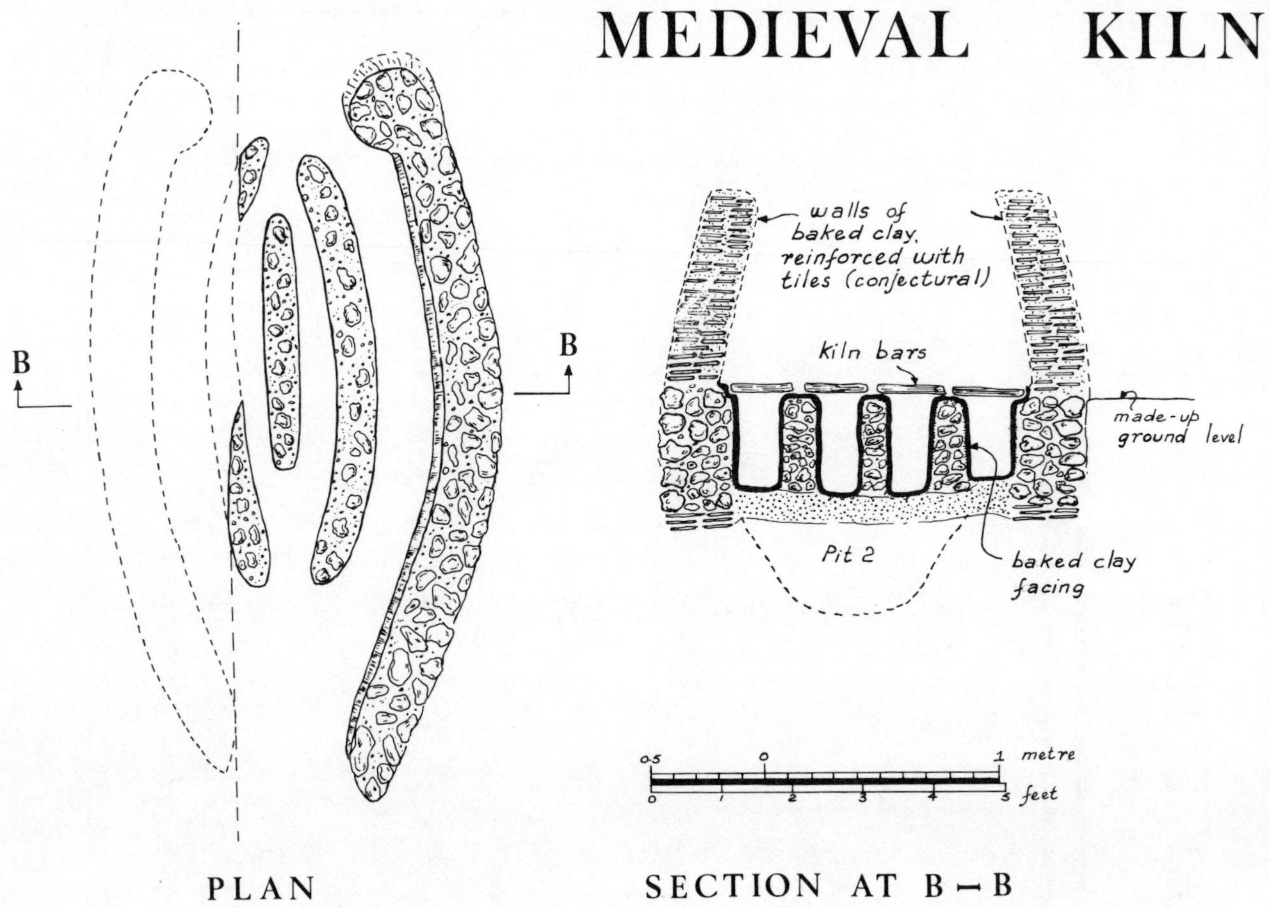

Fig. 9.3 Reconstruction plan and section across kiln.

Fig. 9.4

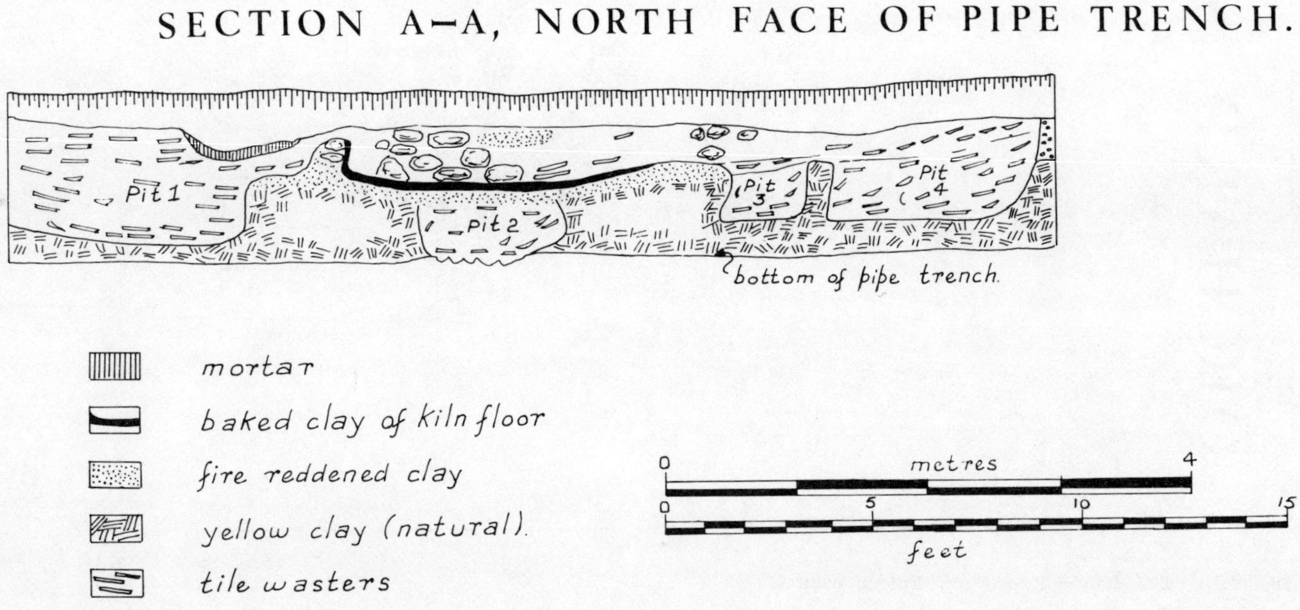

Photo: Thelma Westmore

PLATE 15. Roman lead-glazed and coloured coated wares from the cemetery.
Left: Vessel from Grave 171(f) (p. 79 and Fig. 5.24).
Above: No. 46 (p. 77 and Fig. 5.12).
Right: Colour coated flask from Grave 81(a) (p. 99 and Fig. 5.22).
Scale: Approx. $\frac{1}{3}$.

Photo: Thelma Westmore

PLATE 16. Roman lead-glazed wares from the cemetery.
Two vessels from Grave 247(c & g) (p.79 and Fig. 5.26).
Scale: Approx $\frac{1}{2}$.

recovered were from the kiln itself and from various pits around and under it. The pits had obviously been dug for suitable clay and the wasters used as a convenient fill. Two other spots were noted as possible kiln sites during the street works; an area of burnt clay was sectioned by the pipe trench outside Nos 4 and 5 Orchard Street, and another area at the junction of St. Pauls Road with Orchard Street was noted (Fig 1.) It is evident that this area of the City, just outside the defensive ditch, was where the city's potters plied their trade. The total amount of waste material involved would have been prodigious and it is remarkable that until 1967 no traces of a pottery industry had been recorded.

Site History

The Gardner Map of 1769 (Fig. 2.5) shows a lane running on the line of modern Orchard Street. This is not named, but it is almost certainly the Scuttery Lane mentioned in the Chichester Common Council Minute Book of 1783 – 1826. "Scuttery", or "Scutterithe" appears to be the area outside the City walls from Westgate to Northgate, and the origin of the name is obscure. The houses at present occupying the site are mainly 18th and 19th century, the earlier suburbs having been destroyed during the siege of Chichester in the Civil War in 1642.

There are references in the Chichester Chartulary[3] to a Walter Pot who was granted a house in Chichester by the Dean, Simon de Perigord in 1218, and in the 3rd quarter of that century a Walter Potter (Potarius) is recorded as having sold six houses in Parislane (Chapel Street) to a John de Oving. This man, who may have been a descendant of Walter Pot, owned property very close to the kiln site[4]. His name suggests that potting was his trade, and it is just possible that there may be a connection between the younger Walter and the pottery industry outside the north and west areas of the City.

In 1378 a new ditch, 50 feet wide was dug around the city[5]. The course of this ditch is not known exactly on the north-west corner of the city, but elsewhere[6], excavation has shown that the outside lip of the new ditch was approximately 90 feet from the city wall, and had partially destroyed the earlier Roman outer defensive work. The kiln is only 140 feet from the wall, and assuming, as is likely, that Scuttery Lane (Orchard Street) followed the perimeter of the 14th century ditch, then the kiln would have been slightly less than 50 feet from the edge if it had been functioning as late as 1378.

Although it is thought to be highly unlikely from the date assigned to the wares (see p. 163 below) and also for strategic reasons, that a pottery industry would be allowed to develop immediately adjacent to the newly reconstructed town defences the possibility must be considered. If the kiln was in use after 1378 it is certain that some of the wasters would have found their way into the ditch. It may be possible to prove this point at some time in the near future, when demolition of some of the property on the South side of Orchard Street as part of the scheme for providing a ring road around the City may give us an opportunity to cut some sections across the medieval ditch.

The Products by K.J.Barton F.M.A., F.S.A.

A noticable feature at this site is the small number of finds, whereas from the majority of medieval kiln sites the quantity is enormous. There is however little doubt that all the products detailed here are from the same source of production; many are overfired and as a result are crazed or fractured, with glaze splashed on the fractures. Form and other primary features are common to all the material examined; that this explanation is necessary is due to the phenomena of a varied fabric, which can be wholly

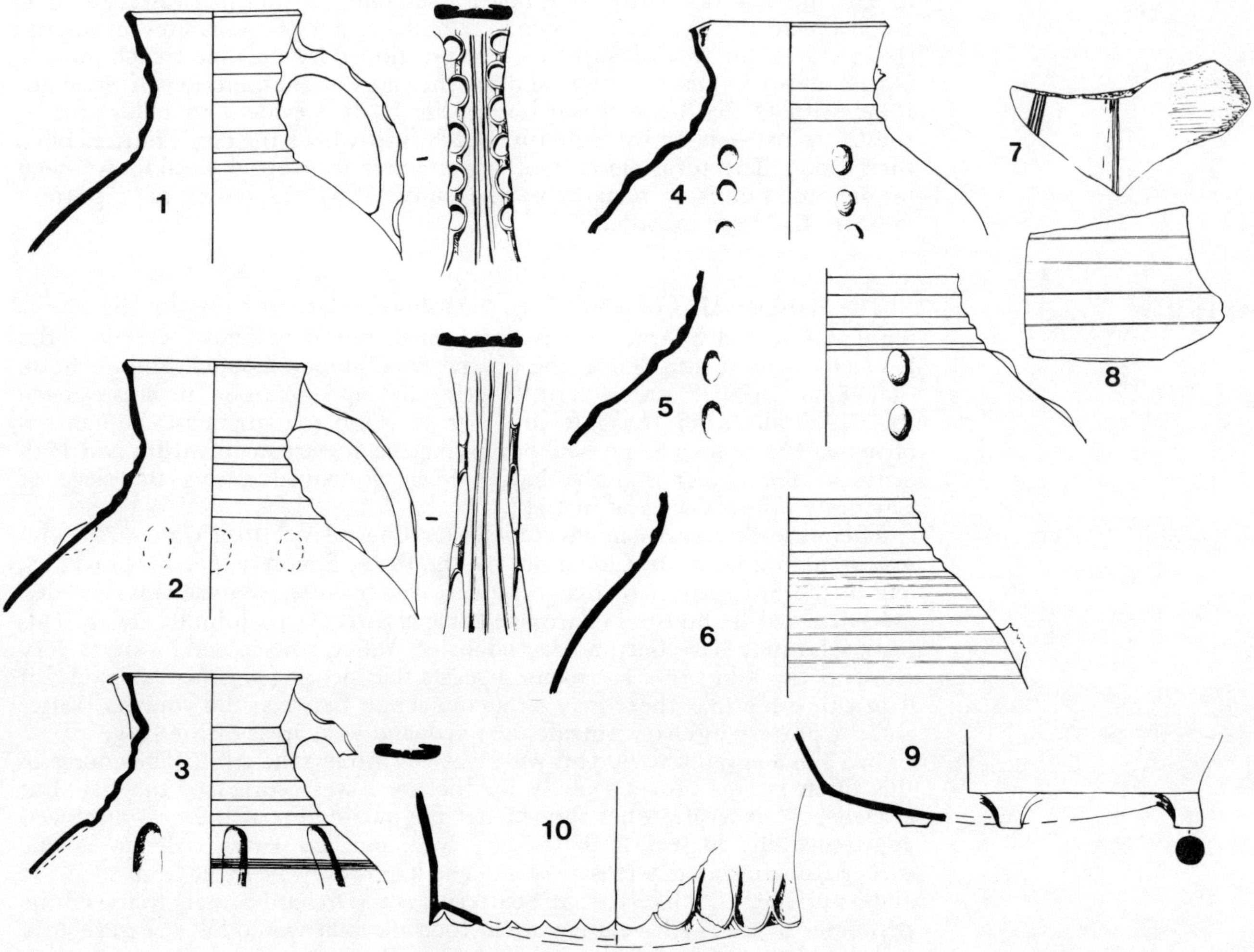

Fig. 9.5 Medieval jugs. (1/4.)

untempered, mildly or heavily tempered with a red sand, or heavily tempered with sharp edged small flint grits. A close examination shows all these grits to be opaque right through, and this opacity and the sharp angle of the fractures is probably caused by baking flint and quenching it while hot so that it fractures to provide a regular tempering medium.

The general intention of the Orchard Street potters was to oxidise their wares, and the bulk of them are. Some are reduced by mistake and in some the measure of oxidisation can only be related to the thickness of the pot, for the thicker the vessel the more likely it is to be wholly reduced or have a barely oxidised surface. In some instances, especially on glazed examples, there is evidence of a deliberate terminal reduction in an attempt to obtain a green colour.

The material illustrated includes all the principal types: Jugs Nos 1 to 10; cooking pots, Nos 11 to 14; lids, Nos 15 to 16; pans, Nos 17 to 18; mortar, 19; storage jars, Nos 20 to 24; chimney pots, Nos 25 to 27; flat roof tiles, Nos 28 and 28 a, b, c,; and kiln bars, No 30.

The Jugs (Fig 5, Nos 1 to 10).

The fabric of these vessels can range from totally untempered, filled with a coarse red sand, or filled with sand with an admixture of flint. The principal fabric is the sand tempered form. The colour of the unglazed portions of the body ranges from brick red to dark grey, although a red/buff colour predominates. Some wares have been oxidised with a terminal reduction to achieve a green colour to the glaze, The glaze colour ranges from bright orange through bright green to a dull green/brown. 101 fragments of jugs occurred.

The main characteristic of these vessels is the deep rim form over a heavily rilled neck which is expanded at its lower end. They have a long body with a wide upper shoulder tapering to a narrow and steeply sagging base which may have a heavily thumbed footring or be plain with tripod feet. The handles are of strap form with finger tipping or wiping, and the spouts are all pulled. All the jugs are glazed across the upper portion and handle, but not on the rim, and only odd splashes on the lower portions. With the exception of the decorative motifs those vessels illustrated here can be considered as the standard form produced by this kiln. The handles, although apparently different are all made the same way as a wide pulled strap with raised edges, and the flat central portion slashed longitudinally. In some instances the raised edges were then carfully pressed to give a series of rounded indentations along both edges (Nos 1; 9 examples) while in other cases the finger was drawn along the edge in three wipes (No. 2; 20 examples) This last method was also used on some pans, (No. 17). All these handles could have been made by the same hand as width measurements taken at the same point show, 3 -4 cm, 1 off; 4 - 5 cm, 24 off; 5 - 6 cm 4 off.

The bases of two types are of steeply angled sagging form. Where thumbed (3 examples) this is heavily and carefully executed. The tripod feet are on plain bases; are round in section and are set on the edge of the base. In these cases the fabric is of as wide a range as the jugs although the tripod feet tend to be in a finer quality fabric. All the bases are of a 22 - 23 cm radius. The jugs are decorated on the body in a small variety of forms. Several fragments (Nos 2 - 5) have raised bosses on the body. These are raised with the finger placed inside pressing against something held outside. They radiate downwards from the neck, and it appears that there were seven rows to a vessel. In the case of one vessel (No. 3) the boss is elongated, but insufficient remains to indicate how far down the vessel this reached. Other decorative media include fine horizontal combing (No. 3) which can occur with bosses or fine radial vertical combing (No. 7), or fine horizontal combing. There is no evidence to show how far decoration was carried below the shoulder. One example, not illustrated here is horizontally grooved around the rim band.

Although called jugs here, some if not all these vessels are pitchers, some certainly tripod pitchers, and the definition of a pitcher that does not have tripod feet at this period of time is difficult. It would seem that the only difference as far as these products are concerned is the sort of basal fitting it achieved after it was raised on the wheel. The vessels are mainly uniform in size with a rim form radius of 10 - 11 cm, but in at least one instance (No. 5) the vessel is very large by comparison.

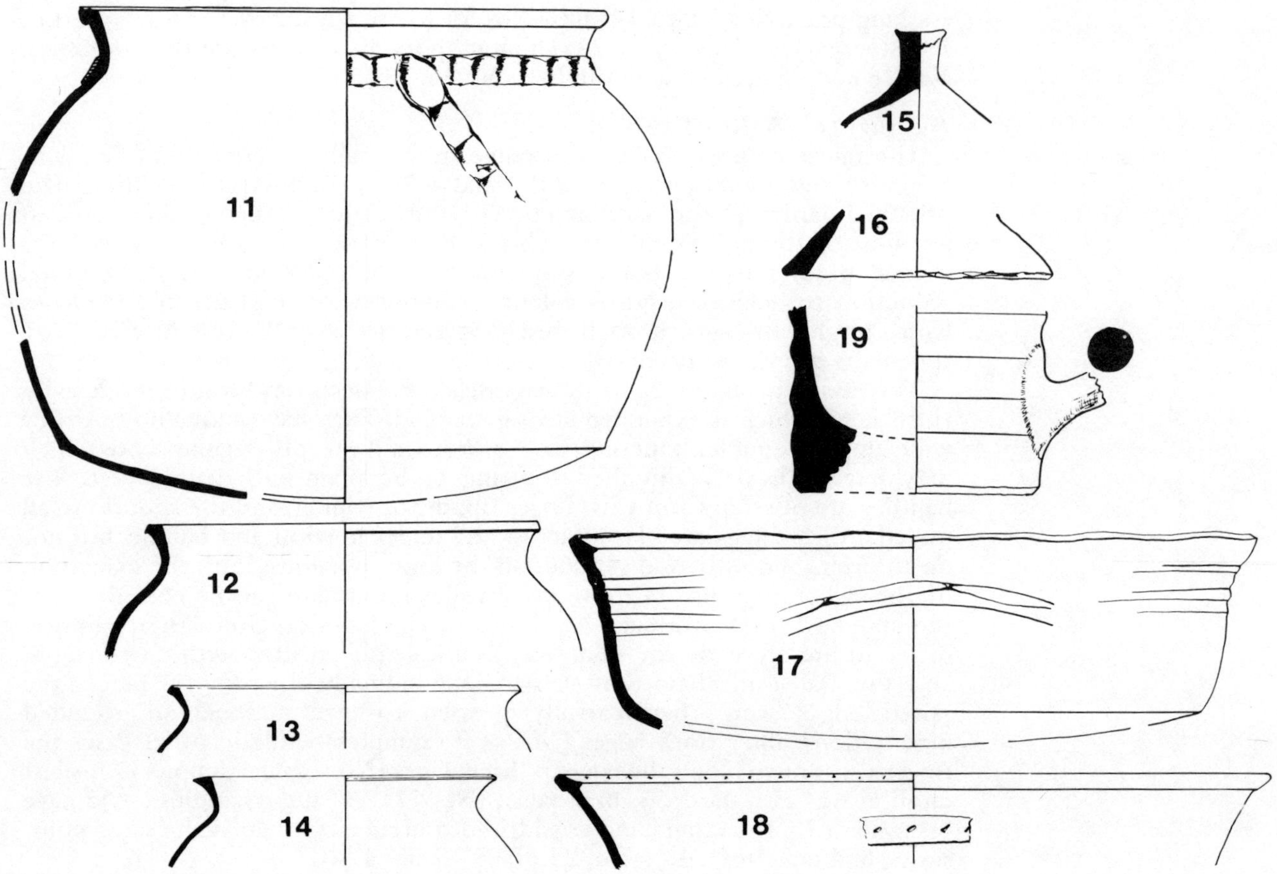

Fig. 9.6 Medieval pottery. Nos. 11-14 Cooking Pots. Nos. 15-16 Lids. Nos. 17, 18, Pans. No. 19, Mortar. (1/4.)

The Cooking Pots (Fig. 6 Nos. 11 to 14)

40 fragments were found which range in fabric from untempered, sand tempered, to very heavy tempering with small angular flints. They are not deliberately glazed, but some bear splashed glaze on them. These vessels are called coarse and fine by virtue of the thickness of the body. Coarse types predominate, 10 as No. 11 and 15 as No. 12 No. 11 is shown here in a reconstruction linking like rim with like base. The applied strap decoration was seen on 6 examples. The flanged rim is seen on a variety of vessels, Nos 11, 13, 17 and 20. The fine wares (No 13 - 8 examples and No. 14, 1 example) are also in the same fabric range as the coarse wares but the throwing of these vessels is very competent and well controlled. The sagging bases (6 examples) are all of the same angle not only in the cooking pots but also in the jugs (Nos. 9 - 10— the pans)No. 17) and the storage jars (No.21). Three sizes of cooking pots occur in this group as represented by the rim radii of c. 30 cm.; 24 cm and 20 cm. There is evidence of a smaller variety as indicated by the lid base No. 16 which is of 16 cm radius.

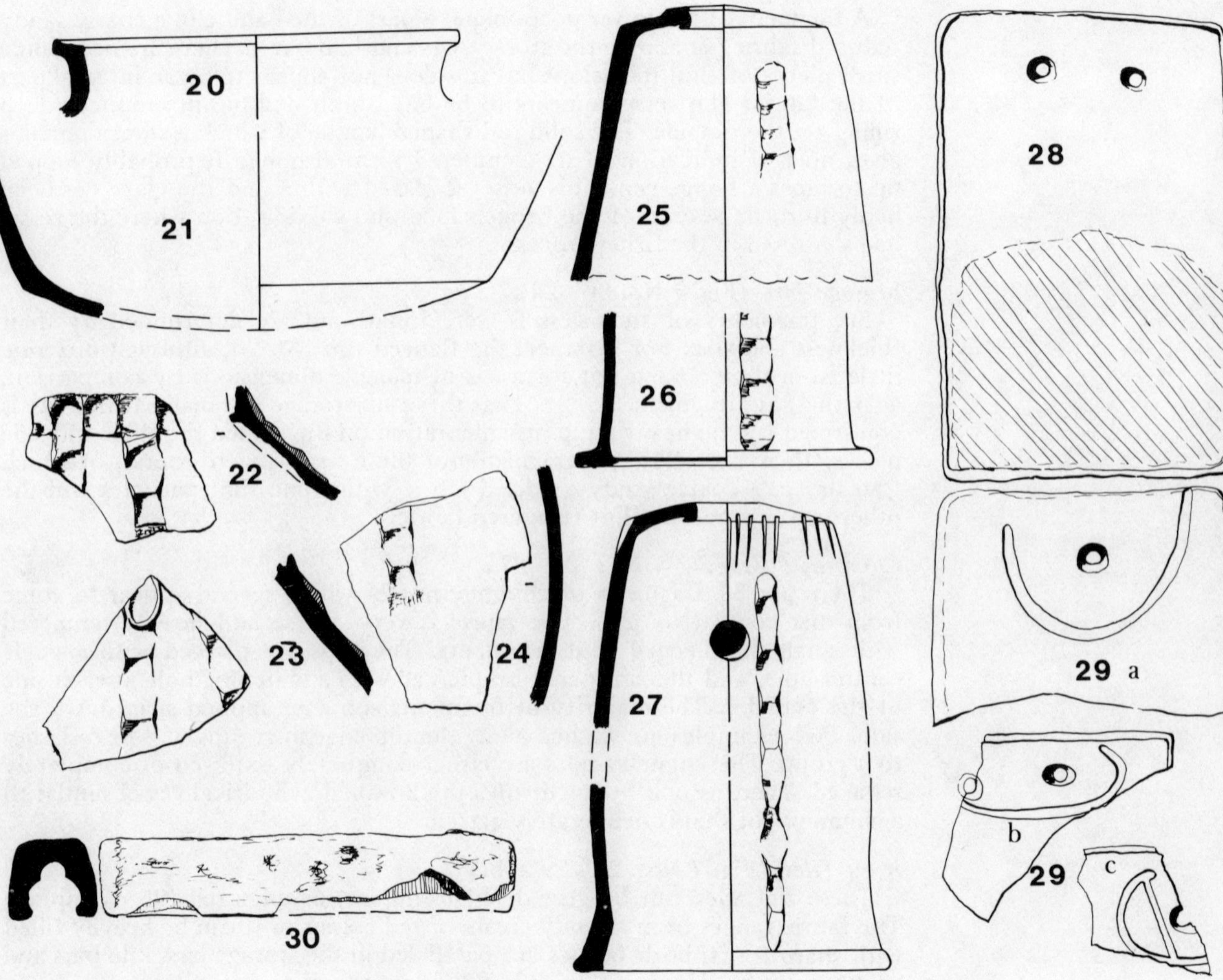

Fig. 9.7 Medieval Pottery. Nos. 20-23 Storage Jars. Nos. 25-27, Chimney Pots. Nos. 28, 29, b and c, Roof Tiles. No. 30 Kiln Bar. (1/4.)

Lids (Fig. 6 Nos. 15 and 16).

Fragments of two lids were found. Their fabric is a fine sandy red form; one example being kiln shattered with spots of glaze on the fracture. They are unglazed and undecorated and have not been thrown on a wheel, but are hand made.

Pans (Fig. 6 No. 17 and 18).

Two types occur; their fabric being the same as the cooking pots. The form of No. 17 is represented by 10 fragments of which 4 belong to the vessel illustrated. In this instance the raised flange has been finger wiped to give a corona effect to the pot rim. The only type of decoration seen here takes the form of stabbing at regular intervals (1.5 cm) with a small tool (.5 cm). This occurs on both types of vessel. No. 18 form is represented by 7 fragments.

Mortar. (Fig. 6 No.19).

A fragment of the lower portion and a part of the handle in a coarse sandy reduced fabric (similar to the storage jars and kiln bars). There are occasional small pieces of flint inclusions but this does not appear to be an integral part of the fabric. The vessel appears to be hand built and has pronounced deep rilling on the outside. The solid rod shaped handle of which a stump remains gives no real indication of its completed form although it probably looped up to meet a flange rim. This vessel is glazed within and the glaze has been badly burned. Several of the broken faces show oxidisation where the vessel had shattered in the firing process.

Storage Jars. (Fig. 7 No. 20 - 24).

Six fragments of such vessels were found and are determined by their thickness and size. For instance, the flanged rim No. 20, although differing little from the cooking pot forms, is of massive dimensions by comparison, as is the base fragment No. 21. That these are storage jars made at this site is confirmed by the heavy strap ornamentation on the angled shoulder and side pieces, (Nos. 22 - 24). Six fragments of these vessels were found, of which four are in a coarse sandy oxidised fabric with some flint particles and the other two in a heavily flint tempered fabric.

Chimney Pots. (Fig. 7 Nos. 25 - 27).

There are 34 fragment of chimney pot of which several appear to come from one vessel (No. 27). The fabric is very coarse and heavily tempered with small sharp-edged flint fragments. The tops are pierced with a single central hole, and the sides are also pierced with a matching hole at each side of the cylinder. The majority of fragments show an applied strip down the side. Two examples are slashed along the top edge in groups of 4 or 5 slashes to a group. The chimney pots are either completely oxidised or completely reduced. There is one fragment of a thick-walled cylindrical vessel similar to a chimney pot that is deliberately glazed.

Roof Tiles. (Fig. 7 Nos. 28 - 29 a, b. c,).

These flat tiles can be glazed (14 examples) or unglazed (25 examples). The fabric ranges from a sandy cream or red colour or it can be heavily filled with sharp flints; both fabrics are paralleled in the storage jars, kiln bars and chimney pots. However in several instances the flat tiles are wholly untempered in which case they fire a dark red and are heavy. The method of manufacture was to press out a tablet of clay into a wooden frame which was set on a sandy bed and the levelling done with a wooden tool. The piercing appears to be double in the majority of cases, but single piercing in the upper centre also occurs. Three fragments have a thumbed semi-circular motif around the fastening holes, these may be batch numbers (No. 29, a, b, c,). The glazed tile fragments indicate that glaze was put over half of the lower portion of the tiles. This glaze colour ranges from dark green to dark brown. The width measurement is 17 – 18 cm No complete lenths occur but assuming that the glazed covered a half (12.5 cm) this would give an overall length of 25 cm.

No ridge tiles were found at the kiln.

Kiln Bar. (Fig. 7 No. 30).

One almost complete example and the fragments of six others were recovered. The fabric is a grey sandy form or a heavily flint tempered form. These bars are made from a rod of prepared clay which has been drawn out underneath with the fingers to give a trefoil form to the section. There are traces of glaze on these bars.

Stacking. As all the glazing was thin, it did not run when fluxed which could have caused the vessels to stick to one another, as is the case in many other medieval kiln. However, some glaze did drip and fall on the cooking-pot fragments, running laterally down the sides, and this suggests that the cooking pots were stacked on their sides on the fire bars and the glazed jugs and roof tiles placed above them. There is no evidence of kiln props, but some pieces of clay had been used to wedge the vessels in place.

Discussion

Until now the kilns of Sussex have always been of a unique form seen at Rye[7], Ringmer[8], and Binstead[9], being derived from the tunnel kiln and not conforming to the common double flue, up-draught form known in the Midlands and West of England, the nearest of which occur at Cheam[10], Laverstock[11], and the newly discovered example at Knighton, I.O.W.[12] That the Orchard Street kiln belongs to this group and not to the "Sussex" group is of greater interest when considering that Binstead is only a few miles to the East. That its internal structure is different from many others sets it aside, but this of itself is not of great importance as kiln interiors have wide variations.

The nearest parallel in form only is the one published from the Maudlin cemetery[13] near Steyning. This vessel occurrred in a pit with cooking pots and unglazed jugs, and was given (without reason) a 13th century date. At Tarring village[14] the base of a similar tripod pitcher occurred in the primary levels in House 1, where a cooking pot with a finger-wiped rim and external strapping also occurred. This group was also given a mid 13th century date on an assumed set of circumstances.

The nearest parallels in form for the cooking pots are those illustrated from Hangleton[15]; these vessels also have a rim flange and external strapwork, and are dated to the middle of the 13th century (without reason). The dating of cooking pots in Sussex must always be considered carefully as their forms are spread wider than the jugs and their development much slower. The applied strap work seen on these vessels has a long history going back at least to the 10th or 11th centuries, and forward into the 14th if the writer's assumptions on the dating of West Sussex wares is correct.[16] An important feature in this group is the incidence of large storage jars which have previously been given early dates but as far as can be seen, without any basis other than a typological one. The chimney pots of Sussex have been thoroughly examined and reported on by Dunning[17] who illustrates examples from Chichester that are parallel to these here and could be from the same source, although the example dated by a coin to *plus* 1199 is of a different form to the rest. He offers a general date range throughout the 13th century for these types but is unable to give terminal dates. It is worth noting that chimney pots were made at Binstead whose products appear to go well on into the 14th century.

So far the material examined could be said to fall into the 13th century if the dating of others were to be accepted, but in the writer's view it is better to place them within the correct sequence of events pending more conclusive evidence from reliably stratified sources. The dominant feature of this kiln's products are the finger-tipped strap handles. This form of handle occurs widely in West Sussex although the commonest variety has central ridge, and not slashing as in this case. At Bramber Castle[18] two thick deposits of medieval pottery were found lying over one another, separated by a plaster floor. The upper layer is dominated by a large quantity of typical West Sussex ware rod handles and has only 3 examples of strap handles, whereas the lower layer contained only strap handles from large globular green glazed jugs and unglazed jugs, and is similar in content to the material from Maudlin. This layer in turn seals a deposit containing a coin of Henry II (issue of 1170); therefore it would seem that such handles occur at Bramber after about 1180 and before West Sussex wares, with a certain overlap at some time. I have suggested elsewhere that West Sussex wares are mainly of 14th century date and possibly later. Whether the Orchard Street examples can be correlated to the Bramber sequence remains to be seen after a good series of stratified material is excavated. What is certain is that these products were never under threat from the massive dominance of the West Sussex forms, although there is a Chichester variety. The bossed decoration is paralleled at Rye and at Laverstock, while the rilled necks are akin to examples from Southampton and Alton. Should the construction of the kiln and the jug forms be any guide it would appear that this ware is influenced from the west rather than from the east of Chichester.[19]

Notes and References

1 "Excavations at Pitlands Farm, Upmarden," forthcoming.

2 *Proc. Hants F.C.* 25 (1968). A late medieval kiln at Knighton I.O.W. by L. Fennelley, K.J. Barton and D. Mynard.

3 *Sussex Record Society,* 46 (1942-3). "The Chartulary of the High Church of Chichester," Ed. by W.D. Peckham M.A.; Ff 146-165, 403.

4 Op. cit. Ff 166-179 "Beate Marie", 522 and 523.

The abuttal on the north side is given as the city wall in deed No. 522 (Folio 177) and in the following deed, No. 523, referring to the same property the northern abuttal is given as the city wall and the southern one as the holding of Juliana de Addesden.

5 *S.A.C.* **90**, 180. Cawley Priory – Walls Excavations, by Alan Rae, citing an entry in the Patent Rolls of 1377-8 (Richard II)

6 *S.A.C.* **100**, 81.

7 *S.A.C.* **74**, 45-64.

8 *S.A.C.* **46**, 236.

9 *Med. Arch.* **11** (1967), p. 316.

10 *Surrey Arch. Coll.* **25**, 79-97.

11 *Med Arch.* **5**, 337.

12 *Proc. Hants F.C.* 25 (1968), op cit.

13 *S.A.C.* **102**, 1 - 9.

14 *S.A.C.* **102**, 21-22.

15 *S.A.C.* **101**, Fig. 10.

16 Op. cit.

17 *Studies in Building History (1961),* pp 78-93.

18 *Excavations at Bramber Castle,* by K.J. Barton & E.W. Holden forthcoming.

19 Orchard Street wares have recently (1969) turned up in stratified deposits at Oyster Street, Portsmouth and are the first recorded instances of distribution outside the City of Chichester. Excavations at Anglesea Court, Oyster Street, Portsmouth", *Proc. Hants. F.C.* forthcoming.

10

Excavations in Somerstown 1965

The area north of the City north gate, beyond the boundary of St. Pauls Churchyard (Fig. 1) has been known as Somerstown since the 19th century. The development of this area is mainly 19th and 20th century, and the Church of St. Paul was built in 1836 to accommodate the new population. The Gardner Map of 1769 (Fig. 2.5) shows it as open fields, and it appears likely that the 19th century development may have been the first to disturb the ground. Until 1965, Somerstown comprised for the most part the houses along George Street, High Street and the west side of St. Pauls Road. These houses or most of them, were demolished by order of the City Council in 1965 when the land was scheduled for re-development and it was thought appropriate that a rapid search of the area should be made by mechanical trenching to test the archaeological potential. The possibility of another Roman cemetery outside the north gate had to be considered, and it was also hoped that some light could be shed on the alignment of the Roman road from Chichester to Silchester, which had not been proved over the approach to the city. Further south towards the city on the south side of St. Pauls Church evidence of Roman suburban development in the 4th century had been noted when the new Fire Station was being built, and the northern limits of this late Roman urban sprawl might have extended as far as the area under discussion.

The Excavations. Fig 10.1

With the kind permission of the City Council, and aided by a grant from the Ministry of Public Buildings and Works, 3 cuts were made from east to west across the site (Fig. 1). These were cut by machine to a width of 2.45 metres (8 ft.) and completed by hand digging. No significant features were found in Trenches B and C, natural brick earth being reached between 0.6 to 1.24 metres, down (2 and 4 feet) and no pottery earlier than the 18th century was found other than a few tumbled sherds of 13th century ware. Trench A was similarly barren except at the extreme eastern end, where a ditch-like feature was discovered, running from north to south, and roughly in line with Broyle Road. This seemed as if it might possibly be the Roman ditch alongside the road, and so further cuts were made to the north to test this possibility. Trench D proved barren, due to the presence of a pit which had destroyed any evidence of a ditch, although some featureless sherds of Roman grey ware were found in the fill. Trench E was again completely barren of features, although again Roman sherds were found in the subsoil. Trench F was dug by machine, and sectioned a ditch dug from a high level, and therefore fairly modern. Against the east section (Fig. 3), most immediately adjacent to the footpath, the machine sectioned a layer of black mud over 30 cms (1 foot) thick. Below this was a thin capping of carefully graded flints which were resting on a thick layer of rammed clay. A further Trench (Trench G) was dug further north, south of, and alongside No. 28 Broyle Road. This was dug by hand and revealed the following features: (Fig. 4)

Fig. 10.1

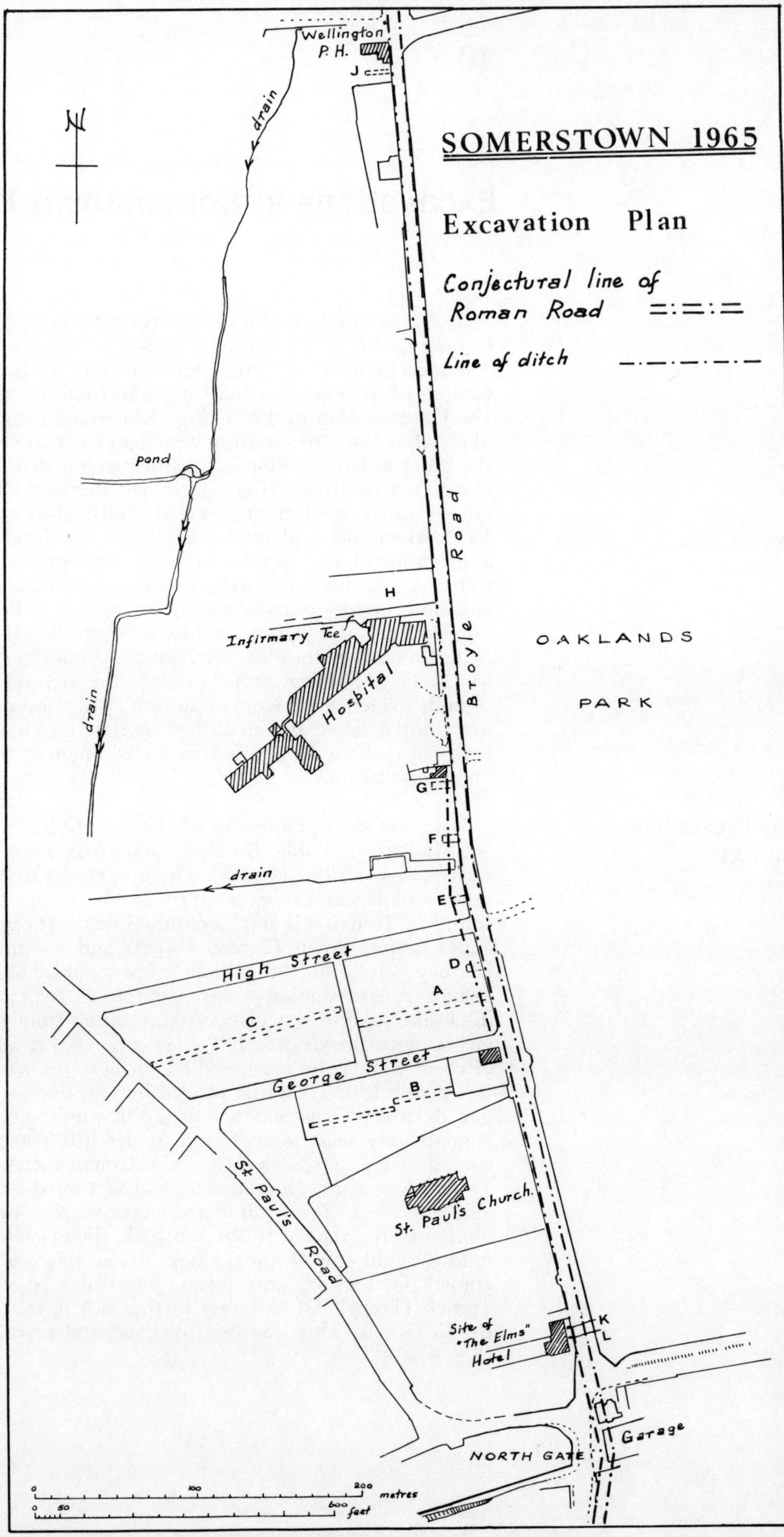
SOMERSTOWN 1965
Excavation Plan
Conjectural line of Roman Road
Line of ditch
Wellington P.H.
J
drain
N
pond
Broyle Road
H
Infirmary Tce
Hospital
OAKLANDS
PARK
G
F
drain
E
D
High Street
A
C
George Street
B
St Paul's Road
St. Paul's Church.
Site of "The Elms" Hotel
K
L
Garage
NORTH GATE
0
100
200
metres
0
50
600
feet

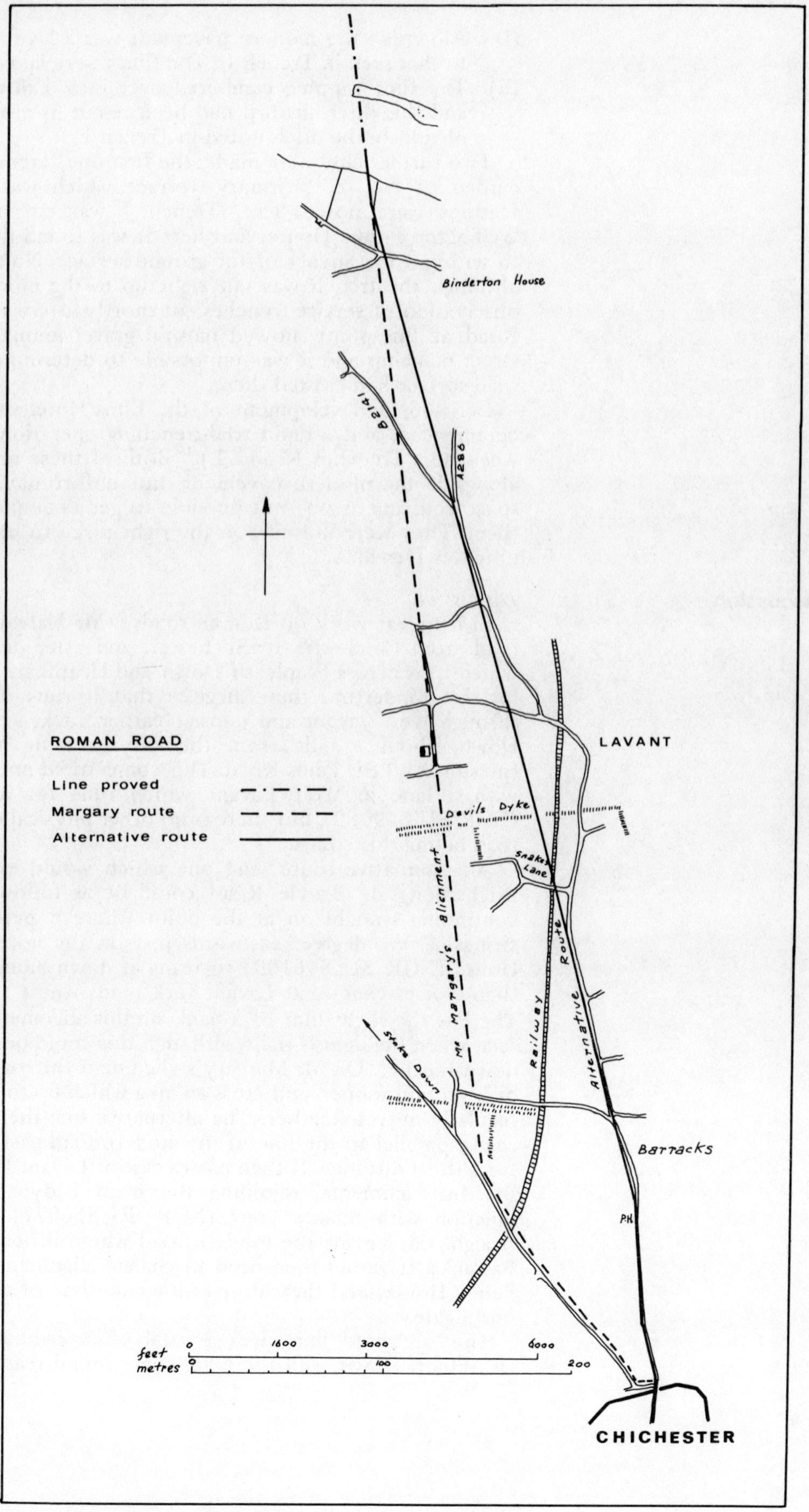

Fig. 10.2 Alternative Alignments of Roman Road from Heath Barn to the City. (Based on Ordnance Survey, by permission of the Director General.)

(i) Alongside the modern pavement was a layer of flint metalling identical to that seen in Trench F. The flints were laid on rammed clay.

(ii) The flint capping cambered over into a ditch immediately alongside, and this ditch in turn had been re-cut in more modern times, and was obviously the ditch noted in Trench F.

Two further cuts were made; the first one, Trench H was made in the back garden of No. 2, Infirmary Terrace which was due for demolition. No features were noted here. Trench J was cut immediately south of the Wellington Public House, and here it was found that the natural gravel came to within a few inches of the ground surface. No trace of a ditch was found, although the trench was cut right up to the modern sidewalk. Subsequent observation of service trenches cut shortly afterwards in the centre of Broyle Road at this point showed natural gravel immediately below the modern street make-up and it was impossible to determine whether or not a Roman road surface had existed there.

In 1966, re-development of the Elms Hotel site opposite Northgate was commenced, and a rapid trial-trenching operation was carried out over one weekend, (Trenches K and L).[1] Both of these revealed a ditch-like feature alongside the modern pavement, but unfortunately, due to restrictions of space and time it was not possible to get a complete section across either of them. They were however in the right place to be an extension of the ditch noted in Trench A.

Discussion

Discussion.

In his great work on Roman roads,[2] Mr Margary discusses the line of the road from Chichester to Silchester, and after dealing with that part of it which runs across Stapleash Down and Heathbarn Down to where the line is lost by Binderton, then suggests that it runs on in the same alignment through West Lavant and joins an earlier trackway coming down from Stoke Down, about a mile from the City, coming into the Northgate along, (presumably) St. Pauls Road. This conjectured line does in fact roughly align with a lane in West Lavant which runs for a distance north – south (NGR/SU 849089), but there is no other physical evidence at present for the road taking this course.

An alternative route, and one which would explain the evidence of the ditch alongside Broyle Road could be as follows: (Fig. 10.2). Instead of continuing straight on at the point where it peters out near Binderton, it swings a few degrees eastwards just on the north west side of Binderton House (NGR SU 846109) to bring it down along the spur of the hill, and then crosses exactly at Lavant fork roads where the A286 and B2141 meet. There is the slight hint of a bank on this alignment which can sometimes be seen when the light is right, although this could be the remains of a ploughed down lynchet. On Mr Margary's alignment the road would descend from the high ground sooner, and cross an area which up to recent times used to flood regularly in wet weather. The alternative line then continues across the fork roads, parallel to the line of the modern road past Yarbrook Council Houses for a short distance. It then passes east of Lavant House and through a gap in the Intrenchments, rejoining the main Broyle Road just south of the junction with Snakes Lane (NGR SU 856077). The road then continues straight on, leaving the modern road where it bends away eastwards by the Barracks. It would then need to change alignment slightly at the Wellington Public House, and thereafter follows the line of modern Broyle Road to the north gate.

This proposed line gives a total of 3 slight changes of direction from Heathbarn Down, and there are some sound reasons why the road builders

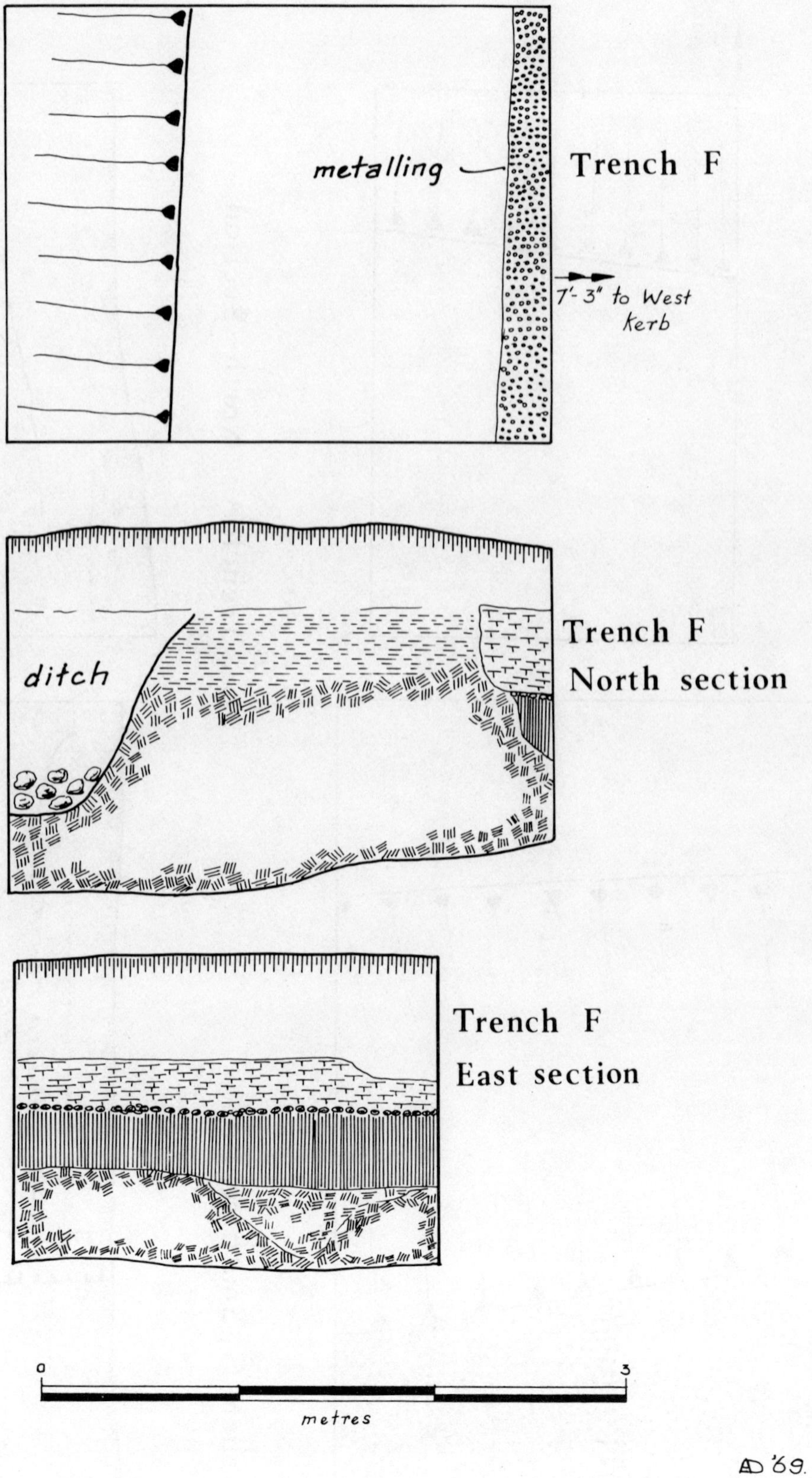
metalling
Trench F
7'-3" to West Kerb
ditch
Trench F
North section
Trench F
East section
0
3
metres
AD '69.

Fig. 10.3

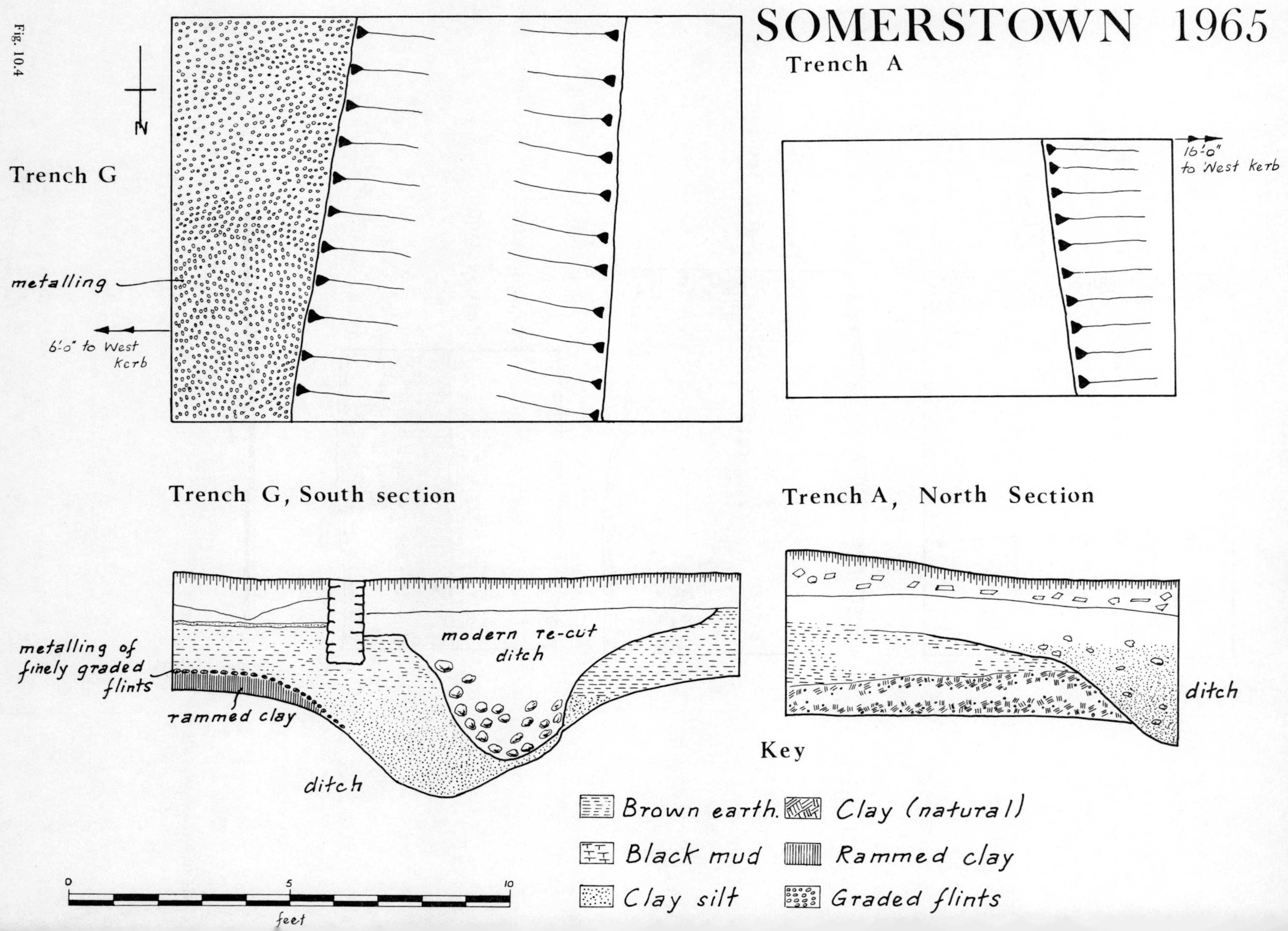
SOMERSTOWN 1965
Trench A
16'0" to West kerb
Trench G
metalling
6'0" to West kerb
N
Trench G, South section
metalling of finely graded flints
rammed clay
modern re-cut ditch
ditch
Trench A, North Section
ditch
Key
Brown earth.
Clay (natural)
Black mud
Rammed clay
Clay silt
Graded flints
0
5
10
feet

Fig. 10.4

should have done this. The first change of direction would be to keep the road to the high ground as long as possible and to bring it down across the driest route, and also possibly to cross the Intrenchments at a convenient spot. The subsequent changes of direction would be to keep the road on the gravel bank which is conveniently close to the surface by the Wellington Public House, and at the same time avoiding the marshy ground to the west. It is possible that the ditch in Trench D was dug for the purpose of draining storm water off the sidewalk alongside the agger, and that it turns at a wider angle than the road, which may explain why it was not noted in Trench E. It is also possible that the modern re-cut dich has destroyed all evidence of the earlier Roman ditch in Trench F, where it, too, swings away from the road. The conjectural line of the Roman ditch is plotted on Fig. 1, but it is no more than conjecture. The modern ditch was probably dug to channel water into the drain shown as running east west across the site (Fig. 1), where it presumably joins the small stream or drain running down from the north. It is possible that a similar system of drainage existed in Roman times.

Conclusions

Conclusions.

The metalled area alongside the ditch in Trench G, and seen again in Trench F was certainly not the Roman road, but it could quite well have been the footway for pedestrian traffic alongside the agger. The new alignment cannot be said to be proved until more field work has been carried out along the stretch from Binderton to the gap in the Intrenchments, but there are certainly good reasons why the road builders should have followed the alternative alignment, the most powerful being the gravel ridge on the approaches to the city which would have provided a ready-made road surface.

Notes and References

1. I am greatly indebted to the Architects Messrs Robt. J. Wood and Partners for permission to carry out this work.
2. Ivan D. Margary, *Roman Ways in the Weald* (1965 revision), p. 278.

List of Subscribers

Mrs. A. Adams
Mrs. B. E. Andrews
Mr. J. C. Armstone
Captain D. H. F. Armstrong, D.S.C., R.D., C.C.
Mr. T. W. Bagshawe, F.S.A.
Vice Admiral H. T. Baillie-Grohman
Mr. D. Barnes
Mr. A. Barr-Hamilton
Miss C. E. Barson, O.B.E.
Mr. T. Beaumont
Mrs. E. Becher
Miss L. Bedford-Forde
Mr. & Mrs. F. H. Bevan
Mrs. F. F. Blakeney
Mr. B. G. Boddy
Colonel E. L. Botting
Mr. Richard Bradley
Mr. Donald K. Braid
Mr. D. W. Bryant
Mr. W. G. Budden
Mr. G. P. Burstow, F.S.A.
Mr. S. M. Caffyn, C.B.E.
Mrs. J. Carpenter
Mr. P. B. Cartwright
Mr. W. B. Caunter
Mr. G. R. Claridge
Mr. H. F. Cleere, F.S.A.
Miss M. Coleman
Mr. A. H. Collins, F.S.A.
Mr. J. Collins
Mr. J. W. Collins
Mr. P. D. Combes
Miss J. M. Cook
Dr. J. G. Cormie
Mr. T. J. Cox
Mr. E. A. Crossland
Mrs. M. Culver
Miss W. J. Curtis, L.L.C.M., A.C.V.
Mr. D. J. W. Daniel
Mr. J. L. Denman, J.P., F.S.A., F.R.I.B.A.
His Honour W. E. P. Done
Mr. J. C. Dove
Mr. J. A. Duke
Mrs. J. P. B. Eastwood
Mr. P. W. Edbury
Mr. F. W. S. Emery
The Hon. Mrs. M. Emmet
Mr. J. Eschbaecher
Mr. H. J. Farrand
Mrs. M. A. Field
Mrs. F. Flanders
Mr. A. L. Foort
Mr. F. E. Ford, A.R.I.B.A.
Miss W. Fox
Professor S. S. Frere, F.S.A.
Mrs. E. W. Fuller
Miss E. W. Garratt
Dr. H. M. Ginns
Mrs. A. M. Glue
Miss A. M. R. Godfrey
Mrs. J. R. Gordon
Mr. R. E. Graebe
Mr. I. Grantham, O.B.E., Ll.B.
Mr. & Mrs. N. G. Graves
Mr. K. W. E. Gravett
Mr. I. W. Griffiths
Miss M. L. Grenfell
Mr. G. M. Haddon
Mrs. B. J. Hales
Mr. J. R. Harben
Mr. H. Harding, I.S.O.
Mr. A. L. Harris
Mr. D. C. Haselgrove, C.B.
Mr. A. W. Hastings
Mr. F. C. Hawkes
T. A. N. Henderson, F.S.A.
Mr. D. S. Herbert
Mr. M. H. Heynes
Mrs. H. M. Hewitt
Mr. C. J. Highton
Miss B. E. Hill
Mr. M. W. Hime
Miss J. Hinde
Mr. E. W. Holden, F.S.A.
Mr. J. Houghton
Dr. R. F. Hunnisett
Mr. D. W. Hutchinson
Mrs. P. M. Ingham
Mr. T. H. Jackson
Mr. R. M. Jackson
Mr. R. H. James
Miss B. Jenkins
Mr. P. Jump, C.Eng., F.I.Mech.E.
Col. J. R. Kellam
Mr. G. H. Kenyon, F.S.A.
Mr. C. E. Knight-Farr
Miss W. E. Kohler
Miss P. J. Lawton
Miss E. R. Lewis
Mr. R. J. Lintott
Mr. M. J. Locke
Mrs. M. E. Lomas
Mr. A. W. G. Lowther, F.S.A.
Mr. M. A. B. Lyne
Dr. R. B. McConnell
Mrs. J. G. McDougall
Miss K. M. Mackenzie
Mr. B. F. N. Mann
Mr. I. D. Margary, F.S.A.
Miss F. M. Markwick
Mr. H. S. Martin, C.B.E., D.L.
The Venerable Lancelot Mason
Mr. R. Merrifield, F.S.A.
Mr. A. G. E. Millington
Mrs. W. Slade Mitford
Mr. M. Milne F.S.A. (Scot)
Commander J. H. C. Minter, R.N.
Miss G. D. Mobbs
Mr. R. R. Morgan
Mrs. R. M. Morice
Mr. J. H. Morrish
Mrs. O. R. Munro
Miss K. M. E. Murray, F.S.A.
Miss D. E. Nethery

Mr. M. Newman
Mr. J. J. O'Hea
Mr. J. R. Osmond
Mrs. H. M. Ouin
The Rev. Dr. T. M. Parker
Mr. F. W. Payne
Mrs. A. W. Peters
Miss J. G. Pilmer
Portsmouth City Library
Mr. J. E. Pratt
Mr. J. G. Puddle
Mr. R. Purchase
Mr. & Mrs. J. R. Rank
Dr.C. W. W. Read
Mr. R. G. Reed
Mrs. R. Reilly
Miss E. M. Rice
Mr. S. E. Rigold, F.S.A.
Mrs. D. I. Martin, Secretary
Robertsbridge & District Archaeological Society
Mr. D. Robertson-Ritchie, F.D.S., H.D.D., L.D.S.
Mr. A. D. Rose
S. H. J. Roth, Esq., F.R.I.B.A., J.P.
The Prior, St. Hugh's Charterhouse
The Rev. S. Salter
Mr. A. E. Sanders
Lady Sayer
Mrs. C. Scott
Mr. W. Shannon
Mr. R. C. Sherriff, F.S.A.
Miss C. F. Shippam
Miss M. O. Sims
Mr. H. C. P. Smail
Mr. L. E. Smith
Mr. S. S. Smith
Mr. J. B. Solomon
Mrs. Somerset
University of Southampton Library
Miss F. E. A. Staffurth
Miss K. M. Stanford
Mr. F. R. Steele
Mr. F. W. Steer, F.S.A.
Mr. M. B. Swatridge
Mr. A. W. Thomas
Mrs. K. M. B. Thompson
Dr. P. Thompson
Lt. Col. H. G. Tranchell
Mr. B. Tunstall
Mr. E. B. Tyler, F.R.I.B.A.
Mr. S. Tyler
Mr. H. R. Underhill, Ll.B.
Miss C. G. Uridge
Mr. H. Vigor
Major Hume Wallace
Mr. C. V. Walthew
Mr. P. L. Wardle
Mrs. W. F. Watson
Mr. N. A. Webb
Mrs. T. E. Westmore
Hon. Mrs. Whistler
Mr. R. E. Wilson
Rev. H. T. Wisdom
Mr. E. E. Wishart
Mr. F. H. Witten, B.A.
Mr. R. H. Wood

Mr. W. J. Rodwell
Mr. M. G. Bell
Mrs. S. Palmer
Mr. M. Morris
Mr. G. S. Burrows, M.B.E.
Miss K. J. Evans
Mr. H. R. T. Compton, B.Sc.

The Sands and Pier, Paignton

Lying in the centre of the magnificent sweep of Tor Bay, **Paignton** is one of the premier resorts in this area with fine sands which stretch for a mile from Hollicombe Head in the north to Paignton's small but busy harbour in the south. Goodrington Sands, on the southern edge of Paignton is one of Tor Bay's most popular beaches. Although commercial fishing has declined, the harbour, which was rebuilt in 1832, is packed with pleasure craft during the summer months. Stretching out some 800 feet from the beach, Paignton Pier is one of very few piers found in the West Country. Opened in 1879, it has undergone a major programme of restoration in recent years and offers a variety of traditional seaside entertainments.

Goodrington Sands, Paignton

Torquay Harbour from Princess Gardens

The Cliff Lift, Oddicombe Beach

The attractive and popular holiday venue of **Oddicombe Beach** is sheltered by high cliffs comprised of an attractive mixture of red sandstone and pale limestone. Situated next to Babbacombe, the sandy beach can be reached by means of a cliff railway.

Torbay has attracted visitors since the late 18th century and with the coming of the railway in 1848 it became one of Britain's most popular areas for seaside holidays. Built on the hillside overlooking the bay, **Torquay** was described by poet Alfred, Lord Tennyson as "the loveliest sea village in England". The spacious, bustling harbour provides moorings for hundreds of small boats. Surrounded by a profusion of sub-tropical plants it has a delightful Mediterranean atmosphere. Torquay is known for its many fine parks and gardens where palm trees flourish in the mild climate.

Oddicombe Beach from Babbacombe Down

Torre Abbey Gardens

Torquay Harbour

Newton Abbot

Shaldon from Teignmouth

The thriving market town of **Newton Abbot** is an excellent centre for exploring both South and Mid-Devon. Situated in the valley of the River Lemon, a tributary of the Teign, Newton Abbot is an ancient town with a number of interesting buildings. Among them is Forde House, a Tudor manor house visited both by King Charles I and William III. In the centre of the town is St. Leonard's Tower, all that remains of a church which was demolished in 1834. Separated from Teignmouth by the estuary of the River Teign, the sheltered resort of **Shaldon** stands beneath a wooded headland known as The Ness. Popular as a yachting centre, Shaldon also offers fishing and beaches of sand and shingle.

Standing on the wide, sandy estuary of the River Teign, **Teignmouth** developed as a port in the early 19th century and is now a popular centre for holidaymakers to the West Country. Known for mild climates and its superb situation, Teignmouth has a colourful riverside harbour, a handsome esplanade and some beautifully kept gardens which attract many visitors. The town has a long and eventful history and many fine Regency buildings remain along the seafront. Ships have long visited the busy quay to load timber and clay and it was also from here that Dartmoor granite was shipped in the 1830s to build London Bridge, now superceded and transported to America.

Ness Point and Teignmouth

Teignmouth Harbour

Dawlish Warren

Lying between the rivers Exe and Teign is the charming seaside town of **Dawlish** where novelist Charles Dickens set part of Nicholas Nickleby. On its way to the sea attractive Dawlish Water, known locally as The Stream, flows over a series of small weirs through The Lawn, a delightful little park inhabited by black swans and some rare species of ducks and geese. Dawlish has a long beach of sand and fine shingle. At one end of the beach high cliffs shelter a little cove where small boats are often pulled ashore. Much of neighbouring Dawlish Warren is now a nature reserve where many species of resident wading birds and winter migrants can be seen.

Dawlish

Bovey Tracey, on the eastern edge of Dartmoor, is a delightful small town and a popular touring centre. It has an interesting history, deriving its name from the de Tracey family who were implicated in the murder of Thomas à Becket. The 14th century parish church was dedicated to St. Thomas as an act of penance. **Buckfast Abbey** lies in a fertile valley beside the River Dart. It was well established by the reign of King Canute but, in common with many other religious houses, it fell into ruin in Tudor times. In the 1880s the site was acquired by French Benedictine monks and the present magnificent structure was built on the original foundations. Buckfast Abbey has one of the most powerful peals of bells in the country and in modern times the monks of Buckfast have become famous for producing tonic wine as well as honey from their own hives.

Bovey Tracey

Buckfast Abbey

Mol's Coffee House Exeter

The Quay and Custom House, Exeter

Founded by the Romans, **Exeter** is an historic city and the most impressive of its many beautiful buildings is the magnificent cathedral. It was established in 1050 although the present structure results largely from re-building begun in 1275. Standing in the tranquil Cathedral Close, the façade of the superb West Front possesses the largest expanse of 14th century sculpture surviving in England. Under the shadow of the cathedral stands Mol's Coffee House, a fine 16th century building which was a popular meeting place for many famous Elizabethan sea captains. The Guildhall dates from at least 1160 and is claimed to be the oldest municipal building in the country. At one time Exeter was a prosperous port and the quay is still well used by pleasure boats. The Customs House was built in 1681 and was one of the first buildings in the town to be constructed in brick.

The Guildhall, Exeter

Exeter Cathedral

One of the few remaining areas of natural, virgin land in the south of England, wild and remote **Dartmoor** is famous for its rugged landscape. Among the numerous scattered granite outcrops which have been carved into curious shapes by the wind and rain are Bowerman's Nose, a distinctive 22 feet high pillar of weathered granite, and Hound Tor which stands prominently on high ground to the north-east of famous Widecombe-in-the-Moor. Ponies have run wild on Dartmoor for at least a thousand years and these sturdy animals, which are so popular with visitors, roam freely across the rock-strewn, heather-clad moorland in all weathers.

Hound Tor

Bowerman's Nose

Widecombe-in-the-Moor

Arguably the most famous village on Dartmoor, **Widecombe-in-the-Moor** is known for its annual fair, immortalised in the traditional song *Widecombe Fair*. The massive 15th century Church of St. Pancras, known as the "Cathedral of the Moor", is a prominent landmark.

Chagford

Moretonhampstead

An excellent centre for exploring the eastern part of the moor, **Moretonhampstead** is a small market town which has some outstanding old buildings. The church, with its fine tower, is a prominent local landmark.

Situated almost in the centre of Devon, the small market town of **Chagford** makes an excellent centre for touring. It was one of the four ancient stannary towns where the tin-miners of Dartmoor would bring their tin to be weighed, assessed for taxes and sold. It lies amidst some of the most beautiful scenery in the National Park, with open moorland, wooded hills and the lovely Teign Valley all within easy reach.

Dartmoor Ponies

The high moorland of the Dartmoor National Park is threaded by numerous pretty little streams and at **Postbridge** the East Dart River is spanned by one of Dartmoor's ancient clapper bridges. Constructed with huge granite blocks supported on four piers, this medieval bridge, which is nearly 43 feet long, provided the main crossing point on the river for many centuries. This was a popular method of bridge building on Dartmoor where large slabs of stone are readily available, and another similar 'Clapper' bridge can be found only a few miles downstream at Dartmeet.

Postbridge

The Bridges, Dartmeet